AMBUSHES AND ARMOUR

To my wife, Laureen.

AMBUSHES
AND
ARMOUR

*The Irish Rebellion
1919–1921*

W.H. KAUTT

IRISH ACADEMIC PRESS
DUBLIN • PORTLAND, OR

First published in 2010 by Irish Academic Press

2 Brookside,
Dundrum Road,
Dublin 14, Ireland

920 NE 58th Avenue, Suite 300
Portland, Oregon,
97213-3786, USA

© 2010 by W. H. Kautt

www.iap.ie

British Library Cataloguing-in-Publication Data
An entry can be found on request

978 0 7165 3024 4 (cloth)
978 0 7165 3025 1 (paper)

Library of Congress Cataloging-in-Publication Data
An entry can be found on request

Printed by The Good News Press Ltd, Ongar, Essex

Contents

List of Illustrations

TABLES

FIGURES

Abbreviations

AD	Archives Department, University College Dublin
Adj-Gen	Adjutant-General
ADP	Army Doctrine Publication
ADRIC	Auxiliary Division, Royal Irish Constabulary
AFDD	Air Force Doctrine Document
ARVN	Army of the Republic of Vietnam
ASU	Active Service Unit
BDE	Brigade
Bn	Battalion
Brig.-Gen.	Brigadier-General
CAB	Cabinet Papers
CAI	Cork Archives Institute
Capt.	Captain
CB	Commander of the Order of the Bath
CBE	Commander of the Order of the British Empire
CIGS	Chief, Imperial General Staff
CMA	Competent Military Authority
CMG	Commander of the Order of Saints Michael and George
Co.	County
CO	Colonial Office
Col.	Colonel
Coy	Company
CP	Cabinet Papers; Command Post
D-C	District Commissioner, RIC
DCIGS	Deputy Chief, Imperial General Staff
DMP	Dublin Metropolitan Police
Div.	Division
DSC	Distinguished Service Cross
DSO	Distinguished Service Order
DSM	Distinguished Service Medal
ER	East Riding
FM	Field Manual
Gen.	General
GHQ	General Headquarters
GOC	General Officer Commanding

GOCinC	General Officer Commanding-in-Chief
HQ	Headquarters
IRA	Irish Republican Army
IRB	Irish Republican Brotherhood
IG	Inspector-General
IGS	Imperial General Staff
ITGWU	Irish Transport and General Workers' Union
IVA	Irish Volunteer Association
JP	Joint Publication
KCL	King's College, University of London
LHCMA	Liddell Hart Centre for Military Archives
Lieut.	Lieutenant
Lieut.-Col. or Lt.-Col.	Lieutenant-Colonel
Lieut.-Gen.	Lieutenant-General
MA	Military Archives (Irish Defence Forces); Master of Arts
Maj.	Major
Maj.-Gen.	Major-General
MC	Military Cross
MM	Military Medal
MS	Manuscript
NA	National Archives
NATO	North Atlantic Treaty Organisation
NLI	National Library of Ireland
NR	North Riding
O/C or OC	Officer Commanding
PAVN	People's Army of Vietnam
PRO	Public Record Office
QMG	Quartermaster-General
RIC	Royal Irish Constabulary
RAF	Royal Air Force
RAOC	Royal Army Ordnance Corps
RASC	Royal Army Service Corps
RM	Royal Marines
RN	Royal Navy
S Constable	Special Constable (in Ulster)
SF	Sinn Féin
SOE	Special Operations Executive
SR	South Riding
STL	Licentiate in Sacred Theology
TC	Temporary Cadet (Auxiliary Division, RIC)

T/Constable or T/Const.	Temporary Constable (Black and Tans)
UCD	University College Dublin
UVF	Ulster Volunteer Force
WC	War Cabinet papers
WR	West Riding

Foreword

The Crossley Tender, so widely used by the Crown Forces in Ireland between 1919 and 1921, is a vehicle of considerable mythic power and reputation, but while celebrated (if that is the right word) in story and song, the lorry itself (in common with the rest of the transport used) has until now attracted almost no serious study. One of the unsung 'realities of war' is logistics – the moving, lodging and supplying of troops – and William Kautt's revealing focus on mechanical transportation demonstrates the importance in Ireland of not just the Crossley Tender, but the whole infrastructure of cars and lorries, as well as railways, telephonic and telegraph communications, carrier pigeons and aeroplanes. Since the Irish war of independence was the first significant *mechanised* counter-insurgency campaign where motor vehicles played a prominent role, their use, their capabilities and their limitations, is absolutely fundamental to an understanding of the conflict. So, too, is that most characteristic feature of the war, the 'ambush', which, for the first time in this book, is systematically and critically examined, from both the British and the Irish sides. Kautt illuminatingly brings his own experience of military organisations and military education to bear on the subject. With an impressively detailed forensic analysis of ambushes accompanied by an appreciation of their human cost, he casts a cool professional eye on IRA and Crown Forces alike and identifies crucial features of these engagements, analysing them and showing how the participants did (or did not) learn from them.

William Kautt wisely observes in this book that direct comparisons and 'lessons' cannot simplistically be drawn from the Irish conflict of 1919–21. He observes, nevertheless, that there are timeless aspects to war such as chaos, fear, hatred and heroism, and there is an undoubted resonance with more recent events in Iraq and Afghanistan in his study of insurgent conflict, ambushes, roadside 'Improvised Explosive Devices' and the like. This important study, therefore, will help us better understand events both in Ireland (and not just in 1919–21) as well as in other circumstances of 'asymmetric warfare', where apparently weak insurgent forces use imagination, improvisation and technical expertise to challenge materially better-resourced, and ostensibly more powerful, orthodox military formations.

Keith Jeffery
Queen's University Belfast

Acknowledgements

There were so many people who helped bring this work to a successful conclusion that it is impossible for me to thank everyone adequately. I should first like to thank the officers and men of the Military Archives at Cathal Brugha Barracks, especially Commandant Victor Laing, Chief Petty Officer Paul Brennan, Private Brendan Mahony and Private Alan Manning. Your assistance, warmth and hospitality are becoming legendary.

I also wish to acknowledge the staff of both the Reading Room and the Manuscript Room of the National Library of Ireland; thank you so much for your patience and assistance. Thanks also to Mr Séamus Helferty and the staff of the Archives Department, University College Dublin, for your wonderful help.

To the Cork Archives Institute, especially Patricia McCarthy, thank you for your assistance and also your commiseration in that horrible second week of September 2001. The library staff of the University of Ulster at Jordanstown were also very helpful and kind during that troubling time.

To the truly wonderful staff of the Public Record Office, you are as nice and cheerful as you are exceptionally capable, and make research pleasurable. I also wish to express my gratitude to Mr David List and Mr George Slowikowski.

There were many individuals who helped above and beyond the call of duty; especially Captain Dev Kostal.

To Dennis Showalter, Geoffrey Parker and Joe Guilmartin, without your encouragement, assistance, generosity, mentoring, and above all, patience over the years, I would never have gotten as far as I did and this work would not have been possible – thank you.

To my supervisor, Keith Jeffery, your guidance, latitude, generosity, great patience, friendship and mentoring made me not only learn, but grow as well. To Sally, thank you for your hospitality and warmth to a stranger.

I also wish to thank the following reviewers: Mr John Borgonovo, Professor Peter Hart, Professor Jonathan House and Professor Niall Meehan, as well as Dr Gil Barndollar.

My thanks also to the following individuals who read and commented on the text: Major James F. Blanton, US Army; Major Michael D. Coleman, US Army; Major Charles A. Hancock, US Army National Guard; Major (Chaplain) H.C. 'Chip' Huey, Jr, US Army; Major Jason M. Norton, US Army; Major Alfonso T. Plummer, US Army; and Major Frank Stølan, Norwegian Defence Force.

Thanks also to David and Nuala McKeogh and Patsy Kitchen for being so kind and welcoming.

I must also thank Lisa Hyde, Karen O Donoghue and Hilary Hammond for their assistance, kindness and patience throughout the publishing process.

If I have missed anyone, I offer my sincere apologies, for it was completely unintentional. I have tried to catch all, but knowing that there will always be something – any mistakes contained herein are my sole responsibility. The views expressed in this book are those of the author and do not reflect the official policy of the Department of the Army, Department of Defense, or the US Government.

W. H. Kautt
November 2009

One

Introduction

When examining the British counterinsurgent effort in Ireland from 1919 to 1921, and the IRA's corresponding countermobility operations against them, anyone who is familiar with the wars in Afghanistan and Iraq in the past several years is struck by the close parallels. Indeed, the present author's students at the U.S. Army staff college, all of whom are majors or equivalent in the American military, as well as from allied nations, on reading earlier drafts of this study for an elective course on insurgency and counterinsurgency in Ireland, were likewise struck by the similarities with this conflict and what they had experienced in the years of combat since 2001. In some cases, the lists of equipment to be carried in convoy operations have not changed.

There are no actual links between Ireland and Afghanistan or Iraq. They are different armies, on two different continents, in different centuries. Most of those students' information and experiences about insurgencies in general, and about ambushes in particular, although seemingly newly learned through bloody trial and error by American and British forces, echoed those of the men in Ireland in 1919 to 1921. In fact, what is evident in the 85-year-old documents were the first instances of the kinds of attacks that have become all too common in Afghanistan and Iraq.

Military commentators and professionals usually will admit that there are timeless aspects to war such as chaos, fear, hatred, heroism. They may, for instance, also be aware that there are modern training methods that date back to the Romans. They will likely know that strategic and operational lessons from the distant past are useful in teaching concepts or demonstrating ideas. Sometimes, there are older military works that remain popular, such as Sun Tzu, but these are usually only of general utility, frequently for the frame of mind they represent. As for more specific information, they say, warfare is too transitional, too fluid and ever evolving for old history to be of 'use' beyond the merely conceptual. By this same logic, therefore, anything learned from the past will be useful only for a short period. This view is narrow and flies in the face of human experience. Would one say this about the discoveries of Newton or Einstein or even Hawking? Yes, one may answer, but these men produced laws of science. Actually, only one produced *laws*, Einstein and Hawking produced *theories*, and yet, the latter has reversed himself on 'string' theory. Why is 'old' science, such as that of Brahe, Copernicus or Galileo, still taught, even though many of their ideas and theories were flawed, or outright wrong? Why do scientists still study them? — because their conceptual frameworks are still valid, even if they did not get all the details right. If 'old' science is useful, why is history not? As already mentioned, history does not repeat itself, because the factors are never the same; the actors and times are different. That is why the historian is critical and controls for these factors when making comparisons.

It is from this view that this study proceeds. It examines situations and looks for links.

Since the invasion of Iraq by the United States-led coalition in the spring of 2003, attacks against ground transport have become one of the most difficult issues for the forces operating there and, to a lesser degree, in Afghanistan. Ambushes and improvised explosive devices (IEDs) brought the issues of road movement and countermobility attacks to the forefront of force protection and route security operations. The situation was serious enough that in the autumn of 2004 some members of the U.S. Army's 343rd Quartermaster Company mutinied rather than transport fuel along a dangerous stretch of road where there had been deadly attacks by insurgents.[1] Such operations against an enemy's movement by road are called countermobility.[2]

The U.S. Department of Defense defines countermobility operations as 'the construction of obstacles and emplacement of minefields to delay, disrupt, and destroy the enemy by reinforcement of the terrain. The primary purpose of countermobility operations is to slow or divert the enemy, to increase time for target acquisition, and to increase weapons effectiveness.'[3] Although the U.S. Army apparently has no separate definition for countermobility, it describes the components as being

> divided into mine warfare and obstacle development, each with an ultimate goal of delaying, stopping, or channelizing the enemy. Mine warfare expands to include mine categories, methods and systems of delivery, employment, reporting, recording, and marking. Obstacle development demonstrates innovative techniques and conventional improvements in planning and emplacing obstacles other than minefield.

The manual continues by saying that the 'countermobility effort is not secluded; rather, it balances with the other major battlefield missions of mobility and survivability, as well as general engineering and topography. The overall teamwork and planning process are both evident and essential with each facet of countermobility.'[4]

Since the beginning of this war on terror, commentators have been saying that this is a singular event in history and that there are no examples to guide it.[5] All political rhetoric aside, however, there were earlier conflicts that could serve as illustrations of success and failure in similar circumstances.

The country with probably the greatest experience of counterinsurgency, in terms of both depth and breadth, is one of America's oldest allies, the United Kingdom. During the twentieth century, Britain dealt with multiple 'small wars' throughout Africa, and in places as diverse as Palestine, Iraq, India, Afghanistan and Malaya, to name just a few. These actions met with varying degrees of success. Mostly though, they were

Figure 1.1 Map of Ireland (pre-June 1921)

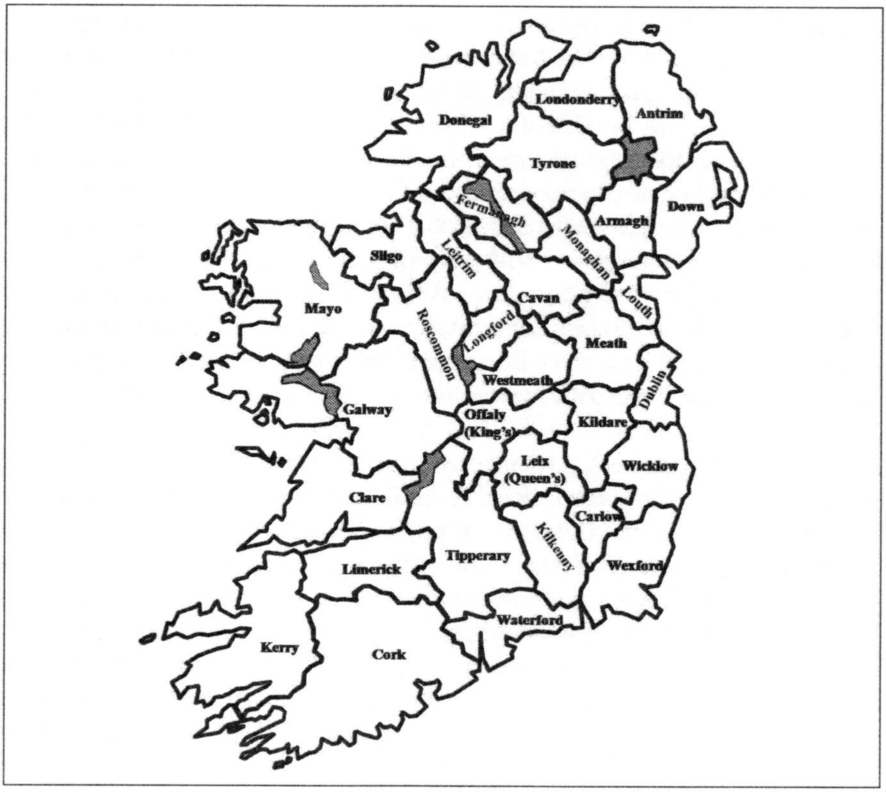

unsuccessful in retaining control; sometimes this was the military's fault and sometimes the politicians', but throughout, one may see significant developments in British[6] doctrine and tactics, techniques and procedures (TTPs).

Probably the most telling of these conflicts was in Ireland during the so-called Irish Revolution of 1916 to 1923[7] and the later 'Troubles' (1969 –2005), because this was one of the first terror wars of that century. It was certainly one of the longest, and is a good example today because, although outside the realm of this work, it involved a populace with fanatical, deep-seated cultural differences and extreme religious hatreds. At the same time, the counterinsurgent forces were 'foreigners' who did not understand the local populace, while the public largely saw the 'native' counterinsurgents as lackeys and traitors. On the insurgent side, the Irish Republican Army (IRA), just as with insurgents everywhere, conducted some of its war against the civilian population to prevent cooperation with the government and the fighting forces – the police and the military.[8] Another, wider-reaching issue of this campaign is that it served as a model for later rebellions around the globe, such as the militant Zionist campaigns in Palestine in the 1940s that led to the creation of the modern state of Israel.[9] Most importantly, however, this was the first rebellion where motor vehicles played a prominent role; thus, counter-mobility operations became a major factor in the IRA strategy. Between 1919 and 1920, the republican rebels became adept in countermobility operations in the various media of transportation in Ireland. At the same time, British forces slowly learned the significance of, and how to deal with, these rebel operations and were preparing a massive counteroffensive in 1921 when politicians ended the war suddenly. But the British had, indeed, learned to fight effectively against these operations. More to the point, while the British did not execute their counterinsurgent plan in 1921, the new Irish Free State National Army, largely former rebels, used significant ideas from it. In the Civil War (1922–3) that followed, the National Army fought their former comrades of the IRA who refused to stop their war for a republic in Ireland. The Free State National Army won. Importantly, that the national army used the same types of ideas as the British plan indicates the former rebels' recognition that the British had learned to fight against the insurgency.

What is also interesting and unfortunate is that the U.S. military is not the only one that forgets its own counterinsurgent lessons out of a mistaken belief that the age of information has anything to do with its validity and viability. The British army appears to have forgotten the lessons of the war in Ireland – they experienced great difficulty with similar conflicts, especially in post-Second World War Palestine and Africa. The British have demonstrated in Basra, Iraq that the concepts they learned in 1920, and paid for with blood, are just as alien to them as the lessons from the Philippine Insurrection (1901–5) appear to be to the U.S. Army today.[10]

A careful examination of the conflict in Ireland might yield some truths and ideas that have not changed despite the distance of time and the obvious qualifier of the macro-level situation. Simply, Iraq and Afghanistan are too far removed in so many factors from the Philippines of 1905 and Ireland of 1921, that most comparison above the tactical and doctrinal level would be useless except, perhaps, for overarching concepts. This study focuses on the IRA's countermobility war in Ireland, specifically ambushes and attacks against transportation infrastructure (roads, bridges and rail), and the British means of defeating them.

BACKGROUND TO THE CONFLICT IN IRELAND

The British had been in Ireland since AD 1170 and spent much of the intervening seven hundred years trying to subdue the country, mostly through military means. There was cultural exchange, to be sure, but this was muted by enmity. A substantial emigration of Gaelic-Irish and immigration by ethnic Britons created a large non-Gaelic population in Ireland, especially in the north of the island, where there is still a high concentration. Further, unlike previous waves of immigrants, these northerners did not assimilate into Irish culture. The Protestant Reformation found adherence mostly among the non-Gaelic Irish newcomers, setting the stage for religious conflict and sectarian politics up to the present. Since 1798, rebellions were republican in nature; the government was usually concerned more about the island's political stability than with keeping peace through justice or efforts to enfranchise the Gaelic-Catholic majority. The southern part of Ireland finally succeeded in obtaining self-governance in 1921, through the creation of the Irish Free State.

If one were to examine nationalism in the early twentieth century, one might be tempted to say that it was somewhat muted in Ireland due mostly to the relative economic prosperity. This would be partly deceptive, because the desire for separation from Britain, the basis of all Irish nationalism, was fulfilled by 1914 with the home rule movement. One could say that republicanism, the desire for a republican government completely separated from the empire, was muted due to the growth in support for home rule. Home rule was making slow progress through the constitutional-legislative solution to Irish independence with the successive home rule bills.[11] The initial reaction of the violently pro-British, anti-separatist unionists to the successive home rule bills, subsequently passed in 1914, was to prepare for war. They created a private army in 1912 and, in reaction, the nationalists followed suit in 1913, but the passage of the Home Rule Act the next year technically placed the government on the nationalists' side, although many in the government and military were sympathetic to the unionist cause.

The outbreak of the First World War in August 1914 changed Ireland. Home rule would be the law by September, but was placed on hold for the duration of hostilities; the empire could hardly make due in the war without Ireland. The unionist private army, the Ulster Volunteer Force (UVF), saw the war as an opportunity to demonstrate their loyalty and volunteered to fight in the British army. The home rulers were divided; some felt they should join the British forces and fight for the United Kingdom, while others saw the war as an opportunity to strike at their traditional enemy. At odds was the truth that home rule did not offer total independence, but only a limited autonomy for Ireland to run its own affairs, as is the case in Scotland after devolution.

The republicans were militant nationalists who saw their chance to break away from their rulers during the world war. In 1916 a small group of rebels seized government buildings and key positions throughout the city of Dublin on the day after Easter, giving the Easter Rising its name. Although the rebels were poorly trained, pitifully armed and badly led (in terms of planning and strategy; unit leadership was generally very good), the fighting to retake the city was savage, street-by-street, and lasted for almost a week. On Saturday, 29 April 1916, the rebels surrendered.

Through a series of major, and in most cases avoidable, blunders, the British military and political leaders lost the support of the Irish people in Dublin. By conducting what appeared to be questionable courts-martial,[12] executions without appeal or court review, and what appears to have been a general mistreatment of the population of Dublin, who had originally cheered and supported the British troops as they came to put down the Rising, the British leadership was partly responsible for reigniting the desire for a republic and complete independence among ordinary Irishmen, which had lain dormant for almost two generations.[13]

During the period that followed the Rising, the surviving imprisoned rebels distilled their experiences of urban combat in an after-action review. For ease of handling and lack of space, the British had concentrated the rebels into mainly one large prison camp in Frongoch, Wales. There they discussed their failures in the Rising, generally agreeing they would not succeed in forcing the British to leave by open, *conventional* rebellion. No, they decided, the next war could be a guerrilla war. They spent so much time training and in other educational pursuits during their captivity that they usually referred to their time in prison as 'Rebel University'.[14]

It is important to understand the regular role of the national police force of Ireland, the Royal Irish Constabulary, during times of trouble, since it was not a 'normal' police force as seen in the United Kingdom. It was a civilian force, but was organized and trained much like the military police. There were both officer and enlisted ranks; the officers being trained first as police cadets, while the enlisted constables received about six months of basic training that included marksmanship, drill, law, procedures, physical training, and so on. After 1920, the country was eventually divided into four divisions based on the four ancient provinces of Ireland, each with a divisional commissioner.[15] Counties, under the command of county inspectors, were divided into districts, which, in turn, had several barracks under a district inspector. The constables were grouped into barracks (police stations) throughout Ireland, with each being under the command of a head constable or sergeant, depending on the number of men, which was, in turn, a factor of the size of the local population.

Table 1.1 RIC Rank Equivalencies

RIC Officer Ranks	Army Officer Ranks	RIC Enlisted Grades	Army Enlisted Grades
Inspector-General	General	Head Constable	Sergeant Major
Deputy Inspector-General	Lieutenant-General	Sergeant	Sergeant
Assistant Inspector-General	Major-General	Acting Sergeant	Corporal
Divisional Commissioner	Brigadier General	Constable	Private
County Inspector	Colonel		
District Inspector, 1st Class	Major		
District Inspector, 2nd Class	Captain		
District Inspector, 3rd Class	Lieutenant		
Cadet	Cadet		

The RIC was also unusual in that it was the only armed police force in the United Kingdom, by 1919, using the 1907 Lee-Metford .303 Cavalry Carbine for the enlisted, and the .38 RIC Webley Service Revolver (although later many preferred to carry the more powerful .455 army variant). Although they had arms, most men did not carry them on a regular basis, prior to the War of Independence, unless ordered to do so. Most of the policemen, officer and enlisted alike, saw weapons as a hindrance to their duties of keeping the peace; they usually found that arms separated them from the community. The reason for being armed in the first place, however, was the seemingly ever-present danger of rebellion; the RIC was the first line of defence. Yet, if the RIC performed the functions adequately, it knew, keeping watch on 'troublemakers', monitoring political activities of individuals and groups, and providing intelligence to the Irish government, it would have sufficient warning.

The other main police force in Ireland during the conflict was the Dublin Metropolitan Police (DMP), which had purview within the environs of the city of Dublin. The DMP was organized much the same as the RIC, but with the important distinction that their men were unarmed. Their primary threat to the militant republicans lay in their exceptional intelligence-gathering capabilities. The force was divided into geographical divisions, designated 'A' through 'F'. The last was 'G' Division, which was the detective division and oversaw the collection of information, especially political information and intelligence.[16]

Of the ten DMP killed during the war, six were 'G-men', a seventh was carrying intelligence despatches and an eighth, Second Assistant Commissioner William C.F. Redmond, was assassinated as a result of Michael Collins' campaign against intelligence; Redmond had commanded 'G' Division just before his promotion. Further, four of these 'G-men' were killed in 1919, when Collins targeted British intelligence capabilities overall.[17] A fifth was killed in April 1920.[18] This targeting worked: of the fourteen remaining men of the original nineteen in the political branch in 'G' Division in early 1920, four retired early, five transferred out on request and one was incapacitated by wounds and only fit for duty inside the Castle. The four remaining men were young and inexperienced in intelligence work. Worse yet, they were all known to the IRA, who actually composed a poem listing the names of all the members.[19]

While this is not meant to be a history of the war itself, a brief outline of the conflict is necessary for clarity. The War of Independence does not break down neatly into the clean and clear categories of which historians and soldiers are so enamoured; however, one may generally fit it into a people's war model.[20]

Revolutionary warfare is a means to overthrow an existing government, whether 'legitimate' or not, and replace it. The replacement element is critical to establish legitimacy.

There are two types of legitimacy: external and internal or 'popular'. The former is based on relations with other countries and how they relate to the government. This does not necessarily mean that these governments will particularly like it, only that they recognize it. Other governments may hold a government in contempt, while still recognizing its legitimacy. Such recognition is usually demonstrated by the exchange of diplomatic relations, formal negotiations and entrance into treaties.

Internal or popular legitimacy is usually based on the 'will' of the people of the country in question. 'Legitimate' governments, in the eyes of the people, are those that govern, with all its attendant functions, providing services such as national defence, public administration, policing, fire fighting, postal services, judicial and penal services, and so on. These are the same factors that other governments look for when determining international recognition of legitimacy. It must be noted, however, that these two types of legitimacy are not necessarily related to each other; the international community may recognize a government as legitimate while the people it purports to govern may reject it. The reverse may also be true; the people may support a government that is unrecognized by other countries.

The obvious question, then, is when does a government lose or establish its legitimacy? External legitimacy is rather simple: governments either recognize each other or they do not. The problem comes with popular legitimacy. This may come easily, such as with elections, but as events in Zimbabwe demonstrate, the fairness of such elections may be in doubt. With elections come the ever-possible issues of fraud, intimidation, denial of voting rights and other such tampering. This leads to questions of how much tampering must there be to invalidate the results and who decides?

If there are no elections, or their veracity is in question, other factors determine legitimacy. For if legitimacy is based merely on obedience, is a government legitimate only because of the force it may bring to bear to compel obedience? If, during a revolution, both sides compel obedience through force, what does that say about legitimacy? If a revolutionary movement uses force to cow the people into submission and defeats the government, does it then gain legitimacy? These are questions that are virtually impossible to answer.

Revolutions may be violent, but they do not have to be. The so-called Catholic emancipation of 1829, the extension of voting rights to all men,[21] and the final passage of the Home Rule Bill in 1914 may all be classified as a bloodless revolution. Unfortunately, revolutions normally appear to be violent.

While there are several types of revolutionary war, the most common of the twentieth century appears to have been people's war. Revolutionary warfare existed *before* the formal articulation of people's war theories in the mid-1930s.[22] Probably the earliest thinker to divide revolutionary warfare into stages that are similar to people's war theory was Crane Brinton in *Anatomy of Revolution*. Although his ideas were not identical to those of Mao, many were parallel and existed in writing fully five years before Mao's classic, *On Guerrilla Warfare*. This point is important because it demonstrates that the ideas of people's war theory are *not* communist, although the term for it is communist in origin and communists were the most common users of it in the twentieth century.[23] Military theorists continue to use the communist term for this type of warfare.

People's war does not recognize any difference in the types of war, such as guerrilla warfare, manoeuvre warfare and positional warfare: there is only one struggle. The types of warfare are merely tools to be used. This attitude is possible because people's war is protracted by its very nature; it takes time to build up a large combat force. Nationalism is a critical element of people's war, because it unifies the people against the foreigner, which is the next element. There is always a foreign invader and also 'collaborators' who work for them against the people. People's war also requires traditional lands, usually held by either the foreigner or the 'lackeys' working for them. All of these elements come together to promote the cultural elements of traditional language and, frequently, a traditional religion. These form the ethnic identity, which tends to foment nationalism.

Table 1.2 People's War Stages

	Mao	Giap	Brinton	Actions
Stage 1	Strategic Defensive	Contention	Stage 1	Political Action
				Get the message out
Stage 2	Strategic Stalemate	Equilibrium	Stage 2	Guerrilla War
				Parity of forces
Stage 3	Strategic Counteroffensive	Counteroffensive	Stage 3	Manoeuvre War
				Conventional war/ manoeuvre
Stage 4			Civil War	Moderates v Radicals

The first stage, contention, has two parts that operate simultaneously: contention and defence, hence the titles given by the theorists. The former refers to the political action among the people, primarily in order to politicize them and get them involved. The methods one may use are rallies and social events, but any public gathering may be converted to this purpose. One may also use newspapers, broadsheets, pamphlets, and so on; whatever will get the message out to the people.

It is important to note that revolutionaries talk much about self-determination and the rights of the people to choose their own destiny, but in practice, they rarely mean it, or at least fail to recognize the inherent dichotomy of their position. For instance, in January 1919, the Irish Volunteers published the following: 'They [the Irish Volunteers] have been the backbone of all the work to secure Ireland's freedom for the past four years. To-day, as always, they stand silent, disciplined, prepared, the stalwart guardians of the right and determination of the Irish people to be free.'[24] Yet they later stated: 'We must show that it is not healthy to be against US, and that those who are not going to be against us must be with us.'[25] Obviously, they did not see the irony of their statements.

In this stage, the revolutionaries begin to terrorize and subdue political opponents, i.e. those who do not share their intended end state. This is not to say they will not make alliances with other groups to form a coalition; for instance, Sinn Féin, the Irish Volunteers, the Irish Citizen Army and Irish Labour. These groups generally agreed that they wanted independence from the empire and some type of republican government. The republicans could not permit the Home Rule Party to join with them because that party wanted to remain in the United Kingdom. Thus, the home rulers were too close to loyalism. It should go without saying that anyone who supported union or the loyalist cause was automatically a target, for while the republicans were trying to enfranchise their supporters, they were also trying to disenfranchise those who did not support them and would use *any* means necessary. Ironically, but not surprisingly, while the revolutionaries may preach universal suffrage or the rights of the people to choose, they ensure that no one is permitted to vote or act in an opposing manner; thus, the inherent self-contradiction, especially in a country with near universal suffrage.

The other element of this phase is frequently called 'defence'; the movement is at its weakest point. Since they are only beginning to arm themselves, they are more vulnerable to governmental forces. During this time, they will recruit, train and equip their military force as best they can. Firstly, there will be the guerrilla force, but one should remember that guerrilla warfare is *not* an end unto itself; guerrilla warfare does not win wars alone. It is merely a stage in the evolution of the revolutionary army and allows it to build its strength. The goal is the creation of a conventional revolutionary army to defeat the enemy forces in a conventional war of manoeuvre.

The second stage, equilibrium, begins some time around when the revolutionaries stop their small raiding operations merely for arms, munitions and supplies and begin to focus on targets with more external military advantage. For instance, they may attack a police station where the police are particularly effective at hunting rebels or gathering information. If they take the station, the rebels will likely destroy it to prevent reoccupation. They will, of course, take everything out of it that they need – arms, ammunition, supplies, etc. These types of raids serve both purposes, but the seizure and removal of a threat is the primary purpose of the raid; the acquisition of supplies is something they will continue to pursue throughout the war.

As the revolutionary army grows, there comes a point when it needs a place to gather that is safe from enemy surveillance and attack. This area will have to be a place where the enemy forces *fear* to go because it is *totally* under the control of the revolutionary forces. In this instance, the guerrilla force will create this sanctuary and hold it, but only for so long, because guerrilla forces are incapable of holding terrain for a long period. Once the region is secure, the revolutionaries must create the conventional force that is, and will remain, separate from the guerrilla force. When it is sufficiently strong, the conventional force assumes responsibility for securing the sanctuary, thus freeing more guerrillas to continue their attacks. In this safe area, the revolutionary forces will train for the conventional war of manoeuvre.

As the two forces increase in size and capability, they undertake larger and more complex operations. Priority in these remains with the guerrilla force until the conventional force is large enough and well-enough equipped to undertake combat operations against equivalently sized enemy units. Once the conventional force is conducting large-scale conventional operations more frequently than the guerrilla force, the focus of the revolutionary movement shifts from the latter to the former. This can only happen once the conventional force has reached parity with the enemy forces.

As the revolutionary focus shifts from guerrilla to conventional, the former's operations do not halt; they continue with those functions that are specific to their medium. They continue to provide internal security, counterintelligence functions, and raiding, ambushing and other small operations. While the security missions do not include guarding buildings or areas, they and the counterintelligence operations are different from the harassment missions such as raiding and ambushing. These harassment missions can provide direct support to their conventional brethren. This type of support is sometimes called 'compound warfare'.[26]

This stage is the final stage of what one may call 'classical' people's war, and begins when the conventional revolutionary army is large enough to take and hold more territory than it needs for its training, rest and reconstitution and other 'sanctuary-like' functions. By this point the rebel army is fighting to *retake* the land, not necessarily just to exploit its resources, although it will, but to deny its use to the enemy. This is truly a counteroffensive and, if successful, ends with the military defeat of the enemy and the fall of the enemy government.

Although the war has been fought against a 'foreign' power, the majority of the fighting may actually have been against the revolutionaries' own people – the 'collaborator' loyalists, unionists and even home rulers, in the case of Ireland – those supporting the status quo. In this sense, the war is automatically a civil war, but as an actual stage, civil war is quite different. The end of the revolutionary phase of the war presupposes that the other groups have been defeated in one manner or another.

None of the classical people's war theorists wrote about this as part of their theories. The only one to examine this was political scientist Crane Brinton. After examining several historical revolutions, Brinton came to the conclusion that just before the fighting began, the moderates, who likely began the movements, were in charge. The radicals sideline the moderates and resort to violence against the enemy; thus the war begins.

At the end of the revolution, the moderates reassert themselves and this causes friction as they vie for power in the new political environment. Another factor is that the various disparate groups that united and created a coalition no longer have the common enemy providing a reason to suppress their specific aspirations. All of these differences must be dealt with somehow. The usual means is civil war, according to Brinton.

People's war is merely a theory, but it is a useful model to use in examining revolutions. It is important to note that there are few absolutes when looking at people's war; the stages are fluid and one may go back and forth between them as necessary. People's war as a strategy is deliberately flexible.

A good example is that of General Vo Nguyen Giap of Vietnam, who, in 1950 in the war against the French, was forced to return to stage two; he had tried to conduct a counteroffensive and was soundly defeated. In most revolutionary wars, such a defeat would likely have doomed the movement, but Ho Chi Minh and Giap returned to a second stage and rebuilt until late 1953. There are two significant points in this example: the Viet Minh were *capable* of falling back to this second stage without it being fatal to the cause due to both the military organization and political reality.

The second point is that not only did Giap and the Viet Minh survive, but they were ultimately successful against the French in Indochina.

One might go so far as to describe the North Vietnamese war against the South as the civil war envisioned by Brinton. After the Geneva Conference of 1954 ended French involvement, approximately one million people fled from North Vietnam, many of them French-speaking Catholics who knew what awaited them in communist-dominated North Vietnam.

Furthermore, the fight against the Americans in the 1960s and early 1970s provides an example of the foreign influence in a people's war. Of course, this war was significantly different in that the North Vietnamese forces, primarily the People's Army of Vietnam (PAVN), tried to fight a conventional war until 1965, when they lost a major battle in the Ia Drang valley. One of the important factors of this battle, made famous in *We Were Soldiers Once ... And Young*[27] was that this was where the U.S. army forces engaged large PAVN forces in a conventional battle. Afterwards, the communist strategy in the south dropped back into stage one.

Probably the most contested of battles in the Second Indochina War was the so-called Tet Offensive of January 1968. Giap planned and executed an operation that was intended to be a stage three counteroffensive of combined Viet Cong (VC – South Vietnamese communists) and PAVN attacks throughout the South. They expected to crush the South Vietnamese army (ARVN)[28] and destroy the Americans in a repeat of the final battle against the French fourteen years earlier at Điên Biên Phù. The place chosen for this military and political triumph was the American Marine fire base at Khe Sanh.

The Tet Offensive was an epic disaster for the communists, the North Vietnamese Polit Bureau and for Giap personally. Although the scale of the attacks was tremendous and the communists certainly had strategic and tactical surprise, they were unable to capitalize on these. This was partly due to the skill with which the ARVN forces responded. They did not crumble, but rather struck back fiercely. The physical results of this campaign were horrifying. In reality, the Viet Cong ceased to exist for all practical purposes after this fight.

There are two further points about this conflict that are important here.[29] The most common icon of the Tet Offensive is probably the infamous Pulitzer prize-winning photograph of Lt. Gen. Nguyen Ngoc Loan shooting a VC prisoner in the head.[30] This came to symbolize the war for many. While for some, this incident was the face of the cruelty of the war, the full story behind the picture is that the man summarily executed was captured after having murdered the family of a Saigon policeman. Without making moral comments on either act of barbarism, one should note that in these wars, including Ireland forty-eight years earlier, police-men and their families were on the front lines and they suffered. None of the policemen's families in Ireland suffered the level of savage violence that those in Vietnam suffered; this comparison is method, rather than means.

The last point about the Vietnam War is that, from a world super-power standpoint, it was a sideshow. The 'real' war for the Americans was the one expected in Germany against the Soviets. This was impor-tant, because it meant that the majority of their military effort was against the USSR – both nuclear *and* conventional. So even had they wanted to, the Americans could not have employed their *full* might in Vietnam. This made victory possible in that it allowed the North Vietnamese a freer hand and the ability to build large conventional forces largely free from the overwhelming attack that could have other-wise occurred. Ultimately, it was conventional force that ended the Second Indochina War, not political intervention.

In the same way that the Americans were limited in their military options in Vietnam, the British were likewise hamstrung in their efforts to operate militarily in Ireland due to their overwhelming global obliga-tions following the First World War. It was largely this preoccupation and lack of political will that doomed the military effort there. Although up to almost one-fifth of the British army was employed in Ireland dur-ing the conflict, this was insufficient for counterinsurgency operations. One must always remember, however, that one cannot solve a political problem with military force, something recognized, at least by General Macready, at the time.[31]

The Volunteers found that most of their arms had been surrendered during the Rising and they needed to rearm. Rearming became one of several critical foci for the rest of the war in 1921. Early in the conflict, the arms effort consisted of simple thefts. By 1919, the Volunteers grad-uated to raids on barracks and private homes. These were also some of the first offensive actions of the war for many rebels units.

Outside of the military arm, de Valera and the political leaders of the republican movement decided to take over the small party called Sinn Féin. Inexplicably, Sinn Féin was blamed for the Rising in the press, although they had nothing to do with it; that name recognition stuck, so the republicans simply took over the party. By 1918, the new Sinn Féin decided to formalize legitimacy by contesting the parliamentary general elections in December. After the election, in which Sinn Féin took almost three-quarters of the Irish seats in Westminster, the newly elected Irish separatist MPs met in Dublin for an Irish parliament (Dáil Éireann). The

Dáil then established an underground rebel government to claim that legitimacy granted them by the people of Ireland.

That same day, Saturday, 21 January 1919, a new violent phase of the struggle recommenced with an ambush of a civilian shipment of high explosives bound for a quarry at Soloheadbeg in the south-western county of Tipperary (see Figure 1.1). The Irish Volunteers of the Tipperary brigade shot the two RIC men escorting the horse-drawn cart of 168 pounds of gelignite.

For the purposes of this study, it was strangely apropos that this official starting date for the War of Independence was in part due to an ambush. What is ironic is that this rural ambush bore little resemblance to the later ambushes that typified and to a great extent defined this war; indeed, the major actions of late 1920 and 1921 were manoeuvre fights. Obviously, the basic components of an ambush remained – the lying in wait, the use of surprise, the nervousness of the attackers, and so forth – but the elements dominating ambushes later, command and pressure-detonated IEDs, automatic weapons, prepared ambush sites, large escorts, and so on, were not present. This small group of rebels waited several days for the cart, without placing obstacles or digging fighting positions; they shot the policemen and took the cart.

With regards to the changes in ambushes during the war, the Soloheadbeg ambush would probably not have occurred just a few weeks later; the escort would have been significantly larger and better organized – some have suggested that the policemen thought this incident was a case of simple armed robbery.[32] It is also doubtful whether the republican leadership would have approved such a violent attack; there were surprisingly few attacks as violent until 1920. In respect to the former point, it is accurate to state that this attack was the last 'officially' independent operation by the Irish Volunteers: for although Dáil Éireann did not declare the Volunteers the army of the underground Irish Republic – the IRA – until 1921, the rebel leader at Soloheadbeg, Seámus Robinson, and his comrades certainly felt that way.

Tipperary brigade commandant Robinson wanted to conduct the attack *before* the meeting of the Dáil; otherwise, he felt obliged to ask permission to attack and he did not think it would be forthcoming. The fact that the attack occurred on the same day as the first Dáil was purely coincidental, although Robinson clearly wanted it to occur earlier in the week.

There were surprisingly few ambushes after Soloheadbeg, primarily due to the IRA's mission of raiding for arms – their violent energies were mostly spent elsewhere. Their other major activities had to do with placing pressure on the men of the RIC and their families to get them to quit the force (see Chapter 3). The year ended with just two additional ambushes of any note, both of which were against policemen on bicycles.

The first of these took place in Co. Clare on Monday, 4 August 1919; the IRA Laraveen Company attacked two policemen, Sergeant John Riordan and Constable Michael Murphy, as they returned to their barracks in Ballyvoreen. Murphy died in the first volley of IRA rifle fire, while Riordan lived long enough to write down that he had wounded some of their three assailants. The pair had been attacked earlier that summer by six men, Martin Devitt, brothers Michael and Thomas Kelleher, brothers John and Michael McGuane, and John Joe Neylon, who overpowered them and took their firearms. In August, the rebels fired without warning. These killings were condemned by the Catholic priest of Lahinch, Rev. Fr M. Mullins, the following Sunday, and also by Rev. Fr Nestor, PPVG, pastor of the Catholic parish of Ennistymon. The bishop of Galway, the Very Rev. Thomas O'Dea, also condemned the killings as murder in a letter to Nestor.[33] The views of the Catholic clergy varied throughout the conflict, mostly over the means used against the government and, to a lesser extent, the targeting of policemen.[34]

The other incident occurred in Co. Tipperary on Tuesday, 2 September 1919, when rebels attacked a three-man bicycle patrol halfway between Lorrha and Carriguhorig. The rebels – John Carroll, John Gilligan, Michael Hogan and John Madden – fired on the policemen from behind a wall, killing Sergeant Philip Brady and wounding Constable Folely in the head. Madden was tried for murder on Thursday, 22 April 1920 and convicted.[35] The remainder of the year saw the IRA raiding for arms and putting severe pressure on the RIC men to quit the force. In both, the rebels were quite successful. Raids for arms continued and barracks attacks grew in number as well. That the police leadership had pulled many of the RIC men out of the hinterlands of Ireland in late 1919 and early 1920, ostensibly to concentrate their power in the population centres, did not hurt the IRA's ability to control, at least partially, those abandoned areas.

There was another hiatus from lethal ambushes of police from September 1919 to March 1920. Such actions resumed on Thursday, 11 March 1920, when an RIC patrol was ambushed at Glanmire, Co. Cork, killing 64-year-old Constable Timothy Scully. For the next two months, the police victims were bicycle-mounted patrols. Two of the three-man patrol died, with their remaining comrade seriously wounded, at Lackamore Wood in Co. Tipperary on Friday, 9 April 1920. Another two RIC bicycle patrolmen died on Sunday, 25 April 1920 at Ballinspittal in

Co. Cork, while the sergeant of another such patrol died at Galebridge in Co. Kerry on Monday, 3 May 1920.[36]

Ambushes against various patrols continued for the remainder of the year, some thirty-seven additional lethal attacks, including the infamous attack at Kilmichael (Co. Cork) in late-November. The earlier incidents occurred before the army received its increase of motor transport, beginning in May 1920, while the police were significantly less motorized.

Beginning in the early autumn of 1920, the police attempted to 'round up' the rebels in their first real offensive action of the conflict, but this was hampered by the decision to consolidate their forces into larger groups (see Chapter 3). Their efforts to arrest the rebels were frequently ineffective, largely due to Collins' counterintelligence war. Indeed, the rebels derided the police and military efforts.[37] Much of the problem lay with the lack of authority on the part of the army and the difficulty of securing convictions against captured rebels prior to martial law (see below).

So, in spring 1920 the IRA came out to fight, but still only as guerrillas and only where they had local superiority, either natural or created by countermobility operations, which had become prevalent by late 1919. During this period, the IRA's ambush planning and execution remained uncomplicated, and there was no need for it to be otherwise. It was only the introduction of motor vehicles into Ireland on a large scale that necessitated the IRA's development of more sophisticated or complex ambush doctrine and tactics. The only exception to this was when the IRA was conducting an ambush in conjunction with an attack on a fixed site, such as a police barracks, as occurred on Sunday, 31 October 1920 at Ballyduff, Co. Kerry, when three policemen were killed.[38] So long as the police patrols were on foot or, more suicidally, on bicycles, the Volunteers continued with simple ambushes.

During the transition period between the introduction of the Auxiliary Division, RIC and the British offensive of autumn 1920, IRA raids remained simple. When the offensive began, rebels were either quick studies or they were captured.[39] Those elusive enough to escape usually landed in the first full-time IRA units. These 'flying columns' carried out more complex attacks as the situation warranted. The IRA were organized by county into brigades, which divided into battalions of several local (town or village) companies. Each company was the local organization into which the individual Volunteers joined. Several companies were placed into a single battalion, each with its own staff and command structure. Likewise, each battalion belonged to a brigade, which usually spanned the county in which it resided. Some counties, like Cork, had so many members that they had several brigades within their county. The membership usually did little to hide their affiliation and lived quite openly until early autumn 1920, when the British conducted what amounted to a counteroffensive against the IRA.

Part of the problem for the army in Ireland was that British law did not recognize a state of rebellion and thus grant soldiers acting in aid of the civil power immunity to prosecution, even during a state of martial law. There was no clear delineation of authority of what a soldier was to do when an action was ordered that was legal under military law, but illegal under civil law.[40] If given an order to fire on a crowd, he could be court-martialled if he refused to obey a lawful order or charged under civil law for murder or attempted murder if he did. Normally parliament passed an Act of Indemnity to shield soldiers from this pitfall, but this did not come until after the war.[41] Thus, martial law granted power to the army, but as the GOCinC, General Macready, observed to the Cabinet, it did not shield soldiers from prosecution under civil law in Ireland, even those conducting courts-martial.[42]

Understanding that they were on a legal tightrope and that there was a need to exercise caution, the military commanders knew that using troops in support of civil authority was risky since not every action used to bring about order would be defensible afterwards. Common law required use of only the force necessary to re-establish order. Moreover, British experience was firm that re-establishing law and order was a civil task, with troops supporting at the proper times. Some military commanders were more concerned about the law, knowing all too well what their restrictions were, and believed they, not politicians, would be held responsible. Making these determinations was one thing; practically implementing them was quite another.[43] Still, the introduction of martial law in December 1920 in several parts of southern Ireland and in Dublin began a new stage in the war. However imperfect the legal situation was, the army took a freer hand than before.[44]

The actual timing of the second phase of this insurgency is difficult to place because of the great variation in levels of support, activity and violence throughout the country. In the north, where the majority of the population was Protestant loyalist, support for the struggle was weak; however, in the south, the opposite was true. Further, the rebels were not operating in a vacuum; they had to react to British operations as well. Offensive operations on any large scale for the rebels were rare, but the IRA would appear to have reached a second stage in some areas of the south by late spring 1920. By this time, the IRA had forced the British to modify governance in Ireland, relieving several officials and reinforcing the police.

In autumn 1920, however, the British counterattacked and reoccupied many of the areas they had abandoned earlier in the year. This drove the IRA back for the first time since the Rising in 1916, but did not defeat them. By November 1920, the IRA struck back with several spectacular attacks (see Kilmichael ambush, Chapter 4) so that by the end of the year there was sufficient evidence to suggest the situation was approaching stalemate, with the IRA unable to dislodge the British and the government unwilling to use any means to defeat them.

One could argue that the IRA never reached a third stage since there was only one large-scale operation in Ireland during the war (see Battle of Crossbarry, Chapter 5). In May 1921 the rebel army was reorganized into divisions, but conducted no major offensives before the truce two months later.[45] In the meantime, the British army was preparing an all-out invasion and had conducted several successful large operations of its own against the IRA when the war ended abruptly with a truce in July 1921 and the Anglo-Irish Treaty in December of that year. From there, a civil war (from 1922 to 1923) raged between republicans who rejected the Treaty and their former comrades who accepted the compromise of the Irish Free State.

Table 1.3 People's War Timeline of the Irish Revolution

First Stage			Second Stage			Third Stage	
Rising	Irish Convention	Preparation	War of Independence			Truce	Civil War
1916	1917	1918	1919	1920	1921	1922	1923

The careful reader will note that this study examines some two-dozen ambushes, which occurred mostly over a period of about ten months. It is not that there were no important ambushes before September 1920 (the Rineen ambush, see Chapter 4) or after June 1921 (the Rathcoole ambush), just that the ambushes which are the primary foci here were incidents that taught the British new lessons or served to reinforce old ones, or should have. Further, there were several actions that the British army included in their reports, from which they drew lessons, that have been included as inserts, primarily concerning types of IRA operations that were not necessarily ambushes. Their purpose was a wider examination of IRA operations generally; therefore, they are reproduced in the appendices.

OUTLINE OF THIS BOOK

Chapter 2 discusses the issues of learning within military organizations, especially the British army in World War I, to provide background on how they normally modified their tactics. The next chapter will establish the state of transportation in Ireland by opening with a description of its transportation infrastructure during the conflict. It then discusses the effects of the Munition Strike (May–December 1920) against British forces, especially with regards to transportation and how it forced the British to use roads as their primary means of manoeuvre and the vulnerabilities this created. The chapter also examines the transport problems stemming from a boycott of the RIC. The chapter ends with the mobility issues of the British counterattack in 1920.

The fourth chapter begins with an examination of the change in IRA ambushes that came about as a result of the British counteroffensive, which actually constituted the rebel response to that offensive. For this reason, it examines the Rineen and Kilmichael ambushes, which collectively cost the lives of some twenty-five policemen. The latter action, almost by itself, was pivotal in the war.

Chapter 5 details the IRA ambushes in rural areas, some of which grew into large battles by guerrilla standards. Chapter 6 examines the IRA's use of improvised explosive devices (IEDs) and the British response to them. It also looks at the British use of armoured vehicles in response, not to explosives, but to rebel gunfire during ambushes. It was against this use of armour that the IRA tried to use IEDs.

Chapter 7 examines ambushes in urban terrain, demonstrating that urban operations were no less lethal, then as now, and concludes by detailing the British military plan for ending the war. The final chapter will examine the British tactics, techniques and procedures as developed through the various official reports, standing orders (see Appendices) and manuals in response to IRA actions. It also showcases the results of following doctrine, with examples of successful counterambush actions.

Figure 1.2 IRA Instructions

OGLAIG NA n-EIREANN.

Ard-Ofig, Ath C Liath.   General Headquarters,
Dublin.
Department...   1921.
Reference No. ....
Training Memo. No. 1.
  1921. Series.

HOW TO REVIEW AN OPERATION.

'The best way to study war in a practical manner is to consider actual operations,' Marshal Foch says on this point. We have said particular cases, not general ones, because in war there are only particular cases. In war exactly the same thing never occurs twice. How, then, are we to study an operation so as to draw profit from it? We must follow its development from start to finish, and dissect the situation at each particular stage in the operation. We thus get into the habit of considering an operation logically and minutely, until it becomes second nature with US to grasp the right alternative automatically and act on it. We shall number the successive stages, as being the surest way of impressing them on our minds.

First.—Information must be considered; whether the information at the disposal of the responsible officer was adequate; was it as good as it should have been, and if not whose fault was it? What was the source of the information, was it old or recent? In short, was it as complete as it could have been, and did it justify his line action?

Second.—His preliminary movements following on his receipt of the information. Were these reasonable and judicious? Did he display sufficient speed and care in starting his operations? Was there any weakness in his machinery that prevented his getting going in good time?

Third.—His selection of ground for his main action. Was it suitable to his purpose and to his numbers? Was it liable to surprise from any direction? Had it good command or could it be commended? Did it afford reasonable facilities for withdrawal in the case of a reverse? If it failed in any of these points, was there any alternative position he could have taken up?

Fourth.—His dispositions.—Including both improvement of his ground and disposal of his troops. Were his engineering measures such as to both remedy the defects of his position and improve its strong point? Were the Action Stations of his troops well selected? Had he too many men here or too few there? Could his parties give one another support by flanking fire? Was there any fear of them firing into one another? Had he a Reserve and was it well placed? Had he too big a force in Reserve? Was his force to open the action strong enough?

Fifth.—*Protection.*—Were proper measures taken to cover the operation? Were covering parties strong and entrenched where that was necessary and weaker where it was safe to have them so? Could scouts observe and signal in time when necessary? Were there too many troops on the Duty of Protection, thus weakening the main force? Was the conduct of the Protective Bodies judicious and skilful? If not, where did they fail?

Sixth.—The conduct of the Main Action.—Was it marked by coolness and steadiness? Was there good fire control? Were the successive stages of the action realized and measures adopted accordingly? Where circumstances called for dash and resource, or stubborn resoluteness, were these qualities displayed? Were there any sign of nerviness or panic? Were all such sternly dealt with?

Seventh.—Closing movements of the operation.—Was the finish of a successful operation drawn out unduly? Was the pursuit keen and skilful? Were the outlying parties smartly called in and got in hand? Were proper measures taken to protect the march away whether it was a retreat or simply moving off after a victory?

And remember, defeats provide lessons just as good as victories—often, indeed, more useful than victory. So analyse defeats with special care.

The above points in their proper sequence should be kept prominently in mind. (1) In preparing for operations, (2) in the reporting of operations carried out, and (3) in the review of such operations which must be regarded as a preparation and training for subsequent ones.

                                                                Director of Training.

NOTES

1. N. Banerjee and A. Hart. 'Soldiers Saw Refusing Order as their Last Stand', *New York Times*, 18 October 2004, p.1. The soldiers were not court-martialled but rather were disciplined administratively, although they clearly violated several articles of the Uniform Code of Military Justice, especially 'Disobeying a lawful order', 'Conduct unbecoming', and perhaps even 'Misbehaviour before the enemy'. What precedent this has set is unknown.
2. See Field Manual [FM] 5-102 *Countermobility*, October 2004.
3. *DOD Dictionary of Military and Associated Terms*, 9 May 2005, p.132.
4. FM, 5-102, *Countermobility*, p.i.
5. The issue depends on what one means. Certainly there were counterinsurgent operations throughout the world in the last century and the West has been variously at war with Islam for over 1,000 years.
6. British here taken to mean both official military and police (of all types) forces.
7. In which historians generally acknowledge the 1916 'Easter Rising', 'Black and Tan War' (1919–21), the Irish Civil War (1922–3). The 'Black and Tan War' is probably the more neutral of names for the 1919–21 conflict since the other common ones, the 'Anglo-Irish War' and the 'Irish War of Independence', are loaded with political symbols.
8. See Peter Hart, *The IRA at War, 1916–1923* (2003).
9. One of the only known Jewish IRA Volunteers was Robert Briscoe, who worked primarily as an arms smuggler in Germany. In the early 1930s, Briscoe met with Vladimir Jabotinsky, founder of the Zionist Israeli terrorist group Irgun Zvei Leumi (Military National Organization), and specifically taught him how to exploit British weaknesses that the IRA had discovered in their long struggle. When Jabotinsky died in 1940, Menachem Begin took over, but their 'training pamphlets issued in 1947 included a study of the Irish independence struggle. He fought a similar struggle against the British as the IRA had.' Briscoe was opposed to the Treaty and fought on the republican side. He was also lord mayor of Dublin. See A. Selth, 'Ireland and Insurgency: The Lessons of History', *Small Wars and Insurgencies*, 2, 2 (August 1991), pp.302–04; see also R. Briscoe, *For the Life of Me* (London: Little & Brown, 1958).
10. The U.S. Army Command and General Staff College at Fort Leavenworth, Kansas has used a case study of the Philippine Insurrection in its field grade officer education course during most of the decade after the events of 9/11.
11. Home rule meant that Ireland would remain within the United Kingdom but maintain its own government in Dublin, which would run its *internal* affairs.
12. Trial by field-general court-martial (FGCM) was legal under the Defence of the 1915 Realm Act (DORA), although one could question the application of it according to the technical requirements. It met the criterion of involvement with the Germans due to Roger Casement's dealings with them, but although he was the only republican leader in contact with the Germans, he was not tried by FGCM. Further, there was no imminent threat of attack, as required under DORA, since the rebels had all surrendered by the time the courts sat. Nor was there a pressing *need* for the trials to re-establish order; the army had already restored order. In the end, fifteen convicted rebel leaders were shot before Prime Minister Asquith halted the executions.
13. For more, see W. Kautt, *The Anglo-Irish War, 1916–1921: A People's War* (1999).
14. For more on the decision to use guerrilla war, see, 'The work before us', *An t-Óglác: The Official Organ of the Irish Volunteers*, 1, 10 (February 1919). For more on the period of captivity, see S. O'Mahoney, *Frongoch: University of Revolution* (1987).
15. General Staff, Irish Command, *Record of the Rebellion in Ireland in 1920–21, and the Part Played by the Army in Dealing with It* (1922), vol. IV, p.18 (National Archives [hereafter NA] PRO WO 141/93). Five divisional commissioners were appointed in late March 1920 and coordinated with the several counties under their purview. By mid-summer, two additional divisional commissioners were appointed for the headquarters of the 5th and 6th Infantry Divisions to coordinate their activities with the army. See, 'Conference Held at Royal Hospital', 4 July 1920 (NA PRO WO 35/90/1/6).
16. For discussion of DMP divisions, see, J. Herlihy, *The Dublin Metropolitan Police: A Short History and Genealogical Guide* (2001), pp.27–30 and 234–5.
17. For specific instances of DMP personnel being targeted, see Statement of James J. Slattery (Military Archives [hereafter MA] WS/445). In addition, two RIC plain-clothed intelligence specialists were also assassinated during the war. See M. Foy, *Michael Collins's Intelligence War* (2006).

18. D/Const. Laurence Dalton was assassinated by the Squad on 20 April 1920 (R. Abbott, *Police Casualties in Ireland, 1919–1922* [2000], pp.72–3).
19. 'Uniform Force D.M.P.', p.3 and 'RE: Detective Department, D.M.P.', p.2, reports to Committee to inquire as to the organization of the uniform and detective branches of the DMP, March 1920 (NA PRO CO 904/24/5); and Herlihy, *Dublin Metropolitan Police*, p.151. See also General Staff, Irish Command, *Record of the Rebellion*, vol. IV, p.40.
20. The stages listed by Vietnamese General Vo Nguyen Giap in his book, *People's War, People's Army*, are clearer than those listed by Mao Tse-tung, and so are used here. See also, FMI-3-24 *Counterinsurgency Operations*.
21. The author does not classify the female suffrage movement as 'bloodless'.
22. See Mao Tse-tung, *On Guerrilla Warfare* (1961).
23. See also Gen. V.N. Giap, *People's War, People's Army* (1961); and C. Guevara, *Guerra de Guerrillas* (1970).
24. 'The Irish Republic', *An t-Óglác*, 1, 10 (31 January 1919), p.1.
25. 'Ruthless Warfare', *An t-Óglác*, 4 (14 October 1919), p.1.
26. See T. Huber, *Compound Warfare: That Fatal Knot* (2002).
27. Harold G. Moore and Joseph L. Galloway, *We Were Soldiers Once … And Young* (1992). There was also a film of the same title in 2001.
28. The 'Army of the Republic of Vietnam'.
29. The author intends to make no moral comments.
30. Associated Press photographer Eddie Adams received a Pulitzer Prize in 1969 for this photograph. He later said that he regretted the photo because it was taken out of context. '"The guy [Lieut-Gen. Loan] was a hero," Mr Adams said, "Sometimes a picture can be misleading because it does not tell the whole story." Mr Adams said in an interview for a 1972 AP photo book: "I don't say what he did was right, but he was fighting a war and he was up against some pretty bad people."' R. Pyle, 'Obituary: Eddie Adams / New Kensington native who won Pulitzer for photo of execution', *Pittsburg Post Gazette*, 20 September 2004.
31. 'Memorandum on the present military situation, and general proposals in regard to troops during the coming winter', 26 July 1920 (NA PRO WO 32/9520, p.4).
32. Abbott, *Police Casualties*, pp.30–2.
33. Ibid., p.43 and R. Marrinan, 'The War of Independence in West Clare: 1918–1919: The Beginning of the War in West Clare, http://www.clarelibrary.ie.
34. Dáil Éireann representative Seán T. O'Kelly, then resident in Italy, had a private audience with Pope Benedict XV on 26 June 1920, during which the Pope expressed his concern about the conflict and the targeting of policemen, especially using ambushes. O'Kelly remarked that the RIC was an armed force and that they used ambushes and raids against the IRA. Pope Benedict XV did not condemn the IRA, but issued a statement against the violence on both sides. Statement of Right Rev. Monsignor M. Curran, PP (MA WS/687, Section 2).
35. Abbott, *Police Casualties*, p.44.
36. Ibid., pp.63, 68 and 74.
37. For instance, see *An t-Óglác*, II, 5A (February, 1920), pp.67–8. The article claimed that the British captured almost none of the wanted men in Dublin, which Lieut.-Gen. Shaw, the GOCinC, confirmed, but they failed to mention that the British captured about 80 per cent of the wanted men targeted outside of Dublin; see Shaw to Cabinet, 'The Military Situation in Ireland', 25 March 1920 (NA PRO WO 32/9519, pp.1–2).
38. Abbott, *Police Casualties*, p.141.
39. For IRA views on this offensive, see, in general, *An t-Óglác*, particularly, 'General Notes', II, 5A (February, 1920), pp.67–8; II, 16 (7 August 1920), p.109; II, 17 (15 August 1920), p.114; II, 18 (1 September 1920), p.117; and II, 20 (1 October 1920), p.125.
40. See War Office, *Manual of Military Law*, 'Powers of Courts of Law in Relation to Courts-Martial and Officers', p.120, especially for this lack of protection, and C. Townshend, *Britain's Civil Wars* (1986), pp.19–20.
41. Maj.-Gen. Sir S. Hare, 'Martial Law from a Soldier's Point of View', *Army Quarterly*, vol. VII (October, 1923 to January 1924), pp.289–300.
42. T. Jones, *Whitehall Diary*, vol. III, *Ireland 1918–1925* (1971), 31 May 1920, p.18. Hare specifically cited the case of *Rex* vs. *John Allen* (Court of the King's Bench, Dublin, February 1921), which decreed that courts-martial in time of martial law were not 'legally speaking, courts at all but merely committees set up by the Executive for its assistance, and that consequently, immediately the state of insurrection has ceased to exist, the proceedings of these courts can only

remain valid by the passing of an Act of Indemnity' (p.297).

43. For more on contemporary views of officers concerning the problems, see Lieut.-Col. H. De Watteville, 'The Employment of Troops Under the Emergency Regulations', *Army Quarterly*, vol. XII (April and July 1926); Major B.C. Dening, MC, RE, 'Modern Problems of Guerrilla Warfare', *Army Quarterly* (January, 1927), pp.347–54; Bvt. Maj. T.A. Lowe, 'Some Reflections of a Junior Commander upon the campaign in Ireland'. *Army Quarterly*, vol. V (October 1922–January 1923). See also Townshend, *Britain's Civil Wars*, pp.19–24.

44. Shaw to Cabinet, 'The Military Situation in Ireland', 25 March 1920 (NA PRO WO 32/9519).

45. While there were multiple and coordinated guerrilla attacks over large areas during the war, for instance, the IRA 1st Southern Division conducted numerous attacks around 14 May 1921 in reprisal for the execution of two IRA prisoners. See J. Borgonovo, *Spies, Informers and the 'Anti-Sinn Féin Society'* (Dublin: Irish Academic Press, 2008), p.88.

Two

Learning Organizations and the British Army

The IRA attacked British forces' abilities to manoeuvre in Ireland in a concerted countermobility campaign beginning in spring 1920. Before examining British counter-tactics to combat these attacks in this phase of the Irish Revolution, it is important to explore how the army established doctrine and procedures; in short, how they learned. This section begins by looking at military organizational learning in general terms and then transitions to high-level learning. It juxtaposes Prussian and German transformations with those of the British. From there, it discusses the British attempts to solve the stalemate on the Western Front in the First World War; leading into their armoured vehicle development not only rounds out the introduction to their institutional learning, but also establishes the baseline for the beginning of the Irish Revolution.

The principal question is: how do military organizations learn? This is not a matter of how they train or educate soldiers, except in that this forms part of *what* they teach. This is an issue of change. It is more than change, however, because learning implies new information has been processed and has made something different in the thinking of the actor involved. This also suggests either a deliberate process for learning or a trauma that the military organization has suffered as a result of something new on the battlefield; the actor is thus forced to change and is unable to deny the reality of his situation.

Training and education both require learning, but they are not the same. Training implies motor skills, or at least, mechanistic or repetitive skills. While education encompasses some of this, it is more conceptual, using principles, theories and other mental models. For example, training will teach a soldier how and where to emplace a machine gun position and then how to use the weapon; education will tell him *when* to use it to the greatest effect. Experience sometimes replaces education through long practice, but it also may be outmoded or superseded by more recent events. One should see these issues of training and education as symbiotic rather than opposing.

In the military, one speaks of an 'organizational' or 'corporate' memory, which tends to personify a military unit. In some senses, this is true, but groups do not have memories, although one might make a case for traditions. Yet, military units, in so far as the people of the unit remember and apply, consciously or unconsciously, whatever positive or negative lessons they have from within the group, may be said to have a corporate memory.

This brings back the original question: how do military units learn? One answer is that a military unit 'harnesses the experience of its people and organizations to improve the way it operates', adopting 'new techniques and procedures that get the job done more efficiently or effectively'.[1] How this is different from a leader's individual learning is difficult to ascertain, except that this occurs at an organization-wide level. There are several steps involved in this institutional learning: recognizing the need for change, development of the idea, forwarding the idea to higher echelons and dissemination and implementation of the new concept.

There is a period when a unit's training crashes headlong into the reality of combat, where they either succeed or suffer based on how their plan works. One of the major factors in this is, of course, the quality of the planning. How well suited was the plan to the reality of war, the situation, the terrain? This does not mean the war one wants, but the war one gets. Assuming a sound plan, while understanding the two applicable old adages that 'the enemy always gets a vote' and 'no plan survives first contact', the next factor is training. If the training matched and met the realities the troops would face on the battlefield, then they should be all right, although anything can happen in battle. If their training was insufficient, the unit must recognize this fact. Not all organizations are capable of this. For instance, in the early part of the First World War, hundreds of thousands died using tactics that were almost half a century out of date. The stalemate on the Western Front was borne of desperation on the Allied side and necessity on the German side. Another of the issues involved is just *who* in the organization needs to learn; who has the authority and capability to make the changes; whether this information gets to that individual; and whether he has the *will* to do this. This is difficult.

Recognizing the need for changes in education and training is complex, but this discernment of the need to change is one of the most important factors in examining an organization's learning abilities, because changes in their education and training demonstrate that they have learned, although not necessarily that they have learned the right lessons. While most who have served in modern military organizations will recognize that, sometimes, unnecessary change masquerades as innovation and advancement, this is certainly not always the case. With regard to substantive changes due to identifiable deficiencies, the results are tested in combat.

At the basic level, one could look for survival and retraining by units going into combat as indicators of effectiveness. Most units provide additional training to inbound replacement troops due to the limitations of basic training. There is, however, a difference between *supplemental* training and unit *retraining*. The former is in addition to, while the latter replaces, insufficient or outmoded training. Retraining, then, is the attempt to correct great problems or gaps in earlier training.

The philosophical question is: when can one state definitively that a military force has learned? Does a change in the training at the company or battalion level mean that the higher-level organizations, the brigade, division, corps, etc., have 'learned'? The issue of level of learning is particularly important because one must ask if a field army has instituted retraining or supplemental training, which realistically speaking is theatre-wide, then why has the rest of the army not followed suit? Perhaps this training is limited to the specific theatre. If the need has been identified, what corrective measures are being taken before the troops arrive in the war zone?

Identifying the level above a field army is rare in terms of a level of learning, but there are some precedents, Germany and the Soviet Red Army probably being the most obvious.[2] The Prussians, and later the Germans of the First World War, do not normally conjure up images of freethinking innovators; automatons perhaps, but not artful transformers. Whenever one examines the First World War, however, one is struck by the stark disparity in the learning climates in the Allied armies in contrast to that of the German army. Although Prussian-centred, the Germany army demonstrated a willingness to entertain new ideas that was unmatched in the war. The stereotype of the Prussian soldier as a stern, stoic, unforgiving, machine-like figure, although not altogether inaccurate, belied his distinct capacity to adapt and innovate quickly. This capacity would seem paradoxical until one scratches the surface of recent (pre-1914) Prussian history.

After the horrendous defeats in the Jena-Auerstadt campaign of 1806, the Prussian Military Reform Commission of 1807, under the leadership of General Gerhardt von Scharnhorst, reformed and reconfigured not only the Prussian army, but Prussian society as well.[3] The new army was that which Marshal Blücher later took to Waterloo, having already been tactically defeated earlier that same day at Ligny – a singular event in the Prussian army's Napoleonic-era history.[4]

Another innovation of the Prussians in 1807 was not only the creation of a general staff for campaign and war planning, but a special school, the Kriegsakademie in Berlin, to train such staff officers. This intensive, competitive and prestigious school taught officers to perform the tasks necessary to serve on the staffs. This allowed the Prussians to exert a degree of relaxed control in which the Chief of the General Staff, for instance Helmuth von Moltke, the elder, allowed his field army commanders greater autonomy during the invasion of France in 1870.[5] Since he knew the capabilities of the general staffs of the three field armies, von Moltke knew when and when not to intervene.

It is worth noting that while France started the revolutionary changes in European affairs, particularly the military changes, Napoleon eventually lost, due, in part, to his inability to continue to adapt his military capability. Further, almost all of his enemies instituted significant reforms in both their armies and societies in response to the threat from France. Notably, the British did not. The British army modified its tactics but did not change its cultural or political bases. Perhaps this was due to the unlikelihood of invasion.

The Prussian military machine continued to develop after Napoleon's fall and the Wars of German Unification (1864–71) demonstrated this dramatically, and yet, the lessons of these wars, particularly the Franco-Prussian War (1870–71), appear to have been lost on the rest of Europe. The true nature of Prussian success lay not just in the tactical realm, but in the conceptual. Prussian military thought, largely embodied in theorists such as Clausewitz and leaders like von Moltke the elder, had little effect on the military elites of Europe at the time; they were only too happy to read their own biases and prejudices into *On War*.[6]

The computer age and the advent of the internet have made dissemination of ideas far easier than in the past, although this may really only be true concerning actual speed of transmittal. Although the volume of information available is certainly greater than ever, the possibility of too much information has likewise increased. With this new standard, many people seem to forget that the transmission of information via print and 'snail mail' was rather limited in terms of time in the staff process – time to ask; time to receive; time to collect and reflect; time to respond; time to collate, evaluate and write; time either to resend and go through the process again, send up to a higher echelon, or to disseminate. When one examines the operations in Ireland, or indeed the First World War, one must remember that this was what they had to do and they knew that while they were doing so, men were dying.

An important question when examining military learning is the location of the new information: does the frontline rifleman know how to fight the war, or does he know how to fight the battle? The same question holds for the platoon NCO, the platoon leader and company commander, all of whom have separate, coexisting functions. The corollary of this question is also valid; does the general know how to fight the battle, or just the war? His function is decidedly different from the rifleman and he may not even have the physical capabilities necessary to perform the rifleman's job, or his skills may be so out of date as to be superfluous. These questions are central to the issue of learning and knowledge transmittal.

Under normal circumstances, if one may speak of 'normality' in war, these questions are almost irrelevant because battle tactics rarely dictate the formal conduct of the war. Certainly, battle tactics have an influence, but as regards planning, it is only necessary for the general staff, which is responsible for examining courses of action, making recommendations to the commanding general and planning the execution of his decision, to identify objectives, routes, contingencies and other such higher-level factors. To be sure, the general staff must have knowledge of battlefield tactics in order to understand what is and what is not possible when they ask subordinate units to perform the missions they lay out for them. At the same time, the general staff is normally unconcerned about the *means* used to execute the missions.

For instance, it would be rare indeed for a general staff to identify a machine-gun position as an obstacle or target; usually, they would identify the enemy unit controlling the area rather than individual elements of such a unit. *If* a general staff noted a machine-gun nest as requiring destruction, they would hardly concern themselves with the *means* (i.e., air strike, artillery bombardment, infantry squad assault) of its destruction. Obviously, as one goes down the chain of command, the more concerned about these issues one becomes; so a platoon leader or company commander is confronted with an obstacle like this more than a division or corps commander. That said, it is possible for such an obstacle to have greater effect than normal. In modern parlance, this is said to be 'asymmetric'.

There may be times when a general staff *should* be concerned with the means and method. This previous discussion assumes a *conventional* war of *manoeuvre*; what happens when there is a significant divergence between strategy, tactics and technology? Such was the case in the First World War, when technology outpaced tactics, which forestalled strategy. While the general staffs concerned themselves with manoeuvre after penetrating the enemy lines, they were not concerned about *how* their soldiers would actually penetrate enemy defences until much later in the war.[7] The results were disastrous. The soldiers were unable to achieve a breakout for most of the war. On the other end of the line, the riflemen were unconcerned about the manoeuvre after the breakout; they worried about the enemy's machine guns and, more so, about his artillery. They worried about crossing no-man's-land. Thus, in the First World War, strategy stalled due to the tactical–technological disparity, which limited the armies' capabilities. This produced the characteristic stalemate on the Western Front. This is an extreme example, yet there were other factors which could limit war.

Restrictions on the fighting of wars are nothing new. The eighteenth-century dynastic wars[8] are sometimes referred to as the 'Age of Limited War', since the cost of maintaining armies became so exorbitant that monarchs were reluctant to fight pitched battles that could produce high casualties. Another era of limited war came about more recently with the advent of nuclear weapons. The potential for annihilation was so high that the 'superpowers' of the Cold War (1946–93) could only fight each other by proxy due to the risks of escalation. In a strange way, this limitation served as one of the 'enablers' of revolutionary and other 'small wars' so common after the Second World War, because, while trained on each other, the superpowers could only bring a small fraction of their military might to bear against their militarily inferior foes. Further, politically, there was a point beyond which they would not, or could not, go, thus effectively limiting their options and capabilities.

This brings back the question of whether the general knows how to fight the battle. Normally the general's understanding of the conduct of combat, the actual meeting of opposing military forces on the battlefield, is not as important as where the armies meet and to what purpose – pitched battle, delaying action, shaping action, and so on. Their meeting or contact is tactical; the choice of where and why are strategic, or operational; and the overarching reasons and effect are grand strategy. It is rare indeed in conventional war for all of these to intersect at one place and time. In Ireland, as in most unconventional warfare, the battle or tactics, to a great extent, overshadowed, or perhaps one could say, became, the strategy. Put differently, the tactical actions within battles in Ireland had grand-strategic consequences far beyond their individual scope and scale. In small wars the *means* became politically, and thus strategically, important when they would hardly have had any normal or conventional military value at all.

Returning to the earlier issue, if the rifleman knows how to fight the battle and this information is important, how did information get from small units to the higher commanders? In a perfect bureaucracy, a detachment or company commander would realize that a certain approach or technique worked or helped in their day-to-day operations. He then would write a report to his battalion commander detailing what he had learned. The battalion commander would then copy the message and send it to his brigade commander, while sending the copies to his other subordinate detachment or company commanders. In Ireland, this process continued at the brigade and divisional levels until it reached the commanding general of the British army; during this conflict, General Sir Nevil Macready. Either this issue or several like it could be collected together and sent back to the field commanders in report form for their information or action. Thus, the information is distributed and could be used throughout the Irish Command. In practice, this process, when it worked, worked slowly. This has been the same basic process used from the First World War up to the present.

Another means was for the division or Irish Command generals to call conferences where senior officers discussed the situation and possible solutions or lessons learned. From such meetings, the Irish Command wrote summaries they distributed throughout Ireland. Since this is not meant to be a treatise on the history of learning within the British army, this section will not examine the Second South African War other than to mention that the army was slow to adapt their tactics to the changed battlefield environment.[9] More importantly, these changes remained local and did not influence the rest of the army. Likewise, the Staff College at Camberley, never popular among the regimentally oriented officer corps, did not take up the innovation cause.[10] So while the British army in 1914 was the most experienced army in Europe operationally due to its constant missions of 'imperial policing', this experience was in small unit engagements, which did not translate well to regular warfare, or what they referred to as 'open warfare'. These issues beset the army at the start of the war in August 1914.

From the outset, the British Expeditionary Force faced problems in France and Flanders. Maj.-Gen. Sir Nevil Macready, who became GOCinC of Irish Command during the War of Independence, came to prominence by eliminating the choke points in the logistics train from Britain to France in August 1914. Not surprisingly, the other important generals in the Irish situation later also came to prominence in the Great War; among them Generals Jeudwine, Strickland and Tudor.[11]

The tactical problem on the Western Front in broad and general terms was also the strategic and grand strategic problem – stalemate. This stemmed from one basic problem: artillery was too powerful and infantry could not cross no-man's-land. Because one arm had grown more powerful, the others (cavalry and infantry) were virtually useless against it, while the newest arm, air power, would not come into its own for many years. One's artillery could obliterate the enemy's frontline trenches containing their infantry, but then as one's own troops moved into no-man's-land, the enemy's corps-level artillery, out of reach of counterbattery fire, fired into no-man's-land on preset coordinates. This was devastating to the advancing infantry.[12] Moreover, the further one's infantry moved into enemy lines, the less effective one's artillery support capabilities became and, conversely, the more effective the enemy's rear-emplaced artillery was. It became a question of range to the target and the ability to adjust fire, which in turn depended on the ability of the artillery to communicate with someone who could actually see the rounds exploding. One reason for the disproportionate casualties among the Allies early in the stalemate was their habit of massing their infantry in the front trenches where just a few salvos from the German artillery could slaughter them. They wrongly believed that dispersal would reduce the fighting spirit of their men and/or the strength of their defences. This disparity of the artillery's power thus caused stalemate throughout all levels. Paradoxically, as powerful as artillery was, it could not win the war; artillery could not take and hold ground, only deny it to the enemy. Further, although artillery could shoot deep into the enemy rear, it could not reach far enough. So artillery could only prevent the other arms from obtaining victory.[13]

The issue then became how to use the heavier artillery, which came into service in conjunction with the infantry. Massive artillery barraging the enemy line in one area for several days and nights without cease *may* have created a breach in the line, or 'softened' the enemy for a charge across no-man's-land. It was equally likely, however, that by doing this, one had also given the enemy not only the location of the pending attack, but however many days and nights of bombardment to bring up rein-forcements; this was especially true for the Germans, because they used a layered defence, or a defence in-depth. This meant that, instead of massing one's infantry into the frontline trench, one would position a relatively small number out front while increasing the numbers and sophistication of each succeeding trench. Thus, when the enemy artillery began its assault, the first few trenches would be overrun rather easily by advancing enemy infantry, while its defenders fell back to the stronger trenches behind them. As the enemy penetrated deeper, the resistance and obstacles grew, making a breakout more unlikely. The BEF did not adopt this type of defence until May 1918, when GHQ promulgated a new manual, 'The Division in Defence'.[14] As soon as the shelling stopped, the enemy knew that the infantry was ready for its attack across the beaten zone and left their bunkers to receive the enemy advance.[15]

Another idea the British army tried was bringing up their artillery in secret and not registering the guns before the opening salvo or doing so surreptitiously.[16] This allowed for greater surprise, but also greater inaccuracy, which meant that the additional attempts, and therefore time, needed to hit the targets negated much of the advantage of surprise. Since the guns were unregistered, the artillery commanders did not want to continue firing as friendly troops closed on the targets for fear of fratricide. If they moved the guns forward, always a difficult process, the gunners still could only fire within visual range of the spotter and so the utility of moving the field artillery forward was questionable, and especially so due to the threat of enemy counterattack.

Along with the offensive use of artillery went the issue of how one should use the infantry in these operations. Clearly, or at least what should have been clear, was that the 'fix bayonets and charge' frontal assault in waves of men moving upright into no-man's-land was suicidal, or simply not working. It is not so much that the generals did not know that frontal assaults caused tremendous casualties and were not working; it was that they had few options due to the political nature of the war. Not fighting the war was not an option for the generals.

The people and the politicians were going to keep the war going as long as there was no military decision. In other words, until someone caved to the military or economic pressures of the war, which Germany eventually did, the war continued. The numerous attempts by Pope Benedict XV and even Blessed Charles of Austria, the emperor of Austria-Hungary, were ignored on both sides. There was a simple reason for this – what politician could remain in office having made a peace that was anything less than total victory, after expending so many lives? To accept any conditions for an enemy surrender would have made the sacrifice of those lives superfluous. The war seems to have become somewhat self-perpetuating in that sense. So the generals had to continue the war. One wonders whether the backlash against the military in Europe, and especially within British society after the war, was partly misplaced guilt over how the British people let such a disastrous war continue for so many years. While this does not exonerate the generals for failing to adapt, one does not always have the means to do so.

This still did not solve the problem of moving men across; artillery was still too powerful. The armies tried many means of getting the infantry across no-man's-land in frontal assaults: in close order, dispersed order, in 'worms', in wave after wave. The futility of it quickly became apparent; many soldiers stopped running – there was no reason to run to one's death.[17] Bidwell and Graham point out that the relatively poorly trained infantrymen in the new armies of 1915 and 1916 were inexperienced enough that they would do what they were told; this led to such high casualties, with their replacements continuing in the same manner.[18]

By 1916, the Allies were still trying to find technological solutions; larger artillery,[19] poison gas in 1915, new hand grenades, lighter machine guns, body armour, etc. had all made their appearance and disappointed.[20] There were also more macro-level attempts such as the landings at Gallipoli to strike at the 'soft underbelly' of Europe; 'strategic' aerial bombardment; blockade and submarines (the latter from Germany). At the highest level, however, it was the crippling blockade of Germany which ultimately ended the war. Although the German army in November 1918 was in a desperate state, many elements surrendered in France, a fact the extremists later used to create the 'stabbed-in-the-back' myth.[21] In truth, the Germans at home were starving.

The unpleasant reality for those who might decry 'teutonophilism' in First World War studies is that the answers to the stalemate were not centred mainly on new technology, but on new tactics borne of experience, training and new ideas of command and control.[22] Some, such as author and historian Paddy Griffith, contend that the British army possessed the constituent elements as early as 1916 at the Somme, while Bidwell and Graham point out that in 1907 Lord Kitchener posited ideas similar to infiltration tactics, but little came of it.[23] While Griffith's point *may* be true, it is also irrelevant because one cannot fire a rifle merely by possessing all its components, but by squeezing the trigger of the loaded, assembled whole. Griffith presents little to prove his theory, and actual events counter his claim.

Germany's army, for all its faults, embraced a culture of innovation and learning. In 1916 the Germans captured in a trench a 1915 pamphlet, written and published privately by French army Captain André Laffargue, which outlined the tactics that could break the stalemate; these would be known later as 'storm troop tactics', 'infiltration tactics' or 'Hutier tactics'. The French military leadership was uninterested in the pamphlet written by one of their junior officers, but the Germans took it and recreated the German army according to its principles. Beginning with General Oskar von Hutier, who validated these tactics in his experimental use on the Eastern Front in 1916, much of the German army reorganized and retrained to fight a new type of war of manoeuvre.[24] By 1918, the great transformation was complete and, during the Spring

Offensive of 1918, they advanced thirty-five miles, when they had only previously been able to advance mere yards. Luckily for the Allies, it was too late for Germany. With the arrival and employment of large numbers of Americans, the Western Front was reinvigorated and there was realistically nothing Germany could do to win.[25]

While the Germans used *sturmtruppen* tactics, specifically to knock out the higher-level artillery and command-and-control nodes, the Allied answer to the stalemate required several factors to come together; maps, improved command and control, and better training. By 1917, British maps were more accurate; enough so to allow Brig.-Gen. Sir H.H. Tudor to build upon the work of Maj.-Gen. Sir Herbert Uniacke to create highly accurate fire and manoeuvre tables for the 9th (Scottish) Divisional artillery's barrage fire to work without the earlier problems of endangering the infantry at Cambrai (20–28 November 1917).[26] The next improvement was in command and control, which made the coordination between the artillery and infantry more efficacious.

Better training enabled the last part of the command-and-control piece; headquarters elements *reduced* their control over the attacking infantry, which permitted lower-level commanders to make decisions based on actual local situations. In this sense, higher degrees of training made it possible for less direct control by senior commanders. This was the 'open warfare' for which the generals hoped since the beginning of the war. Troops also exploited cover in their assaults because their commanders had greater trust in their soldierly qualities and abilities.[27] As the 1920 Committee on Shellshock later explained:

> Killing power, not man power, wins a war. A man merely dressed in uniform and hurried into battle decreases rather than increases the power of an army ... He does not know his weapon; he is incapable ... Before he can be of use he has to acquire killing power, to be trained in the use of his weapon, to gain self-control and the power of endurance. Man power is only converted into killing power by training.[28]

Although 1917 and 1918 saw an increased use of aircraft in all of its rôles, but especially in ground attack, air power's time still had not come. Much of the same is true with tanks, or more appropriately, armoured vehicles, which were another attempt to break the stalemate.

By way of introducing the myriad of issues with motor vehicle ambushes later in Ireland, it is necessary to examine briefly the origins of these vehicles within the British military establishment. Their development in the BEF paralleled attempts to answer the issue of crossing no-man's-land. Vehicles remained relatively new in 1919; the British army went to war in August 1914 with just 950 lorries, they ended the war in 1918 with over 48,000 vehicles of various types in France alone.[29] That said, relatively few of these were deliberately designed for combat duty or to carry troops into battle. Most motor vehicles were used as transport for large amounts of materiel from the rail depots to the front.

Armoured cars had two main functions: protecting their occupants while attacking the enemy. The armoured car was both an offensive and defensive weapon 'system', consisting of the vehicle, its propulsion, armour and offensive weapons, its machine guns. This leads to what they were not; they were not troop transportation vehicles. Thus, the capacity for occupants was quite limited. The armoured car was really a mobile machine-gun platform, where the armour protected the gunners and drivers. While the armoured car could certainly transport a few additional people, its true function was to deliver concentrated machine-gun fire in an offensive or defensive mode.

'Up-armoured' vehicles, to use the modern phrase, were similar to armoured cars, but differed fundamentally in design, purpose and function, which directly affected their employment. When examining the other armoured vehicles, one must remember their purpose: protection. If there was little or no threat to the vehicle's cargo, one would not normally have spent the additional time and money needed to hang heavy armour, usually half-inch or one-inch steel plates, on the vehicles. One did not normally have to protect materiel from enemy fire until it came within range, so the retro-fitted armoured lorry had a different purpose, the one that the armoured car could not fulfil: protecting troops in transit. It is notable that the identified need to protect troops in transit did not come really until after the First World War (see below) and after the normal armoured cars were already in service. This made the un-armoured lorry after the Great War different from the armoured car in two respects: the commanders not only found it necessary to employ armed troops in the defence of convoys, but also the troops' presence necessitated armoured lorries to transport them. Except for munitions and highly combustible materials, the cargo normally rode in regular unarmoured lorries.

The story of how the British developed their armoured capabilities in the First World War not only examines the state of the art in 1918 and 1919, but also highlights the British army as a learning organization. This is significant because it partly prefigures how the British army would react in the War of Independence and, more importantly, why.

Although the idea of armoured vehicles had been around for centuries in various forms, industrialist Jean de Bloch and novelist H.G. Wells gave it new meaning by envisioning the nature of the fighting in the First World War, a decade beforehand. While Bloch thought such heavy casualties would lead to stalemate and, inevitably, to political collapse among the combatants, Wells felt that 'Land Ironclads' would provide an answer to the stalemate. Although Wells thought that these machines would transport combat troops, he also felt they would be capable of destroying machine-gun positions and other enemy strong points without discharging their passengers.[30] Their ideas, however, did not lead to changes in the forces, largely because Bloch and Wells were civilians.

Ironically, the Royal Navy was the first to establish armoured car units in the British Expeditionary Force (BEF) in the Great War. Winston Churchill, then First Lord of the Admiralty, placed a squadron of aircraft from the Royal Naval Air Service (RNAS) in Belgium on 28 August 1914. They conducted not only air operations, but also ground reconnaissance by motorcar. When Allied forces were pushed out of that part of Belgium shortly thereafter, the squadron, under Commander C.R. Samson, moved to Dunkirk and continued operations there. Commodore Murray Sueter, chief of the Air Department, asked for 'fifty armed motor cars to assist in forming temporary forward airfields'. The enthusiastic Churchill gave them one hundred.[31]

These vehicles had machine guns from the beginning and later had armour – simple steel plates welded into place by local contractors. They were apparently not very effective. Sueter answered directly to Churchill, who was also eager about the project, and established the RNAS Armoured Car Centre at Wormwood Scrubs. There, he set about experimenting with determining armour needs against German bullets at varying ranges. The result was the first 'Admiralty pattern' Rolls Royce armoured car in December 1914.[32]

As early as October of that year, army officers were suggesting that tracked vehicles with machine guns and armour could cross no-man's-land. The British originally began with the idea of a troop-transporting armoured vehicle, but eventually gave that up for an offensive vehicle. That said, armoured cars had been around for almost two decades. Further, the Royal Navy's 'Admiralty Landships Committee' envisioned troops deploying from these vehicles like marines.[33] By early 1916, a joint committee designing the tank decided to have two variants, which they called 'male' and 'female'. The difference between them was that the 'male' was armed with 6-pounder naval guns, while the 'female' was armed solely with machine guns and was intended to protect the 'male' tanks from enemy infantry, hence the machine guns. This also demonstrated an early understanding of the threat posed by infantry to armoured forces. Their use on 15 September 1916 at the continuing Battle of the Somme was unspectacular in terms of military results, but the novelty of the machines caught the attention of the press.[34]

With the issue of why it took so long from 1914 to 1915 to get any real support for the idea of the tank, it appears that the overly cautious military structure, especially with Lord Kitchener serving as Secretary of State for War, limited innovation. Further, this would also have led to disputes later about whose ideas led to the development of the tank, with people from the Royal Navy to members of various committees to H.G. Wells claiming absolute credit for the idea. Harris rightly points out that it was a series of ideas from various sources which all came together at the right moment.[35]

Colonel E.D. Swinton was the first to propose formally to the army that tanks could help break the stalemate. He understood that tanks must operate in an all-arms environment – the British artillery would conduct both barrage and counterbattery fire while the tanks crossed no-man's-land. Upon reaching the enemy trenches, infantry would cross and support. The problem was exploitation; if the tanks created a break-out, how could the British move more troops forward to exploit the breach? With horse cavalry, as some suggested?[36] They would have had to do this before the Germans shifted their forces to fill in the gap. Their first use at the Somme on 15 September 1916 was less than spectacular, with most of the vehicles breaking down rather quickly.

One of the important characters of this saga was an obscure staff officer called J.F.C. Fuller, who gained fame after the war for his claims of having come up with modern tank doctrine during the conflict. Fuller was an intellectual and a radical, enjoying a privileged position as a de facto advisor to Lord Milne, chief of the Imperial General Staff from 1926 to 1933. Still later, Fuller moved to the edge of society with his involvement with satanism and, still later, fascism.[37] Despite his oddities, he was a more than competent military historian and theorist. In this examination, his ideas on the November 1917 Battle of Cambrai, especially the use of tanks, merit some review, since they illustrate some of the inherent issues with armour development.

Fuller's critique and observations of tank usage at Cambrai begin with the assertion that there was insufficient space for the armour to operate; that 10,000 yards was too narrow a front. Although this is five and a half miles, it did not matter because this was not an armoured offensive. The tanks were in support of the infantry. This point is rather important, because it decided how the British forces moved forward. The British tanks were incapable of being the main element of attack at this point due to capability – speed, survivability, manoeuvre, and so on. Another reason the space was largely irrelevant was that there were insufficient tanks to cover a larger area.[38] Since there was no battle-tested armour doctrine, it was difficult to determine how many tanks there should have been per yard of frontage. Of course, there was no mention of how Fuller would have controlled such forces over an even larger area without radios. How could one control artillery during such an advance? Arguing that one should do what was arguably correct but impossible due to other constraints was less than useful.

Fuller's first criticism brought into question his second, that there should have been a tank reserve to exploit any breach in the German line. This assumed there were sufficient tanks to spare, which, in turn, assumed that the advancing tanks were, and would remain, mechanically sound, while not succumbing to failures due to various obstacles and other enemy action. The 324 tanks at Cambrai suffered severe losses on the first day (see Table 2.1). The second problem was that it also assumed the attacking tank forces had more than sufficient tanks which could have been spared for a reserve while at the same time still achieving a breakthrough. If they had extended the line of advance, as Fuller said they should in his first point, there would have been insufficient numbers of serviceable tanks with which to advance; the creation of a reserve force would have dramatically reduced the density of forces. Finally, as Harris aptly stated: 'It was, moreover, quite noticeable that the fewer the tanks that were engaged the greater the proportion of casualties they were likely to sustain.'[39]

Table 2.1 Tank Usage at the Battle of Cambrai, November 1917[40]

Action	Tanks
Engaged in Combat Operations	324
Direct Hit by Artillery	65
Broken Down	71
Abandoned by Crews	43

The third critique was more of an observation; that the advance was limited to the infantryman's speed and endurance. This also identified the weakness of armour, to which Fuller only hinted in his fourth observation: tanks did not operate well in urban environments.[41] The corollary of both of these points is that armour *must* have infantry support and is therefore limited to its speed. While all this was true, the issue of speed was not solved until the Second World War. Fuller's critique did not mention that tanks really needed to operate as part of an all-arms team.

Based on these observations, it is difficult to argue that Haig should have acted differently at Cambrai with regard to tanks. Fuller's later pronouncements about tanks were only supportable *ex post facto*, and then only in part. Further, Harris argued that Fuller's later angst with 'Tanks and Their Employment in Co-operation with Other Arms' of August 1918 was unfounded. Quotations from this manual portraying GHQ's response as 'reactionary' to armour were taken out of context and, when read as a whole, the manual demonstrated 'that GHQ was keen to use the existing tank technology to its full potential but anxious not to make claims which would not be legitimate until the next generation arrived'.[42] This point demonstrated a more balanced approach to armour than Fuller seemed willing to admit. To accept or overly rely on untested technology is reckless. Haig may have been myopic, but not because he rejected the grandiose and largely unsupportable claims of theorists like Fuller.[43] The latter's comments and claims may eventually have come to pass, but not in the First World War, and were based on a vision that had not yet been realized.

One may question Haig's soundness for many of his failures, but criticizing him over this is disingenuous. For instance, why should Haig suffer at the hands of historians for his apparent inability to conceive of the 'proper' use of tanks when this remained undecided among most armies in the West until at least 1940? The weapons that caused the stalemate on the Western Front in the First World War, primarily artillery, and to a lesser extent machine-guns and modern rifles, had debuted in the Second South African War fifteen years earlier and in the Russo-Japanese War in 1905. The British army in South Africa developed effective counter-tactics to deal with the effects of these weapons. Why did these lessons not become part of British training?[44] If one wishes to criticize Haig, there is ample cause elsewhere while, at the same time, one would have to criticize those in charge beforehand, beginning at least with Lord Roberts.

The war eventually ended, but not due to the use of tanks. After the war, theorists such as Fuller and Liddell Hart advanced the science of war, but embellished their arguments with claims of widespread incompetence among the leadership of the BEF.[45] Asserting that it took time and bloody experience to develop the right tactics to end the stalemate, or waiting for the Americans to arrive, would not have advanced their theories. While there was much truth in their claims, the BEF leadership were not quite as Blackadder-esque as they are frequently portrayed. Still, it is important to recognize that while both Fuller and Liddell Hart made strides in military theory, these advances would have been impossible for the pre-1917 British army.

The issue of how best to protect troops was not solved definitely in the First World War. As late as spring 1920, the brigade commanders and other senior army officers in the Dublin District debated what materials they should use to protect passengers in their lorries. They considered thick wooden planks, sandbags, and corrugated iron, among others, before finally deciding on steel plates.

Historian J.P. Harris said that the armoured car was an excellent tool for British interwar imperial policing, specifically mentioning India, Iraq and Ireland. He noted that Mesopotamia (Iraq) 'was of particular importance to the development of British armoured forces'.[46] It is interesting that Ireland had the most use of armoured vehicles, in terms of total numbers employed, but does not appear to have influenced armoured vehicle doctrinal development. Was it because the British found that armour did not make as significant a difference as one would think? Interestingly, some army officers questioned the utility of armoured cars in all-but-routine convoy operations, claiming motor vehicles in general were not useful in combat. While one would expect such resistance from cavalry officers during the interwar debate over replacing horses with mechanical transport, one of the harsher critiques came from an experienced infantry officer of the Essex Regiment, who had fought in both the First World War and in Ireland. Still, it is important to remember that the tank and armoured cars were developed to meet a conventional threat in a conventional war. Their application to small wars was as halting and hesitant as the development of an overall 'imperial policing' doctrine. By 1922, neither British armour doctrine nor counterinsurgency doctrine were sophisticated. Thus, it is no surprise that the combination of the two was problematic.

In general, the British military was quite busy after the First World War; they had to police their empire, govern the mandates given them by the League of Nations and perform occupation duties around the world. At the same time, the British military, especially the army, was demobilizing from its wartime strength. In 1919, the British army was 3.9 million men; by 1921, it had reduced to just 250,000. Of these, 163,736 (65.49 per cent) were serving in active operations worldwide. So during a time when their military might was near its historic heights, field commanders around the world had understrength units and simply saw that exceptional might fade away. Furthermore, the war had destroyed the old pre-war army, the 'Old Contemptibles', who had been so effective in their small colonial actions. During the Great War, the 'new army' of 1915 and later were not trained to the same level as the old army, partly due to the lack of time to train properly and partly because the survivors of the old army were too few to provide adequate training cadres.[47] This limited capabilities and necessitated greater or more direct control. The army had found that precision marksmanship, a fundamental skill of the 'Old Contemptibles', was counterproductive on the First World War battlefield. Instead, they used volume of fire. The British army of 1919 and 1920, in comparison, were ill suited to imperial duties. This army was trained to fight in large-scale, corps and field army-sized campaigns in the open field with massive firepower supporting them. They were trained to kill the enemy whose location and identity were quite obvious with a large volume of rifle fire. What they got bore little resemblance to the company and battalion-sized 'policing' actions in which they were engaged.

Added to the obvious mismatch with the structure of these British forces was an anti-intellectual climate inherent in the regimental system, the system to which they reverted after the war.[48] This attitude extended to the reviews of the Great War. The Germans were singular in beginning a quiet and serious examination of their failures in that war almost immediately. Perhaps it was that losers are more inclined to review their loss, but any examination of the First World War reveals the shortcomings of such an argument. The systematic review by General Hans von Seeckt and his hand-picked group of staff college graduates created the new concepts of conducting mobile warfare that the Nazis eventually used so effectively against the other European armies from 1939 to 1942. Nazism's heinous ideology, reprehensible conduct, and evil mass murder notwithstanding, the purely military concepts that English-speakers labelled *blitzkrieg* were sound. These concepts, especially all arms working in conjunction with swift command and control, form the basis of western conventional doctrine today.

While the Germans were minutely dissecting every aspect of the First World War in painstaking detail, the British army merely reverted to its pre-war condition. They did not begin a formal systematic examination of the First World War until 1932. Even then, the committee's report was suppressed by the new chief of the Imperial General Staff, Montgomery-Massingberd. Thus, incorporating any lessons was nearly impossible.[49]

It is important to recognize several of the mitigating circumstances the British army faced. After the world war, Britain wanted peace. There was a decidedly anti-military sentiment due to the association of the army with the conduct and outcome of the war. Rightly or wrongly, British society looked down on professional military men primarily because they were seen, as a group, to have performed so poorly in the war. In the eyes of the public, the professional officers had failed to pre- dict the type of fighting that would occur, they failed to develop work- able tactics or strategies with which to win the war, they failed to achieve decisive results, they proved inept on the modern battlefield, and they continued the slaughter. It was then that the 'lions led by donkeys' myth was born.[50] Unfortunately, many of these criticisms were true, although the regulars did have some idea of what a modern war would look like, especially after the shocks of the Second South African War. As men- tioned above, Jean de Bloch accurately predicted what would occur, but since he was not a military man, his ideas were largely ignored. Military views held that the war would be exceptionally bloody, but short because populations could not sustain the level of casualties expected. Of course, the British public did not seem to hold the politicians account- able for their failures either, but popular sentiment is not normally fair.[51] Many questioned why the war had continued, seemingly not under- standing that the army had no control over the stopping or continuing of the war. There was certainly much blame to go around after such tremendous trauma and these assessments were not logical judgements, but rather, emotional reactions. As a result, they held greater sway.

The horror of the destructiveness of the world war produced not only an anti-military view in Britain, but also a general anti-war sentiment. This was greater than a mere abhorrence of war; it was a pacifistic turn in which for many people there were few causes or circumstances which justified war. These feelings were on a continuum, which produced varying levels of such sentiments, and they combined with a new liber- alism to cut spending for the military after the war. Given the devastat- ing effects of the war on society and the economic system, the vast mil- itary stockpiles built up during the war, and a lack of a 'peer competitor', to use the modern phrase, it was difficult to justify increased military spending, in many cases even for the basics.

Accurate or not, these sentiments produced a political climate in which government decided to declare a policy of 'limited liability', in which the British army would never again be committed to ground combat on the continent of Europe. Obviously, this policy was not really feasible, but the insistence of the RAF that they could destroy any enemy army with bombing, the insistence of the Royal Navy that they could prevent any invasion of the United Kingdom, and the belief that the people of Britain would not support an overseas war again enabled its suspension of reality.[52] As a result of widespread anti-military feeling and the official policy of limited liability and budget constraints, the British army was then reduced to an unsafe level, one at which it could hardly perform the tasks to which it was assigned, let alone participate in any substantial combat.

Probably the worst problem for the army in 1919 to 1921 was their ongoing combat and other active operations. As mentioned above, 160,000 soldiers were serving in fourteen locations around the world. With so much attention focused around the world and such a large part of the army deployed, it is a wonder that they were able to do much at all. As will be detailed later, the army was also just learning to use armoured vehicles (both tracked and wheeled) and was experimenting with a combination of manoeuvres on the Salisbury Plain and trial and error in combat.[53] How useful the lessons of the First World War were was not yet apparent and depended mainly on how one approached war.

So, for the British after the First World War, limitations had nothing to do with superpower rivals or concerns with losing a great ideological battle, but rather with the anti-war sentiment and over-extension. At the same time, there was a general rise of liberalism in the western democracies following the war, but especially in the United Kingdom.[54] This was a sort of 'sigh of relief' after more than four years of war.

All of these factors came together to place effective limits on what was permissible in the mind of the British public. Thus in Ireland, the balance of strategy, tactics and the political objectives was tilted. The politicians were meagre in their guidance to the army, merely telling them to create stability in order to withdraw. As a result, the strategy was unclear. Likewise, since there was no clear political or higher-level military guidance, the tactics, the 'how to', of the war, were muddied. The question for the field commanders was simply: how? That is not to say that Lord French, the Lord-Lieutenant, Hamar Greenwood, Chief Secretary for Ireland, General Macready or any of the higher-level officials in Ireland did not have their own vision of what they wanted to see or do, but that neither they, nor the prime minister, provided an actual stated mission for the Irish Command or formulated any vision into policy.[55]

After formal training, soldiers learned and transmitted information about combat operations in Ireland in several ways. Those who have not served in the military might tend to underestimate the power of informal discussions, but in reality these are surprisingly effective in examining combat and other stressful situations. Frequently, one will find that the troops in the field actually discern what works and what does not work. Once this occurs, the informal communications systems within armies will take over and transmit the information. There are, however, more formal means to perform this function. Probably the most important is the after-action review.

As mentioned above, reports went back and forth between British units and their higher headquarters and, in a manner of speaking, most operational and intelligence reports from the army were de facto after-action reviews in that they summarized the importance of what occurred during the period under review, what happened how, why and with what result. There were four main reports which fall under the more formal after-action review system: war diaries, individual reports, operation summaries and weekly intelligence summaries.

The term 'war diaries' was applied both specifically and generally. Specifically, these consisted of notation in a book or ledger by the duty officer or NCO of anything important occurring, listing time, place and a brief description. They were usually the first link in the chain of more official reporting. All of these links were designed to keep the higher echelons informed, but also to pass on information about what worked against the rebels and what did not.[56]

Individual incident reports largely appear not to have survived, except as attachments to other documents. These were reports by officers and NCOs in charge during a particular event, be it a raid or patrol, convoy or party being ambushed. In these incident reports, the authors laid out the facts, *as they knew them*.[57] Considering that one's perspective becomes quite focused when under fire, these reports were usually full of incomplete, inaccurate and sometimes erroneous information. Thus, it was not unusual for the narrative of an incident to change as more information became available. Sometimes these reports came from other units or individuals who arrived later and conducted a more thorough investigation of the area or incident.

Operation summaries were the next link in the chain and were more considered, daily reports written by brigade general staff officers using the earlier reports, written and oral, to inform higher headquarters of what occurred in their area that day.[58] Oftentimes, these reports, usually not exceeding two typed pages, included copies of the individual incident reports and war diary notations.

The weekly intelligence summaries were longer reports containing the major incidents and occurrences throughout all the brigades and divisions under the Irish Command. Like the other types of reports, these summaries included copies of the various war diaries, incident reports and operation reports.

The final report type which fell under this system was the actual intelligence report. Such reports were based on information received through various means and sometimes included best practices from either side.[59] Frequently, intelligence information confirmed suspicions that certain operational changes worked against the enemy.[60]

In the latter part of 1920, the Irish Command directed the brigades, through the divisions and the Dublin District, to maintain a record of all the major incidents. The General Staff directed that these reports be timely, but not sacrifice accuracy for speed. They were especially concerned about relations which might affect civilians or cause coverage in the press.[61] These were the mechanisms for transmission of lessons learned in Ireland.

All of this demonstrates that the British army was, indeed, capable of learning, albeit at a reduced pace. It attempted many ways of breaking the stalemate in the Great War, but was hampered by high casualties, lack of time and men, poor leadership in some cases, desperation in others, and a parochial sense of propriety. After the Somme in 1916, the commanders began to make changes in the collection of information about the battles. These studies changed how the British army fought the rest of the war.[62] But then, soldiers usually do not like dramatic changes, since they might suffer as a result. The solution they found to the stalemate, all arms, was the same they would eventually try to employ in Ireland. Part of this was the use of mechanical transport. The British General Staff system worked, but was not as efficient as the German General Staff.[63] The Irish Command, or more appropriately, the units, men and officers who comprised it, brought all of this baggage with them to Ireland.

Figure 2.1 'Dublin District Weekly Intelligence Summary',
N°. 118, Copy N°. 83, for week ending 12 June 1921 (NA PRO WO 35/91)

SECRET

3rd Battalion Rifle Brigade,
Phoenix Park
Dublin.

To:- Adjutant,
From:- O.C. "A" Company

General report on operations carried out at BLANCHARDS TOWN
on Morning 17.6.21.

OBJECT.   To make a thorough search of the village, for wanted men, arms,
            ammunition, or seditious literature.

FORCE
EMPLOYED.   (a) Cordon Party, 1 Officer and 26 Cyclists, also 1 Officer and
            23 Other Ranks.
            (b) Search Party, 4 Officers and 20 Other Ranks.
            (c) Reserve, 4 Other Ranks.
               Total, 6 Officers 73 Other Ranks.

CORDON
PARTY.   The cordon troops were in their allotted positions at 0500 hours.
            The formed a circle round the village. Each road was guarded and
            the intervening spaces, watched from vantage points and
            frequently patrolled.

SEARCH
PARTIES.   Divided into 4 groups each under an Officer. Operations by these
            groups stared at 0515 hours.

PROCEDURE.   On arrival all males up to 60 years of age were sent to
            Headquarters (R.I.C. Barrack ruins on East edge of village) their
            names being taken and houses numbered.
                The search then proceeded, parties working towards centre
            of village. All males were detained under guard until completion
            of search.

RESULTS.   Nothing of an incriminating nature was discovered excepting a few
            S.D. Jackets the property of ex-soldiers. These were confiscated.
            All males were released at the conclusion of the operation except
            for 18 young men who were brought in to the barracks for interrogation.

GENERAL.   The possibility of any really satisfactory results from this raid
            was ruined from the start by the non appearance of the Intelligence
            Officers from H.Q. Dublin District. Every effort was made to obtain
            these when it was seen that they had failed to arrive at the appoint-
            ed hour. Teleghone [*sic*] messages were sent at intervals from 0500 hours
            to mid-day. As a result, there was none present who knew any-thing
            about the 127 males detained. The only possible alternative was to
            dismiss those whose account of themselves appeared satisfactory.
            A few doubtful xxxxx looking men were brought away.
            Any operation of this nature is a waste of time if there is none
            about who can identify "Wanted Men".

            The troops carried out their tasks well. The cyclist party were
            particularly useful, not only for cordon purpose but escorting
            men from one place to another and returning quickly.

            The following are attached herewith.
            A. Nominal Roll of Males present in the village with the
            occupations they stated themselves.
            B. Damage Certificate.
            C. Certificate of Looting.

                                (Sgd) T. Massy-Beresford. MC. Captain.
                                O.C. Raid. 17.6.21.

NOTES

1. U.S. Army, FM 6-22 *Army Leadership: Competent, Confident and Agile*, Washington, DC: Headquarters, Dept of the Army, 12 October 2006, p.82. The U.S. Army is one of the few military organizations to study, publish and implement the ideas of a military learning organization. This field manual was born out of their experiences in combat in Afghanistan and Iraq.

2. Since the Red Army's metamorphosis came after the Irish Revolution and the period under examination, the previous example of the Germans will be used, especially since the British army faced the Germans just prior to the Irish Revolution.

3. Social reforms included ending serfdom, allowing all Prussian men to serve in the military at any rank, and a draft. See C. Clark, *Iron Kingdom: The Rise and Downfall of Prussia, 1600–1947* (Cambridge, MA: Harvard University Press, 2006).

4. Prussian forces had always disengaged following a battlefield defeat; that Blücher would re-engage after a defeat apparently never crossed Napoleon's mind.

5. D.E. Showalter, 'The Prusso-German RMA, 1840–1871', in M. Knox and W. Murray (eds), *The Dynamics of Military Revolution, 1300–2050* (2001), pp.94–5 and G.E. Rothenberg, 'Moltke, Schlieffen, and the Doctrine of Strategic Envelopment', in P. Paret (ed.), *Makers of Modern Strategy* (1986), pp.299–300.

6. See also A. Bucholz, *Moltke, Schlieffen, and Prussian War Planning* (New York: Berg, 1991); A.J. Echevarria, *After Clausewitz: German Military Thinkers Before the Great War* (Lawrence, KS: University Press of Kansas, 2000); W. Gorlitz, *History of the German General Staff* (New York: Praeger, 1957); M. Howard, *Franco-Prussian War: The German Invasion of France, 1870–1871* (New York: Routledge, 2001); D. Showalter, *Railroads and Rifles: Soldiers, Technology, and the Unification of Germany* (Hamden, CT: Archon Books, 1975) and G. Wawro, *The Franco-Prussian War: The German Conquest of France in 1870–1871* (Cambridge: Cambridge University Press, 2005).

7. S. Bidwell and D. Graham, *Fire-Power: British Army Weapons and Theories of War, 1904–1945* (1982), p.115.

8. Usually starting with the War of Spanish Succession (1701–13) and ending around the Seven Years' War (1756–63).

9. See D. Graham, 'The British Expeditionary Force in 1914 and the Machine Gun', *Military Affairs*, 46, 4 (December 1982), pp.190–3 and B. Poe II, 'British Army Reforms, 1902–1914', *Military Affairs*, 31, 3 (Autumn 1967), pp.131–8.

10. Bidwell and Graham, *Fire-Power*, pp.10–13.

11. The concept of combined arms requires that all arms be roughly equal in the sense that while artillery counters infantry, cavalry counters artillery and infantry counters cavalry. With this concept, one must have all three, and the mastery of their use is the timing of their use during the battle.

12. J. House, *Combined Arms Warfare in the Twentieth Century* (Lawrence, KS: University Press of Kansas, 2001), pp.34–7.

13. For more on the First World War in general, and these problems specifically, see M. Samuels, *Command or Control? Command, Training and Tactics in the British and German Armies, 1888–1918* (London: Frank Cass, 1995), and T. Travers, *How the War Was Won: Command and Technology in the British Army* (London: Routledge, 1992). For British forces in that war, see also P. Griffith, *Battle Tactics of the Western Front: The British Army's Art of Attack, 1916–1918* (New Haven, CT: Yale University Press, 1994).

14. SS 210: 'The Division in Defence', May 1918.

15. Bidwell and Graham, *Fire-Power*, pp.26–7.

16. Registration is a means by which a gun is fired to measure its range and establish its accuracy under its new emplacement (ibid., p.73).

17. Interestingly, the British sentenced over 3,000 men to death for military crimes such as cowardice, desertion, mutiny, etc., and executed 321. The French sentenced over 2,000 for the same reasons and executed some 600, including forty-nine (of 554 sentenced to death) for the mutinies of 1917. The Italians executed 750 men, while the Germans sentenced 150 men to death and actually shot only 48. The issue today is how many of those executed were, in fact, suffering from Mild Traumatic Brain Injury or Post Traumatic Stress Disorder, what they then called 'shell-shock'. Soon after the war, the Committee on Shellshock started asking these questions. See G. Christopher Oram, *Military Executions During World War I* (London: Palgrave Macmillan, 2003), pp.3, 12 and 18, and 'Report on the War Office Committee on Shellshock', September 1920 (NA PRO WO 32/4748).

18. Bidwell and Graham, *Fire-Power*, p.117.
19. This consisted of the 'creeping barrage', where the artillery fired on specific timetables to allow the infantry to cross no-man's-land while the German forces were still in their bunkers (Bidwell and Graham, *Fire-Power*, pp.83 and 111–12).
20. See G. Raudzens 'War-Winning Weapons: The Measurement of Technological Determinism in Military History', *Journal of Military History*, 54, 4 (October 1990), pp.403–34.
21. Bidwell and Graham offer an interesting criticism of the inter-war era commentators, that by unfairly attacking the British military leadership, they gave fuel to the 'stabbed in the back' myths in Germany (*Fire-Power*, pp.112–13).
22. For a counterview of the 'new' (i.e. post-1871) German army's tactical abilities early in the war, see S.D. Jackman, 'Shoulder to Shoulder: Close Control and "Old Prussian Drill" in German Offensive Infantry Tactics, 1871–1914', *Journal of Military History*, 68, 1 (January 2004), pp.73–104.
23. Griffith, *Battle Tactics*, p.54 and Bidwell and Graham, *Fire-Power*, p.31.
24. House, *Combined Arms Warfare*, pp.51–6.
25. For a new interpretation of the American contributions, see K. Stubbs, *Race to the Front: The Material Foundations of Coalition Strategy in the Great War* (Westport, CT: Praeger, 2002).
26. Bidwell and Graham, *Fire-Power*, pp.90–1 and 103–9; Travers, *How the War was Won*, p.24 and J.P. Harris, *Men, Ideas and Tanks: British Military Thought and Armoured Forces, 1903–1939* (Manchester: Manchester University Press, 1995), pp.108–10.
27. Bidwell and Graham, *Fire-Power*, pp.112–13.
28. 'Report on the War Office Committee on Shellshock', September 1920 (NA PRO WO 32/4748), p.206.
29. Col. R.H. Beadon, *The Royal Army Service Corps: A History of Transport and Supply in the British Army* (1931, pp.86–118 and I. Brown, *British Logistics on the Western Front, 1914–1919* (1998), p.63.
30. Harris, *Men, Ideas and Tanks*, pp.5–8. See J. de Bloch. *Future of War: In its Technical, Economic and Political Relations* (Boston: World Peace Foundation, 1914); H.G. Wells, 'The Land Ironclads', *The Complete Short Stories of H.G. Wells* (London: Benn, 1966); T. Travers, 'Technology, Tactics, and Morale: Jean de Bloch, the Boer War, and British Military Theory, 1900–1914', *Journal of Modern History*, 51, 2 (June 1979), pp.264–86.
31. Harris, *Men, Ideas and Tanks*, pp.10–11 and E. Bartholomew, *Early Armoured Cars* (Buckinghamshire: Shire Publications, 1988), pp.11–13.
32. Harris, *Men, Ideas and Tanks*, pp.12–13 and Bartholomew, *Early Armoured Cars*, pp.12–16.
33. Bidwell and Graham, *Fire-Power*, p.137.
34. Harris, *Men, Ideas and Tanks*, pp.31–3.
35. Bidwell and Graham, *Fire-Power*, p.137 and Harris, *Men, Ideas and Tanks*, pp.36–8.
36. Harris, *Men, Ideas and Tanks*, pp.48–9 and Bidwell and Graham, *Fire-Power*, p.99.
37. Bidwell and Graham, *Fire-Power*, pp.168–9 and Harris, *Men, Ideas and Tanks*, p.1.
38. Travers, *How the War was Won*, p.24; Harris, *Men, Ideas and Tanks*, pp.108–10; and Bidwell and Graham, *Fire-Power*, pp.134–5.
39. Harris, *Men, Ideas and Tanks*, p.179.
40. Numbers taken from Bidwell and Graham, *Fire-Power*, p.137.
41. Travers, *How the War was Won*, p.24.
42. Travers, *How the War was Won*, p.24 and Harris, *Men, Ideas and Tanks*, pp.180–1.
43. Bidwell and Graham, *Fire-Power*, pp.66–72.
44. T. Travers, 'The Offensive and the Problem of Innovation in British Military Thought 1870–1915', *Journal of Contemporary History*, 13, 3 (July 1978), pp.531–53.
45. Griffith, *Battle Tactics*, pp.5–7.
46. Harris, *Men, Ideas and Tanks*, p.197; see also Bidwell and Graham, *Fire-Power*, p.169.
47. Bidwell and Graham, *Fire-Power*, pp.27–9 and 38–40.
48. See, for instance, Bidwell and Graham, *Fire-Power*, pp.19, 33, 152, 156–60; M. Samuels, *Command or Control? Command, Training and Tactics in the British and German Armies, 1888–1918* (London: Routledge, 1995), pp.43–5; and Poe, 'British Army Reforms', p.132.
49. Williamson Murray and A.R. Millett, *Military Innovation in the Interwar Period* (Cambridge: Cambridge University Press, 1996), pp.20–1 and 24; and Bidwell and Graham, *Fire-Power*, pp.132–3 and 144–5.
50. Griffith, *Battle Tactics*, pp.6–7; and Bidwell and Graham, *Fire-Power*, p.38.
51. Many officers felt that the politicians should have borne the responsibility for what occurred in the war because they had not funded the army to a reasonable level in the years leading up to the war (Bidwell and Graham, *Fire-Power*, p.39).

52. Murray and Millett, *Military Innovation*, pp.9–10 and 305; and Bidwell and Graham, *Fire-Power*, p.150.
53. Harris, *Men, Ideas and Tanks*, p.197.
54. Bidwell and Graham, *Fire-Power*, p.65.
55. Bidwell and Graham describe a similar problem for the army in general in the inter-war era; the assumption was that the army would participate in imperial policing, but there was little firm guidance (*Fire-Power*, pp.150–1).
56. See, for instance, 'War Diary', 36th Brigade, RFA, 15 April 1921 (NA PRO WO 35/93A); see also 'War Diaries' (PRO WO 35/90–3), 'Duty Officer's Diary' (WO 35/177) and 'Duty Log book' (WO 35/178).
57. Dublin District Memorandum No. S/712/G., 21 September 1920 (NA PRO WO 35/90/1/49 and 'War Diaries', Dublin District Memorandum No. 102/1 G., 11 December 1920 (WO 35/90/1).
58. See attachments to Weekly Intelligence Summaries generally (NA PRO WO 35/90–3).
59. See, for instance, Dublin District Memorandum No. S/G.1., 19 October 1920 (NA PRO WO 35/90/1/52, pp.1–2.
60. See 'Extract from An tOglac', Appendix C, 'Dublin District Weekly Intelligence Summary', No. 118, Copy 83 for week ending 12 June 1921 (NA PRO WO 35/91).
61. Dublin District Memorandum No. S/712/G., 21 September 1920 (NA PRO WO 35/90/1/49 and 'War Diaries', Dublin District Memorandum No. 102/1 G., 11 December 1920 (WO 35/90/1).
62. Bidwell and Graham, *Fire-Power*, pp.115, 120.
63. For more on the British General Staff system, see Bidwell and Graham, *Fire-Power*, pp.43–8.

Three

Operations Against British Transportation in Ireland

Rebel attacks on British movements led to the development of the IRA war against British communication, but the former seem to have come about more by opportunity and chance than by deliberate targeting in the early months of the war and throughout 1919. Although the republicans conducted many attacks against barracks in the early part of the war to gain arms,[1] they probably understood the inherent strength of fixed or fortified sites, while recognizing that policemen or troops on the move were more vulnerable to certain kinds of attack. At the same time, however, the IRA used British military manuals from the First World War, and frequently even earlier, so considering their distinct lack of military training and experience; this revelation was fortunate for the republican cause.

This chapter continues partly from the previous chapter by further establishing the necessary background. Instead of being primarily chronological, it is more topical. Beginning with a description of the transportation infrastructure existing in Ireland during the war, the chapter continues with discussions of British logistics in Ireland, to include military motor transport, armoured vehicles in the country and issues of up-armouring of regular vehicles. It examines the Munition Strike of 1920 and the ensuing road transportation problems for the British army, as well as other labour troubles that plagued their operations. There is also an examination of the RIC boycott and the problems this created. The chapter concludes with the British offensive of late 1920.

Before continuing, an examination of British transportation in Ireland is necessary. By mid-1920, the IRA's new operations forced the British forces in Ireland to rely on mechanical transport. One should keep in mind that in the early part of the last century, until at least the 1920s, automobiles were not yet a primary means of transportation. There were only two forms of reliable heavy transport – waterways and railways.

Prior to the invention of railways, water was the primary means of transporting heavy cargo. It was the most reliable mode to move people and goods over great distances relatively quickly. In Ireland, there were just under 1,500 miles of navigable waterways, including rivers and man-made canals, which provided communications from the interior of the island to the nine major ports (Arklow, Belfast, Cork, Drogheda, Dublin, Foynes, Limerick, New Ross and Waterford) through which overseas heavy commercial traffic flowed. In addition to being ports, Belfast and Cork also had shipyards; in fact, the SS *Titanic* was built in Belfast. Belfast's port was also one reason many textile mills were built there.

The next mode of heavy transport came with the invention of the railway in the early nineteenth century. Although it took about eighty years to develop the routes, lay the rails, build the bridges and construct the rest of the necessary infrastructure – the marshalling yards, railway works (for manufacturing and repairing locomotives and railcars), goods yards, stations and so on – by the turn of the century, Ireland had a modern rail system. By 1920, there were about 3,000 miles of railroads and around 2,500 rail bridges of varying sizes, while the fourteen major railway companies employed tens of thousands of men and women throughout the country (see Figure 3.1). From the mid-nineteenth century, rail was the primary means of travel over any distance that one would not wish to walk. By the 1860s, rail replaced canals and rivers as the primary means of heavy transport for reasons of speed and capacity. Although it was a faster means of transport of heavy cargo, it was also more expensive, so one had to weigh the speed versus the extra cost (assuming that water could handle the weight of the goods).

In stark contrast to the highly developed railway and canal systems in Ireland were its roads, which were the slowest and least reliable means of long-distance transport in Ireland. Prior to the First World War, the roads throughout the whole of the United Kingdom were insufficient to meet military transport needs,[2] but one must recall that with canals and rail (primarily the latter) providing the majority of the transport already, there had been little incentive to improve the roads until after the war.[3] The early systematic development of the road system in Ireland came mostly through the routes created for the postal service, and thus the roads became known as 'post roads'. By the early nineteenth century, there was sufficient demand for transportation that an immigrant, Charles Bianconi, developed road transport services, beginning in the south; basically what amounted to stage coaches, but the railways started to supplant this system by the 1860s. Due to a declining population throughout the nineteenth century, primarily to emigration and largely to

Figure 3.1 Railway Map of Ireland

the United States,[4] further development of road systems was unnecessary because road traffic did not increase as with the rest of the United Kingdom.[5] Thus the roads in Ireland were still primitive by the time of the conflict, and by the 1950s there were more unpaved than paved roads, which have really only come to a modern standard as a result of European Union funding in the latter part of the 1990s and early twenty-first century. In a less industrialized society, everyday transportation is by muscle power, foot or hoof. With the industrial centre of Ireland in the northern, primarily loyalist, city of Belfast, there was little need to develop anything approaching an intricate or sophisticated and modern road network. Most goods would not have been of a size or weight to require such roads. Since virtually all goods going outside a district moved by rail or water, local roads supported only local commerce, which by necessity had to be light.

So with the exception of the two major cities (Dublin and Belfast) and the larger towns, most of the roads in Ireland were unpaved. Paving was expensive, both to build and to maintain, and was unnecessary except in high-traffic areas, and then only for commerce; hence paved streets in major towns and cities. There were less than 9,000 miles of hard-top-paved (asphalt or cobble stoned) roads in 1920s Ireland.[6] In open debate in 1926, the economically depressed Dáil Éireann discussed the scarce resources they had for roads, yet the minister for local government tried to convince his listeners (unsuccessfully) that they did not have 'the worst roads in Europe'.[7]

It is therefore evident that most roads in Ireland in 1921 were incapable of handling heavy motor transport vehicles. Although no exact figures appear to exist for road capacity, a reasonable estimate was made by the British army, who gave an upper limit of seven and a half tons for both vehicle and cargo, and then only on the best roads.[8] It is unclear if there were any long-distance roads which could have permitted fully loaded motor transport vehicles, whose capacity and total weight was greater than the capacity of the roads.

Further complicating the matter, Ireland was renowned for narrow, winding roads, which required slower speeds. The numerous narrow bridges made the situation worse, since they were usually built only for light traffic and spanned streams or rivers with few, if any, alternate routes. In such an event, it might have been impossible to ford the river or stream with the vehicles in the convoy. Chances were that if the load was too heavy for animals to pull, road and bridges could not handle it anyway. So, except for Belfast, Dublin and, perhaps, Cork City, the roads were insufficient for heavy cargo.

Finally, there was the significant problem of weather, especially rain. With a humid climate and almost forty-seven inches of annual rainfall, in some areas as high as seventy inches, Ireland was a wet country. This meant that unpaved roads were frequently too muddy to be passable to heavy transport. The winter months rarely brought relief because the temperature was usually above freezing and thus the ground remained soft and wet. The British army in Ireland congregated into fewer, but larger, groups to facilitate resupply during the winter, meaning that the number of convoys reduced as a result but whose size and capacity, necessarily, increased in convoys to supply the larger groups. The primary benefit was fewer routes, but it is unclear what effect the increased traffic had on the roads used. Although climate was not mentioned as a reason by the British as being a problem, it certainly exacerbated an already difficult situation in supply and transportation.

Dublin was, and remains, the primary city on the island and is also centrally positioned; facing Britain, in some respects it acted as a gateway to that island. Dublin Castle, in the city centre, was the home of the civil administration of Irish government. The Castle housed representatives from every branch of government, including the chief secretary for Ireland, the RIC inspector-general and their staffs. To remain accessible

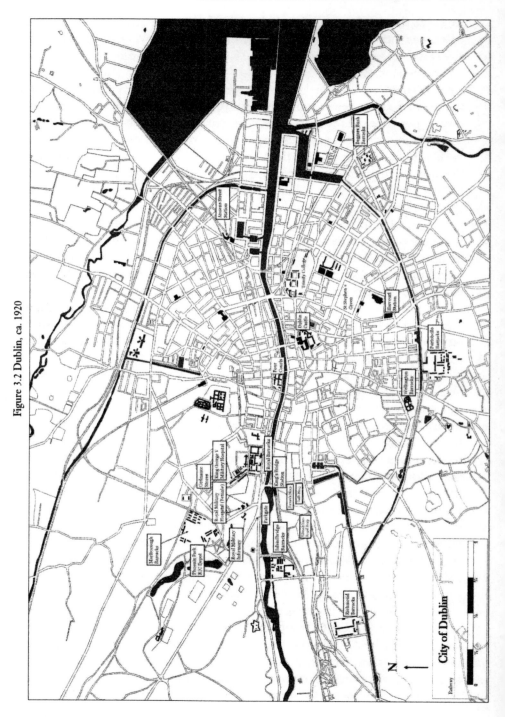

Figure 3.2 Dublin, ca. 1920

City of Dublin

N

to the government, the military leadership was located in the city as well. Considering the many transportation issues, the criticality of moving all classes of supplies to the various military units throughout the country and the fact that most supplies came through Dublin, it should come as no surprise that the British army's Irish Command established its general headquarters, along with their depots, hospitals and major barracks, at Parkgate in western Dublin at the convergence of the Grand Canal, the Liffey River and the major east–west rail line (one could also transport traffic down the Liffey to the major north–south railways) (see Figure 3.2). The Liffey also connected to the Grand Canal, which ringed the southern part of the city and the Royal Canal on the northern half. The military also used both Cork and Belfast for movement of military cargo to units posted in the south and north respectively. The British army relied on the same two old, but reliable, means of transportation, water and rail, primarily the latter. It was at these that the republicans struck in 1920, albeit more by accident than deliberate plan. In 1920, rebel operations and republican labour activism forced the British to increase their reliance on the inadequate roads as their primary means of transport. Although these methods did not work in Belfast, they were widely successful in Cork. One of these first 'campaigns' was an unplanned labour action.

THE MUNITION STRIKE, MAY–DECEMBER 1920

With this background, then, it is possible to examine the effects of unexpected problems for the British military with the transportation system. Even though the Irish government believed that there were concrete links between the Irish Labour Party, the unions and the republican movement, there actually were not. These groups had common interests, and frequently a common membership, but they rarely intentionally *planned* to help each other; assistance usually came only after one of them started an action unilaterally. As a result, when the Irish labour unions began strikes for various issues – increased pay, better working conditions, a 52-hour work-week for instance – Sinn Féin (by then the leading republican political party) might declare support, but it was not consulted beforehand. If Sinn Féin learned of a pending strike, it was normally due only to republican spy networks.[9]

The Munition Strike came at an economically and politically turbulent period; the United Kingdom had lost most of its overseas markets during the First World War, mostly to the United States, while simultaneously experiencing a glut of durable goods, due to the worldwide increase in manufacturing capacity during the war. Added to this were the problems of administering their various colonies, the colonies from the defeated nations, the occupation of the Central Powers and intervention in the Russian Civil War. Further, there was significant labour unrest in Britain itself apart from the situation in Ireland. Finally, there was political pressure at home to demobilize their massive army, which then sent hundreds of thousands of men into an already tight labour market.

At its base, the Munition Strike was a refusal by dock workers and, later, railwaymen to handle military or police cargo or to convey troops. At a deeper level, this was a non-violent, if somewhat provocative attempt by these men to halt or inhibit what they saw as an unjust war against their countrymen. Britain, they felt, was trying to subjugate Ireland once again, and although they may not have been revolutionaries or necessarily supported the republican cause, they would take no part in its violent suppression. This same sentiment seems to have been common in Ireland at the time; while one may not have supported the violent campaign for an Irish republic, or even the republican cause, most appeared not to have been willing to aid the police or the army against their fellow Irishmen.

Probably the more remarkable aspect to the strike is that it was unplanned. The inspiration for the strike probably came from the stevedores in London who refused, on Monday, 10 May 1920, to finish loading the SS *Jolly George* with arms and munitions bound for Poland to fight the Bolsheviks in Russia. This was not the first incident of porters in Ireland refusing to offload vessels in protest; in December 1919 the Irish Transport and General Workers' Union (ITGWU) tried to get the railwaymen to refuse to handle petrol in protest at the motor permit order limiting the driving of motor vehicles to those with permits in an attempt to limit the availability of vehicles to the IRA.[10]

On Thursday, 20 May 1920, the Dublin dockers spontaneously refused to offload a shipment of munitions for British forces at North Wall Quay (see Figure 3.2).[11] They then declared they would not handle any arms or munitions being used against the IRA. The situation worsened for the British three days later on Sunday, 23 May, when the railwaymen joined the strike and halted rail traffic everywhere except the loyalist north. Townsend reports that the railway workers refused to handle the cargo from the SS *Polderg*, which troops loaded on to thirty railway carriages.[12] Their union, the ITGWU, strove to catch up. Although the dock workers started the Munition Strike, it was the railwaymen who gave it the heavy impact since far more military and police, as well as their cargo, travelled inland on a daily basis by rail.

Those who handled cargo were critical regardless, but the railwaymen got most of the attention, credit or blame, depending on one's viewpoint.

At first, British forces and the government were surprised by the strike. Their immediate reaction, according to Townsend, was 'indistinctive'. They then blamed 'Bolshevism' and the republicans (whom they generally considered socialist – which, to them, was synonymous with 'Bolshevik' – anyway). Otherwise, they had no substantial reply other than circulating minutes and scurrying between ministries without any clear ideas on what to do. For, with the end of the First World War, the Transport and Munitions Ministries were basically powerless. During the war, the government used force to halt a similar strike in 1915, but such measures would now be illegal, in addition to the inevitable unpopularity at home and abroad. Their primary concern at first was to prevent sympathetic strikes in Britain, and, indeed, there is evidence to suggest a similar incident in Liverpool was partly another inspiration for the strike.[13]

The railway companies also responded to the strikers – technically this was a 'work stoppage', since they willingly moved any other traffic – by suspending hundreds (up to 1,000), fining some and firing others. Since this was an unplanned campaign, the unions' strike funds, used to help strikers' financial needs, were ill prepared and they, along with the republicans, began collecting donations from the populace and struggled to keep the workers' families from starving.[14] Nevertheless, the workers' resolve remained firm and the strike continued.

By June, the situation had grown no better; at the Haulbowline Royal Naval Dockyard in Co. Cork, soldiers had to offload two ships because, as the police reported, the civilian workers were 'Sinn Féiners' to a man and refused to do so.[15] Of course an equally plausible reason was that, being civilians, their contracts did not require them to do this, although there were, in fact, many IRA men working in the dockyards. Regardless of their motivation, these men were unlikely to help the British,[16] since, as with so many political actions, motivations were multifaceted.

Later that same month, a group of policemen boarded a train at Cloughjordan (Co. Tipperary) bound for Templemore. The driver, guard and fireman refused to move the train until the policemen got off. However, the policemen refused to leave. So the train sat in the station on the only line in or out of Cloughjordan for ten days. By mid-July, whole districts in Ireland were almost completely cut-off by similar incidents. The British military commander, General Sir Nevil Macready, advised the government that 'it must be remembered, however, that owing to the railway paralysis, the troops even with increased [motor] transport which has been lavishly poured into the country, will not be as mobile'.[17] This was precisely how the strike hit its target, and in so doing, the railwaymen confirmed to the IRA a lesson about mobility that they had examined earlier in the year; that if one stops the enemy's movement as well as the means of their movement, one will have greater likelihood of success.[18]

The Munition Strike had seriously hampered British capabilities, but began to fall apart towards the end of November 1920; the men could only strike for so long. The fact that this was a work stoppage allowed the men to maintain some income since most trains were not transporting military or police cargo. Further, at the height of the strike, from mid-October to the end of December, there were only 175 incidents reported. [19] The strikers' actual achievement was to mitigate the effect of the RIC offensive in the autumn by forcing them to rely on the inadequate road system and relatively small supply of motor vehicles, thus reducing their tactical and operational mobility.[20] Further, the IRA used their growing countermobility experience where they could to slow down the British forces. The British, especially the police, were less mobile and became more susceptible to ambushes, something the IRA exploited.[21] A third order effect was that this new reliance on roads and, hence, motor vehicles made the British vulnerable to skilled labour shortages. It is difficult to prove definitively that the IRA could not have withstood the autumn RIC offensive without the Munition Strike, but since virtually every brigade in the IRA experienced losses and disruption, it is difficult to see how even the strongest rebel areas would have survived as they did.[22] No; the railwaymen and dockers performed an outstanding service for the republican cause by their sacrifice and resilience; all the more so because they were non-violent.

British forces' growing reliance on motor vehicles to mitigate their mobility problems was not an intentional result of the IRA actions, nor instantaneous, but came about by necessity. Part of the army's trouble was that their growing forces, about 38,000 men by 1920, were dispersed in small detachments throughout the country, thus making supply and transport more difficult. The Munition Strike only exacerbated this problem. The senior military leadership in Ireland agreed that the strike forced them to plan operations without an expectation of functioning railways, and that the only realistic alternative for heavy or long-distance transport was motor vehicles.[23] But herein lay the problem; the army had too few vehicles.

Other sources of mobility were horses and bicycles, but while there were several cavalry and horse artillery regiments in Ireland, their troops were largely untrained horsemen. In an industrial society that uses automobiles, one might tend to under-appreciate the value of bicycles, but in

Ireland they were (and remain) a prime mode of transportation. In the first half of 1920, there were not enough soldiers who knew how to ride them, and the 'disadvantages are that army bicycles are heavy, they require artificers [mechanics] and repair outfits, and men on bicycles with rifles and so on, and cannot go very long distances, nor can they bring back prisoners … [and a man on a bike is] at a disadvantage when opposed to armed men … [and is] easily ambushed'. Still, the army understood their value and by summer 1920 each infantry battalion was to have 250 bicycles.[24]

With the obvious problem that the road system was poor, one might suggest waterborne transport, but in 1920 the Irish Command had to discount sea transport, not only due to the Munition Strike but also because Macready's official title, 'General Officer Commanding-in-Chief, British Forces, Ireland', applied only to the army and the 11th (Irish) wing, RAF. The Royal Navy and Marines were under the command of the Admiral-Commander, Western Approaches, who generally kept his forces out of the way and so did not readily cooperate with Macready. This was a consistent point of contention between the War Office, the Admiralty, the Cabinet and the Irish government.[25]

In 1914 the British army began the First World War with 950 lorries and 215 cars; four years later, they had 33,500 lorries, 1,400 cars and 13,800 tractors in France alone.[26] Yet this massive build-up did not translate to a surplus throughout the army as a whole, even when the British army began to demobilize in 1920. Many of the vehicles were discarded, given to Allied forces or sold off as surplus. The Irish Command expressed its dissatisfaction in 1922 saying:

> The Disposals Board appeared to have sold all the best vehicles and to have retained those which were nearly worn out, or deficient in the necessary spare parts. The repair of already part worn [sic] could not be carried out because at first there were no workshops. Repairs were numerous … [t]hose were bad days in 1920, and the inefficiency of the M.T. [motorized transport] was a daily cause for complaint. No blame can be attached to the M.T. staffs; they were overworked, and starved for want of efficient personnel and efficient material.[27]

In March 1920 the Irish Command had 549 four-wheeled vehicles and by May they had significant increases, but requirements still outpaced supply capacity and availabilities (see Table 3.1).

Further aggravating the problems of transport in Ireland with the Munition Strike was the increased wear and tear on the motor vehicles that the strike caused. In spring 1920, two months before the strike, the Royal Army Service Corps (RASC) in Dublin had significant problems

Figure 3.3 Disposition of British army Forces in Ireland, ca.1920

with their vehicles in the district. Of the twenty lorries assigned for 'administrative' duties (e.g. transporting supplies), five were down for repairs, while two of the twenty were the extremely heavy Foden steam lorries. Lieut.-Col. L. Moore, commanding the RASC in Dublin, complained that this 25 per cent 'under repair ... on average ... [was] on the low side', but that demands were increasing. In a memorandum the following day, Moore identified one of the problems the motor vehicle fleet experienced – being used for unnecessary duties for which other transport was already provided. He also complained that the RASC drivers, due to the constant demands placed by the overuse, were getting little rest. Further, of the thirty authorized lorries for 'tactical' purposes (i.e. raids), they had only sixteen available.[28]

By mid-summer 1920, the Dublin District Assistant QMG, Lieut.-Col. R.T. Lee, informed the subordinate organizations that the motor vehicle breakdown rates were unacceptably high due to their overuse. He impressed upon the officers of the district that 'tactical'[29] lorries were not to be used for other purposes, such as transporting rations and other supplies, as there was adequate transport for these purposes already. He also informed them that they would 'incur a grave responsibility if they over-rule, except in cases of urgent tactical necessity, the technical advice of the M.T. Personnel'.[30] Of course, it was unclear precisely what 'grave responsibility' this was, but it does demonstrate the frustration of both sides, the conflict between the logisticians and the combatant forces.

Table 3.1 Motor Transport in Ireland as of 31 March 1920.[31]

	Lorries	Cars	Vans	Ambulances	Motor Cycles
In Ireland on 31.3.1920	156	41	290	62	332
Shipped to Ireland between 1.4.1920 & 31.10.1920	319	64	379	42	331
Further increases –					
Completed by 8.12.1920	39	11	68	19	87
To be completed by 2.1.1921	65	-	75	10	80
To be completed by 15.1.1921	24	18	82	-	-

Table 3.2 British Motor Vehicles in Ireland[32]

	Crossley 'Tender' (Model 20/25)	Ford Model T Touring Car	Albion motor wagon, 1914	Y6-1 AEC 'Y' Type Lorry 1916	Triumph Motorcycle
Length:	162 in	134 in	235 in		
Width:	60 in	66 in	86 in		
Weight:	3808 lbs	6720 lbs	6720 lbs		
Engine:	4 cyl, 40hp	4 cyl, 20 hp	4 cyl, 32 hp		225cc/2.25 hp 499cc/3.5 hp 550cc/4 hp
Speed:	55 mph	45 mph			
Fuel:	petrol, 13–15 mpg	Petrol	Petrol	Petrol	Petrol
Capacity:	11 (3 in front, 8 in rear)	4			

	Austin Armoured Car	Jeffrey Quad	Lancia Armoured Car	Peerless Armoured Car	Rolls Royce Armoured Car
Length:	192 in	216 in	225 ins	240 in	194 in
Width:	79 in	76.8 in	78 in	88 in	76 in
Weight:	11464 lbs	9237 lbs	15232 lbs	9259 lbs	
Height:	101 in	96 in	94 in	108 in	100 in
Engine:	4-cyl, 50 hp	4 cyl	4 cyl, 35hp	4cyl 40 hp	6 cyl, 80 hp
Speed:	34 mph	20 mph	37 mph	18 mph	44 mph
Fuel:	Petrol	Petrol	Petrol	Petrol	Petrol
Capacity:	4 crew	4 crew	3 crew+ 10 men	4	3 crew
Armament:	2x.303 Vickers		.303 Lewis Gun	2x.303 Vickers	.303 Vickers
Armour:	4-7.5 mm	2x Vickers .303	6mm	10mm	12 mm

Table 3.3 'Mechanical Transport Tactical'[33]

	Present allotment for tactical purposes					Total now required					Increase required				
	3 ton Lorries	5 cwt. Box Bodies	Ford Vans	Motor Cars	Total	3 ton Lorries.	15 cwt. Box Bodies.	Ford Vans	Motor Cars	3 ton Total	Lorries	15 cwt. Box Bodies.	Ford Vans	Motor Cars	Total
5TH Division	32	20		6	58	60	84	10	19	173	23	64	10	13	
6TH Division	24	65		7	96	50	112		20	182	26	47		13	
Dublin District	30	4	4	1	39	43	13	10	6	72	13	9	6	5	
	86	89	4	14	193	153	209	20	45	427	67	120	16	31	234

This will involve the HQ of an additional Company.
Every unit must be completed with its officer and NCO personnel.
Vehicles supplied must be same type as those in use.
Motor cycles – six for each division, Galway, Kerry, etc.

The British forces used several different types of motor vehicles in Ireland. Probably the most recognizable was the Crossley 'Tender'. This was the Crossley model 20/25, officially designated the 'Type J' by the British army.

There was little or no motor vehicle doctrine in the British army in 1920, since their wheeled vehicle attacks during the First World War demonstrated the need for tracked vehicles. At the same time, the British army was beginning to develop mechanized and motorized doctrine. So the forces in Ireland were still learning to use the vehicles they had, effectively. Simply driving to a location was insufficient, because there was no existing doctrine for using motor vehicles in conjunction with raids and infantry operations and thus no pre-existing means of security, screening and coordination; these ideas were being tested by the army through its experiments on the Salisbury Plain. The army admitted in 1922 that it took them some time, until February 1920, before they even considered using motor vehicles in a tactical mode.[34] It then took time to figure out

Table 3.4 'Statement shewing the number of Vehicles in Service in Ireland on 1st May, 1920'[35]

Cars	40	
3-ton lorries	165	
30-cwt lorries	8	
Steam lorries	3	
Box-body vans	285	
Ambulances	67	
R.E. light sets	4	
Armoured cars and lorries	32	
Workshop lorries	8	
Store lorries	6	
Fire Engines	1	
Tractors	1	
Trailers	21	
Motor cycles	308	
Motor cycles and sidecars	34	
	983	
3-ton lorries	7)	
B.B. vans		
	16)	in transit
3-ton lorries	5)	Due, awaiting shipment
B.B. vans	3)	
Motor cycles and sidecars	7)	
	38	
Not included in the above are :-		
Cars	6	(used by Lord French)

In addition Lord French has 1 private car maintained by us in spare parts, tyres and petrol.
Grand Totol less X   1027

how to coordinate vehicle-mounted and dismounted troops in one movement. But as they began to use them tactically, the demand for vehicles increased too, especially when they began to experience losses.

Most important was the arrival of armoured cars, for the army was not operating in a vacuum. By increasing their attacks on vehicles and convoys, the IRA pushed many of the army's developments in defensive measures. Originally, speed was a primary countermeasure, but through trial and error, the IRA developed the means to nullify this advantage.[36] Therefore, doctrine developed incrementally on both sides.

The difference between a tank, an armoured car and an armoured lorry was that a tank was a tracked, offensive vehicle, usually with a main gun firing explosive projectiles, supported by machine guns mounted in turrets. The armoured car was just that, a wheeled car designed and built with armour and machine guns in turrets for offensive operations, although it could perform defensive fire missions. Both the tank and armoured car had crews of three or more, but were not designed to carry troops.

The armoured troop-carrying vehicles in use were not designed to be armoured. When it became apparent to the army that the troops within these vehicles were unnecessarily vulnerable, they 'up-armoured', to use the modern phrase, many of their main troop-transporting Crossley 'Tenders' by mounting one-inch and half-inch steel plates from their sides (see below).[37]

The 17th (Armoured Car) Tank Battalion arrived in Ireland in January 1919 with three companies, which were spread throughout the country (see Table 3.5). The vehicles of the 17th were a variety of armoured cars, primarily Jeffrey Quads and Austin Armoured Cars, along with Medium A and B, Mark IV, and Mark V tanks.[38]

Table 3.5 17th (Armoured Car) Tank Battalion Assets Under 5th Infantry Division, 1919

5th Infantry Division, Nov. 1919		
H.Q. 5th Infantry Division, The Curragh	8	Heavy Tanks
	6	Medium A Whippet Tanks
	4	Medium B Whippet Tanks
	18	Armoured Cars (2 Tank Corps & 16 MGC[39])†
Mullingar	Detachment 2	Jeffrey Quad Armoured Cars (East Yorks)
Maryborough	Detachment 2	Armoured Cars†
Ulster Brigade Area, Nov. 1919		
H.Q. Belfast	MGC 5	Armoured cars
Dublin Brigade Area, Nov. 1919		

HQ 17th (AC) Tank Bn, Marlborough Barracks	H.Q.	8	Heavy Tanks
		4	Medium A Whippet Tanks
		4	Medium D Whippet Tanks
(Tank Corps)			
		2	Armoured Cars (Tank Corps) †
Ship Street Barracks		2	Medium A Whippet Tanks
		4	Armoured Cars (MGC) †
Vice Regal Lodge		1	Armoured Car (MGC) †

Athlone Brigade Area, 1919			
Galway	A Company	4	Medium A Whippet Tanks
		4	Austin Armoured Cars

† These vehicles were of unspecified type, but probably were Jeffrey Quad Armoured Cars, of which they had twenty-two earlier in the year.

The 17th (Armoured Car) Tank Battalion was deactivated on 1 May 1920, while the 5th Armoured Car Company assumed its place. Attached to it was a section of four Mark IV tanks of the Tank Corps. Virtually all of the Austins had seen action in France. Along with these vehicles went thirty-nine officers and 221 other ranks; these were insufficient to man all the vehicles of the battalion. Further, many of the officers were being demobilized from the war.[40]

In reality, the 5th Armoured Car Company was really just responsible for the maintenance of the vehicles, since they had insufficient personnel to man them. They made up the deficiency by using other soldiers. In many cases, they simply handed the vehicles over to the infantry units. The 5th Division later said that all of these vehicles 'had done a good deal of work and had to be carefully "nursed"'.[41] The tanks given to the 5th Infantry Division were eventually so poorly maintained they became literally *in-situ* – fixed site defences.

The division received replacement armoured cars in July 1920: Peerless for the Austins. The drawback for the Peerless cars was that they were the heaviest of the military vehicles at seven and a half tons when fully loaded, too much for all but the best Irish roads, and then only in good weather. Further, the Peerless were replacements, and so total numbers remained the same. At the same time, the 5th (Armoured Car) Company personnel preferred the Peerless.[42] The advantage of the Peerless cars was that they were 'factory' armoured and carried two machine guns (the light Hotchkiss .303) in two turrets.

In late November 1920, the Royal Arsenal at Woolwich conducted trials with Ford armoured cars. However, the 5th (Armoured Car) Company representatives found that the trials 'clearly showed that the Ford

Armoured Car was most unsuitable for work in Ireland. The armour plating was not bullet-proof and the cars were too light to deal with the large crowds likely to be encountered in Dublin, Cork and Limerick.' The day after the trials, the War Office decided to send Rolls Royce armoured cars to Ireland, some of which had been earmarked for Mesopotamia.[43] Still, this was insufficient to meet the demands of the Irish Command. In January, when the army council asked if they could use the Fords, Macready asked for 100.[44] It is likely that, despite the determination of the 5th Armoured Car Company, these vehicles were insufficient for the environment; the mediocre vehicles one had were better than the excellent vehicles one did not.

The allocation of armoured cars reflected the reality in Ireland, that the 6th Infantry Division covering most of Munster in the south was in greater danger than those in the other three areas of the island. When the ten Rolls Royce armoured cars arrived in January 1921, half went to the 6th, two each were allocated to the 5th Infantry Division and the Dublin District, while the 1st Infantry Division in the north got only one.[45]

A month later, Macready asked for more vehicles and was told that sixteen more Rolls Royce armoured cars were on the way; they arrived on 15 March 1921. When they first began to arrive in January 1921, the 5th (Armoured Car) Company arranged for two weeks of training for the drivers at the Rolls Royce company in Derby.[46]

It is interesting that, rather than creating several offensive units centred on the Rolls Royces, the Irish Command divvied them up between the Divisions and the Dublin District. The 5th Division got six new Rolls Royce armoured cars – which carried twin machine guns (the medium Vickers .303) and were faster and lighter than the Peerless. More of the Rolls Royces would have permitted them to approach quickly with less noise, but since they got only six, the 5th Division commander, Lieut.-Gen. Sir Hugh Jeudwine, gave one to each of his brigade commanders for escort duty.[47] This may not have been the best use for these vehicles, but there was always the issue of which was more important, protecting one's lines of communication or conducting offensive operations. It appears that by the end of the war, new operational concepts rendered this issue moot; the army performed both missions due to increased manning and changes in doctrine. While these vehicles were welcome additions, the Irish Command also decided to retro-fit some of its existing vehicle fleet with armour.

As part of the ongoing effort to increase the armoured vehicle strength in Ireland, the 3rd Tank Battalion arrived on 8 January 1921 with a cadre of men. The three 'skeleton companies' just about had sufficient men to

Table 3.6 Distribution of 5th Armoured Car Company Detachments, 1921[48]

5th Armoured Car Company	Rolls Royce	Peerless	Tanks
HQ & Depot (Dublin)	13	20	4
'A' Company (6th Infantry Division, Cork)	14	27	4
'B' Company (5th Infantry Division, Curragh)	6	24	-
'C' Company (1st Infantry Division, Belfast)	1	8	-

Table 3.7 Distribution of 5th Armoured Car Company Headquarters Detachment in Dublin in 1921

Rolls Royce	Peerless	Tanks
Company HQ (Marlborough Barracks)	9	-	4
Dublin District HQ Section (Parkgate)	4	4	-
24th (Provisional) Infantry Brigade	-	6	-
25th (Provisional) Infantry Brigade	-	6	-
RASC Section	-	4	-

lead once the various infantry, cavalry and RASC organizations produced enough troops to man them. The 5th (Armoured Car) Company had seventy-one armoured cars and eight tanks (see Table 3.6).

Unfortunately for historians, these were not the only armoured cars in Ireland; many were in the hands of the various units themselves and an itemized list appears not to have survived.

As a result of increasing IRA attacks on motor vehicles beginning in the late spring and continuing throughout the summer of 1920 (at the height of the munitions strike and immediately before the RIC offensive in the autumn), the army began to supplement their total armoured vehicle numbers by 'up-armouring' much of their existing wheeled motor vehicle fleet, starting in late August.[49] It appears that all of these were Crossley Tenders (see Table 3.2). The army documents usually refer to these retro-fitted lorries as 'tactical lorries' to differentiate them from the unarmoured Crossleys. They used one-inch thick steel plates for protection against rifle and machine-gun rounds (primarily .303 Lee-Enfield and 7.9x33mm Mauser), and, in towns and cities, half-inch-thick steel plates against pistols (primarily .38 and .455 revolver, .45 ACP and 9mm Parabellum). They further differentiated the 'tactical lorries' as 'armoured' (for the one-inch plated vehicles) and 'protected' (for the half inch plated vehicles).[50] For the pistols, it is important to point out that of the military rounds, only the 9mm Parabellum (9x19mm NATO) is still used with any frequency today. Interestingly, since modern assault rifles fire mostly smaller and weaker cartridges (5.56x45mm NATO and M74 5.45x39mm Kalashnikov)[51] than the .303 Lee-Enfield (7.7x56mm rimmed) or 7.9x33mm Mauser, this armour would still provide similar protection today.

This, however, brings up the important point that the steel plates were meant as protection against small arms fire, not against explosives, although the one-inch plate was sufficiently strong against Mills bombs (the British fragmentation hand grenade; see Chapter 6). Against high explosives the armour gave only limited protection.

In late spring 1920, the Irish Command began to examine the various means of protecting their motor vehicles from these attacks. 'Brigades were asked to experiment with strengthening lorries. Corrugated iron with rubble was suggested as a method, also planks on the outside of each lorry that could be removed in the event of an obstacle such as a trench being met with and used as a bridge for the wheels.' They also looked at sandbags, with a view to making each vehicle 'a defensive position for a few men, whence to cover the remainder'. Sandbags placed in the rear of lorries provided protection for four men against shotguns and pistols. The idea was that these 'four men could return it [fire], whilst the others got out as quickly as they could' in a counterattack.[52]

The Irish Command quickly settled on using steel armoured plates, but these were still a compromise since they could not prevent ricochet of bullets, fragments or shrapnel. Further, the armour plates still failed after multiple small arms hits and were never intended to protect troops for long periods, so staying inside the vehicles was not a realistic option; they had to dismount the vehicle and counterattack or escape inside them and retreat. Further, the armour was made in accordance with the threat; in rural areas, where the IRA used more rifle fire against convoys, the one-inch plate was a necessity; whereas, in Dublin, where the rebels used primarily pistols and shotguns, the half-inch plate was normally sufficient. Ironically, this meant that the areas with fewer paved roads had heavier vehicles, while the lighter armoured lorries operated on the paved streets of Dublin.

They planned to retro-fit an initial total of 354 vehicles; 160 were to receive 'armour' and up to 500 'protection'. The vehicles were retro-fitted in Britain, and also in both the predominantly loyalist north and at the Great Southern and Western Railway Works at Inchicore (Dublin), which lay next to the Parkgate military area in the city (see Table 3.2). The Belfast area was an obvious choice, not simply for the sake of loyalty, but because there was a large shipyard there that could handle such relatively small plates with ease. The Inchicore Western Railway Works likewise provided similar capability and had armoured a vehicle during the Rising by enclosing much of the vehicle with a locomotive boiler, particularly the engine. Later retro-fitting would include removing the entire front bonnet and encasing the large engines with steel plates and roughly shaping them to fit, while enclosing the rear with basically a steel box. Although not mentioned in the official sources, the time required, three months, was probably a result of inexperience in the type of work. Most of all, however, the process was slow; after starting in August, the first six of these refitted lorries were delivered in November 1920.[53]

Perhaps the primary limiting factor with the vehicles themselves was weight, then as now. For every pound of protective steel plate added, one had to remove a pound of cargo. The 9"x 6"x1" steel plate weighed just over 2,000lbs apiece. The railway yard and the shipyards could only attach the plates; they could not reinforce the undercarriage, wheels or tyres. Nor could they provide more powerful engines. They were simply unable to do anything except hang the steel on the vehicles. One cannot underestimate the effect of motor vehicles in that age; very few people had experience with them and those who were qualified to work on them were more highly valued and better skilled workers than today. So safety came with a price; drastically shorter working life for the vehicles, slower speeds, longer stopping distances, and an overall loss of manoeuvrability, cargo capacity, and increased fuel consumption.

Still, the up-armoured vehicles fulfilled a need and the British used them to good effect. While the IRA stated that the vehicles were ineffective, their actions spoke differently. For instance, there was an IRA raid on the Inchicore Western Railway Works on the night of Sunday, 6 March 1921, by F Company, 4th Battalion, Dublin IRA Brigade.[54] Approximately eighty men of the company, divided in four sections, moved into the works, captured the watchmen and went after the steel plates. Inexplicably, they first tried smashing them with sledgehammers, but this, obviously, had little effect. Then they took one of the railway company's six-ton lorries, loaded the plates and headed off south. The lorry, overloaded with men and steel, broke down on the way out of town in the direction of Naas (Co. Kildare), so they dumped the plates into a canal next to the road. The mission did not go well, but why did the IRA risk eighty men on such an operation when the Western Railway Works was right across the road from British army's Richmond barracks, housing the 2nd Bn Welch Regiment and the 1st Bn King's Own Royal Regiment; Islandbridge barracks, housing 'B.B.' Company, RASC and No. 14 Company Royal Army Ordnance Corps (RAOC),[55]and just a mile from the Irish Command's GHQ? It was a high-priority job because of the effect the vehicles had, otherwise they would not have attempted it in the first place. For unexplained reasons, the authorities never recovered the plates, although they knew their location.[56] This raid also demonstrates the stress the plates' weight placed on the vehicles, when, although probably more overloaded than a normal military 'up-armoured' vehicle, the works' lorry broke down within minutes of leaving the area.

The issue of armoured and up-armoured vehicles demonstrates just how detrimental IRA attacks on vehicles in the Irish Command were. Figures and tables do not demonstrate this nearly as well as the supply of meat. There was an incident at the Military Abattoir in Dublin, which was collocated with the Dublin Corporation abattoir on Aughrim Street. On Monday, 14 May 1921, the IRA seized a Peerless armoured car and attempted to use it to get one of their comrades, Seán McEoin, out of Mountjoy jail. Although they were unsuccessful in their attempt to release McEoin, their success in obtaining an armoured car with two twin-mounted Hotchkiss machine guns both in turrets demonstrated their capabilities. The attack was not nearly as important as what the situation indicated, that the state of affairs must have been extreme if the military could only deliver meat by armoured convoy (see Chapter 7 for more detail on this incident).

In addition to the IRA attacks, there were external issues surrounding the motor transport problems in Ireland, especially with personnel and, in an area that may seem all too familiar for today's soldiers, spare parts. The army in general had difficulty attracting sufficient numbers of skilled men despite the relatively high recruiting bonuses. The Secretary of State for War, Winston Churchill, complained to the Cabinet in autumn 1920 that the Irish Command was about to have a 'serious breakdown' in 'essential services', meaning all supply and transport. Part of the problem was an army-wide shortage of men, but especially in skilled labour such as artificers (mechanics), drivers, communications specialists, electricians and engineers.[57] The army was dealing with two competing problems – the requirement to demobilize from the high First World War strengths while maintaining a sufficiently manned and trained force to meet increasing overseas obligations. The government did not make this process any easier when they adopted the policy eventually known as 'limited liability', which reduced troop strengths in the army. This hope led to a reduction in funding for the army at a time when, far from being underemployed, it was engaged worldwide in a broad array of missions brought about by the ending of the First World War. There were only about 250,000 men in twenty-eight commands around the world, including Mesopotamia (Iraq), Palestine, Khartoum, Egypt, and the North-West Frontier (Afghanistan).

Funding and expectations aside, the army's drawdown was neither well planned nor well executed. Their initial responses to the shortages problem might be recognizable today; first they tried recruiting bonuses, but as Britain became more industrialized, these bonuses could not compete with the pay on the open market, for although work for unskilled labour was tight, skilled work was at a premium. The men going into, or staying in, the army generally had no non-military skills, perhaps the reason they joined in the first place. Worse yet, the army even found themselves competing with the police; being a totally separate agency, the RIC had more money for bonuses and salaries than the army (see Table 3.8). Another means they used to alleviate this problem was to retrain active soldiers for the necessary duties, but the training centres could not produce sufficient numbers for ongoing operations at an acceptable rate, so the army reduced the length of training, thereby producing more 'qualified' men at a faster rate. Of course, their skills levels were reduced. This carried over into basic training as well; prior to the First World War the army considered the 'other ranks' (enlisted soldiers) 'fully trained' only after seven or eight years of service.[58] By 1920, having developed training in the Great War to produce soldiers quickly – in twenty weeks – the army then reduced basic training by 40 per cent to help meet demand.[59] Clearly, the situations in which the British army found itself in the post-war era were more complex than in the Great War itself and this created a need for more training. So at a time when the new soldiers needed more training, they got less.

Further, there was additional time and training for their specialisms. Churchill was incredulous that it took months to train a motor driver, especially when the time was used as an excuse seemingly to do nothing.[60] Moreover, this situation was one of the reasons the QMG was delaying sending vehicles to Ireland; he wanted sufficient troops with the armoured cars. The same held with the problem of artificers – the QMG wanted to wait, but Churchill overrode that and eventually they were able to make up the difference with civilians from Britain, since it took three years to train an army artificer.[61]

Macready, through this constant complaining and by delivering dire predictions to the Cabinet, began to receive more support personnel by autumn 1920, and although this was still insufficient to the Irish Command's needs, it was all the army had (see Tables 3.8 and 3.9), and thus, all he was going to get. Of course, it did not hurt that the Chief of the Imperial General Staff, Field Marshal Sir Henry Wilson, was an Ulsterman worried that losing Ireland meant losing the empire.[62] When Macready requested the 100 Ford armoured cars in early 1921, he also asked for sufficient artificers and drivers to go with them. The QMG felt this was simply not possible.[63]

Further aggravating the Irish Command's transport problems was a

Table 3.8 Artificer and Lorry Driver Comparisons[64]

Rate RIC	Army Rates
I-Artificers	
Pay £5-6-6/week & bonus of £25 at the end of each year's service	£1-4-6/week to £1.18.0, according to group or trade classification
Separation allowance/Family allowance if over 26 and married	
Free Clothing Free Clothing	
Messing at wholesale rates	Free messing
II-Mechanical Transport Drivers	
£4-9-0/week£1-4-6 to £1-11-6/week	
Other conditions as in I	Other conditions as in I
No bonus	

Table 3.9 Driver and Artificer Assignments, 26 October 1920[65]

To:	Drivers	Artificers
Ireland	1097	116
India	202	101
Mesopotamia	950	66
Egypt	318	57
Black Sea	405	33
Rhine	447	27
Colonies, Military Missions, etc.	29	0
TOTAL:	3448	400

severe shortage of spare parts. The army's QMG stated that there were forty-one armoured cars in Ireland in March: 'Some of these are now pass repair, but roughly 25 are running.' By December, the prime minister cited only 40 per cent being mission capable. It is difficult to determine precisely, with the evidence available, if the increase of a 25 per cent 'under repairs' rate to 40 per cent non-mission-capable rate or higher, in just the seven months between May and December 1920, in the army's vehicles in Ireland was due to overuse, enemy action or lack of spare parts. Based on incomplete data from the RIC reports covering the same period, however, it is clear that in 1920 the loss rate was a combination of overuse and lack of spare parts. Indeed, the IRA destroyed or stole at least fifty-nine bicycles from the RIC, whereas, in the same period, they destroyed or stole only about eight RIC motor vehicles. The QMG also mentioned that they had shipped forty-eight Peerless armoured cars, that six were leaving the next day and that in a week, he expected another six Rolls Royce armoured cars. He would order twenty-six more and could ship sixteen Peerless from the Home Commands 'if situation in Great Britain permits'.[66]

Table 3.10 'Deficiency of Signal Personnel', 7 May 1920.[67]

	War Establishment of Two Divisional Signals Companies	Present Establishment of Specific Signal Company	TOTAL ESTABLISHMENT	Present Effective Strength of Special Signal Company	Cyclist Brigade Signal Sections	Nuclei of 5th and 6th Signal Companies	TOTAL	Deficiency
Telegraphists Office	56	62	118	16		1	17	101
Cable Men	40		40				-	40
Brigade Section Pioneers	80		80				-	80
Telephone Switchboard Operators	8	18	26	12			12	14
General Duty Pioneers	88	15	103	5	10		15	88
Electricians	2	-	2				-	2
S & C.S.	4	-	4	1				
Drivers & Batmen	94	36	130	7	10	6	23	107
Wheelwrights	4	2	6	1			1	5
Harnessmakers & Saddlers	4	2	6				-	6
Instrument Repairers	4	3	7				-	7
Motor Cyclists	30	57	87				12	75
Permanent Linemen	-	3	3	12	-	2	4	-
Field Linemen Mounted	-	12	13	2	-	3	9	
Field Linemen Dismounted	-	22	22	6	2	1	9	16
Wireless Operators	-	73	73	6			3	70
Wireless Fitters	-	15	15	3			1	14
Wireless Electricians	-	15	15	1				15
Farriers	-					1	1	
	414	335	749	72	22	14	108	643

For his part, the QMG denied there was even a problem, maintaining that his department had shipped 4,000 tons of spare parts to Ireland in the third quarter of 1920. Of course he did not address the Irish Command's shortfalls in the earlier quarters of that year, especially considering the earlier breakdown rates. The QMG also blamed the shortage of maintenance personnel for the vehicle loss rate.[68] While there was probably much truth to the QMG's latter point, although he cited no evidence, it did not change the shortfall, nor could it explain the entire loss rate. Moreover, the 5th Armoured Car Company history clearly stated their problem: 'The great difficulty at this period was the shortage of spare parts for the Austin Armoured Cars', their most numerous armoured vehicle. Further, Macready was unlikely to accept simplistic excuses since he had significant experience in this realm; he had fixed the British Expeditionary Force's severe transportation and supply problems in 1914 and 1915 that were on a much grander scale.[69]

Chastised by the prime minister and, although not always popular with the uniformed military leadership, Churchill sided with Macready and blamed the QMG with harsh words: 'More than six months have passed since urgent orders were given to increase steadily the supply of Irish motor transport … In spite of the enormous staffs which the QMG is maintaining, the actual result for fighting purposes appears lamentably small.'[70] He ended by ordering him to supply Ireland's needs, indeed, by ordering the army of the Rhine to be stripped of motor transport and at least one shipment of armoured vehicles for Mesopotamia (Iraq) diverted to Ireland.[71]

The simple problem was that the QMG did not have the materiel to send, so orders from higher headquarters or even the secretary of state for war meant little. There is no indication what response the QMG received when he pointed out this fiscal and physical problem. Another factor was the effect of the active boycott against the police (which also affected the army).[72]

At this point, it is necessary to divert again slightly in order to explain the effects of another republican campaign that existed alongside their other activities during this conflict, called the RIC boycott. This was a campaign to get policemen to quit the force by applying extreme social and economic pressure to them and their families. Although it targeted primarily policemen, it included the army and the Auxiliary Division of the force (ADRIC). The use of boycott in Ireland went back many years, but had shown itself more recently in the previous century during the so-called 'land wars' of the early 1880s; indeed, it was this era that gave the English language the word 'boycott'.

The land war began after the Irish Land League, formed in 1879 by liberal Irish member of parliament, Charles Stewart Parnell, began to agitate for land and agrarian reform. Since the majority of the populace lived on rented properties, and since their fortunes were largely determined by the crop season and weather, the Land League felt that the rents owed should vary according to the amounts of crops produced rather than by fixed prices. The landlords disagreed and the land war began when tenant farmers refused to pay the increased rents.[73]

Evictions, frequently by force, or threat thereof, with the assistance of the RIC and sometimes even the army, became a common occurrence in Ireland. Many times this meant that the farmstead buildings were burned once the family was outside to prevent reoccupation.[74] As one might well imagine, this could turn violent quickly, and frequently did.

Boycotting got its name from one of these incidents in 1880, when the people of the village of Ballinrobe, Co. Mayo, ostracized the landlords' agent, one Captain Charles C. Boycott, in retaliation for some evictions he had undertaken. The townspeople refused to speak with him, conduct any business with him, sell to him, work his lands (he was also a landowner and farmer) or have any contact with him. In an era where one needed fresh supplies every day, this caused significant hardship. The newspapers in London sensationalized his plight to illuminate the situation in Ireland. His name quickly became a verb. Boycott was actually lucky that he was not beaten or assassinated. Boycotts could be peaceful, but frequently were not.

This was the weapon the republicans unleashed on the policemen and their families beginning as early as 1917, although the main effort began in late 1918. In November 1917 the police began to report growing hostility and that 'a spirit of disloyalty and defiance of authority has been disseminated, and a hostile attitude towards the police has been created (because of their loyalty to the Government)'.[75] 'Boycott' meant no contact at all. Anyone conversing with or even seen in the company of a boycotted person risked being boycotted themselves – or subjected to other types of punishment. It is important to remember that the government deliberately used the RIC as the main force against the IRA until autumn 1920, partly due to constitutional restrictions of using military forces at home. Further, their omnipresence in Ireland made the RIC the natural choice for this role. Yet, this presence also made them the most common and most visible sign of the government's authority, as well as an excellent intelligence source, and therefore the most

Figure 3.4 IRA General Order No. 6 'Boycott of RIC'

GENERAL ORDER NO. 6   4th June, 1920

BOYCOTT OF RIC

Volunteers shall have no intercourse with the RIC, and shall stimulate and support in every way the boycott of this force ordered by the Dáil.

Those persons who associate with the RIC shall be subjected to the same boycott, and the fact of their association with and toleration of this infamous force shall be kept public in every possible way. Definite lists of such persons in the area of his command, shall be prepared by each Company, Battalion and Brigade Commander.

obvious target of any violent backlash. The boycott continued sporadically for the next year and a half, with varying degrees of success.

The boycott, in many respects, resembled an economic blockade and had a tremendous impact in 1919 and onward. Cut off from the basic necessities, the policemen felt the effects immediately, simply because they purchased everything they used, with the sole exception of arms and munitions, locally. If their sources of food, transportation, fuel, hay, wood, and so on were disrupted or cut off, so were they.[76] This also brings up an important point; while the boycott was against the police and military, the ones who were punished for 'infractions' were the common people. So while a policeman might initiate contact, he was not going to be the one to suffer for it.

The punishments themselves ranged from threats to murder. Typically the first instance of violating the boycott usually brought threats and orders not to do it again. If one was a known or ardent anti-republican in a staunchly nationalist area, a single 'violation' might have been one's last, but usually more was required. A second instance would instigate a harsher 'warning' such as a random gunshot into the offender's house, or a beating. Men who violated the boycott were almost always treated more harshly, except for one case – dating. Young women who stepped out with a boycotted man, almost always a policeman or soldier, risked violent and 'symbolic' humiliation. 'Armed and masked' gunmen would drag her from her bed, usually strip her, beat her with their firsts or with straps, and frequently shear off her hair. Men usually were beaten or flogged and, subsequently, risked death. The IRA also used tar and feathers in counties Clare, Cork and Kerry.[77]

Death was reserved for men; although IRA general orders included an instruction on executing women spies, it was almost never done.[78] Men who were murdered by the IRA were rarely killed deliberately for violating the boycott; although there were instances of men being hit by warning shots. Actual 'executions' were against 'traitors', for having passed information to the enemy. It is impossible to say how many of these incidents were real, imagined or contrived.

Violence against people was not the only form of punishment; animals and property also suffered. Animal mutilation and killing were common in this campaign. While theft of goods was almost always unacceptable, their destruction, usually by fire, was acceptable. This usually occurred against goods being sold or against the homes of people violating the boycott.

It is difficult to demonstrate the effects of the RIC boycott against the British army because they were more insulated, but the policemen and their families suffered bitterly. It would be wrong to suggest that the RIC boycott was monolithic and equally applied throughout the country. The campaign varied by location; the northern counties, having much higher percentages of unionists, had little anti-police activity. In the south, especially in more republican counties like Cork, Clare and Tipperary, the boycott was most effective. In the west and central counties, the effectiveness and intensity varied by time and location.[79]

The effects of the boycott began to tell in late 1919, but it was by no means the only rebel activity in 1919 and 1920. Raids on police barracks and ambushes on patrols became common throughout the country. So with the effects of the boycott combined with these other stressors, morale in the force[80] plummeted, resignation and retirements increased, while recruiting dried up. By the end of 1919, the RIC was stagnant. Between January 1919 and December 1920, there were 833 police casualties in Ireland; 333 (40 per cent) were killed in action, in a force that, prior to the war, hardly ever saw death in the line of duty. The records are incomplete, but in the fourth quarter of 1920 (October to December), 205 men retired, 318 resigned and 58 were dismissed, while 2,841 men joined the RIC. On the surface, this appears to be good; 2,841 men joined while 758 men were listed as 'wastage' – 581 plus 177 killed in action. But of the new recruits, only 185 (6.5 per cent) were Irish; the rest were temporary constables hired for the duration of the conflict. The RIC, before January 1920, was completely Irish, by regulation. These temporary constables were a departure from this as a measure against the acute recruiting problem that had been ongoing for the previous year.[81] Another effect of this was that the RIC was becoming more foreign to the population.

These declines came to affect policy and operations by early 1920, when the senior RIC leadership decided that the smaller stations throughout the countryside were too hot to hold, and so ordered their abandonment in March of that year. The idea was to concentrate RIC manpower into urban centres from which they could strike against the IRA. This was a repositioning and a sound operational decision to be sure, but the IRA, the ordinary people and, indeed, the policemen themselves saw it as nothing but retreat.[82] It was also a tacit admission that the IRA was strong enough to push the police out, and thus, was 'winning' against the RIC. Further, it denied the British a valuable source of intelligence. Worse still, the slow build-up of forces necessary to strike at the IRA effectively took time and it was not until the end of the summer that British forces were capable of going on the offensive. It is also clear that the RIC boycott and the IRA's guerrilla campaign directly brought this situation about. In the official history, the General Staff of the Irish Command admitted that 'Crown forces were thrown back on to the defensive' and thus lost the initiative in the conflict.[83] In many ways, the police never regained this initiative.

At the same time, the Cabinet realized that the RIC needed to be reinforced. For constitutional reasons, the army could not provide this support, so they turned to demobilized soldiers from the Great War. The first of these were the so-called 'Black and Tans', former enlisted soldiers from the British army who were brought in, beginning in March 1920, as 'temporary' constables and inserted directly into the existing regular RIC structure. The second group was the force's Auxiliary Division (ADRIC), former officers enlisted as temporary police cadets, who began to arrive in Dublin in July 1920. The problem with both groups was that they were not Irish. Their excellent training aside, the great strength of the RIC had always been that they were drawn from the society they served; with the introduction of the Black and Tans and the ADRIC, this advantage began to evaporate. The Black and Tans moniker was mistakenly applied to both and has become infamous. In actuality, it appears that only the ADRIC, which operated on its own in 100-man companies, actually earned this infamy.[84]

Beginning in early autumn 1920, British forces – the RIC in the lead and the army in support, with a new mandate for participation, along with new motorized transport – moved back out to the countryside, areas they had abandoned only months before. The IRA was largely unprepared for the new campaign against them and much of their leadership was either captured or went on the run in all but the staunchest republican areas of the south, especially in counties Clare, Cork, Kerry and Tipperary, and this was where the Munition Strike (ending in December) had its greatest effect in helping to prevent the offensive from reaching its full potential by retarding British forces' mobility. For although the British forces had the men and materiel, and were starting to get the vehicles, the strike forced them on to the roads.

Although still reeling somewhat from the increased police operations, the IRA began to counter the effects of the still-superior British mobility, primarily through countermobility operations – mostly ambush and, eventually, road obstruction and destruction. The rebels learnt the art of countermobility earlier in the war in 1919, when they cut off the roads in the areas around the police barracks in preparation for their attacks.[85] They became quite skilled at using trenches cut in the roads, dropping trees, placing mounds of earth and stone, as well as bridge demolition. This enabled them to isolate their target as well as cut off any relief. Later in 1919, they began to channel relief forces into ambush sites.[86] Eventually, they became sophisticated enough to attack a barracks as a feint to draw out a relief force and funnel it into an ambush, while simultaneously attacking its barracks. In early autumn 1920, these were the skills the IRA brought to bear against the new mobile British campaign.

One particularly heinous obstruction was wire stretched across a road, attached to sturdy trees on either side. While only one report of this in the war (in 1918) has come to light, it was soundly condemned in the army intelligence report. It occurred near the town of Ballingar, Co. Galway (East Riding) where a 'Mr Rice, Resident Magistrate, was motoring home after holding a Special Court to deal with two men arrested for drilling. He found [it did not state how] 3 strands of barbed wire across the road, nailed from one tree to another. He tried another road and found a tree felled across it '. The magistrate was able to find a constable and get home safely. The potential harm this type of obstruction could cause was horrific; if the wire was low, it could slice into the vehicle and potentially cause grave damage to the occupants. But if the wire was strung slightly higher, it could decapitate its victim. In either case, it had the advantage of being near invisible to travellers until it was too late. Such an occurrence would have slowed British motor traffic for some time, even if there were no other instances occurring. Still, the threat was grave enough that the Dublin District ordered lorries to be refitted with '2 Angle irons about 5' long ... About 16' wire rope ... The wire will be attached to the radiator bar and the front cord support on the top of the lorry, passing through a slot (or over a wheel) on the horizontal angle iron ... Units will carry this out under their own arrangements'.[87] It is not clear how many of these reinforcements of the vehicle frames were done.

Figure 3.5 Sketch from 'Tactical Lorries'[88]

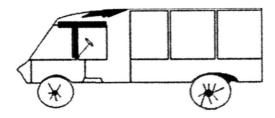

It should come as no surprise that the violence and lethality of the conflict increased during the British offensive. Police casualties increased by two-thirds in both killed and wounded, while the army's more than doubled. Since the police had primary responsibility for the suppression of the republicans until August 1920, the army's casualties actually increased at a higher rate once they became more involved, but never approached the numbers inflicted on the RIC. Further, although the army's role increased, the RIC remained in the forefront of the effort, with military technically only in support. In many ways it is difficult to assess the potential effect of a true military campaign, especially as there are

Figure 3.6 IRA Engineering Circular

GENERAL HEADQUARTERS, DUBLIN

DEPARTMENT OF ENGINEERING

6th January, 1921

Circular No. ½ 4½

ROAD OBSTRUCTION

In general there are two methods of obstructing a highway, by placing an obstacle or making it impassable by excavating or demolition. Both the methods to be effective must be carried out in a large scale. In other cases it may be possible to block a road to wide vehicles while allowing the passing of narrower.

Obstacles placed on a roadway may be anything from a light barricade of hurdles, brushwood or carts to masonry backed with earth. Masonry walls at frequent intervals make a good obstruction, while small vehicles may be allowed to pass by placing one wall across the road leaving a small gap on the extreme left. The next wall a short distance behind the first will leave a small gap on the extreme right. Such pairs of walls should be at frequent intervals.

This idea may be carried out with lighter walls or with other variations.
The subject of variation is to remove just enough of the surface to make it impassible for vehicles above a certain size to pass or to block the road to all wheeled traffic.

Considering first a scheme for complete obstruction, alternate squares, triangular or irregular patches or strips of the road surface are removed. These are explained in the attached sketch. Figures 1 to 4 show examples of complete blockage. The shaded portions are cut out of the surface. No.1 is probably the best as it is the hardest to fill in. in all work of this kind no excavation material should be left about and the walls of the excavation should be as nearly vertical as possible.

Figure 5 shows a good example for a partial stoppage. Figure 6 is a modification.

In choosing a position to block a road, a narrow main road without alternative routes is desirable. Other points to look for are roads bounded by strong hedges or strongly built masonry walls or a road which is a cutting or embankment, the former being the better of the two. The possibility of bringing a vehicle into the fields on either side of the road and so around the obstacles should not be overlooked. To meet this, such a position as is shown in Figure 7 would be advisable. This shows ditches with hedges or other such obstacle at right angles to the road, & position should also be chosen if possible where suitable material for filling up the excavation is difficult to obtain.

Figure 8 shows another method. This is a cross section. The dotted line showing the original surface of the road, the portion shown shaded is excavated leaving a new roadway below the original level and narrower so that wide lorries etc, cannot pass.

DIRECTOR OF ENGINEERING

few records of the casualties among the IRA, but in addition to inflicting casualties, the British captured so many men that they struggled to house the prisoners. But the British counteroffensive hinted at an answer, because although the police still led the attack, most of their reinforcements were former military men. Combining with the rebels' counters, the full effect of the Munition Strike on this offensive is unclear, but the strike clearly mitigated at least some of the effects of the offensive and demonstrated to the IRA that mobility was a particular vulnerability for British forces.[89]

The arrival of the Black and Tans and the Auxiliary Division, in addition to the increase in motor vehicles for both the army and the police, and an IRA finally equipped with sufficient arms to begin or increase their campaigns against British rule, brought about a decided turn in the war. For the IRA had to respond to new threats. This they did in autumn 1920.

Figure 3.7 Typical Antitank Ditches[90]   Figure 3.8 Abatis

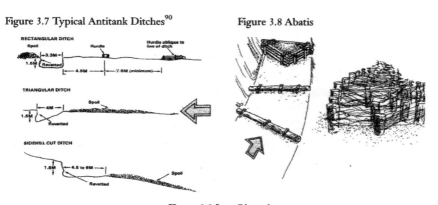

Figure 3.9 Log Obstacles

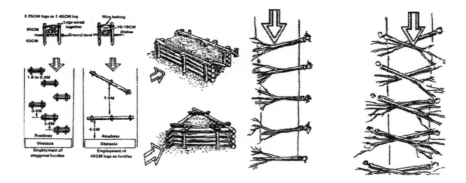

NOTES

1. For an in-depth and statistical examination of barracks attacks in the war, see W. Kautt 'Logistics and Counter-Insurgency: Procurement, Supply and Communications in the Irish War of Independence, 1919–1921', PhD thesis, University of Ulster at Jordanstown, 2005. Of the approximately ninety attacks on barracks between 1919 and 1920, 62 per cent were unsuccessful (p.141).
2. J.E. Swindlehurst, *The Maintenance of Roads in Urban Districts* (1894).
3. *The Northern and Western Motorway: Its Aims and Objects* (London: Northern and Western Motorway, 1923), p.7.
4. Until the later part of the twentieth century, Ireland was the only country in western Europe which had a steadily declining population, from 8,000,000 in 1841 to 3,900,000 in 1911. For more, see R.F. Foster, *Modern Ireland: 1600–1972* (London: Penguin, 1988), pp.599–619.
5. P. Flanagan, *Transport in Ireland, 1900–1910* (Dublin: Transport Research Associates, 1969), p.11.
6. D.J. Reynolds. 'Inland Transport in Ireland: A Factual Survey', Economic Research Institute, Dublin, Paper No. 10, November 1962, and the *CIA World Factbook*. There were only some 9,500 miles of hardtop-paved roads in Ireland by 1950, of 49,000 total miles of roads. Today there are 59,000 miles of paved roads in Ireland.
7. Mr Burke, minister for local government and public health, 1 June 1926, 'Estimates for Public Services', Dáil Éireann Debates, vol. 16.
8. General Staff, Irish Command, *Record of the Rebellion in Ireland in 1920–21, and the Part Played by the Army in Dealing with It* (1922), vol. IV, p.94 (NA PRO WO 141/93).
9. See E. O'Connor, *A Labour History of Ireland, 1824–1960* (1992).
10. Ibid., pp.108–9. See also S. Sagall, 'Solidarity Forever', *Socialist Review* (September 2002); B. Winslow, *Sylvia Pankhurst: Sexual Politics and Political Activism* (London, UCL Press, 1996), p.121; N. Davies, *White Eagle, Red Star: The Polish–Soviet War, 1919–1920 and 'The Miracle on the Vistula'* (New York: 1972), pp.172–82; and C. Townsend, 'The Irish Railway Strike of 1920', *Irish Historical Studies*, vol. 21, no. 81 (1978), pp.265–82.
11. Presumably this was the SS *Anna Dorette Boog*. See Townsend, 'Irish Railway Strike', p.266.
12. Ibid. After a meeting with railway officials, the railway men allowed the train to proceed after they were shown that ther were no munitions onboard; the consignment for the military was beef (p.267), although later in the strike they would probably have moved even food stuffs for the military.
13. Ibid, pp.269–71, and O'Connor, *Labour History*, pp.108–9.
14. Townsend, 'Irish Railway Strike', pp.268 and 273. For the possibility of forced 'donations' see 'Report on the Situation in Ireland by the General Officer Commanding-in-Chief', 29 June 1920 (PRO CAB 27/108/10); 'Weekly Survey of the State of Ireland' for 12 July 1920 (CAB 27/108/13 SIC 13); and 'Weekly Survey of the State of Ireland' for 19 July 1920 (CAB 27/108/14 SIC 20).
15. RIC Inspector-General [hereafter IG] Monthly Confidential Report for June 1920 for Cork (NA PRO CO 904/112).
16. Identity politics was contentious in Ireland throughout the twentieth century, as it remains today. It is probable the foremen giving the instructions to the workers were as 'Irish' as the workers themselves, and thought of themselves that way.
17. Macready Memorandum of 26 July 1920 (NA PRO CAB 24/110 C.P.1750); 'Notes of General Officer Commanding's Conference Held at Dublin District Headquarters', 3 June 1920 (WO 35/90/1/5, p.3); Statement of Michael O'Leary (MA WS/797); and 'Vote to End Rail Boycott', *New York Times*, 21 December 1920. The RIC reports continued this way for months.
18. Townshend, 'Irish Railway Strike of 1920', p.270.
19. 'Report on the Situation in Ireland by the General Officer Commandig-in Chief', 18 October 1920–12 December 1920 (NA PRO CAB 27/108/233–336 SIC 46–66) and Townsend, 'Irish Railway strike', p.278.
20. See, for instance, Dublin District Memorandum No. S/124/G., 12 July 1920 (NA PRO WO 35/90/1/34).
21. See, for instance, 'Lorry Fighting I' and 'Lorry Fighting III', *An t-Óglác: Official Organ of the Irish Volunteers*, II, 22 (22 February 1921), p.136 and III, 1 (15 March 1921), pp.147–8.

22. Townsend is more direct in his assessment: 'military evidence indicates that it created severe difficulties, which could have been acute. In fact, if the embargo had been made total in scope and indefinite in duration, it is hard to see how a functional military presence in the hinterland could have been maintained', 'Irish Railway Strike', p.281.
23. British Army Quartermaster General (QMG) to the Secretary of State for War, 26 October 1920 (NA PRO WO 32/9540) and Dublin District Memorandum No. S/124/G., 12 July 1920 (WO 35/90/34).
24. General Staff, Irish Command, *Record of the Rebellion*, vol. IV, p.16 (NA PRO WO 141/93).
25. The IRA began attacking coastguard stations as early as September 1920. The protection of these facilities and their aids to navigation was a constant struggle between the Royal Navy, police and the army. For more, see 'Malicious Injury to Coast Guard Stations' (ADM 116/2146); 'Employment of Marines in Ireland' (ADM1 8574/329); 'Coast Guard Service' (ADM 1/8550/26); 'Destruction of Coast Guard Stations' (ADM 116/2084); 'Eighth R.M. [Royal Marine] Battalion in Ireland' (ADM 178/39); and 'Raids on Irish Coast Guard stations, 1920–1921' (ADM 178/106–8).
26. Beadon, *Royal Army Service Corps*, vol. II (1931), pp.85–103.
27. General Staff, Irish Command, *Record of the Rebellion*, vol. IV, p.16 (NA PRO WO 141/93). See Admiralty to Viceregal Request, 27 November 1919 (NA PRO ADM 1/857/329) and 'Admiralty Memorandum', 27 May 1920 (NA PRO CAB 24/106 C.P.1353).
28. RASC, Dublin to HQ Dublin District, Memorandum No. 21101/D, 'Transport (MT) Dublin District, 10 March 1920 and RASC, Dublin to HQ Dublin District, Memorandum No. C/134, 'Transport (MT) Dublin District, 11 March 1920 (NA PRO WO 35/90/1/9).
29. These were lorries retro-fitted with steel plates as armour.
30. Dublin District Memorandum No. S/124/G., 12 July 1920 (NA PRO WO 35/90/1/34).
31. Table 8.9 (WO 32/9541); Table 8.10 (NA PRO WO 32/9522; Table 8.11 (NA PRO WO 32/9540); Table 8.12 WO 32/9541) and Table 8.13 (WO 32/9522). The records are scarce, but it appears that they kept to this timetable.
32. Crossley Motors Ltd; P. Collins, *British Motorcycles Since 1900* (1996), p.110.
33. Draft Conclusion of a Conference of Ministers held at 10 Downing Street', Appendix III, 11 May 1920 (NA PRO WO 32/9522); table original to document.
34. General Staff, Irish Command, *Record of the Rebellion*, vol. IV, p.16 (NA PRO WO 141/93); see also 'Summary of a Conference Held at Dublin District Headquarters', 22 May 1920 (WO 35/90/1/5, p.2).
35. Draft Conclusion of a Conference of Ministers held at 10 Downing Street', Appendix, 11 May 1920 (NA PRO WO 32/9522); table original to document.
36. General Staff, Irish Command, *Record of the Rebellion*, vol. IV, pp.16, 85 and 251–2 (NA PRO WO 141/93); BMH Chronology; 'Proceedings of a Conference of Ministers', 8 June 1921 (WO 32/9522); 'Report on the Situation in Ireland by the General Officer Commanding-in-Chief', 10 August 1920 (CAB 27/108/13 SIC 28); and 'Weekly Survey of the State of Ireland', 13 December 1920 (CAB 27/108/20 SIC 4.12.1920). See D.V. Duff, *Sword for Hire: The Saga of a Modern Free Companion* (1937), pp.55–6.
37. For clarity, although the terms were not fixed at the time, the author will use 'mechanized' in reference to tracked vehicles and 'motorized' to describe wheeled vehicles. Further, the first actual armouring of unarmoured motor vehicles for the British came in October 1914 when the Royal Navy experimented with its armoured car squadrons. By December of that year, they received factory-armoured vehicles and so did not have to deal with the consequences of up-armouring for long.
38. 'History of 5th Armoured Car Company', 8 January 1923 (Tank Museum, Bovington [hereafter TMB] RH.87 RTC 5ACC: 8008), p.1, and General Staff, Irish Command, *Record of the Rebellion*, vol. IV, p.85 (NA PRO WO 141/93).
39. Machine Gun Corps.
40. 'History of 5th Armoured Car Company', 8 January 1923 (TMB RH.87 RTC 5ACC: 8008), p.1, and General Staff, Irish Command, *Record of the Rebellion*, vol. IV, p.85 (NA PRO WO 141/93).
41. General Staff, Irish Command, *Record of the Rebellion*, vol. IV, p.85 (NA PRO WO 141/93). Interestingly, the 5th Armoured Car history stated that these vehicles were in good working order.

42. 'History of 5th Armoured Car Company', 8 January 1923 (TMB RH.87 RTC 5ACC: 8008) and General Staff, Irish Command, *Record of the Rebellion*, vol. IV, p.85 (NA PRO WO 141/93), p.3.

43. QMG to Secretary of State, Memorandum No. 79/Irish/715, 10 October 1920 (NA PRO WO 32/9540) and 'History of 5th Armoured Car Company', 8 January 1923 (TMB RH.87 RTC 5ACC: 8008), p.3.

44. 'War Diary of General Staff, GHQ Ireland', p.6, 24 January 1921 (NA PRO WO 35/93A).

45. 'War Diary of General Staff, GHQ Ireland', pp.1–2, for 5 January 1921 (NA PRO WO 35/93A).

46. 'History of 5th Armoured Car Company', 8 January 1923 (TMB RH.87 RTC 5ACC: 8008), p.3.

47. 'War Diary of General Staff, GHQ Ireland', p.5, 19 January 1921; p.6, 24 January 1921; p.9, 18 February 1921; p.1, 4 March 1921 and p.1, 14 March 1921 (NA PRO WO 35/93A) and General Staff, Irish Command, *Record of the Rebellion*, vol. IV, p.85 (WO 141/93).

48. 'History of 5th Armoured Car Company', 8 January 1923 (TMB RH.87 RTC 5ACC: 8008), p.4, table original to document.

49. General Staff, Irish Command, *Record of the Rebellion*, vol. I, p.32 (NA PRO WO 141/93).

50. 'Report on the Situation in Ireland by the General Officer Commanding-in-Chief', 7 December 1920 (NA PRO CAB 27/108/311 SIC 61 and WO 32/9534, p.2).

51. Most of the NATO countries use the 5.56 x 45mm NATO standard round instead of the 7.62 x 51mm NATO round, which is primarily now a machinegun round, although the AK-47 uses the 7.62 x 39mm m1943; all of these rounds are variously weaker than the .303 Lee-Enfield round. See I. V. Hogg and J. Weeks, *Military Small Arms of the 20th Century* (1992).

52. 'Summary of a Conference Held at Dublin District Headquarters', 22 May 1920 (NA PRO WO 35/90/1/5, p.2) and Dublin District Memo, No. S/712/G/1/-, 17 May 1920 (WO 35/90/1/23, p.3).

53. Sir H. Jeudwine, 'Report on the Situation in Ireland', 7 December 1920 (NA PRO WO 32/9534); 'Mechanical Transport, Armoured Cars and other forms of Protection for Troops in Ireland', 7 December 1920 (WO 32/9541); General Staff, Irish Command, *Record of the Rebellion*, vol. I, pp.32, 37; and vol. IV, pp.69 and 236 (WO 141/93).

54. See 'Lorry Fighting III', *An t-Óglác*, III, 1 (15 March 1921), pp.147–8. For simplicity's sake, all units referred to are British; IRA units are referred to with 'IRA' in the title.

55. Royal Army Service Corps and Royal Army Ordnance Corps respectively.

56. 'Operation Report', Dublin District Memo No. S/G/1/A., 7 March 1921 (NA PRO WO 35/90); J. White, *Dublin's Fighting Story, 1913–21: Told by the Men Who Made It* (1947, nd), pp.157–9; and 'Railway Situation for Week Ending 14 March 1921' (CO 904/157). It is likely that F Company was reinforced by its sister companies, if not by other battalions. This incident also demonstrates the problems with weight since the stolen lorry broke down.

57. Memorandum by Gen. Macready; Appendix to Appendix II, C. 29 (20), 11 May 1920 (NA PRO CAB 23/21). This was at a time when people only rarely *saw* motor vehicles and the majority did not know how to drive at all; so this was considered a special 'skill'.

58. Brown, *British Logistics on the Western Front*, p.54.

59. Director of Organization to Adjutant General, 5 March 1920 (NA PRO WO 32/9522) and War Office to Macready, 8 February 1921 and 16 February 1921 (WO 35/172/1).

60. Secretary of State to CIGS, QMG, Memorandum No. 92/7209, 21 October 1920 (NA PRO WO 32/9540).

61. 'History of 5th Armoured Car Company', 8 January 1923 (TMB RH.87 RTC 5ACC: 8008), p.5, and British Army QMG to Secretary of State for War, 26 October 1920 (NA PRO WO/32/9540).

62. 'War Diary of General Staff, GHQ Ireland', p.6, 24 January 1921 (NA PRO WO 35/93A).

63. 'History of 5th Armoured Car Company', 8 January 1923 (TMB RH.87 RTC 5ACC: 8008), p.5, and British Army QMG to Secretary of State for War, 26 October 1920 (NA PRO WO/32/9540).

64. British Army QMG to Secretary of State for War, 26 October 1920 (NA PRO WO/32/9540).

65. British Army QMG to Secretary of State for War, 26 October 1920 (NA PRO WO/32/9540). The number of military motor-transport drivers in Ireland increased to 1,680 by 7 December 1920 and would increase to 1,770 two days later – QMG to Secretary of State, 7 December 1920 (WO 32/9541).

66. 'Mechanical Transport, Armoured Cars and Other Forms of Protection for Troops in Ireland', 7

December 1920 (NA PRO WO 32/9541) and Jones, *Whitehall Diary, vol. III*, p.43. The RIC files 'Outrages Against the Police', 1920–21, contain reports of attacks against motor vehicles (NA PRO CO 904/148–51).

67. 'Deficiency of Signal Personnel', 7 May 1920 (NA PRO WO 32/9522).

68. 'Mechanical Transport, Armoured Cars and Other Forms of Protection for Troops in Ireland', 7 December 1920 (NA PRO WO 32/9541) 2; QMG to Secretary of State for War, 26 October 1920 (WO 32/9540); and Jones, *Whitehall Diary*, 1 December 1920, p.43.

69. British Army QMG to Secretary of State for War, 26 October 1920 (NA PRO WO/32/9540), p.1, and Brown, *British Logistics*, pp.31–4 and 56.

70. Secretary of State to CIGS, QMG, Memorandum No. 92/7209, 21 October 1920 (NA PRO WO 32/9540) and Jones, *Whitehall Diary*, 1 December 1920, p.43.

71. QMG to Secretary of State, Memorandum No. 79/Irish/715, 10 October 1920 (NA PRO WO 32/9540).

72. These statistics do not include the IRA's attacks against facilities, such as the firing of the GHQ Motor Repair and Ordnance Depôt at National Shell Factory, Parkgate Street, Dublin on 3 June 1921. The fire destroyed numerous vehicles, at least some of which were armoured cars. Although the official record does not contain an itemized list, the IRA claimed to have destroyed six armoured cars and sixty-seven motorcycles. The government claim of damage was £1 million. Court of Inquiry, 4 June 1921; 'Government Department Decree for Property and Loss at National Shell Factory', July 1921 (NA PRO TS 46/87); General Staff, Irish Command, *Record of the Rebellion*, vol. IV, p.250; and *An t-Óglác*, III, 15 (1 July 1921). For the advanced warning the Dublin District received, see 'Dublin District Weekly Intelligence Summary', no. 116, copy no. 63 for week ending 29 May 1921 and 'Operation Report', 6 July 1921 (WO 35/91, p.1).

73. Townshend, *Britain's Civil Wars: Counterinsurgency in the Twentieth Century*, pp.46–7.

74. There are two types of land ownership in the United Kingdom, 'freehold' and 'leasehold'. Under the former, one literally owns the land and structures on it, while in the latter, the land is held by one party and the structures are owned by another.

75. RIC IG Monthly Confidential Report for November 1917 (NA PRO CO 904/104). This boycott and ostracizing of the police was not a foregone conclusion since, via demographic studies, historian Peter Hart demonstrated that the IRA and the rank and file of the RIC were drawn from the same communities.

76. RIC IG Monthly Confidential Report for October 1919 (NA PRO CO 904/110).

77. General Staff, Irish Command, *Record of the Rebellion*, vol. I, pp.13 and 20, vol. IV, p.150 (NA PRO WO 141/93); and 'Outrages Against the Police', April 1920 (NA PRO CO 904/148/89) and 11 December 1920 (CO 904/159/291).

78. A Mrs Mary Lindsay was 'executed' by the IRA for giving information to the British; she and her driver were killed, without confirmation of IRA GHQ. See General Staff, Irish Command, *Record of the Rebellion*, vol. IV, p.172 (NA PRO WO 141/93) and P. O'Farrell, *Who's Who in the Irish War of Independence and Civil War, 1916–1923* (1997), p.55; see also Chapter 5.

79. For RIC reports on boycott-related incidents, see RIC IG Reports from 1917 to 1921, primarily for the southern and western counties (NA PRO CO 904/108–16).

80. There were actually two police forces in Ireland. The RIC had purview over the entire island, but the Dublin Metropolitan Police functioned in the city. The DMP was subject to abuse, but also suffered an assassination campaign.

81. RIC 'Outrage Summaries', 1919 to 1920 (NA PRO CO 904/148–51).

82. RIC IG Report for February 1920 and for June, July and August 1920 for counties Sligo, Mayo and Carlow (NA PRO CO 904/111–12); Jones, *Whitehall Diary*, 31 May 1920, p.17; Macready Memorandum to Cabinet, 26 July 1920 (CAB 24/110 C.P.1750); Herlihy, *Royal Irish Constabulary: Short History and Genealogical Guide*, p.107 and 'Note by Mr Long', 15 July 1920, SIC (CAB 27/107 CP1636). See also Macready Memorandum 26 July 1920 (WO 32/9520).

83. General Staff, Irish Command, *Record of the Rebellion in Ireland*, vol. I, p.12.

84. See D. Leeson, '"Scum of 'London's Underworld", British Recruits for the Royal Irish Constabulary, 1920–21', *Contemporary British History*, 17, 1 (Spring, 2003); D. Leeson, 'Imperial

Stormtroopers: British Paramilitaries in the Irish War of Independence, 1920–1921', PhD thesis, McMaster University, 2003.

85. RIC IG Report for December 1920 for Co. Cavan (NA PRO CO 904/113); see also RIC IG Report for January 1921 for counties Antrim and Kilkenny (CO 904/114); and P. Hart, *The I.R.A. and its Enemies: Violence and Community in Cork, 1916–1923* (1998), p.103.

86. 'General Notes', *An t-Óglác*, III, 11 (3 June 1921) and 'Cutting Roads', *An t-Óglác*, III, 14 (24 June 1921); C. Browne, *The Story of the 7th: A concise history of the Battalion, Cork No.1 Brigade, Irish Republican Army from 1915 to 1921* (2007), pp.48–9; IRA Cork No. 2 Brigade Memorandum, 'Enemy Road Traffic', 24 April 1921, Siobhán Lankford Papers (CAI U169/2); and Statement of John O'Mahoney (MA WS/1662).

87. IRA Operation Memorandum No. 2 1921, Siobhán Lankford Papers (CAI U169/34); Monthly Confidential Intelligence Report for Midland and Connaught District, June 1918 (PRO CO 904/105) and 'Tactical Lorries', Dublin District Memo No. S/26/G.M.T., 24 August 1920 (WO 35/90/1/49).

88. 'Tactical Lorries', Dublin District Memo No. S/26/G.M.T., 24 August 1920 (NA PRO WO 35/90/1/49).

89. For evidence that the munitions strike slowed British forces, see 'Notes of General Officer Commanding's Conference Held at Dublin District Headquarters', 3 June 1920 (NA PRO WO 35/90/1, p.3), in which it is directly referenced as a cause. See also DAQMG, Dublin District, Memorandum No. S/124, No. S/124/G., 12 July 1920 (WO 35/90/1/34); and 'District Headquarters' Conference', Memorandum No. 1067 'Q', 9 November 1920 (WO 35/90/1/9, p.3). See also General Staff, Irish Command, *Record of the Rebellion*, vol. I, pp.15–6; vol. IV, pp.18, 24, 28, 35, 89, 135, 151–2. For discussion of a wider IRA campaign against logistics, see Kautt, 'Logistics and Counter-Insurgency'.

90. Note: Figures 3.7, 3.8 and 3.9 are from FM 5-102 *Countermobility*.

Four

Kilmichael and the IRA Counter to the British Autumn 1920 Offensive

The IRA did not simply roll over during the RIC offensive; for although the British captured many rebel leaders and put many IRA men on the run, there were still sufficient 'safe' areas in the south and in the most rugged parts of Ireland in which they could escape. The IRA rank and file were reassured in August that the police campaign of 'frightfulness' would fall apart as the IRA struck back. By September, they were being told to hold firm; in October, that the enemy was incompetent and barbaric. By January, the IRA learned from their leaders that the RIC offensive had failed.[1] While not entirely correct, the IRA certainly scored some important victories in autumn 1920. The offensive also had an unexpected third order effect; being on the run, the rebels congregated in some of the largest groups seen since the Rising four years earlier by bringing the more active of the part-time rebels into the full-time fight by forcing them to leave their families and work. As a result, they had more time to devote to the republican cause. This enabled the remaining rebels to fight harder and so made the war more violent; attacks and casualties increased dramatically on both sides. This chapter explores the beginning of the IRA counters by first examining a typical IRA ambush of the pre-British offensive and then the major turning point critical for the IRA to check the government offensive.

By autumn 1920, the IRA's ambush tactics had begun to change. Prior to September, the rebels halted British police or military columns with gunfire, although sometimes they used obstructions, as noted above. Before the counteroffensive, British convoys used higher driving speeds as a primary countermeasure, racing through to their destinations. Obviously, this was not always possible, so in addition, British forces began to develop other means of dealing with rebel tactics – specifically countermeasures in the event of attack. These tactics, techniques and procedures (TTPs), what one might call a sort of 'proto-doctrine', combined with speed and not stopping for damaged vehicles, were generally effective. An additional result of the offensive was that the two principle units within the IRA brigades for conducting ambushes and other attacks came to the fore, the 'flying

Figure 4.1 IRA After-Action Report, August 1920[2]

1st Tipp. BDE
4/8/20

To: – ADJUTANT GENERAL
  G.H.Q.

ACTIVITIES REPORT
Hold up of military vehicles near OOLA.

OBJECT: –
  To Capture 12 or 16 Rifles: 1 Lewis Gun : 1 (40 H.P.) crossley car :1 Triumph motorcycle & Military mails:

Information in our hands: –
  Motor lorry carrying military mails from LIMERICK to TIPPERARY passed regularly through OOLA between 10 AM & 10-15AM. It contained from 12 to 16 military & carried 1 Lewis Gun (The tenders of military carried from 12 to 16). A motor cycle normally preceded it at a distance varying from 100 to 300 yards; basically the motor cycle was carried in the lorry (probably having broken down). Speed about 30 miles an hour.

ATTACK.
  V. Comdt, 1st Tipp. BDE in charge:
  About 55 men in all took part in attack: Vice Comdt 1st Bn. 4 Volunteers each from A & B Coys and 6 Volunteers each from C, D, & E Coys BTNI. and 8 Volunteers [illegible] Tipperary BTNS, who are on the run. These latter [illegible] two motor drivers and one Machine Gunner.
  Men were mobilized all 2 am [illegible] while S.E. of Oola at 9A.M.; Took up position on Oola-Tipp Road at 8-45 AM. Position selected was : – Bend on OOLA-TIPP. Road about ½ mile S.E. of OOLA. About 10 AM two Cavalry passed from TIPP direction but didn't see our ambush: The Lorry arrived at 10-20 AM but was not preceded by Motor Cycle: The Lorry passed through our ambush as far as the Barricade, where it was halted: The enemy immediately opened fire while our Troops returned shooting one in the act of getting for [illegible] fight lasted about 15 minutes during which time about two of the enemy was killed and [illegible] wounded: [illegible] leader for retreat was sounded as it was realised another lorry was coming from OOLA direction.

Result: –
  Attack was a failure.

Probable Reasons: –
  I. The Ambush was too long, as the motor cycles didn't happen to travel with the car.
  II. Second lorry came along as we were about surrounding the mail car.

Diagram shewing position etc
          (not drawn to scale)

columns' and 'active service units' (ASUs). Although the terms were frequently used interchangeably, technically the first were full-time and roamed about, while the latter were similar guerrilla bands that remained local and part-time, coming out primarily to support the operations of the former although they also conducted operations on their own or with the support of the rank and file of their brigades. Flying columns and ASUs were the elites of the rebel brigades and were frequently used to lead the less experienced part-time rebels in the regular companies and battalions. The columns and ASUs did not come to prominence until later in the autumn; the regular IRA units retained primary responsibility until then and were capable of significant action of their own.

Rineen Ambush, 22 September 1920

One such operation was the Rineen, Co. Clare ambush of Wednesday, 22 September 1920, which saw the 4th Battalion, IRA Mid-Clare Brigade attack a lorryload of police. The stated objective of the operation was revenge for the killing of the Mid-Clare Brigade vice-commandant, Martin Davitt in February 1920,[3] but the secondary purpose, and perhaps the more important, was to gain arms and munitions because the battalion was, like most IRA brigades, poorly armed. During a battalion meeting in mid-September, the leadership, including the battalion officer commanding, Ignatius O'Neill, decided to attack the RIC lorry that went from the RIC barracks in Ennistymon to Miltown Malbay, some nine miles south-west, twice a week at regular intervals on the same route (see Figure 4.2). Planning for the next Wednesday trip, which usually left at 1130 hours and returned by 1530, the rebels chose Dromin Hill at Rineen as their ambush site because, at 400 feet high, the hill commanded the surrounding area.[4]

The fifty-three rebels from seven of the battalion's nine companies marshalled at the Moy Church around 0200 hours on the morning of the ambush. They were pitifully armed: eight had rifles, two had revolvers, sixteen shotguns and one man had two hand grenades, the rest were unarmed. In total, they had sixty rounds of various types of ammunition. By 0400 hours, the rebels took up their positions in a ditch at the base of the west side of Domin Hill between the railway track and the road. On the opposite side of the road lay the ocean and, thus, no cover.[5]

The Volunteers made no preparations for their site – no fighting positions or obstacles; they only laid down straw for comfort in their long wait. It may have been that the ditch was sufficient to their needs or that they were inexperienced in ambush operations. The eight riflemen were under the command of former Irish Guardsman Cmdt Ignatius O'Neill,

4th IRA Battalion commander. The remaining men were under the command of Capt. Curtin, commandant of the Moy IRA Company. Commentators have pointed out that at least two trains must have passed the ambush site, but did not report the IRA presence to the police.[6]

Although no one warned the police, someone betrayed the rebels' plan to the British army. Some time early on the 22nd, an NCO of the 2nd Battalion, Highland Light Infantry in Ennistymon received information about the ambush; the Highlanders subsequently sent out at least one patrol to strike at the rebels. This patrol went out in three Crossleys, and they also sent out a second patrol mounted on bicycles.[7]

After awaiting the arrival of the RIC lorry for some eight hours, one of the rebel scouts, inexperienced and overly excited, gave the wrong signal to the ambushers as the lorry approached; the rebels, in accordance with their plan, let the policemen pass through unmolested, since the signal received said that there was more than one lorry in the convoy. Fortunately for the rebels, they remained under cover and the ambush position was sufficiently hidden that the police knew nothing of their presence. As a result, and knowing that the RIC men would be returning by the same route, the Volunteers remained in position for another three hours. Their patience paid off when the RIC Crossley returned, and the rebels engaged it.

The attack began when Volunteer Peter Vaughan, a former U.S. Army soldier, threw two hand grenades at the lorry; both overshot their target, but their detonation was sufficient to kill four of the six policemen – Constables Hardman, Hodnett, Kelly and McGuire – outright, while wounding a fifth, Const. Harte. When the vehicle finally came to a halt, Harte and Sgt. Hynes dismounted; the driver, Hardman, was dead. Hynes rushed, probably for what he thought was cover, straight towards the Volunteers' position, where he was gunned down. Harte, wounded and on the other side of the vehicle, crawled west towards the ocean, desperate for cover; Volunteer brothers Tom and Donal Lehane followed him and mercilessly shot him to death. Harte was unarmed, for, according to the rebel accounts, five rifles were handed out to the remaining Volunteers; only Hynes was carrying a service pistol.[8] Harte simply left his rifle when he tried to escape. He may have been in the driving compartment with Sgt. Hynes and Hardman; if this was the case, he likely would have left his rifle in the rear of the vehicle. Of course, it also means that Harte was unarmed when he was gunned down.

Meanwhile, as the shooting started, after the blast of two grenades, the Crossley-mounted Highlanders, having arrived at the intersection of the Miltown and Liscannor Roads, immediately set out for the hill. At the same time, the bicycle-mounted soldiers also converged on the site.

The republicans claimed that they fought for three hours with the Black and Tans, but the truth is that O'Neill's riflemen, receiving a third again as much firepower and at least several hundred rounds of .303 Lee-Enfield ammunition,[9] fought a fairly competent rearguard action while the other thirty-nine rebels under Curtin retreated. Both Cmdt O'Neill and Capt. Curtin displayed excellent leadership and were wounded in this action.

Table 4.1 IRA Companies' Participation in the Rineen Ambush

Company	No. of Volunteers taking part
Ennistymon	4
Inagh	10
Lahinch	10
Moy	6
Glendine	8
Miltown Malbay	10
Letterkenny	5
Total:	53

Figure 4.2 Map of Rineen Ambush, 22 September 1920

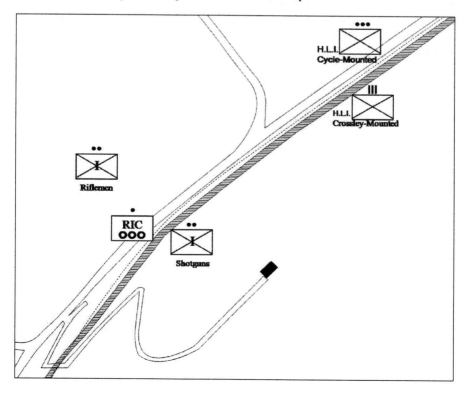

Republicans claimed to have killed at least four more Black and Tans, but since there was only one in the entire engagement, T/Const. Reginald Hardman, the Crossley driver, killed in the opening attack, and no other policemen than those in the first engagement died, this is impossible. Further, the claim that the bodies of the six policemen in coffins were processed through the streets of Ennistymon the following morning (the 23rd) is likewise impossible, since Sgt. Hynes was only wounded when he rushed the IRA position and succumbed to his wounds on the 24th. The Highland Light Infantry had one RASC driver wounded as they drove up.[10]

At some point in the fighting, the soldiers got a Lewis machine gun into action, possibly from the top of Dromin Hill. This brings up an interesting point: the rebels made no attempt to secure their flanks, designate a reserve or identify a line of retreat. All of these came into play about nine weeks later at Kilmichael. Although both O'Neill and Curtin fought courageously, their ambush site was poorly located, they did not attempt to hold the high ground, or even, it appears, to place scouts on top of it. Further, if not for the effective fire of O'Neill's riflemen, the Volunteers certainly would have taken more casualties than just their two commanders. It is interesting to note that there were neither obstacles nor IEDs (although, perhaps, one could classify a hand-thrown grenade as an IED); the ambush was almost amateurish and was significantly different from what would come later in the war.

There are some interesting points with regard to this attack and subsequent events. In addition to rather simplistic planning and execution, the rebels and later republican writers appear to be completely unaware that they were betrayed. None explained how three lorryloads of soldiers just appeared on the scene along with those who came on bicycle. This omission is unusual since the IRA intelligence system was quite good; they knew enough that they would not have expected the troops to arrive on the scene by accident. Further, it is unusual that they misidentified their attackers, although it was certainly possible that they exited the area so quickly that they never got a good look at the enemy troops. Further, the republican sources did not comment on the British charge that the rebels used 'dum-dum', or soft-lead bullets, in the attack. These bullets flatten and fragment on impact, causing horrific wounds; they were outlawed for use in war by the two Hague conventions which were then in force.[11] There are two problems with this idea. The first is that the IRA captured or stole most of their ammunition from the British army or from the RIC, thus this would have meant that they were, in fact, using these bullets, which the republicans have also claimed. The other possibility is that the IRA were reloading spent cartridges. Unless one has access either to a smelter or to pre-cast full metal jacketed bullets, one will use a bullet mould to create the bullets. Lead would be the most common material used and, therefore, this would have been a factor of military necessity rather than a simple violation; the equipment captured by British forces suggests this to be the case.[12]

There is, of course, the problem that, under the laws of war as written and interpreted at the time, the rebels were not accorded the protections of the laws of war and were under no *legal* (versus moral) obligation to do so. Further, there were accusations from the rebels that the British used dum-dums at the Battle of Crossbarry in March 1921 (see Chapter 5).[13] In fact, IRA adherence to the laws of war in past and future events of the era meant nothing to the British authorities.[14] So decrying that those whom one has declared criminals are not obeying the law is rather odd.

In the end, although the military and police made extensive searches, none of the rebels were captured. In reprisal for this ambush, RIC men, including Black and Tans, 'set fire to buildings in Ennistymon, Lahinch and Miltown Malbay in Co. Clare and killed three people'.[15] Although the rebels claimed a greater victory than occurred, and although their successes were due more to luck than skill, there is no denying that this attack was a victory for the IRA Mid-Clare Brigade.

The republicans had developed their countermobility capabilities during their raids in 1919 for arms. As they grew in experience and capability, the rebels became more audacious and began more organized and coordinated raids against RIC barracks for firearms and ammunition, which entailed greater risk. The police, in turn, developed countermeasures against these raids, including calling for help. The arrival of relief forces was potentially disastrous for the IRA, so they learned to block roads and, eventually, to ambush the relief forces. For instance, at Bruree, Co. Limerick on Thursday, 29 July 1920 rebels ambushing a patrol of eight RIC and soldiers were attacked by a relief force from the 1st Bn. The Machine Gun Corps. After losing two men, the Volunteers prudently fled. At Lislevane, Co. Cork, on Monday, 17 January 1921, twenty-five Volunteers preparing an ambush site surrendered after being surprised by troops from the 1st Bn Essex Regiment.[16]

So the rebels learned to guard their flanks by placing guards and unarmed scouts, although each guard took one weapon away from their attack. They also blocked means of advance by trenching roads and dropping trees. Additionally, they learned to attack the relief forces too. Their tactics became sophisticated enough that they could block every road except the one leading to their ambush site. During an attack on the

Figure 4.3 British Standing Orders for Convoys (undated)

Dublin District Standing Orders for Armed Parties Moving by Lorry, and for Lorry Convoys.

Part I. – General.

1. The term 'lorry' in these orders includes all vehicles of 15 cwt. carrying capacity and upwards.

2. No armed party or escort will consist of less than one officer or selected N.C.O., and six men. The maximum number in one lorry will not exceed one officer or N.C.O. and 12 other ranks, except when it is necessary in an emergency to convey a greater number for a special duty and no additional transport is available.

3. Rifles will have magazines charged, and safety catches back. A round will not be placed in the chamber, except in the case of men detailed for 'immediate action,' *vide* paras. 5 and 6.

4. Revolvers and pistols will be loaded. (Automatic pistols will not have a round in the chamber, and the mechanism will be set at 'safe')

5. Normally, bayonets will not be fixed, but it is left to the discretion of Brigade Commanders to modify this if they should consider it necessary.

6. Every lorry which carries armed personnel will have the following minimum number specially told off for duty, and for immediate action: –

(a) A forward 'lookout' sitting beside the driver.

(b) Two side 'look outs,' one on each side of the lorry.

(c) A rear 'look out' by the tail-board.

7. The 'look outs' mentioned above will have their revolvers or rifles for 'Immediate action.' In the case of rifles, 'Immediate action' will mean that a round is in the chamber with the safety catch back, the rifle being held muzzle pointing up, the barrel resting, if desired, on the side, or tail-board of the lorry.

8. All 'look outs' in lorries will stand or sit in such a position that they can use their rifles without delay. The sides of the tarpaulin hood will always be rolled up to allow of this.

9. In addition to the 'look outs,' one or two men will be told off specially to drop the tail-board of the lorry if required.

10. A N.C.O., or selected private, will be detailed to command the party inside the body of each lorry. Should there be only one N.C.O. on the lorry, he will be in the body of the lorry and not on the seat beside the driver.

11. The officer, N.C.O., or selected private in command in the body of the lorry will be responsible that the 'look outs' are posted, that they are always on the alert, and that reliefs are arranged.

12. N.C.O.s and men not detailed for the above-mentioned duties will hold their rifles in their hands, and may be allowed to sit down if there is room.

13. Look outs, officers, and N.C.O.s in command of troops in lorries must always, when away from barracks, be suspicious of harmless looking parties of civilians on the road-side.

In several cases parties of civilians playing 'pitch and toss' have suddenly produced revolvers and held up our patrols and lorries.

Groups of civilians sitting by bridges with steep approaches thereto will also be watched carefully.

14. In case of hostile attack or ambush, the 'look out' will immediately open fire from the lorry, whilst the remainder get down as quickly as possible and go for the enemy.

15. The officer or N.C.O. in command will impress on all ranks before starting off on a lorry journey that, in the case of ambush being met with, it is essential that there should be quickness, obedience to orders and complete absence of panic.

Rapid fire from the 'look out' will greatly disconcert the enemy, and will give the remainder of the party time to get out and counterattack.

16. 'Lorry drill,' *i.e.*, action to be taken if ambushed, will be practised on every possible occasion, and this drill is to be *rehearsed either before the start, or soon after the start at some quiet part of the road by each party or escort*.

As a precaution against hostile fire from behind hedges, banks, or walls along the road-side, certain men will be detailed *before starting* for the duty of getting through or over the hedges etc., on both sides of the roads, and thus enfilading the enemy.

17. Should the lorry break down on the road an isolated party of troops will be specially on its guard against attack. Civilians are not to be allowed to collect near the lorry, and will only be allowed to pass by in twos and threes at good intervals. Should there be a hedge or wall by the roadside some of the party will be so stationed as to cover the far side.

An *unarmed* man will be sent to the nearest detachment or police barrack for assistance in the case of a serious breakdown to the lorry.

18. It is better to appear ridiculous in the eyes of civilians by over-caution than to risk the lives of your men or loss of rifles and ammunition.

19. (*a*) *All tactical lorries will carry*: –

One pick.
One shovel.
One wire hawser (for towing purposes, or for dragging away obstructions).
One hand axe.
One cross-cut saw.
One pair wire cutters.
One crowbar.
Four planks (for use as wheel bases, to allow the lorry to cross over the filled in earth of any trench dug across the road).
Three trench mortar bombs, with slow fuses.

(*b*) *In the Dublin Metropolitan area*, including Kingstown and Dalkey, lorries other than tactical lorries will carry: –

One wire hawser.

(*c*) *Outside the Dublin Metropolitan area*.

(*i*) Lorries, other than tactical lorries employed in rushing troops out to meet an emergency will, at the discretion of the Officer Commanding on the spot, carry all, any, or none of the stores in para. 19 (*a*), according to the urgency of the call and the time available.

(*ii*) In any convoy conveying troops, prisoners, or stores, at least one lorry will carry the stores enumerated in para. 19 (*a*). Subject to sub-para. 19 (*c*) (*i*).

20. Officers and N.C.O.s in command of lorry parties and escorts must be prepared to meet the following road obstacles: –

(*a*) Trees felled across the road.
(*b*) Stone walls across the road.
(*c*) Trenches (covered with camouflage material or left open).
(*d*) Barbed wire entanglements.

Instructions for the removal of (*a*) have already been circulated.

21. Every lorry carrying troops will be provided with a cover as a protection against bombing. This cover must not prevent a clear view from the sides.

22. Instructions will be posted up in all lorries explaining how to stop the lorry if the driver should become a casualty, and in every armed party travelling by lorry there must be at least one soldier who is capable of stopping the lorry if the driver should be disabled.

23. Arrangements are being made to provide armour for tactical lorries, and it is hoped that this work will shortly be completed.

24. The attention of all ranks is directed to this Office letter No. 242/4 S.T., dated 12th July, 1920, with reference to the proper use of motor transport vehicles.

25. If two or three lorries are moving in convoy, one lorry will act as advanced guard, keeping about 200 yards ahead of the others. The escort to be divided between the front and rear lorries.

26. (*a*) With more than three lorries a convoy will have an advanced guard lorry, moving 200 yards in front of the main body. The main body will move close up, with 20 yards distance between each lorry.

(*b*) If a motor cycle (preferably a combination cycle) is available, it will be utilized as a vanguard 100 yards in front of the advanced guard lorry. An additional motor cycle, if available, should be used for purposes of communication. If no motor cycle is available and the country is suitable for cycling, a few cyclists can be used with advantage as a vanguard.

27. The strength of the escort will depend on the size and importance of the convoy.

28. The forward 'look outs' and rear 'look outs' respectively, will pass back and forward the usual military signals, such as 'Halt!'; 'Enemy in sight,' etc. Rear 'look outs' will be responsible for, reporting at once, any stoppage or opening out on the part of following lorries, and when overtaking vehicles require to pass.

29. The officer (or N.C.O.) commanding the convoy escort will be in tactical command of the whole convoy, including the drivers of the vehicles and any other personnel travelling in the convoy.

He will travel with some of the escort in the leading lorry of the main body, himself being *inside* the lorry.

He will be responsible: –

(a) For the safety of the convoy, and that all military precautions are taken.

(b) That each lorry containing armed personnel is under the command of a N.C.O., or selected private, and that the 'look outs' are posted before starting.

(c) That all ranks receive instructions before starting as to their action in case of attack, and that such action is rehearsed.

(d) That the convoy moves in formation laid down, and that lorries are not left behind. Halts are unnecessary, except for meals and purposes of nature, unless required by the A.S.C. for mechanical reasons.

(e) That the convoy does not exceed a maximum speed of 12 miles per hour on the open road, slowing down to 8 miles per hour when passing through towns and villages. The speed of the convoy should be that of the *slowest* vehicle. *Low speed vehicles should be at the head of the main body of the convoy*, but if necessary, the high speed vehicles in a convoy may be moved in bounds to cover the advance of the remainder of the convoy, so long as the high and low speed proportions of the convoy are each provided with an adequate escort.

(f) That in the case of a lorry breaking down completely (*i.e.*, that it cannot be towed), he shall have transferred to other lorries all its movable stores. He will use discretion as to whether he can spare a guard over the broken down lorry until it can be brought in. In any case the driver (unarmed) of the lorry must remain with it.

(g) That he keeps a log of any incidents which may happen on the journey, and that he reports on arrival at his destination to the proper quarter.

30. A copy of these orders will be in the possession of every officer, and Commanding Officers will be responsible that these orders are made known to all ranks.

Commanding Officers, or Officers Commanding detachments at the departure point will ensure that the officer or N.C.O. in command of the convoy or lorry party is thoroughly acquainted with his duties.

RIC barracks near Ardmore, Co. Waterford, on Monday, 1 November 1920 a second group of rebels ambushed the relief from the 2nd Battalion Hants (Hampshire Regiment), killing one soldier.[17]

The means they used to block the roads depended on location and circumstance; some methods were more permanent than others, such as destroying a bridge versus trenching a road or felling a tree. The last was the least permanent. The design of British vehicles also came into play and spurred the rebel trenching tactics, because early in the war, 1919, Co. Tipperary IRA volunteers noted that the then primary British vehicle, the Crossley Tender, would break down or even break an axle on large potholes in the poorly maintained roads. So the rebels began digging shallow trenches across the more common routes. The trenches were only a few inches deep, but when combined with the initial British countermeasures of driving high speed, they were remarkably effective – too much so, since they blocked civilian traffic as well. Townspeople complained to Dáil Éireann's Home Government minister, founder of Sinn Féin Arthur Griffith, and the underground rebel government, eager to bolster legitimacy, ordered a halt to the trenching operations. The rebels, obedient, stopped. Of course, the IRA leaders then got around the order by merely having their men 'maintain' the existing potholes.[18]

Regardless of semantics, potholes were not going to stop British forces for long, nor were ambushes like that at Rineen, so the IRA stepped up its attacks, both in ambushes and against fixed sites. By November 1920, in the midst of the RIC and ADRIC offensive against the rebels, IRA violent attacks were still on the rise and demonstrated increasing sophistication in doctrine and TTPs. At the same time, British forces learned from these encounters. It is important to note that while the British army examined many of the ambushes detailed in this study, they were usually only partly involved; the attacks examined here were primarily against police convoys. The obvious question, then, should be, why examine attacks on police? There are many good reasons, not least of which is that they were the most common victims of IRA ambushes, but the most important reason is because the British army did. The army took an interest in police ambushes because they had to operate against the same enemy, with the same weapons, on the same ground, and, most importantly, with the same tactics and doctrine; especially since the police were increasingly filling up with former military men. IRA tactics did not vary according to whether the victims were police or army, especially since they were increasingly working together.

As stated above, the British reinforced the RIC with the Black and Tans and the Auxiliary Division and went on the offensive in late August and September 1920. The IRA fought back while at the same time being forced to go on the run. It is unclear which came first, the going on the run or the increase in attacks. Perhaps they were simultaneous. Still, in early November 1920, the war was going poorly for the republicans, but by the end of the month they were beginning to hold their own against the British advance. They stemmed the tide on the last Sunday in November on a lonely road in a rural part of west Cork. Here, at a place known as Kilmichael, the Cork IRA changed the conduct of the rest of the war by massacring an ADRIC patrol almost to the last man.

Kilmichael Ambush, 28 November 1920

The Macroom, or Kilmichael ambush, as it is more commonly known, was a pivotal event in the War of Independence, not only because it signalled the end of the RIC offensive or because it followed exactly a week after 'Bloody Sunday' in Dublin, but because it demonstrated the fighting capabilities of the full-time rebels in the flying columns. This, in turn, pushed the army into their own offensive. In this manner,

Kilmichael ended the police leadership in the offensive, while ensuring the army would take over with another. It showed they were not mere amateurs and that to disregard them was perilous indeed. The facts of what occurred that Sunday evening in rural Co. Cork on the Dunmanway–Macroom Road speak to the horror of war in general, but specifically to this type of conflict, while demonstrating Clausewitz' famous 'fog' and 'friction',[19] or confusion, in war. That these events spoke differently to the British than to the republicans, the latter getting a boost to their sagging morale while the former decrying it as horrible murder, demonstrated that the British army and leadership did not have a firm grasp of the situation in Ireland. Or perhaps it is more accurate to say that they did not understand the republican view of the situation in Ireland, for one must understand one's enemy's views in addition to those of the population in this type of war. The enemy is not beaten until he believes he is.

Part of the shock of Kilmichael, beyond the scope and scale of the carnage and abject savagery of it, was the larger issue of group identity for the British leaders. Due to their standing and class, they had an innate sense of their own inherent superiority. Kilmichael, whether one sees it as a legitimate act of war or as outright murder, challenged that cherished belief. Up to November, the men dying on the British side were mostly Irish-enlisted men; officers of the RIC or the army died primarily due either to luck on the part of the rebels or to deliberate assassination. Even the officers who died on Bloody Sunday were gunned down in their beds or under circumstances where they had no chance to defend themselves. This, the British could explain away as mere crime or terrorism; Kilmichael, on the other hand, they could not explain away as easily.

The Auxiliary cadets who died at Kilmichael were not enlisted men or 'mere policemen'; they were elite. As former military officers, they were born to the gentle class or raised to it due to their martial qualities displayed in the fields of Flanders and elsewhere. They had been excellent soldiers; they had fought 'real war' and survived. In many cases, the cadets of the ADRIC had displayed personal valour on the battlefield; there were three Victoria Cross recipients among their ranks.[20] The IRA were, according to the British view, nothing but criminals, layabouts, ruffians; men who would do no honest work. The IRA were, to the police and army, cowards.

So if one could discount the fighting capabilities of the IRA flying columns, one would not have to face the harsh realities of the conflict in Ireland. Sinn Féin was a popular, well-organized and legitimate political entity. The IRA were not the enthusiastic, but largely incompetent, Irish

Volunteers of Easter Week, 1916; they were successful in many parts of the country and far from beaten at the end of autumn 1920. The British offensive had certainly made significant strides and had hurt the IRA, but did not go far enough. While their enemy was demonstrating not only resilience and the ability to adapt quickly, the British *would not* see this, or that the IRA possessed potent leaders and tactical competence. The British appear to have been unwilling to admit these points in late 1920, so they turned back to their original assumptions: if the IRA were nothing but murderers and ruffians, they could only have defeated the Auxiliaries from Macroom through perfidy and murder. Even in this, the British commentators seemed to be embarrassed and seem to hold that any true gentleman bearing arms should have been able to defeat these mere 'criminals'.

It is important to state that the author believes that neither the British nor the republicans *deliberately* attempted to falsify or manufacture evidence for propaganda or any other purposes; the best propaganda is true or, at least, believed to be by the producers of it. The author believes that the known facts of the incident at Kilmichael support much of what both sides claimed. It is from this position that the examination will continue. Finally, the available evidence, carefully examined, reveals details that have gone unmentioned, but also offers ideas apropos to the concept of ambushes themselves. Therefore, there is greater dialectic involved in the examination of this ambush than the others in this study.

The British army eventually drew some lessons from the events at Kilmichael, but they were appalled by the sheer savagery of it. This attack demonstrated the necessity of existing route security doctrine, specifically the placement of flank, rear and advance guards. For the rebels, this was a much needed boost to sagging morale. On both sides it demonstrated the ferocity and earnestness of the opposing sides. In terms of sheer violence and success for the rebels, the Kilmichael ambush was one of the most deadly during the entire conflict.

Around dusk on Sunday, 28 November 1920 the IRA 3rd West Cork Brigade flying column under Cmdt Tom Barry ambushed a patrol of Auxiliary police on the Macroom–Dunmanway road near Kilmichael. The patrol consisted of two Crossley Tenders and eighteen policemen.[21] In the end, twenty-five men became casualties that day; twenty were killed outright or died of their wounds within hours, and five wounded men survived. Seventeen of the eighteen 'Auxies' were killed, including their commander, District Inspector Colonel Francis Crake, O/C, C Company, ADRIC.[22] Three IRA Volunteers died and four were wounded. The twenty-fifth casualty, Cadet H.F. Forde, survived only because he was so badly wounded the rebels thought he was dead. Forde was physically and mentally disabled for the rest of his life.[23]

The facts of what happened at Kilmichael are still very much in dispute, with one side maintaining that the rebels murdered helpless and unarmed men and the other claiming the Auxies surrendered falsely; both of these charges violated the Hague conventions on the laws of war in force at the time. The intervening eighty-seven years have not quelled this debate because, with the last deaths of the participants, those with first-hand knowledge of the truth of what happened that day are gone. Further, the events have not only passed literally into song, but have become part of the legends of the independence of the Irish Republic. By entering into the debate of what occurred in terms of atrocities on either side, it is possible to examine this ambush as a military operation on either side. Such an examination also yields information about the conduct of the war. This is possible since there are facts upon which all agree that permit some reconstruction of the events of that terrible day and which will help in understanding ambushes. Thus, this section examines the attack and the arguments surrounding it by contemporary historians, and poses plausible explanations for the evidence.

The ambush party consisted of the flying column of the IRA 3rd West Cork Brigade, divided into four sections with some local Volunteers acting as scouts. Strangely, Cmdt Barry established his command post (CP) in line with the three attacking sections rather than on the higher ground behind them; in addition, it was not centrally located where he would have been able to see those sections and the Auxiliaries as they engaged and thus have been able to command the IRA fight. This is extremely odd, especially since he was out of communications with the No. 3 Section detailed as a reserve. He was, therefore, unable to commit his reserve force. One could expect from Barry's personality that he would have wanted the most dangerous function for himself and that thus his command post had to be in the position it was. In reality, this was still quite foolish; how a rebel leader could be so careless is surprising. Probably the only reason would have been a poor choice of ground, one that did not provide sufficient cover in any of the otherwise more appropriate locations or deployment configurations.[24]

The command post was at a stone wall on the easternmost end of the ambush site. This, according to both republican and British sources, was 'loopholed' to allow riflemen to shoot from cover rather than exposing them while shooting over the wall. After the command post came the three sections numbered one to three, lined east to west (see Figure 4.4). No. 1 Section was the first one west of the command post, about 10

Figure 4.4 Kilmichael Ambush, 28 November 1920

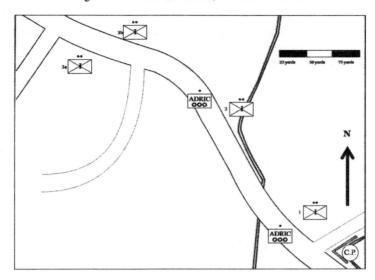

yards away; No. 2 Section was about 150 yards to the west of them; while the third (westernmost) section was about forty yards distant. Barry divided No. 3 Section, with six men detailed to the north of the road and the remainder on the south side of the road. These were to be prepared if a third vehicle should arrive, to prevent the ADRIC from taking up defensive positions and to act as the reserve.[25]

In a downright foolhardy move, Barry claimed that he deliberately established the ambush site to allow for no line of retreat.[26] Assuming this was true, it was recklessly irresponsible for a guerrilla leader to jeopardize his force in such a manner. In guerrilla warfare, the survival of the guerrilla force must always be of paramount importance for the movement to continue; to risk annihilation in this way was just arrogant and foolish. Assuming that Barry was neither foolish nor arrogant, there may have been other reasons for him to have claimed this.

The accounts generally agree that the two ADRIC vehicles were travelling at least fifty yards apart; proper spacing was a security measure and was in accord with standing orders. Barry claimed to have stepped out into the road as the first Crossley began to slow down as it neared the command post, having been allowed to pass by all three sections. Whether it was because Barry appeared on the road or if it was already slowing is unclear. Barry appeared to be a British officer in his trench coat, a Volunteers' blouse, and, according to the British army, a steel helmet. When the lead vehicle halted, Barry said he threw a Mills bomb (fragmentation grenade, see Chapter 6, Figure 6.2) into the driving compartment, killing the driver and the convoy commander, Col. Crake, but the British accounts say that the Auxies came forward on foot. There is likely an element of truth in both, because Barry said the fighting went hand-to-hand very quickly. At this point, the men in the uncovered rear of the vehicle began to dismount and the Volunteers in Barry's command post fought them at close quarters. By the end of this immediate fight, nine men laid dead, dying or wounded.[27]

Around the same time, the No. 2 Section began firing on the second lorry's passengers, who were also attempting to dismount. Having dealt with the first nine, Barry said that he took his four men of the command post and moved west along the north side of the road to assist against the others. They made quick work of the rest, having them in interlocking fields of fire. The seventeen policemen were dead or dying, while the last was so badly wounded they thought him dead.[28]

This is about all that the different sides agree upon, with one side charging Barry with wearing a British uniform to get the police to stop, killing prisoners, most of whom were wounded and defenceless, and allowing his men to mutilate the corpses of the slain. These are serious charges, all of which violated the laws of war at the time[29] (as well as now), but historian Meda Ryan notes that Barry disputed the last two while not bothering to comment on the first.

The British believed that Col. Crake had sent out no advance or flanking guards.[30] If it was true that a group from the first vehicle went forward to investigate the suspicious man on the road, they clearly took no security precautions. Of course, if Barry had appeared to be a British officer, then they may have let their guard down – fatally. In Barry's account, he did not say that they had not come forward on foot, but implied that they were still in the vehicle. In any case, advance or flanking guards and proper security certainly would have made a difference there; they would have inflicted greater casualties on the IRA while providing extra time for those in the vehicles to dismount and counterattack. Further, if the men in the first vehicle had simply waited for the second to get closer, they would have been able to take some additional precautions, especially deploying men out to their flanks. Obviously, Colonel Crake did not feel sufficiently threatened and he and his men paid for this inattention with their lives. Just how many Auxies would have survived had Crake followed sound march security practice is unclear, since Barry's ambush site was so expertly chosen. Whatever one may say about Barry, one cannot deny that he was a master at preparing and executing ambush operations, the author's criticisms of the placement of the command post notwithstanding. Threat of counterattack might have prevented commencement of the ambush, unless Barry's claim of no retreat was real; the British most assuredly would have inflicted greater casualties on the rebel column than they did. By November 1920, the British army had developed procedures for dealing with ambush; since these will be dealt with in the final chapter, there is no need to discuss them here.

As mentioned above, the Kilmichael ambush provided the IRA with a much needed victory, enduring as they did almost three months of onslaught from sizeable British forces, mostly the RIC with the Black and Tans and ADRIC reinforcing them, during the most difficult period of the war to date. This attack was a pivotal event, coming just a week after the brutal killings by the IRA Dublin Brigade of fourteen British officers in the episode since called 'Bloody Sunday'.[31] It had a stunning effect on combatants on both sides, tending to steel resolve. It was a badly needed boost to rebel morale. It was a victory that Bloody Sunday could not provide, for all arguments of atrocity aside; it was a clear military victory for the republicans.

From the outset, there were questions about what happened on that road, questions that continue today. The two most notable figures in the modern debate are historian Peter Hart and author Meda Ryan. Hart has described the killings of the policemen at Kilmichael as unnecessary war crimes[32] and has likened Barry to a 'serial killer'.[33] On the other side,

Figure 4.5 Disputed IRA Report of Kilmichael Ambush[34]

REPORT OF THE AMBUSH AT KILMICHAEL, 28TH NOVEMBER, 1920.

The column paraded at 3.15 a.m. on Sunday morning. It comprised 32 men, armed with rifles, bayonets, five revolvers, and 100 rounds of ammunition per man. We marched for four hours, and reached a position on the Macroom–Dunmanway road in the townland of Shanacashel. We camped in that position until 4.15 p.m., and then decided that as the enemy searches were completed, that it would be safe to return to our camp. Accordingly we started the return journey. About five minutes after the start we sighted two enemy lorries moving along the Macroom–Dunmanway road at a distance of about 1,900 yards from us. The country in that particular district is of a hilly and rock nature, and, although suitable to fighting, it is not at all suitable to retiring without being seen. I decided to attack the lorries. The action was carried out in the following manner: – I divided the column into three sections, viz.: One to attack the first lorry; this section was in a position to have ample cover, and at the same time to bring a frontal and flank fire to bear on the enemy. The second section was in a position about 120 yards from the first section, and at the same side of the road. Its duty was to let the first lorry pass to No. 1 section, and to attack the second lorry. The third section was occupying sniping positions along the other side of the road, and also guarding both flanks. The action was carried out successfully. Sixteen of the enemy who were belonging to the Auxiliary police from Macroom Castle being killed, one wounded and escaped, and is now missing.

The captures were as follows: – 14 rifles, 5 bayonets, 17 revolvers, 719 rounds of .303, 136 rounds of .450, with equipment and two lorries, which were subsequently burnt.

Our casualties were one killed and two who have subsequently died of wounds.

O.C. [Tom Barry], Flying Column
3rd Cork Brigade.

> P.S. – I attribute our casualties to the fact that these three men (who were part of No. 2 section) were too anxious to get into close quarters with the enemy. They were our best men, and did not know danger in this or any previous actions. They discarded their cover, and it was not until the finish of the action that P. Deasy was killed by a revolver

Ryan takes the view that Barry's claim of military necessity was justified based on the situation at the beginning of the fight as well as the conduct of the Auxiliary cadets towards the end of it. As these shed light on the conduct of the ambush, as well as common practices during the war, they are examined here in detail.

The first accusation Hart made in his groundbreaking study, *The IRA and its Enemies* (1998) was that 'Here the treachery is Irish. British uniforms were falsely worn (an act punishable by death under international legal conventions)'. Hart, taking his cue from the official history, later stated that members of the column 'were wearing steel helmets and Barry was wearing something very much like an officer's uniform ... [as] a ruse'.[35] This is certainly a violation of Article 23 of Hague IV which, in part, prohibits wearing enemy uniforms. It is important to note that the convention does not prohibit wearing protective kit.

Yet the argument that Barry, in fact, wore a British officer's uniform is groundless if Barry did not wear it. It is simply unlikely that Barry had access to an officer's uniform since he served in the British army as an enlisted man, so his claim of borrowing an Irish Volunteer's uniform blouse is more likely; Meda Ryan said that Barry wore an Irish Volunteers officer uniform he borrowed from Volunteer Paddy O'Brien two days earlier (26 November).[36] The next issue is whether this was a *ruse de guerre* or a war crime. Wearing a uniform of one's own organization, regardless of how much it may resemble the enemy, cannot be considered a war crime. Further, Article 24 of the 1907 Hague Convention states: 'Ruses of war and the employment of measures necessary for obtaining information about the enemy and the country are considered permissible.' Finally, one must question the justifiability of British outrage at this, considering that their proclamations had made merely wearing a Volunteer uniform a capital offence, which is *ipso facto* a war crime.[37]

The most serious accusation against Barry and the column was that they killed the policemen after they had surrendered, that these men were wounded and unarmed prisoners. This is and was a war crime – violating Article 23 of the Hague IV convention, which states (in part):

> In addition to the prohibitions provided by special Conventions, it is especially forbidden ... To kill or wound an enemy who, having

laid down his arms, or having no longer means of defence, has surrendered at discretion; To declare that no quarter will be given; To
employ arms, projectiles, or material calculated to cause unnecessary suffering; To make improper use of a flag of truce, of the
national flag or of the military insignia and uniform of the enemy,
as well as the distinctive badges of the Geneva Convention ...[38]

For his part, Barry and his defenders have stated that the policemen surrendered falsely during the fighting and that, after suffering casualties as
a result, the Volunteers killed those Auxies remaining, even when they
later tried to surrender again.[39] This is where the situation gets legalistic:
for if a soldier surrenders, he immediately becomes a prisoner of war and
loses his belligerent status (the right to kill enemy soldiers in war); thus
he cannot legally fight or kill and must be protected from injury or death
by those capturing him. If a prisoner kills, he can be tried for murder.
Likewise, when a prisoner of war is attempting to escape, he may not
violate civil law or take up arms lest he also may be tried.[40] Every soldier
has the inherent right to surrender without being abused or killed. At the
same time, however, while a soldier is required to take prisoners, in
accordance with the laws of war, no soldier is required to *risk his own life*
to permit an enemy to surrender.

In practical terms, if there was a false surrender, Barry would not be
expected to take them prisoner unless he could do so safely, which, for
instance, was frequently the problem facing the Allies in fighting the
Japanese in the Second World War. Such a false surrender would have
been a significant defence if such a case were to go to a war crimes trial.
For these reasons, the issue of the false surrender makes the difference
between a militarily justifiable action and outright murder. Neither side
wanted to *appear* to be violating the laws of war, the British classification
of the IRA as criminals notwithstanding. Still, while calling the IRA
'criminals' and gloating over rebels' executions, the British decried the
IRA's violations of the Hague treaties.

Although the British honestly saw nothing wrong with executing
rebels while at the same time complaining that the rebels were not following the laws of war, most captured rebels were interned in one of the
half-dozen 'military prisons in the field' in Ireland.[41] Further, when looking at the records of the convictions by the field general courts-martial
in Ireland during the war, one is struck by the fact that many people
were acquitted by the courts-martial officers of the charges against them.
This demonstrates that while the courts-martial were not necessarily the
full protection of the law, neither were they 'kangaroo courts'.[42]

For their part, the rebels were hardly the rough band of cut-throats and murderers they were portrayed to be by the British. Throughout the war it was usually safe for a soldier or policeman to surrender to the IRA. The only time one was likely to be killed, outside of 'combat', was when specifically targeted for assassination, or in retaliation for some action by the British forces; there were far more instances of the IRA sending their prisoners off with wounded pride, having taken their arms, munitions and kit, than simply killing them.

The story then becomes muddled by Hart's analysis, when he presents evidence he claims as proof that the Auxies did not surrender falsely. By far the most damning was a series of interviews Hart conducted in 1988 and 1989 with former IRA men who had taken part in the Kilmichael ambush. Based on his reconstruction from his and others' interviews, he suggests that Barry was out to make a name for himself and that this action was a perfect opportunity for this. The attack occurred much as Barry claimed, just that the wounded were shot even as they tried to surrender. His interviewees were adamant that no Volunteers were killed as a result of a false surrender and 'Two of these veterans considered Barry's account to be an insult to the memory of these men.'[43]

The issue that many researchers have had, Ryan included, is that Hart refuses to name the sources of these interviews. This is a considerable obstacle because Hart states that he was able to get these men to talk only by promising confidentiality, likely for fear of reprisal. Ryan has taken Hart to task in her excellent biography, *Tom Barry: IRA Freedom Fighter*, where she notes that Hart has been steadfast in his refusal to give information on these sources. But then Ryan attacks directly, saying:

> If, including scouts and helpers, records show the last Kilmichael ambush survivor Ned Young (whose faculties were impaired during his final years) died on 13 November 1989 aged ninety-seven; the second last, Jack O'Sullivan in 1986; Tim O'Connell 1983; Patrick (Pat) O'Donovan 1981 (all rifle-men) then who are these people who could not stand over their names and the information that they gave regarding the Kilmichael ambush when Peter Hart interviewed them in 1988, 1989? Who were, 'all of the men interviewed [who] agree on this point: McCarthy and O'Sullivan did not stand up and did not die because of a fake surrender'? Who were the 'Two of these veterans' who 'considered Barry's account to be an insult to the memory of these men' who were killed? [44]

She continues, noting that the scouts were all dead by 1971 and says, 'Perhaps if Peter Hart revealed their names, the credibility of these two witnesses who claim to give a first-hand account could be examined. Their version of events to Peter Hart contradicts so many others'.[45]

The argument against Hart's witnesses is difficult to overcome, but one should assume Hart is telling the truth. One should not, however, accept his interpretation based on his evidence. Nor should Hart have introduced evidence that could not be verified or examined. Likewise, he should not be expected to break his word, so the only reasonable course is to reject the anonymous witnesses altogether.

Another contentious piece of evidence Hart used in his analysis of the Kilmichael incident was the so-called 'Rebel Commandant's report on the affair', purportedly written by Barry about the attack, and is widely held by the pro-Barry side to be a British forgery. The original document does not appear to have survived, a point critics say is because it never existed, and Hart's and Ryan's analyses are based on a typescript of it in a draft copy of *The Irish Rebellion in the 6th Divisional Area from after 1916 Rebellion to December 1921*, written by the General Staff of the 6th Infantry Division in 1922 for inclusion in the General Staff, Irish Command *Record of the Rebellion in Ireland in 1920–21, and The Part Played By The Army In Dealing With It*, Volume IV, Part II. The version used was a draft copy housed in the Strickland Papers in the Imperial War Museum. The final version of the work, in all four volumes, appears only to exist in the National Archives at Kew (formerly the Public Record Office). In any event, the only significant difference between the draft and the final copies are the page numbers (66–7 in the former and 166–7 in the latter).

An important point about the report is that the IRA maintained far greater information on paper than most revolutions, some of which was captured and most of which appears to have survived. Many of these records were detailed after-action reports (see Figure 4.1). These points mean that it would not have been unusual for Barry to have written it, especially since this was a primary means of transmitting techniques and procedures as well as anything the rest of the IRA needed to know.

Barry's being able to write it does not mean that he did; so much seems to hinge on the authenticity of the 'Rebel Commandant's report', and Ryan strongly criticizes the document in her book on Barry. The following points were raised by Ryan and are discussed for other plausible explanations besides outright forgery. The first of her criticisms concerns what might be minor details in the document that are believed to be in error: times of events, number of men present and how much ammunition they carried.[46] These are minor, but important, points and Ryan is right in identifying them, but fails to consider why they might be wrong without making the report a forgery. The simplest answer is what Clausewitz called the 'fog' and 'friction' of war, meaning that not only are situations unclear in combat, but details are frequently lost.[47] For instance, Barry's account of the Battle of Crossbarry, 19 March 1921 (see Chapter 5), differs from that of Liam Deasy, especially as regards the time of day. Should we then assume that one of them was lying or that their account was false? Of course not. Another reason could be exaggeration to justify his actions, thus providing excuses.

The next issue Ryan raises was whether the column moved out or remained in position during the day just before the attack. The report states that they 'started the return journey. About five minutes after the start we sighted two enemy lorries'. To this Ryan responds: 'How could any commander get his men into the sections and a sub-section and be so well positioned to instantly take on the enemy?'[48] This is a good question, but it makes several assumptions. First, that after being in position on the Macroom–Dunmanway road for about eight hours, the rebels had not already prepared their positions. Considering that the column was in its ambush site most of the day, this is not a valid assumption. As seen in many of the ambushes detailed in this study, the IRA frequently dug fighting positions and erected or dug obstacles in preparation for their attacks. Further, to move out from their positions, spread over 250 yards, five minutes is an insignificant amount of time and they could not have got close to rallying in one spot or towards their debarkation point when they saw the vehicles just over a mile away on the winding road. To have done so would have required them to run from their positions, but there was no reason to run. They certainly would have had time to get back into those same positions since the report states they were still on that road, thus giving them good reason to run at that point. That Ryan did not consider the issue of how far they got from their original site (assuming they, in fact, moved) is evident when she asks why Barry would expose himself to such a danger. Still, there are many instances of IRA ambush forces changing positions just before an attack. Reoccupying their ambush site was far safer than attempting to leave since, as Barry claimed, there was no safe line of retreat.

Ryan mentions that the report does not contain references to the armed command post or to the sub-section of Section 3, but then she implies that the actual focus in the report on terrain was a waste of space and thus he would not have written this. Barry, for all his foibles, was a soldier, and to soldiers, terrain is more important because it determines both the tactics and distribution of the forces. Further, it could also bolster a claim that he had no choice but to fight there due to the nature of the terrain and the impossibility of escape due to the exposed terrain. Yet Barry, in multiple statements which he undisputedly made, never specifically mentioned the 1st or 3rd Sections having engaged; perhaps they were superfluous. This is interesting since the second vehicle stopped 'thirty yards at our side of No. 2 Section' and Barry took his three men from the command post and moved to the flank of the second vehicle's troops.[49] This means that he had to pass in front of No. 1 Section to do so. Why were they not engaged? If they were, then the Auxies that Barry was going towards to 'flank' would already have been 'flanked' and thus his approach was unnecessary or would have drawn fire. There are, therefore, inconsistencies in his verifiable statements. Still, No. 1 Section remaining in place would have been critical if he moved to the flank as he claimed, because they then became his rearguard, so staying in position was critical. The same holds true for No. 3 Section as well. Indeed, No. 1 Section came up only after Barry and his command post had got into position.[50]

Ryan questions the terminology of the report and much of this is valid, but only two comments come to mind. First, IRA reports usually read as if they were trying to sound 'official' and 'soldierly'. Barry had been a soldier in the British army and certainly knew what terms to use, and thus it is not inconsistent. The second point has to do with Pat Deasy's name in the report. Ryan asked why Barry would have written the name out in full and why Deasy was singled out from the others. The IRA rarely used anything more than a single name or just initials in their reports for the sake of security. It was common for both the British army *and* the IRA reports to use just the first initial and surname (if mentioned at all). However, since Deasy's brother Liam, vice-commandant of the brigade, would be reading such a report, it is only natural to mention how Pat died. Further, saying that he was aggressive was better than saying he was stupid for exposing himself needlessly to enemy fire. Finally, it is important to bring attention to Ryan's questions about how, when and where the volunteers died as mentioned in the report; it is a valid point and perhaps explainable by 'fog and friction', of which soldiers know so much.[51]

Why would anyone forge a document like this? An obvious point would be to exploit its propaganda value, but there is nothing spectacular in the report, nor was it ever released to the public. Ryan examines the value of the document for insurance claims for the families of the dead and mentions Barry's assertion that he was approached during the truce by Castle official Andy Cope, who asked him to make a written statement about the ambush. She suggests that 'Barry's refusal of Cope's request meant the invention of "an alternative"' was necessary. She then discusses the machinations of a solicitor's firm and dealings with the Castle on the matter.[52]

This line of reasoning runs into the realities in Ireland at the time, however, when one remembers that coroners' juries were not functioning in that area. The army only needed a medical opinion from a medical officer and the opinion of a court of inquiry to make a legally binding determination of death.[53] This sufficed for both insurance and claims against the county council in multiple other cases.[54] Thus, there was no need to 'create' such a document. The failing point of this argument is that Cope was, in all manners, a realist. Why would he approach Barry, a rebel officer, albeit during the truce, to write a document that would put Barry's neck in the noose? Few in the government, the military or even the IRA honestly believed that the negotiations and truce were anything but temporary, thus Barry would be signing a confession to murder. Barry would not only have refused, but the realist Cope would not have asked.

In terms of what was captured by the rebels, Ryan says that the 'forgers' got the list of captured items wrong compared to what Barry wrote in later accounts and that they put in the report what was carried in the vehicles. But then they did not get the list correct: where was the required 1,200 rounds of boxed .303 ammunition carried in the vehicle, in accordance with standing orders? This was, by far, the single most important item captured in such an action.[55] Indeed, it would have been a coup.

Finally, Ryan questions why Barry did not mention himself in the report as having stood in the road, because if he had written the report, 'he surely would have mentioned the daring ploy that marked the opening of the attack'.[56] It could also have been that he was embarrassed by such high casualties among his men and did not want to mention what was, in point of fact, an astonishingly stupid act for a combat veteran. For a commander to expose himself like that did not indicate valour or daring, but rather outright, inexcusable and criminal negligence.

The next problem with this document is when it was written, which Ryan strongly implies was during the truce.[57] But the timing of the report may also have had something to do with why it was written. Ryan points out that Barry was on the move through the rest of November and then in hospital from 2 to 28 December. When would he have written such a report? Also part of this question was another Ryan asked in her earlier examination, when she said: 'Why [would Barry] suggest that "the ambush was an accident"?'[58] Much of the confusion is due to the assumption that the document was forged during or after the truce, but if it was written earlier, there might be other, equally plausible, reasons for Barry to have written it.

When Barry was recovering in hospital, he learned that, after a month of attacks and reprisals in Cork, the Roman Catholic bishop of Cork, Dr Daniel Cohalan, DD, promulgated a decree against murder and, specifically, ambushes. He said:

> Beside the guilt involved in these acts by reason of their opposition to the law of God, anyone who shall within these spaces of Cork, organize or take part in an ambush or kidnapping or otherwise be guilty of murder or attempted murder shall incur by the very fact the censure of excommunication.[59]

The bishop's reasoning was that the victims of an ambush had no realistic ability to defend themselves, nor to surrender and this thus constituted murder. This was what is called *latae sententiae* excommunication; it is incurred by the very act itself, no further decree is necessary. Cohalan was merely stating and clarifying existing Catholic Church teaching.[60]

This decree ended up doing little to curb the IRA's actions, but during his hospital stay, Ryan says Barry was concerned about the effect of it. Why would Barry or any IRA members be concerned beyond their personal souls? According to Ryan, Barry was worried that it would discourage his men.[61] Further, such a decree reminded the populace that assisting the rebels in these acts would incur this same, severe penalty.

This decree also came out after IRA attacks and British reprisals almost every day since Kilmichael, including the burning of over five acres of Cork City on the night of 11 December.[62] It is not difficult to expect that the IRA leadership in Cork were under pressure over the attacks. Further, if Barry actually did depart the ambush site before the attack and returned only because of the threat to their survival, he had stated that there was no line of retreat and thus, they were exposed and had to move *back* – this then creates a *de facto* excuse of this not being a 'pre-planned ambush', but an attack born of military necessity. It could not then be murder if it was carried out in defence of their own lives (securing their line of retreat) or, as is stated in the report: 'The country in that particular district is of a hilly and rock nature, and, although suitable to fighting, it is not at all suitable to retiring without being seen.' This provided an excuse to argue that it was not a case of murder, but of self-defence and therefore not incurring *latae sententiae* excommunication. This provides excellent reasons for Barry to have written this report and would explain why he, an outstanding tactician, would claim to have done something so stupidly unjustifiable as to choose a site without a sufficient line of retreat deliberately.[63]

This still does not deal with the inherent mistakes in the report or its timing. The mistakes come as no surprise to military historians. In dealing with the confusion of war, military historians are taught to expect reports to be full of errors.[64] In fact, if one does *not* find errors in after-action reports, one is taught to question their authenticity. Yet, if, as Ryan claims, the document did not exist prior to July 1921, it must be a forgery.

There is a significant problem with this position since the document demonstrably existed *before* the truce. There is an earlier version contained in the little-known Irish Command paper, 'The Irish Republican Army (From Captured Documents Only)', prepared in April and May 1921 and published in June.[65] This document is important because it destroys two assumptions: first that the document did not exist until after Barry refused Cope's supposed request and that the British manufactured the document. Since the army was working with the document up to three months prior to the truce, the suggestion that Cope created it later is unsupportable.

The Irish Command certainly believed the document to be genuine, not because they included it in 'The Irish Republican Army (From Captured Documents Only)', but because they changed operational doctrine as a result of it. The entire work consists of documents captured by various agencies, turned over to intelligence chief, Brig.-Gen. Ormonde de l'Epée Winter and then used as examples of IRA attack doctrine and how best to defeat them. The British simply were not so incompetent as to base combat doctrinal changes and risk their men's lives on a forgery; however amateurish republican legend might want to suggest they were.

Taken as a whole, and with conscious regard to Ryan's valid questions, it seems clear that the document existed before the truce, that neither the British police nor the military forged it, and that the admitted errors in it are plausibly explained, with exceptions as noted above.[66] Thus the document *could* be genuine.

The final charge laid by the British against Barry and the column was that of mutilating the dead after the fight was over. Barry strenuously denied this charge.[67] There is sufficient evidence that the bodies were brutalized, but insufficient evidence produced thus far to claim by whom. The evidence that Ryan provides described the battle as being ferocious, and going hand to hand in the case of the first lorry.[68] This would not have produced the types of wounds that were described by those who viewed the corpses, witnesses who were certainly familiar with the wounds created by close-quarters fighting, as seen in the trenches of Flanders. Ryan is quite correct when she says that the IRA were not carrying axes, but the lorries did.

What has not been explained by Barry's detractors is why a fairly large group of full-time guerrillas would stand around watching while several of their comrades hacked away at the dead with axes. To what purpose: rage at the false surrender? But those who say the bodies were mutilated claim there was no false surrender. Surely such an act of wanton barbarity would have been spontaneous and have come with whatever was immediately at hand. Is it not much more likely that such aggression would have been let loose with their rifles – butts and bayonets? Axes would have required premeditation because they would have had to retrieve them from the lorries and then attack the dead. Finally, why would the column not have exfiltrated the area as quickly as possible? They knew they were in a known location as soon as the first shots went off; they had to expect a relief force. It does not make sense that rebels disciplined enough to have ambushed the enemy and hold their positions (Sections Nos. 1 and 3) would have done this.

The problem then becomes: how can one explain the credible reports of physical damage to the British dead by trained observers? A possible answer to this lies in the BMH witness statements and demonstrates a salient point as well. The statement of the Very Rev. Thomas Canon Duggan, MA, STL, cited earlier, contains a curious section in which he says:

> The Battle of Kilmichael was fought on a Sunday, a dirty November afternoon in 1920. There was some mix up about the Black and Tans surrender, and, as we know, the thing ended in carnage. Tom Barry himself told me this. His men were cooling down and the horror of twenty-four bleeding corpses was growing upon them. At that critical moment, an old man, in his clean Sunday flannel jacket, drove twelve cows down the road and over the bodies. The old patriarch stood in the middle of the corpses, he lifted his head, and with the solemnity of an Old Testament prophet, he intoned, 'Jesus Christ be praised that I have lived to see this day.' A vision of the mills of God grinding out retribution for the wrongs of fifty years before. Daniel of Cork was born within a couple of miles of the scene of the ambush and Daniel's out-look was little different from that of the old man, who drove the cows.[69]

This story may be apocryphal, but it would definitely account for the damage. The other part of this is that while the appearances look bad, there simply is not enough information to make condemnations of Barry and the column for what they did that day when there are other, equally probably, explanations.

In taking stock of the evidence, Hart's interviews should be merely ignored and the 'Rebel Commandant's report' accepted as possibly being real. The most important question then becomes: what actually happened? It is impossible to say for sure because those who know took their knowledge to the grave – unless their known, verifiable statements were correct. But it is likely that the battle occurred much the way Barry said it did – he got them to stop in the manner described; he used the hand grenade; they fought 'tooth and nail' at the first lorry and then went to support the second; there was likely a false surrender and IRA men might have died as a result; the rebels at that point took no prisoners.

This seems to be a resounding chord in favour of Barry's supporters and one against Hart's version, but not necessarily. For as much as Hart denies this in the main text, he actually lays the groundwork for the argument in favour of a false surrender occurring in his footnotes when he says: 'The Auxiliaries were spread out and it is reasonable to suppose that, while the others were giving up, another wounded Cadet (whom Deasy thought was dead) did not see or care, and fired at Deasy when he approached (as Barry reported in 1920 [in the disputed report]).' Hart continues in the footnote: 'one [anonymous] witness ... saw several Auxiliaries surrender *after* [original emphasis] the three Volunteers were hit, but then heard further firing, some of which he believed came from the Englishmen. Because of this, he says there was a sort of false surrender, but that not IRA men died as a result'.[70] This would also agree with the disputed report, if Barry actually wrote it.

If this occurred, there is no question then there *was a false surrender*. What most people do not understand is that the act of surrendering is extremely dangerous because forces are normally expecting to make hostile contact and usually fire as quickly as possible. This means that the surrendering enemy has to take the risk that they will be shot if they must expose themselves to indicate surrender; hence the reason one would use a white flag if possible. Mistakes happen, but the problem is so common that it escapes most people. Sir John Keegan described a similar event from 1917 in his seminal *Face of Battle*: Australian troops had just succeeded in getting German soldiers to surrender their bunker; they were filing out unarmed when a shot from a German in an upper storey who did not know of the surrender – the building had not been cleared – killed one of the Australians. The grouped soldiers believed the deed 'to be the vilest treachery and they forthwith bayoneted the prisoners'. Keegan continues, citing the Australian Official History: 'The Germans in this case ... were entirely innocent, *but such incidents are inevitable in the heat of battle* [emphasis added], and any blame for them lies with those who make wars, not with those who fight them.'[71]

A more likely scenario at Kilmichael than outright murder is that Auxies, out of view from each other, were firing and reloading, fighting for their lives, when one individual or group called the surrender, out of sight or hearing of the others. The others continued reloading and shooting – they may have been reloading and out of a firing position (one does not stay exposed when reloading) when the call went out. If so, what would they have seen when they came back into firing position? An easy target if the Volunteers had stood up. It is difficult to imagine a soldier, unaware of his comrades' attempts to surrender, not taking the shot. Would this be a false surrender? Most definitely. Would it be done on purpose? Certainly not.

What is strange is that in all this, no one has mentioned why an Auxiliary would expect that he could surrender safely after deliberately committing such a heinous act. Once done, the fight goes to the death. The fact that the Auxiliaries tried to surrender later suggests they did not know what had happened earlier. What would happen if such an incident occurred? Precisely what happened – it is hard to imagine soldiers who would risk their lives *again* to take prisoners. In an unscientific poll of military officer students,[72] this author has yet to find one (of about 200 thus far) who would not have 'taken the shot' when seeing an enemy stand up, or who would risk their lives to take prisoners after a false surrender. If Deasy had done this, it was a stupidly amateurish act that cost him his life; would Barry have told Liam this, or would he have portrayed him as killed valiantly in action?

Although the debate has been heated, there is no way to prove what happened. There is also no way to prove that this suggested scenario occurred, but the evidence fits this supposition as well, or better, than any other suggested by other commentators and also explains why the document might be genuine. Further, there is no reason to presume that this was deliberate murder or deliberate perfidy on either side, when what is suggested here is as plausible. Accident or confusion explains this situation and evidence better than deliberate violation of the traditions of war on *either side*. To do so, one assumes that both sides were equally vile; this is certainly more implausible. The effects of the entire episode are hardly in dispute and are examined throughout the rest of this study.

British forces suffered a significant defeat at Kilmichael, one that was far more psychological than military, although one should not discount the military effects of either the ambush itself – the unit was effectively destroyed – or the boost to IRA morale. Fighting, or at least attacks, continued in Cork for the rest of November and into the first two weeks of December 1920. The events of December 1920, the burning of Cork City and the British military innovations against IRA attacks will be examined more fully in the chapter that follows.

NOTES

1. *An t-Óglác*, II, 16 (7 August 1920), p.109; II, 17 (15 August 1920), p.114; II, 18 (1 September 1920), p.117; II, 20 (1 October 1920), p.124; and II, 22 (22 February 1921), p.134.
2. South Tipperary Brigade Papers, Collins Collection (MA A/0509/XXIX).
3. Although stated by the primary sources, the accounts of Davitt's death do not demonstrate wrong-doing; he clearly was not 'murdered', but was killed in action while leading his men in an operation. The IRA did not normally take revenge unless there was some heinous act of brutality, an outright murder, torture or other such actions by the enemy.
4. R. Marrinan, 'War of Independence in West Clare, and A. Nelligan, interview with Andrew O'Donoghue.
5. Nelligan, interview with Andrew O'Donoghue.
6. R. Abbott, *Police Casualties in Ireland, 1919–1922* (2002), pp.123–4.
7. General Staff, Irish Command, *Record of the Rebellion in Ireland in 1920–21, and the Part Played by the Army in Dealing with It* (1922), vol. IV, p.160 (NA PRO WO 141/93); Marrinan, ' War of Independence in West Clare'; and Abbott, *Police Casualties*, p.123.
8. Marrinan, 'War of Independence in West Clare', and Abbott, *Police Casualties*, pp.122–4.
9. The claim that they captured 1,000 rounds of .303 ammunition is plausible since military standing orders required lorries to carry a box of 1,000 rounds of additional ammunition in the back, but none of the sources mentioned removing ammunition from an ammunition box, only bandoliers (fifty rounds each) from the policemen.
10. Marrinan, 'War of Independence in West Clare' and Abbott, *Police Casualties*, pp.122–4.
11. They were first outlawed for use in war by the Declaration of St Petersburg of 29 November 1868. See also 'Declaration on the Use of Bullets Which Expand or Flatten Easily in the Human Body', 29 July 1899. E. O'Malley, *Raids and Rallies* (1982), pp.67–84; R. Bennett, *The Black and Tans: The British Special Police in Ireland* [1959], p.94; T.P. Coogan and G. Morrison, *The Irish Civil War* (New York: Seven Dails Press, 2001), p.85.
12. For capture of rebel ammunition of this type, see Operation Report, Dublin District Memorandum No. S/G.1.A, 21 January 1921 and No. S/G.1.A., 1 April 1921 (NA PRO WO 35/90).
13. D. Begley, *The Road to Crossbarry: The Decisive Battle of the War of Independence* (1999), p.89.
14. See General Staff, Irish Command, *Record of the Rebellion*, vol. III, *Law*, War Office 1922 (PRO WO 141/93), and 'Laws of War', *An t-Óglác*, III, 10 (27 May 1921).
15. S. McConville, *Irish Political Prisoners, 1848–1922: Theatres of War* (London: Routledge, 2003), p.692. This incident was preceded by the burning of twenty-five buildings in Balbriggan, Co. Dublin on 21 September 1920, in retaliation for the killing of Head Const. Peter Burke.
16. General Staff, Irish Command, *Record of the Rebellion*, vol. I, p.21 and vol. IV, p.211 (NA PRO WO 141/93). These men, some of whom may have been armed, were trenching the road. They apparently did not place adequate guards.
17. General Staff, Irish Command, *Record of the Rebellion*, vol. IV, p.218 (NA PRO WO 141/93).
18. Robinson Statement (NLI MS 21265), pp.54–5; Statement of Gilbert Barrington (MA WS/773) and Statement of Francis Davis (MA WS/495). See C. Townshend, *Political Violence: Government and Resistance Since 1848* (1983), pp.320, 334 and 337; and General Staff, Irish Command, *Record of the Rebellion*, vol. IV, pp.42 and 245 (NA PRO WO 141/93).
19. For discussion of the concept of fog and friction in military operations, see C.M. von Clausewitz, *On War* (1984), especially, Book 1, 'On the Nature of War', Chapter 7, 'Friction in War', pp.119–21.

20. A.D. Harvey, 'Who Were the Auxiliaries?', *Historical Journal*, 35, 3 (1992), pp.665–9. According to Harvey, the recipients of the Victoria Cross were J.H. Leach, James Johnson and George Onions, and he specifically mentions that 'Leach resigned from the Auxiliaries after six months; Johnson deserted after two months' (p.665).

21. The two drivers, Constables H.F. Forde, the sole survivor, and A.F. Poole, were temporary constables (the 'Black and Tans') rather than ADRIC cadets. See Abbott, *Police Casualties*, pp.156–63.

22. The commanders of the ADRIC companies held the rank of district inspector in the RIC.

23. P. Hart, *The IRA and Its Enemies: Violence and Community in Cork, 1916–1923* (1998), pp.22–9. For more on the debates surrounding Kilmichael, see M. Ryan, *Tom Barry: IRA Freedom Fighter* (2005), and A. Gregory, 'The Boys of Kilmichael', *Journal of Contemporary History*, 34, 3 (July 1999), pp.489–96. Abbott, *Police Casualties*, p.157. M. O'Riordan, 'Forget Not the Boys of Kilmichael!', *Ballingeary Historical Society Journal*, 2005. M. Ryan 'Tom Barry and the Kilmichael Ambush', *History Ireland*, 13, 5 (September/October 2005); and features and letters, *History Ireland*, vol. 13, no. 2 (March/April), no. 3 (May/June), no. 4 (July/August) and no. 5 (September/October), 2005.

24. See T. Barry, *Guerilla Days in Ireland: A Personal Account of the Anglo-Irish War* (1995), pp.41–2 and 'Auxiliaries Wiped Out at Kilmichael in Their First Clash with the IRA', in M. Keegan, ed., (1947) *Rebel Cork's Fighting Story*, pp.108–9; and Barry, *Tom Barry*, pp.48–50.

25. Barry, *Guerilla Days*, pp.41–2 and Ryan, *Tom Barry*, pp.48–50.

26. Barry, *Guerilla Days*, p.40 and 'Auxiliaries Wiped Out', p.108.

27. Hart, *The IRA and Its Enemies*, pp.22–9; General Staff, Irish Command, *Record of the Rebellion*, vol. IV, pp.166–7 (NA PRO WO 141/93); and Barry, *Guerilla Days*, pp.43–51.

28. General Staff, Irish Command, *Record of the Rebellion*, vol. IV, pp.166–7 (NA PRO WO 141/93).

29. See Hague IV 'Laws and Customs of War on Land', 18 October 1907.

30. 'The Irish Republican Army (From Captured Documents Only)' (Dublin, June 1921; NA PRO WO 141/40), p.27. How a convoy could travel with flank guards is unclear, but upon the approach of a potential threat, a man in the road, Crake should have halted and had flank guards dismount to search forward of his position.

31. In this incident, famed IRA leader Michael Collins ordered his men to assassinate a dozen and a half men he suspected of being British intelligence agents. Of the sixteen gunned down, two of whom survived, most were simply working for the army, but some appear to have been working in intelligence.

32. Hart vehemently opposes this characterization of his description, saying he never used the words 'war crimes'. This is true, however, when he said 'Here the treachery is Irish. British uniforms were falsely worn (an act punishable by death under international legal conventions)' on page 24 of *IRA and its Enemies*, he is referring to a crime – one would not be 'punished' with 'death' under 'international legal conventions' for something which is not a crime.

33. Hart also strenuously denies referring to Tom Barry as a serial killer in *The IRA and its Enemies*. The statement comes after naming 'Tom Barry at Kilmichael, and Dathaí O'Brien at Carrigtwohill' when Hart states: 'As time went by, these political serial killers and their methods became virtually indistinguishable' (p.100). Although the beginning of a new paragraph, this sentence clearly refers to the men named in the previous paragraph.

34. The anti-Hart critics take issue with this report, stating that it is not a proper IRA after-action report and that it contains mistakes that Barry would not have made, especially the mention of 'P. Deasy'. While there is truth to this in terms of consistencies, the report reads like many other legitimate IRA documents. The veracity of the document is, in fact, irrelevant to this study because the British certainly *believed* that it was genuine and made doctrinal modifications as a result of its 'exploitation'.

35. Hart, *The IRA and its Enemies*, p.24. See also the General Staff, Irish Command, *Record of the Rebellion*, vol. IV, pp.166–7 (NA PRO WO 141/93).

36. Ryan, *Tom Barry*, pp.48 and 51, and Barry, 'Auxiliaries Wiped Out', p.106.

37. The issue of the British refusal to grant the rebels legitimate combatant status will not be dealt with here. Volume III of the *Record of the Rebellion in Ireland in 1920–21, and The Part Played By The Army In Dealing With It, Law*, dealt with this issue, specifically stating that there was precedent to grant belligerent status – the American Civil War – but that the IRA did not follow the rules of war and thus did not merit such consideration.

38. See Hague IV 'Laws and Customs of War on Land', 18 October 1907.
39. Barry, *Guerilla Days*, p.45 and 'Auxiliaries Wiped Out', p.110; and Ryan, *Tom Barry*, pp.64–89.
40. Art. 8. 'Prisoners of war shall be subject to the laws, regulations, and orders in force in the army of the State in whose power they are. Any act of insubordination justifies the adoption towards them of such measures of severity as may be considered necessary. Escaped prisoners who are retaken before being able to rejoin their own army or before leaving the territory occupied by the army which captured them are liable to disciplinary punishment.' Hague IV, 'Laws and Customs of War on Land', 18 October 1907.
41. These were at Spike Island, Bere Island and Ballykinlar; Sligo prison; detention barracks, Cork; and the Cork male jail; 'Military Prisons in the Field' (NA PRO WO 35/141/4); 'Detention Barracks and Soldiers Detained' (NA PRO WO 35/50/1); and 'Report of the QMG' (WO 35/50/6). They also wanted to place prisoners on the Isle of Man: see General Staff, HQ, Irish Command, War Diary, 3 December 1920 (PRO WO 35/93/p.4).
42. Judge Advocate General's Office to Secretary of State, 29 July 1921 (PRO WO 141/53); 'Notes on the Administration of Martial Law', 1921, Strickland Papers (IWM EPS 2/2); see also Jeudwine Papers (IWM 72/82/2). For acquittals, see 3 August 1920 and 'Report on the Situation in Ireland by General Officer Commanding-in-Chief', 8 August 1920 (PRO CAB 27/108/13); and 'Weekly Summary of the State of Ireland' (PRO CAB 27/108/15 SIC 26/27).
43. Hart, *The IRA and its Enemies*, p.34. It should be noted that others have taped interviews which are also held in confidence and Hart should not be singled out in this insistence of maintaining anonymity.
44. Ryan, *Tom Barry*, p.69.
45. Ibid. Professor Niall Meehan has also attacked Hart's sources based on the same lines, that none were alive when he claims to have interviewed them; see N. Meehan 'After the War of Independence: Some further questions about West Cork, April 27–29 1922,' *Irish Political Review*, 23, 3 (March 2008).
46. Ryan, *Tom Barry*, p.76.
47. In teaching soldiers who have seen a great deal of fighting in the last six years, this author has yet to find one who disagrees with his description of combat as causing 'tunnel vision' when the shooting starts. One's view necessarily narrows when one is trying to save one's life.
48. Ryan, *Tom Barry*, p.77.
49. Barry, *Guerilla Days*, p.44.
50. Barry, 'Auxiliaries Wiped Out', p.110.
51. Ryan, *Tom Barry*, pp.79–81.
52. Barry, 'Auxiliaries Wiped Out', p.113; and Ryan, *Tom Barry*, p.83.
53. See Inquest Files (NA PRO WO 35/180 (Part 3)/4).
54. See, for instance, 'Opinion of the Court of Enquiry Relative to the Death of A/Corp John Howard', 23 December 1921; Mr R. McCarthy to Adjutant, 3rd Royal Fusiliers, 29 December 1921; and Deposition of Capt. M. Shipsey, RAMC, Limerick, nd (NA PRO WO 35/180 (Part 3)/4).
55. Ryan, *Tom Barry*, p.79.
56. Ibid., p.80
57. Ibid., pp.82–4.
58. Ibid., pp.76 and 77.
59. Text cited in full in ibid., p.394.
60. Statement of Very Rev. Thomas Canon Duggan, MA, STL, former secretary to Very Rev. Daniel Cohalan (MA WS 551).
61. Ryan, *Tom Barry*, pp.101 and 104–5.
62. See G. White and B. O'Shea, *The Burning of Cork* (2006).
63. Another possibility is that the document was written by another IRA officer, such as Charlie Hurley or even Liam Deasy, while Barry was recuperating. They could have done so for many of the same reasons Barry might have written it. The other, probably likely, scenario is that the British edited the document before publication. Since the original has yet to come to light, this is unknowable. Still, why would one place Auxie treachery (intended or otherwise) in an official publication?
64. In the words of one of this author's mentors, military reports 'are exercises in creative fiction'.

65. General Staff, Irish Command, 'The Irish Republican Army (From Captured Documents Only)', June 1921 (NA PRO WO 141/40). A copy of this paper also exists, according to historian David Leeson, in the Strickland Papers in the Imperial War Museum.

66. This, of course, does not mean that the entire document was written by Barry. It could be that it was embellished by unknown editors, but there is no way to tell for sure.

67. Barry, 'Auxiliaries Wiped Out', p.113.

68. Ryan, *Tom Barry*, pp.84–5.

69. Statement of Very Rev. Thomas Canon Duggan, MA, STL, former secretary to Very Rev. Daniel Cohalan (MA WS 551).

70. Hart, *The IRA and its Enemies*, pp.34–5, and n. 61.

71. J. Keegan, *Face of Battle: A Study of Agincourt, Waterloo and the Somme* (London: Penguin, 1978), p.47.

72. U.S. and allied foreign military officers in the U.S. Army Command and General Staff College. Interestingly, about 98 per cent of these officers have engaged in combat operations in Iraq or Afghanistan; about 70 per cent have been to these wars (either or both) twice and some 40 per cent have been more than three times. At least ten have four tours in both and one has seen combat on three continents. There are several foreign officers who have been both guerrillas/rebels, have overthrown governments and then conducted COIN operations afterwards. All have experience, under fire, in convoy operations. This is all simply to say that soldiers may look at these incidents differently than historians.

Five

The British Forces and IRA Rural Ambushes

Up until this point the discussion has focused mostly on the generalities of the situation in Ireland and the effects of the general IRA raids. The previous chapter laid the groundwork for the rebel attacks by juxtaposing two substantial IRA ambushes. These actions yielded spectacular results for the republicans, but demonstrated the shift in the war caused by the British offensive against the rebels in autumn 1920. Where Rineen was a somewhat amateurish, albeit very deadly, operation carried out by the 'regular' IRA battalion, Kilmichael was a more 'professional' job perpetrated by the elite flying column of the highly experienced IRA 3rd West Cork Brigade.

Most IRA ambush operations fell somewhere in between these two discriminators. This chapter examines the IRA's ambushes in the countryside for the rebels' TTPs and the British responses to them. The first of these was in late January 1921, in Co. Kerry.

Toureengarriv Ambush, 28 January 1921

Rebels had noticed that two RIC cars had driven through Castleisland, Co. Kerry on their way to the RIC district headquarters at Listowel on Thursday, 27 January 1921. This two-car convoy carried Divisional Commissioner Major Philip A. Holmes, who was investigating the 20 January killing of RIC District Inspector Tobias O'Sullivan. Under the command of the Newmarket IRA Battalion commandant, Seán Moylan, the flying column of the Cork No. 2 Brigade (North), then resting at the remote village of Kishkeam,[1] mobilized to prepare an ambush for Holmes' return journey. The rebels did not know that Holmes was in the convoy, but they prepared in the hope that the cars would use the same route back through, knowing that touring cars usually held high-ranking officers. Moylan had his approximately sixty men dig a trench across the road; there was no report about how deep the trench was, but it proved a sufficient barrier. Moylan emplaced a Hotchkiss .303 machine gun on a hill to sweep to the north-east side of the road and then put riflemen to cover the south-east of the road to prevent escape. Then the rebels waited in the wet and the cold.[2]

On the return trip the next day, Friday, the 28th, the first car missed the trench because the driver spotted it in time to skid to a stop before reaching it, whereupon the rebel machine gunner opened an ineffective fire. This was likely due to the gunner's inexperience. The IRA did not have sufficient ammunition to practise firing 'full-sized' rifles, so they usually practised with .22 calibre 'miniature' rifles and thus firing practice with .303 Lee-Enfield and 7.9mm Mauser ammunition was rare. With rifles, the shooting skills transferred directly, so the calibres made little difference. With fully automatic weapons, however, the function was significantly different that an inexperienced gunner would probably have been too excited to deliver the necessary controlled, short bursts of gunfire at enemy targets. Lynch explained that the gun was prone to jamming, but that is true of most light machine guns when one does not fire them properly.[3]

Figure 5.1 Ford Armoured Car

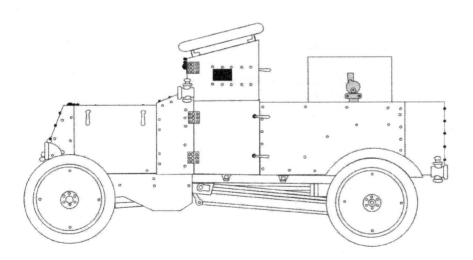

Meanwhile, the policemen were able to dismount their vehicles, under fire, and take cover, albeit in a poor position, and return fire. Outnumbered almost seven to one, the policemen obeyed the order from the dying Holmes to continue fighting until they had expended all of their ammunition before finally accepting the multiple rebel calls to surrender. By this point, all of the RIC men were wounded, with two of them dying.

According to Abbot, while they were searching the wounded RIC men, the rebels took and discarded personal effects from their pockets. When Cmdt Moylan came up, he became so incensed at this that he threatened to shoot these Volunteers if they did not retrieve and restore these items immediately to the wounded enemy.[4] Moylan had a civilian car transport the more seriously wounded to hospital. In the end, Major Holmes and Const. Thomas Moyles died of their wounds, while Sgt. Arthur E. Charman and Constables John H. Andrews, Francis D. Calder, Francis Callery and James Hoare survived.[5]

The death of Major Holmes was a blow for the British because he had served as an army intelligence officer after being wounded twice and gassed once on the Western Front in the First World War, while serving first in the Royal Irish Regiment and later in the Royal Irish Fusiliers. He was an Irishman and came from an RIC family; both his father and grandfather were county inspectors. Holmes was also a county inspector when he was promoted to replace D-C Lieut.-Col. G.B.F. Smythe in August 1920 after the latter was assassinated by the IRA. Holmes' depth of knowledge of the situation in Ireland based on his time in intelligence work was far better than that of most RIC officers, and his three years' experience in the British army must have made cooperation between his police division (Munster) and the army significantly better.[6]

What was unusual about this ambush was that the army did not use the attack as a prime example of the effects of poor route security. The RIC, by January 1921, certainly knew the IRA was capable of conducting fairly sophisticated ambushes and that their intelligence network, while republican hyperbole has inflated its reach, was nevertheless capable of catching such a simple error like using the same route on a return journey. The British army mistakenly believed that this attack was related to the Dripsey ambush and used it in their later written analysis of it as a lead-in into the Dripsey ambush (see below). The two incidents appear to have had no relationship.

Furthermore, the rebels practised good march security. In his account of the Battle of Crossbarry (see below), Diarmuid Begley explained that the 3rd West Cork Brigade flying column used fourteen men in its sections rather than the seven to ten of the British army. The additional men allowed the column or section to deploy flank and other guards. If moving with the entire column, the additional men permitted sufficient men for both advance and rear guards, in addition to having a strong main body and flank guards. The IRA learnt this through two years of operations while around the same time the British army was advocating similar measures. At Crossbarry, the rebel column would use a strong rearguard to allow the main force time to retire.[7] These were the types of actions the British needed to adopt, and eventually they did.

Dripsey Ambush, 28 January 1921

It seems that the British believed this ambush was also laid for Major Holmes' convoy, although it was not. The flying column of the IRA 6th Battalion (Firmount), 1st Mid-Cork Brigade decided to attack a known and commonly used RIC route. Under 6th IRA Battalion Vice-Commandant Frank Busteed, the column chose an area called Godfrey's Cross near the bridge at Dripsey, Co. Cork to wait for police or military, who commonly used the road. Busteed prepared his ambush site by digging fighting positions along the road for about 300 yards, using conscripted locals for labour. Normally, the IRA used forced labour to dig

Figure 5.2 Crossley 'Tender'

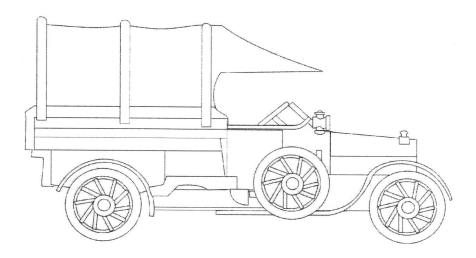

trenches and other positions whenever they could do so without violating security or otherwise endangering themselves. When the operation ended, the British usually rounded up local men – who were often the same men the rebels had used – to fill in the trenches. As one may well imagine, this caused considerable resentment against *both* sides. In this instance, Busteed did not trench the road. He decided, apparently, to use two large trees to block it; they would be held in place by ropes after being cut down, then dropped.[8] Once settled, the rebels remained *in situ* most of the day. This proved fatal.

The plan, according to O'Callaghan, was that the twenty-four men armed with shotguns would rake the vehicles after trees, dropping into their path, halted them. Busteed hoped to kill as many with the opening volley as possible and kill more with his six Mills bombs as the survivors dismounted the vehicles.[9] This plan, however, never came to fruition.

That same day, Mrs Mary Lindsay, a Co. Mayo transplant, drove from her home at Lemount House to the nearby town of Coachford, Co. Cork, and stopped at Timothy Sheehan's grocery store. One of Sheehan's employees, John Sweeney, had been moved out of his house earlier that morning, along with another family, by Busteed's column. It is likely that Sweeney took part in the digging too. Unfortunately for the rebels, they let Sweeney go to work, presumably to keep him from losing pay and/or being fired. Sweeney told Sheehan about the ambush, who then warned Mrs Lindsay because she was going to Ballincollig by that route to get her motor permit.[10]

When she arrived at Ballincollig, Mrs Lindsay went to the RIC barracks and reported the pending ambush. But unfortunately for Mrs Lindsay, a member of IRA Cmdt Walter Murphy's family, who lived across the street from the barracks, observed her. The RIC informed the local army commander of the 1st Bn Manchesters, Lieut.-Col. Frederick Dowling, who then sent out a raid of seventy men of C Company under the command of Lieut.-Col. Gareth Evans to attack the rebels.[11]

On her return trip, Mrs Lindsay unexpectedly ran into Fr Edward Shinnick, the Coachford Catholic parish priest, and told him of the coming ambush and her warning to the British. Fr Shinnick, in turn, informed the local IRA company O/C that the British knew about the ambush site, but they discounted his report because he was known to be anti-republican in general, and was in line with Bishop Cohalan of Cork in his condemnation of ambushes, specifically. It is likely that Mrs Lindsay informed Fr Shinnick only because, being anti-republican, he would not betray her. His warning did not include any mention of her and was probably made in the hope of preventing bloodshed.[12]

Figure 5.3 OC 6th IRA Bn, 1st Cork Bde After-Action Report of Dripsey Ambush

Oglaic Na h-Éireann
Headquarters,

1st Cork Brigade

31st *January*, 1921.

To Adjutant-General –

1. Herewith is a report from the O.C., 6th Battalion, dealing with the engagement near Dripsey on Friday last.

2. Further information to hand this morning is to the effect that seven of our men is the total captured by the enemy, and one, believed to be Barrett, is dead. None of the others are seriously wounded, and those who were wounded and escaped have been attended to.

3. Will report further to-morrow.

(*Signed*) 'Brigade Adjutant.'

Headquarters,

1st Cork Brigade

30th *January*, 1921.

To O.C.,
Cork Brigade No. 1.

This Battalion flying column had arranged an ambush on the Coachford Road on Friday last, and at 7.30 a.m. we got into position and remained there until 4.30 p.m., but during that time no lorry turned up. At that time we got word from the priest in Coachford that the military were aware of our position, but as he is against the cause and ambushes, we did not pay much heed to him, but at the same time we decided that there was no use in remaining any longer, and as we were making arrangements to retreat, I discovered a party of military advancing along the road from Dripsey. I at once realized what was taking place, and we got out of the position and into one suitable to deal with that party almost immediately. I got word from one of the scouts that the military were on our left and trying to surround us, so, for that reason, and as the fields were very large, I thought it better to retreat as quick as possible. In the retreat three of our men were wounded, but were able to come along with us, and, as far as I can ascertain, there are seven others missing. The reason I cannot be certain about the missing is there were men outside the attacking party acting as scouts and flank guards who did not move into the position with us, so I must get in touch with their companies. We lost about three rifles and some shot guns, also some bombs. Some of these articles were hidden by the men, and we may recover them. The military attacked from the front, rear and left flanks, and also scoured the roads all round, so it is evident they got information. I will give further information as soon as obtainable. The wounded have been attended to by a doctor, and will be all right shortly.

The names of the missing men are as follows: – Patrick Mahoney, Denis Murphy, James Barrett (Adjutant), Daniel Callaghan, Thomas O'Brien, Jeremiah Callaghan.

(*Signed*) O.C.,

6th Battalion

Evans split his force, Lieuts Sykes, Orgill, Todd and Vining each leading a section, while a Lieut. Green commanded the armoured cars. Evans led a section, along with Sergeant-Major Brown. After dismounting from their vehicles at Dripsey, they attempted to envelop the rebel ambush site. According to the 6th IRA Battalion O/C John O'Leary's captured report of the action, at about the same time the rebels decided that their quarry did not appear to be coming and so decided to abandon their ambush site. Then Busteed decided to beat a hasty retreat; he wanted to use one section of the column to cover the retreat of the others and then use them to cover the retreat of the first group, but could not due to the two other British sections approaching from his flanks. According to the British report of the incident, were it not for the falling darkness, the Manchesters would have killed or captured more rebels. The darkness probably had more to do with their escape than any actual planning on the rebels' part. In the ensuing brief action, two rebels were killed, five wounded and five captured. The army also captured ten shotguns, three rifles and four revolvers in addition to a cache of documents. The five prisoners, named in a captured rebel after-action report, were later tried by courts-martial and executed.[13]

Figure 5.4 Cover Letter to Mrs Lindsay's Note

To General Strickland,
Sixth Battalion Headquarters,
Sixth Southern Division,
Victoria Barracks, Cork.

We are holding Mrs Mary Lindsay and her Chauffeur, James Clarke as hostages. They have been convicted of spying and are under sentence of death. If the five of our men taken at Dripsey are executed on Monday morning as announced by your office, the two hostages will be shot.

Irish Republican Army

Figure 5.5 Mrs Mary Lindsay's Note to Gen. Strickland

Dear Sir Peter,

I have just heard that some of the prisoners taken at Dripsey are to be executed on Monday and I write to get you to use your influence to prevent this taking place and try and reprieve them – I am a prisoner as I am sure you will know and I have been told that it will be a very serious matter for me if these men are executed. I have been told that my life will be forfeited for theirs as they believe that I was the direct cause of their capture. I implore you to spare these men for my sake.

Yours very truly,

  M. Lindsay.

For her part, the IRA in Cork kidnapped Mary Lindsay and her driver, James Clarke, on Thursday, 17 February 1921 and held them hostage in an attempt to halt the executions of the five rebels. The British did not back down and hanged the prisoners on Monday, 28 February and so the Cork IRA shot the pair on 9 March 1921, without approval from IRA GHQ as required by IRA General Orders N°. 13, of 9 October 1920.[14]

Figure 5.6 Excerpt of Rebel Commandant's Report on Mill Street Train Ambush, 11 February 1921[15]

MILL STREET TRAIN AMBUSH

Headquarters,
Cork No. 2 Brigade.
To Chief of Staff
   3rd March, 1921.

   1. Attached is report of above ambush which, owing to pressure of work by all concerned, has been delayed in being forwarded to you.

   2. Great credit is due to the local companies, as they were lying in position for a week before being assisted by Battalion A.S.S. The local Company's O.C. got the intelligence and worked up the plans. It was well the A.S.S. came to their assistance to perfect and work up the attack.

   3. The Press report on this was satisfactory, and it described the whole affair correctly.

COMMANDANT.
Headquarters, A.S.S., 7th Battalion.
To O.C., Cork No. 2 Brigade
21st February, 1921.

   1................
   2................
   3................
   4................

   5. On the evening of 11th February the 6.30 train from Mallow to Killarney was boarded at Mallow by 14 men of the 1st Battalion, R.F., also an officer.

   6. Two men from 'D' Company had instruction from the Commandant and O.C., A.S.S., 7th Battalion to watch same train, and if it contained enemy forces to board the engine as soon as the driver moved from Rathcoole Railway Station, and order him to stop at a certain point where a signal was placed – this, of course, they ordered to be done at the point of the revolver – each of the two men being supplied with a revolver.

   7. In order to be more accurate about the strength and equipment of the enemy on the train one of the men met the train and Banteer Station each evening, having more time at this station to examine carefully their strength and the compartments they occupied. The other man waited, in the meantime, at Rathcoole Station with both revolvers.

   8. Both men thoroughly knew the cutting where the train was to be stopped and with the assistance of a lamp placed on the bank, at the left-hand side of the railway, brought the train to a standstill just at this point – the ambush party being posted on either side.

   9. The signal for exposing the light on the bank was a whistle from the engine, which they ordered the driver to do a quarter of a mile before the train reached the cutting.

   10. The orders for the men lying in ambush were: – When the train stopped

each rifleman to fire one volley (riflemen numbering 8 altogether – 4 magazines and 4 singles – 2 singles and 2 shot-guns being left to cover guard's van, for fear of Military travelling with the guard). When the first volley was fired the enemy was called on to put up their hands, which they refused to do, but instead took cover, and one of them was heard to shout 'no surrender'. The firing was kept up at a steady rate for about two minutes, another of these was heard to shout 'fire straight'; this order the attackers complied with, with the result that after about 10 or 12 minutes firing when called upon again to come out they did so immediately with the exception of one, who was apparently dead.

11. Having taken their arms, numbering 14 M.E. rifles, and ordered them to get into their compartments again the driver was told to move off.

12. The attackers withdrew then into a remote part of 'E' Company area, where A.S.S. remained in training for week following.

O.C., A.S.S.

        Adjt, A.S.S.

              (Sgd.)   Cm. Commdt.

The executions were of questionable legality, although perhaps acceptable under martial law,[16] and were poor policy; in the end, they did nothing to halt or impede the rebel war effort. Executions were certainly unable to halt the almost daily destruction of bridges and blocking of roads. Furthermore, with the government's inability to force the local county councils to repair the damage, the British forces slowly began to realize (by May 1921) just what the rebels had actually accomplished. In the 5th Infantry Division area,

> most of the damage was done in counties Leitrim and Longford and in King's and Queen's counties [Offaly and Laois respectively]; the Portarlington–Tullamore–Clara area was particularly bad throughout this period. Curiously enough the main Dublin–Curragh road was scarcely interfered with; and little damage was done to the Dublin–Athlone–Galway road; but the map on which were marked up the 'road obstacles reported' showed a distinct attempt to cut off the Curragh [military camp and 5th Infantry Division headquarters] from direct communication with the north-west, west, and south-west.[17]

Even this statement from 1922 demonstrates a lack of clear understanding of what the rebels had accomplished. Yet by May 1921, the British could only regularly transport forces from one coast to the other by sea – it was easier to travel *around* the island by sea than to travel the relatively short distances directly across due to the condition of the roads.[18] Travel inland was normally possible only in force, and then only with difficulty, and preferably with engineers.[19] This should have shown the army the limitations of their tactical mobility, but it appears not to have occurred to them.

Ballyvourney Ambush, 25 February 1921[20]

Another major attack from which the British army adjusted their TTPs, or specifically, confirmed the need to plan properly, took place in the last week of February 1921, when Seán O'Hegarty, commandant of the IRA 1st Cork Brigade, decided to exploit a known ADRIC weakness; the local Auxiliary company regularly travelled west on the Macroom–Killarney Road and always left just after 0900 hours. This, again, was the lethal mixture of predictability and poor discipline that hurt British forces throughout the war. This meant their convoys usually reached the village of Ballyvourney, a total distance of nine miles, by 0930. Therefore, O'Hegarty gathered an unusually large force (for the IRA) of over sixty men: thirteen from the 1st IRA Bn (Cork City), three from the 2nd IRA Bn (Cork City), twenty-one from the 7th IRA Bn (Macroom), and twenty-two from the IRA 8th Bn (Ballingeary and Inchigeela). The group was well armed; he reported '56 rifles, 2 Lewis guns, 10 shot guns'. It is not clear if he had more men or if some carried extra weapons.[21] Nevertheless, by IRA standards this was a *heavily* armed force. Of course, this also demonstrates how weak the IRA actually was, since 'Rebel Cork' was the most violent county, as well as the best-armed and supplied county, during the war and could hardly acquire the weapons they needed for what was, in fact, a fairly small force.

O'Hegarty certainly knew his business. Beginning early on Friday, 18 February, he occupied the high ground about two miles east of Ballyvourney in multiple positions. The rebels trenched a side road that could have allowed the police to head due west instead of following the main road to the south-west. O'Hegarty also stationed a small section there to hold the position and to guard the northern approach. He placed the two Lewis machine guns, under ex-British army Volunteers Eugene O'Sullivan and Patrick O'Connor, along with a section of riflemen for each, in high, rocky ground overlooking the south-westerly road. Commandant Dan Corkery, O/C of the IRA 7th Bn (Macroom), commanded his detachment from the rocky high ground in the centre, just south of the main road. Several hundred yards south of Corkery was an observation post with 'flag signallers' on Rahoonagh Hill, to guard the southern flank. O'Hegarty placed his command post north of the road, between the machine-gun positions. A section of riflemen in the western-most position concealed a cart ready to block the road if the convoy broke through the intended ambush site.[22] O'Hegarty's careful use of guards to cover his flanks made the difference between surprise and capture and escape and freedom when the fighting started later (see Figure 5.7).

At this point, however, O'Hegarty's care and expertise failed him, for

Figure 5.7 Map of Ballyvourney Ambush Site

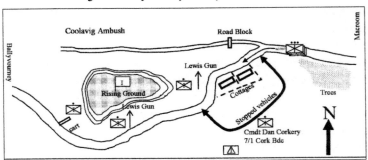

the rebels occupied their positions over four non-consecutive days; they prepared them, occupied them before first light and went home each evening at dusk. Remaining basically *in situ*, along with movement back and forth, for so long, even with breaks in between, compromised their position and the Auxiliaries in Macroom received word of the intended ambush site. Rebels were usually extraordinarily careful about security, except with regard to rural ambushes, where they frequently occupied sites for days, perhaps thinking that the remoteness would protect them. Likely wanting revenge for the Kilmichael ambush the previous November, along with other attacks since, Major James Seafield-Grant, MC, commander of ADRIC J Company, decided to attack the rebels.[23] This was not a surprising place for an ambush as the area saw two ambushes against the Manchesters – on 20 July and 18 August 1920.

Using an abnormally large force for police operations (seventy men), due no doubt to the expected size of the rebel force and their new-found respect for 'Rebel Cork's' ferocity and fighting abilities, the men of ADRIC J Company moved out. Finally following standing orders, the column left two hours earlier than expected (at 0730 hours) and came in a much stronger force than normal; usually only about twenty men went on convoys, but since Kilmichael they had increased convoy sizes. Still, the company was only 100 men at full strength and ADRIC companies were rarely at full strength. It is fairly certain the policemen did not have armoured vehicles, although some rebel accounts claim there were armoured lorries with mounted machine guns. As advance guard, the first of three Ford cars was in the lead, followed variously by the other two and then the five Crossley Tenders. In contravention of policy, Major Seafield-Grant rode in the lead vehicle. The leading vehicle of the convoy was to form the advance guard, while the convoy commander was to ride in the first vehicle of the main body. Otherwise, the convoy was in proper form.[24]

As the convoy turned south-west into the ambush site, it is not clear if they ever saw the trenched side road, but the men in the leading Ford saw a rebel to their right (north) scurrying for cover among the rocks. A police cadet leaped from the vehicle while it was stopping and fired on the man with his service revolver without warning at a distance of over 30 yards. The Ford stopped and the men got out. The remaining vehicles also halted and the men began to dismount. At that point, the rebels knew the lorries would move no further and the ambush was 'sprung', so they opened fire. Major Seafield-Grant was killed in the first rebel volley as he foolishly stood upright, exposed on the right (north) side of the road in front of his vehicle. In his defence, he may not have known at that instance which side of the road was safer, but standing straight up in the open was decidedly ill advised. As the major fell, and the rest of ADRIC column came under fire, the Auxiliaries broke into two nearby vacant cottages on the south side of the road for cover. Seeing this, the second (the western) Lewis gunner, O'Sullivan, an experienced machine gunner from his time in the British army, fired his controlled bursts directly into the cottage doors.[25]

When the shooting started, the first (eastern) Lewis gunner, identified as former British soldier 'Croxy' O'Connor,[26] fired a burst before abandoning the weapon and his section. O'Connor supposedly later claimed the gun had jammed and he could not clear it, but since the weapon was captured when the rebels fled, there was no way to verify his claim. Still, permitting one's weapon to be captured was one of four death penalty offences in the IRA.[27] According to rebel statements, O'Connor's fellow Volunteers did not believe him. Both O'Hegarty and the British agreed that O'Connor's action was pivotal and allowed the ADRIC cadets to escape further harm.[28]

After supposedly fighting for four hours, one of the lorry drivers succeeded in either turning the last Crossley around or driving in reverse until he was clear, to summon help from Macroom. Why this would have taken four hours, or where the driver had been in the intervening time, is unclear, especially since such prolonged contact was uncharacteristic of IRA attacks; although if they thought success was near, this might explain their willingness to remain exposed. There apparently were no homing pigeons in the column, also in contravention of standing orders, with which to summon help.[29] According to republican historians, thirty-four lorries and 600 soldiers came after them. This is hardly credible simply because there were no troop formations of that size near enough to send such a number of men who were dispersed in small detachments throughout the counties, and because it would have taken days to marshal that many men and lorries, but clearly a strong relief force came from the surrounding areas. The British account mentioned a relief force, but did not state its size, just that they 'forced the rebels to retire in haste'.[30]

While some of the rebel flank guards obviously failed in their duties, others succeeded in spotting the army's approach. The rebel withdrawal was hasty and disorderly, but due more to poor communications between the greatly dispersed forces than to cowardice or indiscipline, which was unavoidable since their tactical communications were severely limited (no field radios, lack of visual contact, and so forth). Also at odds were the casualties, which are difficult to determine; neither side disputed that the rebels took no losses, but the rebels claimed to have killed sixteen ADRIC and wounded from eighteen to twenty-four. The British claimed only one killed and eight wounded in their report of the incident, but since the official police casualty lists include Major Seafield-Grant, T/Const. Arthur William Cane and Cadet Clevel L. Soady all being killed that day, the British account is also lacking.[31]

The British version admitted that this was a rare instance where they received accurate information in sufficient time to act and that this 'was a case where an excellent opportunity of defeating the enemy was missed, owing to bad tactics, and failure to work out a proper plan of operations based on information received'.[32] This was remarkably honest in an official account, but since they were talking about police failures, the army likely did not mind assigning blame. At the same time, however, the army recognized that extra caution was necessary, even when one knew where the enemy lay in wait.[33] Clearly, this caution was lacking in the police movement and approach, which, even though they knew where the enemy was, they were careless enough that they basically fell into the ambush anyway. Seafield-Grant's disregard for his personal safety, while admirable in a young subaltern, was foolish for an experienced officer and may have betrayed a carelessness for the rest of the operation. It is difficult to explain how J Company, ADRIC, expected to attack effectively when they drove blithely into the ambush, a site chosen for its poor cover. While one might forgive these issues on account of a belief that IRA leaders were incompetent, which was most definitely false, even a basically competent rebel leader would have annihilated the ADRIC column. It is likely that O'Hegarty would have done so except for O'Connor's possible treachery, or at least failure to get his Lewis gun into action. Seafield-Grant's actions up to the point of his death were reckless, amateurish and cost not only his life but also two others, and at least ten more wounded. Further, there are republican sources that claim that the ADRIC column contained hostages in it and that this was another reason for not inflicting more casualties on the police.[34] There is nothing to indicate that there were hostages present other than these accounts; the British sources mention nothing of them and were generally not shy about their use of these human shields.[35]

More specifically, Seafield-Grant was negligent in not deploying flank guards; the lack of guards exacerbated the problem, making it impossible for them either to avoid the trap or help in recovering from the error of falling into it when they knew it was there. Much of this was probably due to the all too common rush to use 'actionable' intelligence, and thus failing to plan properly. There was then, as now, a delicate balance between time-sensitivity and thorough planning. It is unclear how much time elapsed between the ADRIC receiving the information and the very real necessity of moving out on their offensive operation in time to arrive significantly before they were expected, thus there may not have been sufficient time to plan properly. One would think, however, that in the available time the plan established would not have included merely wandering into the known trap, at least not without a secondary force to strike simultaneously from another direction. It may have been that Seafield-Grant expected his large force would strike fear into the rebel group and that a ferocious counterattack would carry the day. Surprisingly, this type of thinking was popular among army officers. Although harsh and swift counterattack has long been the most efficacious means of dealing with ambush, his men showed no signs of being ready for such an assault. How, after the First World War, any officer could think that charging up a steep slope into the mouth of concentrated rifle and machine-gun fire was the best means to defeat the rebels, is beyond comprehension. Yet, Seafield-Grant had been an experienced infantry officer of the King's Own Scottish Borderers, had won the Military Cross and been mentioned in dispatches twice;[36] he knew what worked in combat. His failures in this are still difficult to explain.

Another issue the army raised was of vehicle spacing in this operation, the failure of which brought all the vehicles 'under fire simultaneously'. The rebels knew that if the column was properly spaced – 300 to 400 yards apart – their preparations would have been worthless and firing on the convoy would have been foolhardy.[37] Seafield-Grant's carelessness and his men's poor road discipline allowed the rebels an opportunity to exploit an obvious weakness. When the army came on the scene, at about noon that day, they had no trouble moving forward in a dispersed order on foot. That they came in a stealthier mode did not hurt their chances. This, again, speaks to the *ad hoc* nature of this operation, but that an officer would merely mount up seventy men and ride out into a location where the enemy was known to lay in ambush, then actually ride right into the ambush, having taken no precautions whatsoever,

Figure 5.8 Commandant Seán O'Hegarty's Report

REPORT OF AMBUSH AT COOLAVIG, 25TH FEBRUARY, 1921.

The scene of the ambush was laid 1 mile east of Ballyvourney and 7 miles west of Macroom.

Number of men engaged – 56 rifles, 2 Lewis guns, 10 shot guns, riflemen and gunners made up of 21 men, 7th Battalion; 22 men, 8th Battalion; 3 men, 2nd Battalion (City); 13 men, 1st Battalion (City).

At 8.30 on 25th the hum of motors found many of our men in the position from W to Z not in their places. There was a great deal of scampering, therefore, and confusion. The cars came on very slowly and the first car (small) stopped, as marked on main road (1) the others also as marked – 6 lorries, 2 small cars.

Car No. 2 stopped first and the men jumped out – 2 of our riflemen firing and Gun No. 1 opening then. Car No. 1 continued until within view of Gun No. 2, which opened on it as soon as No. 1 had started. A hostage was running in front of the small car and he escaped into the southern side of the road. The action then developed – the enemy using 1 machine gun from a position between Car No. 2 and the northern side of the road; but some of our men in the eastern portion from W to Z evacuated their posts without orders, and so gave the impression to some of the men in the western portion, and who were not in action, that something like a retreat was on foot. Some of them, too, became demoralized. On the southern side of the road our men maintained steady fire – being in a position commanding both No. 1 and No. 2 cars. The other cars never came beyond point 3 on the road and never got under our fire. After more than half an hour's fight, a movement to encircle the eastern cars seemed desirable, but when orders were sent to the section in the west position to move up, it was found that the Section Commander had evacuated his post practically at the first shot and demoralized 9 men, all of whom had retreated. This delayed the movement, and when been evacuated and 2 paus left in the position of Gun No. 1. The enemy was now using 2, possibly 3 machine guns from points not easy to place, and many of his men had, under a sniping fire of half a dozen of ours, taken shelter in houses A and B. We concentrated, from a point H, rifle and machine-gun fire upon a window in B exposed to the north and we believe with good effect, but shortly after 10 a.m., upon the arrival of reinforcements from Macroom, it was found necessary to break off the action, and a general movement north was carried out without any enemy pressure.

The action was under the direction of the Comdt., 1st Batt., and I was present. The Comdt., 1st Batt. Is O.C., flying column.

Shorly after 3 p.m. 3 enemy lorries partly surprised up to 30 of our men at a point 3 miles north of Ballyvourney at the base of a hill – the road running right into the point at which we, with a similar number of unarmed 'refugees,' were grouped.

The O.C. column being with the remainder of the men at the point XX on the side of the mountain, I broke the men from the point X at which we were grouped for cover along the fence A. We had had information that there were 24 lorries in Ballyvourney and, therefore, making for higher ground, we put the men up through BB, which was a bouldered stream with very high banks, emerging at C. I gave the order to make for F, a commanding point, under cover and with bursts of firing. There were two routes – first to E, a farmhouse, and then up or along D, a low ditch with less cover.

The majority made west towards E and three of us up D. We all had a lot of time, as the refugees running light carried most of our men west beyond E and these did not fight. Only 7 men in all fought this every way. Some of the men also had continued in the stream beyond C, did not get my order and did not fight. That evening I had made touch with 19 of our men – the following night with 10 more, and 12 hours later with the O.C. column and the remainder of the men. When these latter had endeavoured to work round from the point XX to our assistance and the enemy had observed the movement, he broke off his advance and retired. In this second action the enemy, in our view, suffered a couple of casualties in wounded, and we none.

In the first action the second man on the No. 1 Gun abandoned his post at the first shot, leaving the gunner without loading help and in the position that, being under heavy fire, he had to abandon his two pans to bring his gun out safe. Some of the lorries had stopped right under the position of Gun No. 1, and had this second man used the bombs which were in the gun next to hand the enemy casualties would have been heavy and the final result different.

Information which has since come to us points to the fact that the enemy came prepared to meet an ambush, though personally, I believe he would have come in greater strength and in open order.

As it was, I believe, that as his cars approached our positions, he must have seen our men scampering to their posts on the high rocks, and so not run in under our fire as expected.

There was also a failure of scouts, a line of which from Geata Ban, ¼ of a mile east to a point above our positions, were to signal the enemy's approach. No signal reached us, which explains to an extent the fact that all the men were not at their posts.

Another thing. The O.C. column had himself taken up a position very advanced near the road, and consequently when the unexpected happened, had difficulty in getting back to a position from which he could assume control. There is no doubt that the running of men in the eastern points to their posts as the enemy approached was taken by others as a retreat, and had a demoralizing effect.

BRIGADE COMMANDANT
[Seán O'Hegarty]

is not only suicidal, but criminal negligence in the deaths of Cane and Soady.

Clearly, proper procedure – especially the spacing of vehicles – would have made a difference. It is doubtful if the rebels would have opened fire if the column were stretched out far enough for the lead vehicle to be towards the furthest end of the ambush while the rearguard vehicle was still outside the entry to the ambush site. Assuming O'Connor's actions were not treacherous, but that he did not want to fight under what were ideal conditions, and considering his flight sparked others to retreat; what would have happened if the policemen had moved in properly? The Volunteers did not want to worry about policemen turning their flanks. Even with rebel flank guards it is difficult to determine if they would have held against a determined flank attack. The survivors of J Company actually were just plain lucky. Another factor in the rebel retreat in 'haste' may have been faulty ammunition: 'At least 25 per cent. of the .303 [rifle and machine-gun ammunition] which came out last was *duds* [sic] [emphasis original]'.[39] Obviously, fighting with misfiring ammunition is a problem. This may also help explain O'Connor's weapon malfunction.

Almost a month passed without major attacks in rural Ireland after

Figure 5.9 Captured Rebel Diagram of the Action at Ballyvourney[38]

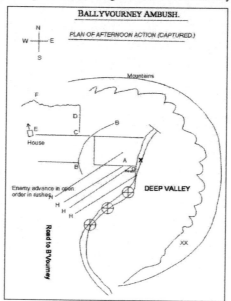

Ballyvourney; participant Charlie Browne stated that a result of the ambush and ongoing countermobility operations (trenching) was that British forces only patrolled this district west of Macroom 'in very large numbers, such as full scale round ups, often involving up to two thousand men' and that it became 'in truth a Little Republic from then until the end of the fighting'.[40] Even making allowance for hyperbole, this was a strategic success, well above the achievements of a mere tactical victory.

Yet in that time, seventeen RIC, both regulars and ADRIC, died in smaller rural incidents. If one adds the killings of three constables in Belfast on Friday, 11 March and the major engagement on Great Brunswick Street in Dublin (see Chapter 7) on Monday the 14th, the death toll rises to twenty-two. All of these, however, pale in comparison to the fighting in Co. Cork on 19 March 1921.

The Battle of Crossbarry, 19 March 1921
In the early hours of Saturday, 19 March 1921 the British army sought a decisive battle with the flying column of the IRA 3rd West Cork Brigade, then still under the command of Cmdt Tom Barry. This engagement is known variously as the 'Battle of Crossbarry' and the 'Crossbarry Ambush'; considering the size and scope of the fighting in comparison to the rest of the war, the former is more appropriate. This action was an ambush that evolved into a far greater action, and while it

was not a decisive battle, in that it did not bring about an end to the war or any significant change, it demonstrated the IRA's capabilities.

There are two versions of what happened, one republican and the other British. Not surprisingly, the accounts differ, but not so much in context as in minor or unimportant details. There are many facts, upon which both sides agree. These different vantage points, however, offer clarity and so both are presented.

Republican Version
The IRA 3rd West Cork Brigade flying column, the same that had massacred the ADRIC cadets at Kilmichael the previous November, received information that the British army, specifically the 1st Bn Essex Regiment, was to reinforce several garrisons in the local area by convoy along the road from Bandon to Kinsale. Early on Thursday, 17 March 1921, after being reinforced by the Innishannon IRA Company, Barry decided to ambush that convoy at Shippool, approximately halfway between the two towns, a route the army travelled almost daily. He moved his 100-man plus column into position and placed two mines in the road. After waiting all day for their quarry, two young Cumann na mBan women bicycled up to the rebel position and reported that the army column had turned back after having travelled about a mile; Barry thought: 'Obviously they were recalled because of information received that our Brigade column had moved across their line of march.'[41]

Vacating the ambush site at dusk and moving to Skough after receiving word of the enemy's returning to barracks, Barry said that a reconnaissance aircraft appeared nearby and the rebels took cover immediately, but were spotted. It is doubtful that this was actually a reconnaissance aircraft sent out that late in the day (it was 1600 hours when they abandoned the ambush site). Such an event suggests far greater coordination and control of the RAF's 11th (Irish) Wing than the Irish Command had. Further, Ryan states that the Cumann na mBan women reported that the military authorities in Kinsale, elements of the 1st Essex Regiment, knew the column was there.[42] This meant that any request for air support had to go through their battalion commander, through the 17th Infantry Brigade, to the 6th Infantry Division at Cork City and, perhaps, to the Irish Command GHQ in Dublin before it would have reached the 11th (Irish) Wing. From there, it would have gone to the nearest squadron, No. 2 Squadron at Fermoy RAF station, for execution. To coordinate this without telephones – because the military had stopped using them due to republican infiltrators listening in – meant that encrypted messages would have been the safest and most expeditious means. To send the approximately five encrypted messages and to assume such coordination could have been accomplished in one day, boggles the mind of any experienced staff officer.[43] Even if one accepts that it *might* have been possible simply to call the airfield, it takes time to prepare and launch an aircraft. Finally, no experienced aviator would launch a biplane-mounted reconnaissance mission at 1600 hours, at dusk, in March in Ireland; the observers would not be able to see anything and would, in fact, be in threat of their lives.

What is more probable than an impromptu reconnaissance mission is that the aircraft was landing at Ballincollig on an airmail flight from Fermoy. Still, such a flight *could* have observed the column, but all the pilot could have done without a radio was fly to the nearest troops, the 1st Bn Manchester Regiment at Ballinhassig, some ten miles away, since no other British troops were in the field yet, and literally drop a hastily scribbled message out of the plane (since he could not land there).[44] This did not happen, since the Manchesters did not engage or act on the information during this engagement. Finally, it is more probable that the aircrew did not observe anything since it was getting dark, they were probably not looking for anything and the ground was extremely difficult. The British, by this time in the war, already knew that the IRA regularly misunderstood the presence of RAF aircraft and had disproportionate reactions to them.[45] Whether they were observed from the air or not, the leaders present – Barry, the column commandant, Liam Deasy, IRA 3rd West Cork Brigade adjutant, and Captain Thomas Kelleher, Ballyhandle IRA Company O/C – decided to move out quickly to Crossbarry. The column spent part of the evening celebrating St Patrick's Day and then marched through the night, arriving at Ballyhandle at 0100 hours on 18 March. Furthermore, they route-marched in a tactically sound formation, having advance, flank and rear guards. The advance guard was under the command of Tom Kelleher.[46] That the IRA was using these formations was significant and speaks to their professionalism; perhaps even more so since the army and RIC were not always doing so.

The column remained at Ballyhandle through Friday, 18 March and moved to Crossbarry at dusk. They then designated Patrick O'Leary's house as headquarters and sent the column into billets for the night with orders to gather at 0600 hours. Barry and Deasy reconnoitred the proposed ambush site and then went for a drink at Cronin's pub.[47] Kelleher's Ballyhandle IRA Company stood guard so the column could get some rest. In the early morning of Saturday, 19 March, British army forces entered the area from several directions simultaneously. Around 0230 hours, rebel scouts reported hearing and seeing lorries approaching in the distance.[48]

Barry roused his men and prepared to take offensive action. He claimed that the army sent 1,400 troops after the column,[49] but British sources tell of smaller groups moving on different axes of approach. Barry's decision to fight, therefore, was all the more remarkable, since he clearly believed he was outnumbered. His view was based on four factors: the belief that they were outnumbered and thus could not expect to get out without a fight. With limited ammunition, forty rounds per man, closing with the enemy to fight at close quarters was necessary. Not having had a 'real' fight for several months, he thought it was necessary to engage one of 'those large British roundups'; and attacking before all the enemy columns were in place would even up the odds. So Barry chose to attack the enemy 'column' that was converging on Crossbarry.[50] At 0300 hours Barry issued orders to the column for the coming fight: no retreat without orders; no one was to show himself until the enemy leadership reached the eastern mine in the road;[51] runners would carry communications between the several sections; and there would be no predetermined line of retreat, presumably to ensure no one would run as well as not knowing what the dispositions of the British forces would be. The column took up its positions at the Crossbarry site at 0430 hours.

British Version

What Barry did not know – could not have known – was that fortune had placed him at the weakest part of the British line. The men of the 1st Bn Essex Regiment had captured some IRA Volunteers at the Upton train station ambush (15 February), one of whom gave information to save his life. How, exactly, this worked is unclear, since there was no way this individual would have had the necessary information about where the flying column would be in one month. Ryan also mentioned this individual's treachery, saying that he was court-martialled by the IRA, convicted and had his death sentence commuted to life in exile.[52] In any event, the British 17th Infantry Brigade, headquartered at Bandon, detailed two battalions to support a joint sweep to attack the IRA 3rd West Cork Brigade flying column.

Two separate raiding parties set out, one from the 2nd Bn Battalion of the Hants (Hampshire Regiment), including eighty-one men (five officers and seventy-six enlisted men) under a Captain Atchison, and left Victoria Barracks in Cork City at 0230 hours, Saturday, 19 March, via Crossley convoy. The second raiding party consisted of five officers and sixty men under a Major Halahan of the 1st Essex Regiment at Bandon, Co. Cork.[53] None of the sources name him, but it is reasonable to assume that Halahan, being the senior officer, was overall mission commander.

Figure 5.10 Map of Crossbarry

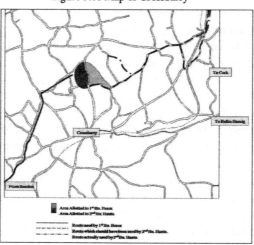

At some point, Company O, ADRIC sent men to the fight, but they are only mentioned peripherally in any of the sources, even though they lost one man; apparently they were lost and ended up in Kilbarry, Co. Cork.[54] They were not, however, the only British group that got lost that night.

While on the move, the 2nd Bn Hants missed their first waypoint, mistook their second waypoint for the first due to the darkness and were considerably delayed in getting into position. Then they dismounted their vehicles some five miles out and proceeded on foot. In the unusually dark night, they had difficulty transiting the terrain and got lost again. Out of an overly developed sense of light discipline, the Hants officers did not use any lights to check their maps. They finally got into position around 0600 hours.[55]

The detachment from the 1st Bn Essex Regiment left their barracks at Bandon in a Crossley convoy at the same time as the Hants. They dismounted their vehicles on reaching their position at the Brinny Crossroad and marched five miles into position without difficulty. The *Record of the Rebellion* claimed that they sent their Crossleys back to Bandon, but both Lowe and Percival claimed the lorries were sent to Crossbarry for a 0730 hours rendezvous and that they were, in fact, ambushed as they approached Crossbarry. It is unclear what the Hants did with their transport, but these vehicles made an appearance later and, considering that these vehicles came reloaded with troops, this would explain the overestimation of the enemy on Barry's part (two groups on foot and two groups of vehicles; perhaps six groups in all since the ADRIC company had its own transport). Begley claimed that a Miss

J. Forde reported being told by a Hants major that they had 300 men. This was highly unlikely since that would have meant bringing out the entire 2nd Bn Hants, which would take considerably more time than was available. Why he would have said this to an 'enemy' civilian, other than for misinformation, is likewise questionable.[56] At any rate, the army was in position for its raids into the IRA area.

The Battle

When Barry made the decisive choice to attack when the British forces were closing in on his position, he did so believing that he was outnumbered almost fourteen to one. To even the odds, he decided to attack in one direction and at one point, instead of dispersing to avoid detection and to increase the chances of some getting through the closing cordon. So while most guerrilla bands would have tried to 'fade away', Barry chose to concentrate and to attack, a bold move, or a foolhardy one, depending on one's view. He had no way of knowing that when he decided to ambush the vehicles at Crossbarry, he had actually chosen the weakest point in the British line; the vehicles converging there were mostly empty, except for a skeleton guard force, under an apparently inexperienced lieutenant. Because, despite republican claims of massive British forces, the 1st Bn Essex sent one officer and eight enlisted men armed with rifles along with the eight vehicles, whose drivers were armed only with pistols. Begley disputes these numbers, claiming that each vehicle was partly full, with eight or ten men each, which would have been the maximum they could carry, but stated that 'Some of the complement of each lorry had been moving forward on foot, in tandem with the lorries, as part of the round up'.[57] This was actually merely sound march security, as these men acted as advance and flanking guards and this was in accordance with standing orders, rather than being part of the roundup.

The republican account says the lead vehicles came into the ambush site, but stopped short of the easternmost mine because one Volunteer moved out from cover early. The lorries stopped and the troops began to dismount their vehicles, whereupon the rebel column opened fire. Here, Barry's recounting becomes almost unbelievable:

> Begley played martial airs on his warpipes as four of our Sections attacked. Volley after volley was fired mostly at ranges from five to ten yards at those British and they broke and scattered, leaving their dead, a fair amount of arms and their lorries behind them ... Three of our Sections were ordered out on the road to follow them

[the fleeing men] up. Using rapid fire they chased the enemy who lost many men.[58]

This republican account does not jibe with the British version, especially since Ryan included the 1st Bn of the Manchester Regiment as having sent a detachment; there is no mention of them participating in the *Record of the Rebellion*, Percival's lecture or Lowe's article. Further, there was no reason for any of these sources to lie if the Manchesters had been present.

The seven sections of the rebel column, designated A through G, were spread out over approximately 600 yards of frontage on the road, with A being the first in the west and E being last in the east. Section E, under the command of Volunteer Denis Lordan, was responsible for the easternmost mine. A deserter from the Royal Engineers called Peter 'Scottie' Monahan, who had been attached to the Cameron Highlanders when he deserted, was to detonate the mine on command. They laid a second mine further west, on Harolds Old Lane, under the charge of Dan Holland.[59]

The British version is unclear why the vehicles were caught the way they were. Lowe said that the drivers were anxious to have breakfast when they stopped, while the *Record of the Rebellion* simply said that Lieutenant A.F. Tower, the officer in charge, 'considered he was safe, being in sight of his destination; he accordingly called in the escort and got on the vehicle for the last few hundred yards'. This latter version coincides with the republican accounts of the flank guards. Begley reported that the column of vehicles came forward in proper form, but Tower called in his guards. Then, only the first three vehicles of the five- or six-lorry convoy had entered the ambush area when a Volunteer exposed himself and the lead vehicle came to a halt. The rebels opened fire and the fighting was intense.[60]

Begley stated that Barry was surprised by the firing, since the vehicles, which were heading east, had not reached his easternmost section. Caught in the open, the British soldiers tried to fight back, but being exposed there was little they could do. At some point they tried to take cover at the railway embankment south of the road, but D and E Sections moved out of cover, headed south-west and engaged them. When finished, they resumed their positions.[61]

The official history also contradicts Barry's timing and force size, saying the ambush occurred at 0700 hours instead of 0800 hours and that only thirty rebels attacked.[62] Both are actually unimportant because Barry's men would not have exposed themselves to view and he only said that the attack occurred 'about 8 a.m.' Since they were due at 0730 and Percival times the attack at about the same time, to rendezvous with the infantry, which had not arrived, the earlier time is likely more correct and would continue to explain the poor visual conditions. In addition, Lieut. Tower fired a distress flare, which would have been more visible in the darkness, whereas in daylight he would normally have fired a sound rocket to attract attention. Finally, although the British got the rebel leadership wrong – they thought Seán Hales, called 'John' in the *Record of the Rebellion*, was commanding the column – their understanding of rebel movements in the days leading up to the attack were in accord with rebel accounts.[63]

When they heard the firing at Crossbarry and saw the flare, various dispersed groups of British troops and ADRIC moved south and west towards it. A Lieutenant Hotblack took his 1st Bn Essex men to try to hit the rebel flank, but was mortally wounded in the attempt. A group of '15 men of the 2nd Hants arrived (under Lieut. Terry) ... [moving] in order to turn the rebel flank. There was some delay in carrying out this movement.' The column worked its way north-west to escape, so 'the Hants' transport was called up, and they were sent round in it to endeavour to head off the rebels, but it was too late'.[64] One of the various British groups converging on the ambush site under Major Percival ran into the IRA E Section as it fought its way out of the area to the relative safety of Skeheenahaine hill west, where the column was rallying. During this action, Peter Monaghan was killed while trying to get his mine to fire. Lordan, E Section commander, tried to retrieve the detonation plunger and accidentally set off the mine. This unexpected blast killed Monaghan, but had the effect of keeping the advancing British forces at bay long enough for E Section to escape. The last of the rebel sections arrived at the hill and exited the area without further incident. In the end, the IRA column escaped with just three dead and several wounded.[65] The British did not take the scores of casualties that Barry claimed,[66] but they were bad enough (see Table 5.1).

The army also lost two Crossleys, burned by the rebels (having taken the extra ammunition in them – three rifles, two pistols, two bandoliers of ammunition, eighty rounds of ammunition and six hand grenades). The rebels claimed that they captured a Lewis gun and ten magazines of ammunition.[67]

The republicans were right to claim a victory; inflated enemy strengths aside, Barry's victory was sufficiently clear in this case, no hyperbole necessary. This engagement, for a guerrilla force, was victory since they inflicted casualties on the enemy, captured valuable arms and munitions, and

Table 5.1 British Casualties in the Battle of Crossbarry, 19 March 1921

	Officer KIA	WIA	Enlisted KIA	WIA	Total
1st Essex	0	2 (1*)	4	3 (1*)	9
2nd Hants	0	0	0	0	0
RASC	0	0	3	0	3
ADRIC	0	0	1	1	2
Total:	0	2	8	4	14
* Died of wounds					

escaped alive. Further, the republicans were justified in pointing out that the British army tried to explain away their failures there; the British pointed to bad luck as being their chief failing, but listed six points to be learned from this encounter.

Foremost, the 6th Infantry Division's General Staff condemned the over-vigilance of the officers of the 2nd Bn Hants in getting lost and then failing to fix their errors.[68] It is understandable that they would not want to be seen at night due to using a light, but there were certainly ways for them to mitigate or prevent such 'violations' of light discipline. They simply failed to act in a decisive manner in this case.

The next criticism was the failure of the leadership to emplace the transport in a defendable position in which the escort would be capable of stronger, albeit static, defence rather than having to defend on the move. The rebels had the advantage of a fixed site along with the inherent weakness of an enemy force in transit. An advance or van guard would have made earlier contact with the rebels, while the main body was sufficiently far away to organize either a defence or a counterattack. The official history concluded by stressing the vulnerability of transport in motion.

The escort – eight enlisted men and one officer – was insufficient to guard the eight vehicles. In this criticism, the General Staff emphasized that the escort should include the previously mentioned part of a regular convoy; the advance guard, main body and the rear guard. In this case, Lieutenant Tower had flanking guards, but insufficient men to have a proper van and rear guard.

Communication with the main force once the vehicles were emplaced was another, more serious, problem, as visual communications, beyond flares, was almost impossible at night. Further, wireless could be carried in a Crossley, but then one would not have sufficient room for the troops. Of course, dismounted infantry were unable to carry wireless telegraphs without great difficulty. To get around these problems, General Staff recommended that the vehicles move forward in timed and limited 'bounds'. This was insufficient to their needs, but since the technology was so limited, there was really no other choice.

Lieutenant A.F. Tower's actions cost the lives of the eight men who died as a result of the ambush. One cannot criticize someone for 'invincible ignorance',[69] but Tower's mistakes were in contravention of standing orders, proper security and plain common sense. Although he had insufficient men for the van and rear guards, Tower deployed the flanking guards, in accordance with the standing orders, but called them in once he was in sight of the destination. One might regard keeping the guards out as over-vigilance, but the official history went so far as to state: 'Neglect of this, even when it seems ridiculous, may lead to disaster, as occurred on this occasion.'[70] A high level of vigilance and security should have remained in place until the convoy was as 'fortified' as it could get.

The last criticism had to do with the loads soldiers were carrying and their relative physical fitness. The 'young soldiers we now have, who tire easily' should not have been overburdened with their kit while on the march. In this instance, the soldiers' rucksacks were too heavy to maintain the inherent agility of dismounted infantry. Although unstated, this suggested that the failure of the detachment of the 2nd Hants under Lieut. Terry was due to the troops' fatigue. At this time, it made little sense to use motorized infantry, dismount them and proceed to overburden them with heavy packs, which thus nullified their agility. The critique/lessons ended with the recommendation that the 'young troops' be constantly physically trained. How this was to be possible is unclear, as it was difficult for the troops to exercise in their garrisons and the dangers outside their barracks were too great.

Although the Battle of Crossbarry was not decisive in terms of the number of casualties inflicted, despite of the relatively large numbers of men engaged, it sent a needed propaganda victory to the rank and file of the IRA, who, although they had not been 'losing' the war, needed to see progress. Crossbarry gave them that boost. Tom Barry later reflected that Crossbarry 'may have been a decisive factor in getting the British establishment to think of a Truce. I am not claiming that it was, as there were other fights all over the country, but it is quite possible that it was very important for this nation, for the army and for the Republic.'[71] It is unlikely that Crossbarry was a factor in deciding to accept the Truce, since the Cabinet, the chief secretary and the army were all prepared to 'soldier on' for months and the decision for the Truce was not taken until June. For the British, this was another in a string of unsuccessful actions but, as detailed above, they learned from it. This does not take away from the IRA successes there, and especially Barry's decisive leadership at a critical moment; these were essential to the republicans. In terms of what this victory meant to the rebels, it had a strategic effect.

The IRA, as detailed above, used every advantage in their rural ambushes. It is impossible to say how many attacks were thwarted by good security, attention to detail or even mere chance. The rebels were most violent in the southern counties of Ireland, but the actions there were primarily in rural settings; urban actions were almost the exclusive domain of the Dublin IRA.[72]

NOTES

1. Many period sources use 'Kiskeam', while others use 'Kishkeam'; since the latter is the contemporary variant, it will be used for the sake of simplicity.
2. S. Moylan, *Seán Moylan in his own words: His memoir of the Irish War of Independence* (2003), pp.90–1; P. Lynch, 'Rapid Evaluation of Military Intelligence Paved the Way to Success of Seán Moylan's Men at Tureengarriffe', in M. Keegan, (ed.), *Rebel Cork's Fighting Story, from 1916 to the Truce with Britain* (1947), p.127; and R. Abbott, *Police Casualties*, pp.189–91.
3. Lynch, 'Rapid Evaluation', p.129. Moylan did not mention the machine-gunner in his later versions of events, but the treatment in his writing was actually quite cursory (Moylan, *Seán Moylan in his own words*, pp.90–1).
4. Abbott, *Police Casualties*, pp.189–91.
5. Lynch, 'Rapid Evaluation', p.131.
6. J. Herlihy, *The Royal Irish Constabulary: A Complete Alphabetical List of Officer and Men, 1816–1922* (1999), p.169; and Abbott, *Police Casualties*, pp.189–91.
7. D. Begley, *The Road to Crossbarry: The Decisive Battle of the War of Independence* (1999), p.82.
8. S. O'Callaghan, *Execution* (London: Muller, 1974), p.19.
9. Ibid., p.19.
10. General Staff, Irish Command, *Record of the Rebellion in Ireland in 1920–21, and the Part Played by the Army in Dealing with It* (1922), vol. IV, p.172 (NA PRO WO 141/93); S. Fox, 'Chronology of Irish History 1919–1923'; P. Hart, *The IRA and its Enemies: Violence and Community in Cork, 1916–1923* (1998), pp.248 and 300; and M.A. Hopkinson, *The Irish War of Independence* (2002), p.112.
11. General Staff, Irish Command, *Record of the Rebellion*, vol. IV, p.172 (NA PRO WO 141/93); O'Callaghan, *Execution*, p.25; and Fox, 'Chronology of Irish History 1919–1923'.
12. General Staff, Irish Command, *Record of the Rebellion*, vol. IV, p.173 (NA PRO WO 141/93); Fox, 'Chronology of Irish History 1919–1923'.
13. General Staff, Irish Command, *Record of the Rebellion*, vol. IV, p.173 (NA PRO WO 141/93); Fox, 'Chronology of Irish History 1919–1923'; and O'Callaghan, *Execution*, pp.13, 20–3, 27–9. Interestingly, O'Callaghan described Evans' treatment of the prisoners as being quite benevolent and that the 1st Manchesters had a good reputation for being fair and humane (p.32).
14. General Staff, Irish Command, *Record of the Rebellion*, vol. IV, p.173 (NA PRO WO 141/93); Fox, 'Chronology of Irish History 1919–1923' and *New York Times*, 'Charges of Cruelty to Woman Prisoner Held by Republicans', 24 March 1921.
15. 'The IRA (From Captured Documents Only)', pp.28–9 (NA PRO WO 141/40).
16. Sir S. Hare, 'Martial Law from the Soldier's Point of View', *Army Quarterly*, vol. VII (October 1923 and January 1924), p.297; C. Townshend, *Britain's Civil Wars: Counterinsurgency in the Twentieth Century* (1986), pp.19–24. See also 'Court of Inquiry in Lieu of Inquest', 5 May 1921 (PRO WO 35/149A); and Macready to Secretary of State, 1 September 1920 (PRO WO 32/9537); T. Jones, *Whitehall Diary, Vol. III*, 31 May 1920, p.18.
17. General Staff, Irish Command, *Record of the Rebellion*, vol. IV, p.42 (NA PRO WO 141/93).
18. Field Marshal Sir Henry Wilson to Jeudwine, 7 December 1920 and Jeudwine to the Chief Secretary of Ireland, 5 December 1920 for naval transport, Jeudwine Papers (IWM 72/82/2).

See also RIC IG Reports for May and June 1921 (PRO CO 904/114–5), especially in counties Clare, Cork and Tipperary.

19. Statement of Captain E. Gerrard (MA WS/348).
20. Also known as the Coolavig Ambush or Coolnacahera Ambush.
21. Cmdt S. O'Hegarty, 'Report of Ambush at Coolavig, 25th February, 1921', 'The Irish Republican Army (From Captured Documents Only)', June 1921 (PRO WO 141/40), p.32; and P. Lynch, 'Strong Enemy Reinforcements Prevented Complete Victory by the IRA at Coolavokig,' *Rebel Cork's Fighting Story*, p.139–40.
22. 'The Irish Republican Army (From Captured Documents Only)', p.32; Lynch, 'Strong Enemy Reinforcements', p.141; General Staff, Irish Command, *Record of the Rebellion*, vol. IV, pp.178–9 (NA PRO WO 141/93); N. Browne, *The Story of the 7th: A concise history of the 7th Battalion, Cork No. 1 Brigade, Irish Republican Army from 1915 to 1921* (2007), p.55; and J.P. and J.D. Cronin, 'Activities of Ballingeary IRA 1920–21', *Ballingeary History Society Journal* (1998).
23. Abbott, *Police Casualties*, p.203. There was no indication how they got this information.
24. 'Standing Orders for Armed Parties Moving by Lorry, and for Lorry Convoys', 20 June 1921, see paragraph 29; 'The Irish Republican Arm (From Captured Documents Only)', p.32; *Record of the Rebellion*, vol. IV, pp.178–9 (NA PRO WO 141/93); and Cronin et al., 'Activities of Ballingeary IRA 1920–21'.
25. Browne, *Story of the 7th*, p.55; Cronin et al., 'Activities of Ballingeary IRA 1920–21; and Lynch, 'Strong Enemy Reinforcements', p.142.
26. Patrick 'Croxy' O'Connor was also known as 'Connor' and 'Connors'; and Browne called him 'Cruix'. See J. Borgonovo, *Spies, Informers and the Anti-Sinn Féin Society* (2008), p.89 and Browne, *Story of the 7th*, pp.55–7.
27. The Cronin brothers claimed that O'Connor was later court-martialled by the IRA for 'treason', sentenced to death, but escaped to New York. He was, in fact, court-martialled for identifying IRA men, some of whom were killed, after being captured. The British helped him to escape to New York, but he was shot there by IRA assassins. Somehow, he survived. Browne apparently accepted the weapon-jamming theory. Borgonovo, *Spies and Informers*, pp.89–90 and Browne, *Story of the 7th*, p.57. See also IRA General Order No. 17 (New Series), 2 April 1921.
28. 'The Irish Republican Army (From Captured Documents Only)', p.32; Cronin, et al., 'Activities of Ballingeary'; Lynch, 'Strong Enemy Reinforcements', p.143. Knowingly conveying information to the enemy, knowingly breaking operations security and grave insubordination or during an operation endangering either one's comrades or the mission's success. How and why this weapon was captured, or why one of the rifle squad members did not take up the weapon, is unclear; it could have been something so simple as none of the others knew how to operate it. Clearly, there is much more to the story.
29. Although if Seaford-Grant had brought most of his men, the remainder would have been useless until they could get word to the army. See 'Standing Orders for Armed Parties Moving by Lorry, and for Lorry Convoys', 20 June 1921, paragraph 29.
30. 'The Irish Republican Army (From Captured Documents Only)', p.32 (NA PRO WO 141/40). Browne alleges in *Story of the 7th* that the rebels knew there were hostages in the convoy and that is why they did not inflict heavier casualties (p.59). This is unlikely.
31. Herlihy, *Royal Irish Constabulary*, pp.162, 222 and 225 and *Royal Irish Constabulary: A Complete Alphabetical List*, pp.52, 421 and 436; Abbott, *Police Casualties*, p.204; 'War Diary of General Staff, GHQ Ireland', 25 February 1921 (NA PRO WO 35/93A); 'The Irish Republican Army (From Captured Documents Only)', p.32; *Record of the Rebellion*, vol. IV, pp.178–9 (WO 141/93); and Cronin, et al., 'Activities of Ballingeary '. Cane died at the scene and Soady died of wounds in the Cork Military Hospital, 1 March 1921.
32. General Staff, Irish Command, *Record of the Rebellion*, vol. IV, pp.179 (NA PRO WO 141/93).
33. 'The Irish Republican Army (From Captured Documents Only)', p.33 (NA PRO WO 141/40).
34. Browne, *Story of the 7th*, pp.57–8.
35. Ibid., p.57.
36. Being mentioned in dispatches is still an honour in the British military and can be a precursor to a decoration for valour.
37. 'The Irish Republican Army (From Captured Documents Only)', p.32 (NA PRO WO 141/40).
38. Ibid.
39. 'Report of Ambush at Coolavig', p.32 (NA PRO WO 141/40).
40. Browne, *Story of the 7th*, p.61.
41. T. Barry, *Guerilla Days in Ireland: A Personal Account of the Anglo-Irish War* (1995), pp.122–3; M.

Ryan, *Tom Barry: IRA Freedom Fighter* (2005), p.132; Begley, *Road to Crossbarry*, p.76 and T. Kelliher, 'Vastly Superior Numbers of Encircling British Forces Routed by West Cork at Crossbarry', *Rebel Cork's Fighting Story*, p.157. Just how they were 'recalled', since they did not carry wireless radios, is unclear, but this incident is not implausible. See also E. Neeson, *The Battle of Crossbarry* (Cork: Aubane Historical Society, 2008).

42. Ryan, *Tom Barry*, p.132.
43. For an example of the bureaucratic mentality with regard to such coordination, see paragraph 4, Dublin District Memo, No. 3/386/1/G, 3 May 1920 (NA PRO WO 35/90/1/21) and 'Summary of a Conference Held at Dublin District Headquarters', 3 May 1920 (WO 35/90/1/3. p.2).
44. K. Hayes, *A History of the Royal Air Force and United States Naval Air Service in Ireland, 1913–1923* (1988), pp.50–1.
45. Ibid; Sir O. Winter, *Winter's Tale: An Autobiography* (London: Richards Press, 1955), p.311; and P. MacCarthy, 'RAF and Ireland, 1920–22', *Irish Sword*, XVII, 68 (1989), pp.177–9.
46. Barry, *Guerilla Days*, pp.123–4; Begley, *Crossbarry*, p.77; and Kelliher, 'Vastly Superior Numbers', p.157.
47. Begley, *Crossbarry*, pp.76–7. Begley stated that the drink took place at 0030 hours; one-half hour *before* the column arrived.
48. Barry, *Guerilla Days*, p.124; and Begley, *Road to Crossbarry*, p.77. Neither Barry nor his subsequent biographers have explained why the army, having supposedly been in such a rush to find the column that they launched a reconnaissance aircraft, then waited about thirty-six hours to send forces out after them on the 17th.
49. Barry, *Guerilla Days*, p.124; Ryan, *Tom Barry*, p.133; and Kelliher, 'Vastly Superior Numbers', p.159.
50. Barry, *Guerilla Days*, pp.125–6; Ryan, *Tom Barry*, pp.133–4.
51. They had reused the mines they laid on the 17th. Barry, *Guerilla Days*, pp.125–6; Ryan, *Tom Barry*, pp.133–4; Begley, *Crossbarry*, pp.78–82.
52. Percival, 'Guerrilla Warfare Lecture, Ireland 1920–1921', in W. Sheehan, ed., *British Voices: from the War of Independence, 1918–1921* (2006), p.126; General Staff, Irish Command, *Record of the Rebellion*, vol. IV, p.183 (NA PRO WO 141/93); Bvt. Maj. T.A. Lowe, 'Some Reflections of a Junior Commander upon the campaign in Ireland'. *Army Quarterly*, vol. V (October 1922–January 1923), p.53; Ryan, *Tom Barry*, pp.124–5; and Begley, *Crossbarry*, p.78. See also Seán MacCarthy to Liam Deasy, 18 July 1963, quoted in full in Begley, *Crossbarry*, p.78.
53. General Staff, Irish Command, *Record of the Rebellion*, vol. IV, p.183 (NA PRO WO 141/93).
54. See RIC IG Monthly Confidential Report for Co. Cork for March 1921 (NA PRO CO 904/114, p.602); Abbott, *Police Casualties*, pp.210–11; Ryan, *Tom Barry*, p.134; and Begley, *Crossbarry*, p.96. The RIC man killed-in-action was T/Const. Arthur F. Kenward, (76391).
55. General Staff, Irish Command, *Record of the Rebellion*, vol. IV, p.183 (NA PRO WO 141/93).
56. Ibid.; Percival, 'Guerrilla Warfare Lecture, Ireland 1920–1921', p.126; Lowe, 'Some Reflections', p.53; and Begley, *Crossbarry*, p.80. It appears that the ADRIC transport was near the 1st Essex transport, since their casualties were two of their drivers.
57. Percival, 'Guerrilla Warfare Lecture, Ireland 1920–1921', p.126; Begley, *Crossbarry*, p.85; Kelliher, 'Vastly Superior Numbers', p.159.
58. Barry assigned IRA Captain Florence Begley to play his bagpipes during the fighting in the belief that 'the best of soldiers will fight even better still to the strains of their traditional war songs' (Barry, *Guerilla Days*, p.123). Diarmuid Begley is the son of Capt. Florie Begley, and Thomas Kelleher said 'that man's music was more effective than twenty rifles' on that morning (p.86).
59. Begley, *Crossbarry*, p.80; and Kelliher, 'Vastly Superior Numbers', p.160.
60. Lowe, 'Some Reflections', p.53; Begley, *Crossbarry*, p.85; and General Staff, Irish Command, *Record of the Rebellion*, vol. IV, p.184 (NA PRO WO 141/93).
61. Begley, *Crossbarry*, pp.80–5.
62. Lowe, 'Some Reflections', p.53; Barry, *Guerilla Days*, p.128; and General Staff, Irish Command, *Record of the Rebellion*, vol. IV, p.184 (NA PRO WO 141/93).
63. Ryan, *Tom Barry*, p.134; General Staff, Irish Command, *Record of the Rebellion*, vol. IV, pp.183–4 (NA PRO WO 141/93); Barry, *Guerilla Days*, p.128; and Percival, 'Guerrilla Warfare Lecture, Ireland 1920–1921', p.126. Kelliher stated that the lorries came into the area around 1000hrs (p.157).
64. General Staff, Irish Command, *Record of the Rebellion*, vol. IV, p.184 (NA PRO WO 141/93).
65. Begley, *Crossbarry*, pp.90–1. Barry named the dead as Volunteers Con Daly, Jeremiah O'Leary and Peter Monahan (*Guerrilla Days*, p.130).
66. Barry, *Guerilla Days*, p.130. Barry described the aftermath as one of carnage: 'British corpses

were strewn on the Crossbarry road, in the fields south of it, in front of Denis Lordan's Section, near Christy O'Connell's Section, and now here were several more of them lying around Kelleher's Section'.

67. General Staff, Irish Command, *Record of the Rebellion*, vol. IV, p.184 (NA PRO WO 141/93). Strangely, since no one has mentioned it, the Crossleys appear not to have been carrying the additional 1,000 rounds of .303 ammunition as required in the standing orders.

68. General Staff, Irish Command, *Record of the Rebellion*, vol. IV, p.185 (NA PRO WO 141/93). The following six points come from this source.

69. Invincible ignorance is a theological concept that someone did not know something and could not have known. Conversely, vincible ignorance occurs when someone did not know something, but should have known, or had the responsibility to know, but did not.

70. General Staff, Irish Command, *Record of the Rebellion*, vol. IV, p.185 (NA PRO WO 141/93). Sgt Frank Poole (Service No. 5998840), 1st Bn. Essex Regiment, was awarded the British Empire Medal for 'having displayed great gallantry in leading a party of young soldiers in an action on 19th March 1921. He also made repeated attempts to bring in a wounded officer lying in an exposed position under heavy fire'; presented in Dublin, 14 January 1922. See *London Gazette*, 1 June 1921. Lieut. A.F. Tower died of wounds on 9 June 1923. The author is indebted to Mr Ian Hook, Keeper of the Essex Regiment Museum.

71. Tom Barry to Kate O'Callaghan, nd, RTÉ Sound Archives, quoted in Ryan, *Tom Barry*, p.139.

72. This is not to say that urban operations did not take place elsewhere, but that those instances in Cork were against single targets or used bombs, which the author covers in a subsequent chapter, while those in Belfast open up issues that are too large for this book.

Six

Improvised Explosive Devices and Ambushes in Ireland

The first attempted use of a road mine by the IRA during an ambush took place on the Dingle Peninsula on Wednesday, 18 August 1920, where a single lorry from the 2nd Bn The East Lancashire Regiment was attacked near the village of Annascaul, Co. Kerry. Four other ranks were wounded. From this attack and the meagre description available, it appears that the rebels command-detonated the mine and the men of the East Lancs surrendered. At this period of the war, the rebels simply took the soldiers' weapons. It is likely that, since the lorry was destroyed by the blast, the East Lancs were incapable of resisting.[1]

So, the British had developed countermeasures to IRA convoy ambushes, which, by mid-1920, usually commenced with rifle or machine-gun fire. Primary among these counters was the use of armoured vehicles, which, as detailed above, became increasingly more available towards the beginning of autumn 1920. The IRA, suffering from the combined effects of the increase of motor transport among British forces and the onslaught of police and Auxiliaries this enabled, found some means of retarding this offensive.

Although the relatively small attack at Annascaul marked the first use of an electrically command-detonated roadside[2] IED, as well as the first use of an IED by insurgents against motor vehicles, roadside IEDs were not the norm in Ireland. It is also important to note that the IRA also used explosives *defensively* during the war; the use of multiple bombs planted in the line of march served to attack, but also to defend the rebel positions, since they frequently did not always fire all of the bombs available. There were many other types of explosive devices that should properly be called 'IEDs' – most of these were hand-thrown, such as various grenades, or were hand-carried, such as either breaching charges or satchel charges. Indeed, it appears that hand-thrown bombs were the majority. For example, of the approximately 172 ambushes noted in the various war diaries in the Irish Command, 109 (63 per cent) used explosive devices of some type, only four of which were mines.[3] These other devices, constructed from various and sundry parts and components, were also IEDs, but were employed either against people or against walls. These other IEDs differed in their construction, mostly in that they had to be smaller in order to be portable enough to be used by one man with little or no time to set up. Thus their design was usually simpler, using primarily flame or commercial spark 'igniters'.[4]

An armoured vehicle in a convoy was problematic for the rebel ambushers for, unless they were lucky, rifle or machine-gun fire was unlikely to stop it. If it was an armoured car, it carried several machine-gun turrets, which usually had dual-mounted .303 machine guns apiece. This meant that an armoured car could operate offensively against the rebels as well as defensively. If the vehicle was one of the up-armoured 'tactical lorries', usually 3-ton Crossley Tenders, it likely carried armed troops. In this case, the rebels needed to knock it out before these troops could dismount; otherwise, they represented too great a threat to the attackers. An armoured car was still a threat, but no one was going to dismount from it, take up multiple defensive positions or charge the ambushers.

This chapter examines one of the IRA's responses to these threats by looking at their development and use of roadside IEDs, in addition to the British countermeasures employed. There were several spectacular successes, as well as significant failures. This chapter scrutinizes both, including the consequences of such failures for both sides.

Toureen/Ballinhassig Ambush, 22 October 1920

The ongoing British offensive was stinging the rebels throughout much of Ireland, but the men of western Co. Cork wanted to strike back. So the leadership of the 3rd West Cork Brigade flying column decided to attack a military convoy that regularly travelled on the Innishannon–Ballinhassig road. They originally wanted to attack it on Tuesday, 19 October, but two of their comrades, Volunteers Jack Fitzgerald and Michael O'Neill, had been captured and the rebels expected that these men would be transferred around the same time.[5] Not wanting to kill their friends, they waited. Word quickly reached them by Thursday that the two men had arrived in Cork City and so they decided to attack the next morning. The officers of the brigade had already scouted the road to find the best ambush site.[6]

The IRA brigade commandant, Charlie Hurley, and his vice-commandant, Liam Deasy, had come by train through Crossbarry to participate in the attack. The column established the ambush site around 0400 hours in front of a local family farmhouse, where Hurley and Volunteer Con Crowley evacuated the family (the Roberts) to a room in the rear of

Figure 6.1 Austin Armoured Car

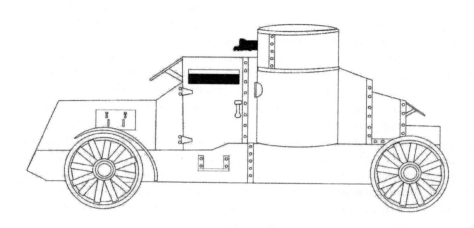

their house under guard, where they would be safe. Hurley also intercepted the Roberts' three workmen when they arrived for the day, spir-
iting them to the backroom with the Roberts family. Hurley had his
section place a large mine in front of the Roberts' house and remained
there behind a wall with Volunteer Jack O'Neil to detonate it. Deasy
commanded the eastern section of nine riflemen, while Tom Barry, who
had not yet assumed command of the column, had ten on the western
side. There were a total of six flank guards posted to prevent surprise, as
well as numerous unarmed scouts in the area to provide early warning.[7]

The military convoy of two Crossley tenders carried approximately
twenty-three troops from the 1st Bn Essex Regiment on their way to
Cork City. As the first lorry came into view, Hurley tried to detonate the
mine, but it failed, so the riflemen opened fire on it; however, it sped on
to its destination. The second vehicle, some 200 yards behind the first,
was not so lucky. As the first vehicle moved out of sight, the second came
under rebel fire and was disabled and swerved into a ditch. Under fire,
Lieut. W.A. Dickinson[8] and his eight men dismounted the lorry and took
cover in the ditch. Dickinson was hit in the right shoulder as he got out
of the driving compartment. The soldiers put up some resistance, ineffective fire according to Barry, but shortly after Dickinson was killed by
a round through the head, they surrendered.[9]

The ceasefire was sounded when the soldiers called out, wanting to surrender. The column collected the weapons and ammunition and then set the lorry ablaze. Five men, including Dickinson, were killed; the remaining four men were wounded. Barry claimed that five died, four were wounded and four were unharmed. It is unclear from the official accounts whether there were more soldiers present or not. The British said there were unconfirmed reports that the rebels lost seven men, but that 'This is not considered probable, as they were not seen removing any dead bodies, though they may have done so.' The republican sources state that the rebels sustained no casualties.[10]

There were some unusual aspects to this ambush; especially, the claim from the British that the IRA charged with bayonets. They rarely had sufficient rifles, let alone bayonets. The army also claimed that at least 150 rebels attacked them; there were about 100 rebels present. That the first vehicle did not stop when the second came under fire initially appears to be an example of the earlier and outmoded British counterambush doctrine of not stopping for disabled vehicles, but when one considers that the first vehicle was carrying an 'important witness and secret despatches from Bandon to Cork', it becomes clear that it was more important to complete their mission than to assist their comrades. One can only imagine the feelings of the men in the lead vehicle as they heard their comrades being attacked while they sped away to safety. It is not surprising that the army dropped this as a countermeasure. Barry was not so understanding, which is not surprising considering he did not know the nature of the mission, when he said that 'The Essex left their comrades to their fate, and were guilty of shameful desertion.' He went on to say that if the first vehicle had stopped out of range and counterattacked on foot, 'they would have made matters awkward'.[11] This is undoubtedly true, but irrelevant since the Essex men put mission above personal emotions in this instance.

Furthermore, Dickinson used then current counterambush doctrine of having the first vehicle acting as van or advance guard, while he commanded the convoy from the second vehicle. His choice to put the documents and witness in the first vehicle was unusual; one would normally expect them to be in the main body near the commander, but for the mission, this turned out to be a good choice. In addition, the road discipline, maintaining 200 yards between the vehicles, was also in accord with standing orders.[12] Unfortunately for the soldiers, the doctrine did not help them personally, but allowed sufficient time for the critical vehicle to accomplish the primary mission; getting the documents and witness through to the destination. Unfortunately for soldiers, sometimes they are sacrificed for the sake of the mission.

It is also interesting that there were two bomb failures during this attack. Although not mentioned in Deasy's or Crowley's accounts, Barry said that he threw a GHQ-made three-pound bomb that struck the first vehicle but did not explode. The likelihood of a large grenade-like bomb failing could have been high, especially since Barry admitted later in his memoirs that he had a poor knowledge of explosives.[13] But what were the chances that the road mine failed, especially since Charlie Hurley deliberately examined it before they buried it, specifically to check its functionality? Unfortunately, the rebels appear not to have examined it later to discover the cause of the failure. Crowley said that they captured 'fourteen rifles, one revolver and about 2,000 rounds of ammunition'.[14] From this attack, the 3rd West Cork IRA Brigade flying column went on to Kilmichael and infamy.

Ambushes in Cork, December 1920

After the violence of the Kilmichael ambush, the rest of November and the first ten days of December saw daily attacks – at least fourteen reported attacks since Kilmichael – by the IRA in Co. Cork. There was no let-up for the British forces. This culminated with the killing of ADRIC Cadet Spencer Chapman at Dillon's Cross in Cork City on Saturday, 11 December 1920. The final act was an attack on an ADRIC Crossley filled with men that day. Travelling from the military barracks into the city, the vehicle was bombed and fired on with pistols by the local IRA company. During the attack, an IRA bomb landed in the back of the lorry, wounding eleven men and killing T/Cadet Spencer R. Chapman.[15] That night, Spencer's comrades of K Company, ADRIC, 'broke out' and began a violent reprisal against the city. They looted, fired their weapons indiscriminately and killed at least two IRA men, as well as setting fire to a number of buildings in the city centre; the fire spread, destroying over five acres and causing some £20 million in damage.[16] Interestingly, few among the British forces denied that this reprisal occurred; in fact, the ADRIC commander, Brig.-Gen. Frank Crozier, transferred K Company to Dublin where, according to Bennett, they wore burned pieces of Cork in their berets as souvenirs.[17] What is unclear is why the Crossley did not have wire mesh protection against bombs and grenades, since, at least in Dublin, they were already using it.[18]

The British army intended their deployment of armoured vehicles in Ireland to mitigate some of the dangers of rebel attacks on road transport, specifically those initiated by small arms fire. The deployment took time: it took a while to manufacture or up-armour vehicles and then to deliver them, and the munitions strike necessarily slowed this. Although the retro-fitting began as early as August, by the first week of December the Irish Command had only twenty (fourteen 1-in. and six ½-in.-plated vehicles) 'on the road'. By 14 December they expected a further twenty-six (eleven 1-in. and fifteen ½-in), with the remainder arriving 'shortly'. This was to complement the forty-eight Peerless armoured cars, with a further forty expected (although no time frame for delivery was given), and the six Rolls Royce armoured cars expected by the 11th. Macready was also promised another ten Rollses by the 15th. He wanted a Tank Corps battalion converted from tanks to armoured cars to assist his limited force; he did not get it.[19] Macready's complaints paid off; the Irish Command's schedule for delivery sped up.

So, at the end of December 1920 the army received their final expected shipment of armoured cars; these were vehicles designed specifically to bear the weight of armour, so this did not harm their structure and the engines were sufficiently powerful to make them manoeuvrable, if not exactly nimble. Their only restrictions were weight on the Irish roads and size – relative to manoeuvrability in confined areas in towns and cities. They also received more retro-fitted vehicles. So, by the first week of January, with their new tactics and vehicles, the British forces began to deal with the IRA ambush threat. They were unprepared for the immediate results. In the second week of that month, the police confusedly reported that IRA ambushes had ceased almost entirely in many areas except in Co. Cork itself. Further, the police reported that the rebels were focusing on countermobility operations – trenching roads, felling trees, dropping bridges (both road and rail) and disabling lengths of railway line (the munitions strike ended in December 1920). These activities were mostly non-violent and subsequently safer than violent attacks, a factor not lost on the British commentators, who derided them as 'cowardly'.

It was incorrect of the inspectors to suggest that the IRA ceased all of their 'combat' (violent) operations after the shock of greater numbers of armoured vehicles in January 1921; there were fourteen deadly attacks against police during that month, with an additional one where ADRIC cadets were wounded (see Table 6.1). Interestingly, of the fourteen attacks, only three were against motor vehicles, none of which were armoured. Of the remaining, all but one were against foot-bound police, the last was against two policemen on bicycles (in Co. Cork on the 21st). Three of these attacks were assassinations, while one, in Co. Monaghan, had a preparatory ambush laid against a potential relief force. There was an ambush at Kilroe, Co. Galway, on Saturday, 17 January 1921, where rebels ambushed a D Company, ADRIC, lorry carrying eight cadets, wounding seven before one of the policemen was able to take a horse and get help.[20] There was another attack in the Dublin District at

Drumcondra on Thursday, 21 January 1921 (see Chapter 7). With forty-seven RIC casualties, January was hardly uneventful for either the RIC or the IRA.

Starting in August 1920, the British forces began receiving new body armour for their drivers.[21] This armour was significantly different than one would envision on a modern battlefield, but was certainly the ancestor of it. These were of two types: 'body vests' and 'body shields'. It is difficult to say with certainty what the 'body vests' were; the British had experimented as early as 1915 with heavy silken coats that could keep bullets from piercing the skin, or at least prevent fragmentation and minimize tissue damage. It is possible that these vests were of that variety, although a Dr Welply, apparently a British army surgeon, supposedly told Florence Begley that Maj Halinan wore a steel plate inside his uniform blouse at Crossbarry when raiding the home where the IRA 3rd West Cork Brigade Commandant Charlie Hurley was killed. Hurley shot the major, but the plate prevented serious injury.[22]

They were also issued 'body shields' similar to those developed during the world war. These pieces of armour consisted of metal plates welded together to fit the body, more like the armour of a medieval knight than a modern soldier. There were also makeshift attempts that merely protected the driver by placing roughly fitted steel plates around him, but these new body shields were more sophisticated in their manufacture and shaping. This armour was heavy enough to stop bullets, but too heavy to permit movement outside the vehicle. There is little information on how many drivers actually wore these suits or how well they worked, although in August 1920 the Dublin Brigade ordered all of its drivers to wear body armour, but the order was rather obscure in its wording:

1. R.A.S.C., Drivers of Tactical M.[otor] T.[ransport], Lorries or other lorries carrying armed troops will wear body armour.
2. Steps will be taken to explain to all ranks concerned the importance to themselves of the driving being protected.

There was no reason given why this was necessary. Was it the case, for instance, that the armour had been available and the drivers were simply not using it, or was the armour just then made available and they were issuing instructions that its use was mandatory? It would appear, by the relatively high number of casualties among military and police drivers, that they were not wearing them. Why this might have been the case is unclear. Further, the second paragraph was rather cryptic; why would anyone object to the drivers protecting themselves?[23]

Likewise, in January 1921 the RIC received permission to purchase

1,001 'body vests' and other protective equipment from the surplus army stores being disposed of by the Munitions Ministry. In February 1921 the Dublin District issued four sets of armour to protect soldiers travelling in touring cars.[24] Again, there is little evidence about the effectiveness of the vests or shields, although the shields should certainly have deflected the inbound fire, but to where? In the case of the army, they directed that the armour 'need not necessarily be worn by the occupants of the car, but if not worn will be placed along the back and sides of the car, thus creating protection for the occupants'.[25] One would hope that all travellers in the front would have such shields, but what if they deflected the rounds down towards one's legs or in other unsafe directions?

It is also difficult to quantify the costs of the body armour in today's money, but the body vest cost £2.15, worth roughly £676.86 today, and the double body shield was 67/6 or £3.7.6, which is roughly £830.70 today. These shields and vests cost the same for both the army and the police.[26] However, they were too heavy and bulky to be used outside the motor vehicles.

The army's use of armoured vehicles in Ireland in greater numbers caught the IRA by surprise. In some cases this became almost comical, as with an ambush near Kilrush, Co. Clare, where local IRA leaders decided to assassinate an RIC intelligence officer. Four men took up a position on the Ennis–Kilrush road on Tuesday, 10 August 1920. They waited for several hours and finally saw what they thought was a delivery van. One of the Volunteers jumped out and flagged it down. The vehicle slowed and came to a stop,

> whereupon one of the party went around to the back – to look into the muzzles of half a dozen carbines in the hands of as many RIC.
>
> A bold move on the part of the volunteers and the lorry was undoubtedly theirs; the occupants being completely non-plussed [sic] at the audacity of the proceeding.
>
> But the lorry again quickly moved off; the police opened fire which the volunteers were on their part too non-plussed to return. Instead they fled thru [sic] a small grove near at hand while the police fled just as ingloriously in the opposite direction.
>
> It was an armoured lorry, received in Kilrush a few days previously, and strange to say, minus rifle vents. This was a new introduction to the area, and something which caused all the volunteers furiously to think.[27]

In other cases, the vehicles saved lives.

When the army began using its new armoured vehicles, the IRA, unable to attack the vehicles directly, began to attack the roads, as mentioned above, but neither the police nor the army understood the significance of these actions. Both used derisive language when describing the IRA road-trenching operations. Since they saw no practical military function, they attributed this activity to simple cowardice or to a desire not to engage combat forces.[28] For instance, late in the war (June 1921), when he should have known better, the RIC Inspector-General, Lieut.-Gen. Sir Hugh Tudor, noted (for Co. Meath) that 'the IRA is active, but a remarkable point is noticed: that of late the operations are of a kind that involve the least amount of risk'. Although there are no exact figures, the Irish Command's QMG noted over 2,000 IRA countermobility operations in Ireland between summer 1920 and the truce in July 1921 affecting just the rail lines.[29] The true effects of this campaign took several months to surface, but by May 1921, British military and police commanders had begun to complain about their inability to manoeuvre due to the state of the roads. By June, so many roads and bridges had been blocked or destroyed that even horse-mounted cavalry had difficulty travelling, Tudor's comments in his report of that month notwithstanding. One cavalry officer, when encountering such difficulty while riding on an offensive drive with the 10th Lancers and the 12th Hussars, asked the commander: 'If it is like this within twenty miles of the Curragh [British Cavalry Brigade headquarters], what is it going to be like in Cork [the rebel stronghold]?'[30] Countermobility operations took time to 'mature' because one downed bridge or trenched road did not normally cut off communications with the surrounding countryside. It was the cumulative effect of many such operations that made the difference. While it necessarily took time to conduct sufficient countermobility operations, the objectives of such campaigns were not always clear. For just as lines of circumvallation are used to isolate a stronghold in a classic siege, what they hold in may also be used to defend against external attack. They are offensive *and* defensive at the same time. The British forces were perhaps too mired in the situation to see these as offensive and defensive in nature, or as circumvallating them, and, thus, had difficulty understanding their nature and value. They were not necessarily at fault for their ignorance, and had few examples from which to draw conclusions. Their points about the IRA avoiding battle were true; the rebels did not want to encounter the British armoured vehicles in the open. Why should one be derided for not wanting to engage an essentially impregnable target? This was not cowardice, but prudence; they needed to find means to counter the armoured threats.

Along with the increase in IRA anti-road and anti-bridge attacks came a new countermobility threat to British forces, what is today called an improvised explosive device (IED). These weapons were nothing new – there was a roadside bombing assassination attempt against Napoleon in 1803. Many IRA bombs fell into this 'roadside' category, but in their modern idiom of roadside IEDs or mines, this was their first real appearance on a large scale in Ireland.[31] Their introduction indicated a hardening will and, indeed, a new desperation or, perhaps, determination in IRA operations.

It is important to note that while there were numerous actions during the month of January 1921, none took place against armoured vehicles, primarily because the IRA did not have sufficient explosives to deal with this threat. Obtaining sufficient amounts of explosives was always problematic for the IRA during the war, and attempts to do so began early on. Indeed, the opening action of the war was to steal explosives at Soloheadbeg in January 1919.

The explosives in the IRA's IEDs came from three sources: they were stolen either from civilian companies or the military, or manufactured by the rebels. Those of the second category were primarily Mills bombs, a type of fragmentation grenade (see Figure 6.2), and were rarely used as a means to begin an ambush (Kilmichael notwithstanding), but rather, deployed when the vehicles stopped. There were instances of the rebels dropping grenades into the open beds of lorries, until the British responded by putting wire mesh over them.[32] Strangely, no evidence has come to light of the IRA using 'Molotov cocktails' against the mesh-covered lorries, or that they even considered doing so. Such weapons were known; perhaps they would have been seen as too horrible.[33]

The bombs or IEDs made from stolen civilian explosives used mostly gelignite – a nitric-based high explosive in the same category as ammonite, cordite, dynamite and tonite – as the main charge, with some simple trigger or fuse (electric or flame). There was a problem with gelignite, however, as it was susceptible to freezing and so could not be left in the ground for long periods in cold weather (not more than three days or so) since the device would likely fail.[34] The second problem with gelignite was that careless handling with bare hands or letting it touch skin allowed the oily residue to absorb into the skin, causing headaches, vertigo or nausea, symptoms known to the rebels as 'gelignite head'. Further, being a commercial civilian explosive, it was simply not powerful enough for the rebels' purposes because the relative weakness meant the bombs had to be bigger to deliver a higher yield, thus requiring more gelignite and causing problems with transportation of the weapon, which also then became a security concern.

Figure 6.2 British Grenades of the First World War Era

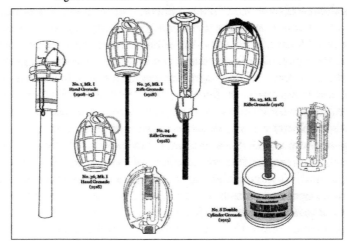

The IRA-made bombs were also of two basic types: crude bombs thrown together by non-experts and those manufactured by IRA experts. The former the army held in distain, calling them 'home-made'.[35] Where the IRA really broke new ground, however, was in their manufacture, from raw materials, of explosives, casings, springs and all other necessary bomb components. The extensive IRA arms smuggling network throughout Britain, especially in Liverpool, Manchester and Glasgow, supplied some of the parts for the bombs. In the case of civilian explosives, Glasgow was the primary source, the material being stolen from the numerous Scottish quarries and mines – the source of most of the gelignite. There was also the further problem of using flame ignition, making stealthy approach at night difficult. For some unknown reason, the IRA did not use commercial 'strikers' as much as they could have. These consisted of simple ignition materials encased in metal, that, when struck, would light the fuse without worrying about light sources or the elements. There is ample evidence that they had these, but did not use them to full effect.

The rebels needed better, more powerful explosives, so they commissioned a republican, University College Dublin post-graduate chemistry student James O'Donovan, to develop them. O'Donovan spent several years working on various explosive concoctions at his apartment on Richmond Road in Dublin. As early as 1918, he and an unnamed professor were producing mercury fulminate and even more complex explosives, indicating that someone in the republican leadership knew that gelignite-class explosives were insufficient *before* the war actually began. Commercial explosives were weaker and more difficult to use than military explosives. This was key, because most Volunteers had no experience with explosives until the war began. Likewise, the republican leadership was similarly ignorant, but someone, likely Michael Collins, identified the problem and brought about a means to solve it. In 1919, Collins directed O'Donovan to develop an explosive that was not only more powerful, but whose manufacture 'had to be made so simple that men with practically no technical knowledge would make them in a farmhouse kitchen and places like that. Yet they had to be fairly foolproof, because we could not have people all over the country having their heads blown off.'[36] This was a tall order.

O'Donovan eventually came up with a substance he called 'war flour',[37] due to its cornmeal-like texture. It was highly explosive, but somewhat unstable, and so not as useful as he had hoped, since the explosives had to be sturdy enough for rough handling. He continued working but was slowed by supply problems during a chemicals ban in spring 1920, but the IRA smuggled and stole what he needed through their arms network. Using simple materials gained locally and those from other sources, he developed their primary high explosive, a mixture of paraffin and potassium chlorate. He called this mixture 'Irish cheddar' (due to its colour). With O'Donovan's and others' work, the rebels had the prime ingredient for their bombs.[38] Next, they needed the mechanical components.

While O'Donovan was working on the chemicals, the IRA smuggled bomb components to Ireland. There are few records remaining, but IRA leader Michael Collins ordered his agents in Britain to purchase springs for bombs by the gross in January 1921. By February, he increased his order to 1,000 springs per week (and received them).[39] Other good sources for bomb-making components were telephone and telegraphic equipment, which the IRA also stole in large quantities. Another indicator of the number of bombs they produced was the amount of specialized coal – hard foundry coke – Collins had shipped by the ton into the rebel foundry in Dublin in late 1920.[40] The foundry was in the basement of the small Heron & Lawless bicycle shop at 198 Parnell Street, right in the centre of Dublin (the IRA eventually had eleven foundries in eight regions throughout the country by the end of the war). It was derelict when Joseph Lawless took over the site in 1918, on release from Frongoch camp, but he quickly got the smelter there working.[41] Collins ordered Lawless to get the machinery working. They cast grenade cases there along with all other bomb parts for assembly elsewhere. The IRA eventually developed a pineapple-style fragmentation case of their own design as the standard and produced them at the Lawless shop.[42] There were also machinists in the Royal Naval Shipyard at Haulbowline in

Cork secretly making bomb cases as well as replacement gun parts.[43]

The natural question would be how powerful were the IRA bombs and grenades? It is difficult to say exactly, but in several lethal accidents, unfortunate rebels found out first hand. There really are few means to measure the effectiveness of IRA bombs of the day, except by how they were used operationally. Here still, there are few clues, primarily because the rebels in the field were inexperienced in both handling and using explosives, so it is difficult to know if the many accidents and failures were the result of design, manufacture, assembly or employment. One of the more definitive instances was of a failure. On 20 June 1920, the IRA Kerry No. 2 Brigade complained to Collins saying:

> I beg to report that 5 Mills bombs [of IRA manufacture] supplied by G.H.Q. to our brigade [illegible] Feb 5th 1920 @ 12/.6 [12 shillings and sixpence] each failed to work when used in the attack on the Gortatlea R.I.C. barracks on March 24th. The attributed failure to explode to the possibility of the strikers being faulty [sic]. As these bombs were quite useless to us in fact they were more dangerous to ourselves than to the enemy as they were in the burning building whilst we were removing etc – we expect that you will replace them with fresh ones.[44]

Embarrassed, Collins replaced the bombs after having them shipped back to the IRA factory to be analyzed for their failure.[45] This suggests that this incident was an unusual occurrence for this brigade, although common elsewhere, and that they had expected severe damage. Unfortunately, while the IRA blew up many buildings, bridges, vehicles and troops, they did not keep good records of such actions; most of their reports detailed attacks on convoys or troops. Although the police noted many bombs failing to destroy their intended targets on detonation, they too appear not to have kept concise records of IRA bombings during the war.

Figure 6.3 IRA Improvised Explosive Device, ca. 1920

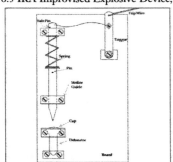

British records note many instances of IRA bomb failures during the conflict. Of the approximately 109 ambushes using bombs of various types reported in the War Diaries, there were about twenty-three where the bombs either did not explode or failed to cause appreciable damage.[46] There were several reasons for this. In some cases, the bombs failed; in others, they were not powerful enough when they hit their intended targets, or the bombers missed their targets when they threw the bombs. Finally, one should note that during the World War the army originally viewed the hand grenade as a sapper's weapon. It gradually became an infantryman's weapon, but the infantry grenade training in 1915 consisted of nine thirteen-hour days of instructions.[47]

One issue in the background when discussing the IRA's countermobility reaction to British armoured vehicles in January 1921 sheds light on this issue of the power of IEDs. Why did the IRA seemingly stop or at least slow down ambushing British convoys when the latter began using their armoured vehicles? The simple answer is that Collins was unable to acquire anti-armour weapons. Specifically, he wanted armour-*piercing* weapons, but his sources could not get them at any price.[48] So they used the only means immediately available to stymie British manoeuvre – bridge destruction and attacking the vehicles' under-carriage through road attacks as described above. Yet on 2 February 1921, the rebels tested their first IED against an armoured motor vehicle in Clonfin, Co. Longford, killing three outright and wounding nine.[49] This indicates that some of their IEDs probably had sufficient yield to damage regular armoured vehicles. Soon the IRA were back in the ambush business, but continued their attacks on roads and bridges.[50] The serious countermobility campaign using anti-bridge and anti-road attacks did not begin earlier than January 1921 because the IRA attacks/ambushes were already effective in stopping British vehicles. When the British developed effective counter-tactics to

Table 6.1 Ambushes on Police in January 1921[51]

Date	Location	County	Casualties	Remarks
1st	Ballybay	Monaghan	2 KIA, 3 WIA	Four-man RIC foot patrol ambushed. Three RIC from the barracks reinforced them; three RIC holding barracks fired distress flare. Joint ADRIC & military respond, travelling 16 miles via lorries, cover last 8 miles on foot due to warning of impending IRA ambush on their route.
4th	Parnell Bridge,	Cork City	2 KIA, 5 WIA, 5 civilians wounded	Foot patrol of 10 RIC attacked with bombs & small arms fire. Reinforcements drove attackers away. cont.

Table 6.1 Ambushes on Police in January 1921[51]

Date	Location	County	Casualties	Remarks
7th	Near Ballinalee	Longford	1 KIA	Attempting to capture Longford IRA Brigade Commandant, Seán MacEoin, DI McGrath was killed when MacEoin fought his way out.
13th	Cratloe	Clare	1 KIA, 3 WIA	RIC patrol of 8 ambushed when their lorry came under small arms fire from both sides of the road.
	Crossmaglen	Armagh	1 KIA, 1 WIA	Five policemen escorting a postman[52] came under small arms fire. Firefight ensued, with the postman being shot in the back by IRA. S/Const. R.W. Compston was first of the USC[53] to be KIA.
14th	Armagh City	Armagh	1 KIA, 1 civilians wounded	Sgt J.J. Kemp killed by IRA bomb blast while walking.
17th	Cappawhite	Tipperary	1 killed, 1 civilians wounded	Const. R.A.E. Boyd was killed while drinking in a pub with his back to the door.
	Kilroe	Galway	7 WIA	Rebels ambushed eight man ADRIC patrol in Crossley Tender.
20th	Listowel	Kerry	1 KIA	DI Tobias O'Sullivan was assassinated while walking with his young son.
	Glenwood	Clare	6 KIA, 2 WIA	Ten man RIC patrol in Crossley Tender ambushed by small arms fire alone. DI William Clarke killed in first volley. Seriously wounded, Sgt Egan did not allow the IRA to take his rifle when they collected the weapons from the dead. Unusually, he was not killed for it.
21st	Waterfall	Cork	1 KIA, 1 WIA	HC Larkin & Sgt H.J. Bloxham ambushed while bicycling to Waterfall from Ballincollig. Sgt Bloxham was killed.
	Drumcondra	Dublin City		See Chapter 7
22nd	Stranooden	Monaghan	3 Killed	Three off-duty constables were executed by the IRA.
26th	Belfast	Antrim	2 Killed, 1 wounded	Three RIC constables on special escort duty, shot in their beds. Const. Gilmartin, shot, but survived.
	Trim	Meath	1 KIA, 2 WIA	Six-man RIC foot patrol ambushed from behind a wall.
28th	Toureengarriv	Kerry	2 KIA, 6 WIA	DC P.A. Holmes & 5-man escort with 2 drivers in two cars ambushed.

Totals: 23 RIC Killed, 24 RIC Wounded and 7 Civilians wounded

these ambushes along with their use of armoured vehicles, the IRA began to attack the roads and bridges in a more deliberate campaign. Eventually, they incorporated explosives into this response.

Clonfin Ambush, 2 February 1921

The first IRA road-borne IED attack of 1921 was carried out by the Longford IRA Brigade against a police patrol at Clonfin, halfway between Ballinalee and Granard. Eighteen ADRIC cadets of M Company, under District Inspector Lieut.-Cdr Francis W. Craven, DSO, DSC, DSM, were on their way to Ballinalee from Longford, travelling in two armoured Crossley Tenders, when they became the first victims of IEDs in the IRA response to the new British mobility.

Seán MacEoin, the famed 'Blacksmith of Ballinalee' and commander of the North Longford IRA Brigade, with approximately fifty men, established the ambush site at the base of a slight hill where a small bridge or culvert crossed the road (see Figure 6.4). He placed one group of men approximately 300 yards south of the road at a small rise in a bog. He put a second group of riflemen several dozen yards to the left of the first. One of these two groups detonated the mine placed in the road next to the culvert. MacEoin, commanding the third and final group, took up a position about 70 yards north of the road at another small rise, where they dug a shallow trench as a fighting position.[54]

The rebels waited until the two lorries came down the hill, around 1400 hours, travelling at high speed and less than 200 yards apart. When the first Crossley reached the culvert, the rebels command-detonated the mine electrically, killing one man, Cadet John A. Houghton, instantly and wounding everyone else in the vehicle. The lorry came to a halt and, while taking fire from the two rebel positions to their south, the Auxiliary cadets poured out from the lorry and on to the north side of the road, trying to find cover.[55]

Meanwhile, the second Crossley stopped as it came upon the first and, while also taking heavy fire from the south, the occupants dismounted and joined their comrades north of the road. At this point, MacEoin's own third section of rebels opened fire on the Auxies from his concealed position 70 yards north of the road. The Auxies were caught between the three rebel positions. Although all eleven men, including Lieut.-Cdr Craven, were wounded, they fought until they had almost expended all of their ammunition; there was little else they could do, even though they had a Lewis gun. When Craven suddenly took a round through the neck and died, the policemen surrendered after first destroying the machine gun.[56]

According to the police and army accounts, MacEoin prevented his men from summarily executing the policemen right there. By this period of the conflict, the British were executing IRA prisoners, albeit after field general courts-martial. The most common charge against captured

Volunteers was murder, although mere possession of arms or ammunition as well as the wearing of the Irish Volunteers uniform were also capital offences. To some members of the IRA, the laws of war, embodied at the time in The Hague conventions of 1899 and 1907, were luxuries that the British had denied them since the 1916 Easter Rising when the Irish Volunteers had fought 'by the rules' while the British still executed their leaders.[57] In this sense, many Volunteers saw no reason to abide by them.[58]

Still, unless the operation was an outright assassination, it was rare for the IRA not to take prisoners, Kilmichael and Tourmakeady (see Chapter 8) notwithstanding. It remained generally safe to surrender to the IRA. MacEoin, according to British accounts, commended the cadets for their spirited fight, had their wounds dressed and, after taking the weapons, equipment and remaining ammunition, sent them back to Longford in the second Crossley. Before they left, however, MacEoin made a point of denying that he had killed RIC District Inspector McGrath on 7 January, a crime for which he was wanted and for which he would eventually be condemned to the gallows.[59]

The British noted that the success in this ambush was due to the mine, MacEoin's excellent choice of ground and his outstanding positioning of his men that day. They stopped short of mentioning that this was due to the skill of the rebel commander. Of the eighteen policemen, four died[60] and eight were wounded. There were no IRA casualties. The army also strangely noted that MacEoin's prevention of 'the massacre of the wounded and prisoners was noticeable and unusual; it counted much in his favour when he was subsequently brought to trial for the murder of a District Inspector, RIC.'[61] In fact, his rendering aid and releasing the prisoners were *not* unusual for the IRA as noted above, and in MacEoin's case, it counted little at his 7 June 1921 trial as he was not only convicted, but sentenced to death. His condemnation to death came in spite of the testimony of three of the Auxiliary cadets he had spared that February day, as well as an appeal from DI McGrath's mother and two surviving brothers to the Lord-Lieutenant and the Chief Secretary for Ireland asking that his life be spared as 'the sorrow and loss sustained by us will be all the greater should it entail the loss of a single additional life'. MacEoin was elected to Dáil Éireann (technically, to parliament at Westminster) in May 1921 while awaiting execution and was released during the truce. The British strenuously refused to release him, until Collins and de Valera insisted. The fact that the ADRIC men were willing to testify on his behalf belies their reputation for being 'thugs' and 'murderers' to a man. As with so much else in war, conduct and quality were frequently

Figure 6.4 Captured IRA Map of the Clonfin Ambush, 2 February 1921

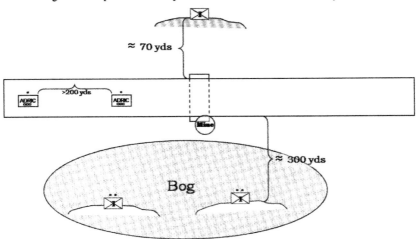

obscured by time and propaganda. Most sources accept MacEoin's guilt in the killing of DI McGrath; nevertheless, he survived the war and Civil War and served in Irish politics until his retirement in 1965. He died of old age in 1973.[62]

What is also interesting is that the use of this IED by the IRA was against an *unarmoured* vehicle rather than the plethora of armoured ones, although it proved of sufficient yield that an armoured vehicle would probably not have saved them. What likely occurred was that the Longford Brigade acquired (or manufactured) the weapon and decided to use it at the next attack regardless of the need. Another notable flaw with the ADRIC movement that day was the high speed and poor spacing of the vehicles mentioned above. This was poor march discipline on the part of Lieut.-Cdr Craven, which cost him and three others their lives. In many respects, this poor attention to proper security was indicative of ADRIC convoys and may have betrayed a distain for the fighting qualities of the IRA, which, by this period of the conflict, was simple recklessness.[63]

Strangely, the British view of the IRA's new emphasis on counter-mobility against their offensive – as evidence that the rebel campaign was losing steam – persisted, even after its effects were becoming known. Both the army and police saw the mass trenching of roads and bridge destruction as signs that the rebels were resorting to safer activities. Further, IEDs, sometimes command-detonated by women, according to the British, were the ultimate 'cowardly' act for the security forces. They saw the participation of women as an additional sign of weakness and fear on the part of the men.[64] Clonfin only signalled the change in IRA tactics; the rest of February saw an overall increase in attacks, while March saw the army taking casualties as never before.

Clonbannin Ambush, 5 March 1921

Probably the worst outright British army defeat in the war came at Clonbannin, Co. Cork in March 1921, where a large party of soldiers was attacked by combined Kerry and Cork IRA brigades. The British army's Kerry Brigade (nominally under the 5th Infantry Division),[65] commanded by Colonel H.R. Cumming, CMG, DSO, received information that a large force of rebels was lying in ambush on the Killarney–Rathmore road between the towns of Barraduff and Rathmore (see Figure 6.5). Cumming sent a detachment of the East Lancashire Regiment at Buttevant, Co. Cork to Rathmore to search for the rebels' site, while he took a party of the Royal Fusiliers from Killarney bound for Barraduff. After searching their respective areas, the East Lancs found the original ambush site empty. Sending the Fusiliers back to Killarney, Col. Cumming went with the East Lancs on their return to Buttevant.[66]

The rebels had combined forces of the IRA North Cork column and the IRA Kerry No. 2 Brigade column for an ambush. The Cork men had tried to attack an RIC postal escort patrol, but called it off when the policemen returned by a different route. So, under the command of the infamous (to the British) IRA Cork No. 2 Brigade Vice-Commandant Seán Moylan, they moved to support the Kerry column. They linked up and laid in wait for an expected small ADRIC convoy for several days, when they received information that their ambush position was compromised. Moylan and the other leaders decided to vacate the site but remain together to execute another ambush. They eventually, after a series of long night marches, selected the area of the Clonbannin cross-roads. On Friday, 4 March they also apparently received word, or at least thought, that another convoy was to come through the same area carrying Lt.-Gen. Sir Peter Strickland, GOCinC of the 6th Infantry Division along with Col. Cumming. The report of Strickland being in the convoy was incorrect, but they could not pass up such potential high-value targets. Establishing a new ambush site to the east of their original position, they laid mines in the road, at the east and west ends of the site, and placed their defences expertly, with both flank guards and reserves. Interestingly, they fully expected at least one armoured vehicle in the convoy.[67]

After waiting all day, Friday the 4th, without contact, the rebels finally got their chance on Saturday, 5 March at around 1400 hours, after Cumming's original push to find them. Earlier in the day, the convoy

Figure 6.5 Map of Clonbannin Ambush

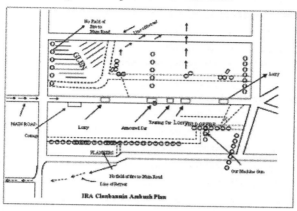

had approached, and Moylan decided to let it through. Having placed himself with the eastern mine, Moylan tried to detonate it, but it failed. At the same moment, the Volunteer next to him, Cmdt Paddy O'Brien, tried to fire on the British, but his weapon was on safe. Since these were to constitute the general order to attack, the rest of the rebels did not open fire. Moylan also said that he believed the convoy would come back again and so was little worried about it getting through. After the convoy left, the rebels examined the mine and found that they had used the wrong type of battery for the detonator. With the same problem in the western mine, they decided to await the convoy's return.[68]

Although the East Lancs did not expect the rebels to be in the area, they came carefully down the road toward the east. The British column had two Crossley Tenders in front, and then the car carrying Cumming, the Rolls Royce armoured car immediately following and a single Crossley Tender bringing up the rear. The Crossleys were covered with wire mesh as a countermeasure. The mines again failed to explode, but the driver in the lead Crossley was seriously wounded in the opening volley of gunfire from the Hotchkiss gun manned by Liam Moyland. This halted the lorry. The second lorry slammed on its breaks to avoid hitting the first lorry, while the car behind it did likewise. The armoured car, being too heavy to allow it to stop quickly, swerved to the right to avoid crushing the Ford touring car and then slid off the road into soft earth, whereupon it was trapped. The republicans claimed that the armoured car actually collided with the car and then veered off. The final lorry safely halted on the road.[69]

The rebels poured 'heavy concentrated fire … into the convoy from many directions'. The fighting reportedly lasted about two hours, during which the soldiers tried to counterattack on the flank, led by the brigade

Figure 6.6 IRA Brigade Commandant's After-Action Report

Kerry No. 2 Brigade
8th March, 1921
To Chief of Staff
A. Chara.

On Monday, 28th February, I sent orders to Commandants of the five battalions in this Brigade that they were to supply five men each to form a flying
column. The men were to mobilize on Sunday, 6th March.

On Wednesday, 2nd March, I received a dispatch from the Commandant,
Rathmore Battalion, asking for permission to get the men appointed from
Castleisland and Firies battalions for the flying column, to aid his men to ambush
two pay lorries on the 3rd instant on the Killarney-Rathmore road in Rathmore
areas. Permission was granted, and our men, reinforced by a section of the North
Cork flying column, laid in ambush for two days, but the lorries failed to turn
up. In the meantime, a dispatch from our Intelligence department in Killarney
arrived, stating that General Strickland, General Cumming, and their Staffs
were in Killarney, and intended to travel to Cork by road, via Rathmore.

As the position our men had taken up became unsafe, they moved into the
Cork area, and took up fresh positions to await arrival of the Generals. On
Saturday, 5th March, at 3 o'clock, that attack took place on the five lorries, one
armoured car and one touring car. The road mines were fired, but failed to
explode, owing to heavy rainfall the previous days. Fire was concentrated on the
touring car, and all the occupants appeared to be wiped out, together with the
occupants of the pilot lorry and rear lorry, as well as some of the enemy, who
endeavoured to outflank our men. Our men retired in good order suffering no
casualties or losses before superior numbers. It is impossible under the circumstances to make an accurate estimate of the enemy casualties.

The flying column mobilized in full strength on the 7th instant, and are now
undergoing a course of training.

(*Signed*) 'Adjutant'

major, C.R. Congreve, DSO, unsuccessfully. Although called upon to surrender, the soldiers continued to resist. The turret machine gunner in the
armoured car was reported by both sides as spraying the surrounding
areas with heavy fire, but the British report stated he only expended 770
rounds – hardly 'heavy' fire for two hours' fighting, especially when he
admitted he could not see the rebel positions. It is likely that the Rolls
Royce armoured car, having slid off the road, was canted to one side and
therefore unable to bring its gun turrets into proper firing position to
engage the IRA positions, even though Lynch claimed that the Vickers
'prevented the IRA from pressing home their advantage to complete victory'.[70] The rebels finally withdrew at around 1600 hours and left the area.

There were no rebel casualties reported by either side, although the
British reports seemed incredulous that this was the case. The IRA
claimed they inflicted heavy casualties (thirteen dead, fifteen wounded),
but the British reported four dead and six wounded. Among the dead
were Col. Cumming and another, unnamed, officer.[71]

The British write-up of this in 'IRA (from Captured Documents)' stated that this ambush was a good example of both sides using intelligence to

determine their actions and decisions. Further, they acknowledged, at least tacitly, that the IRA did better on this occasion. It did not admit, however, the excellence of Moylan's command decisions and preparations, which obviously led to the rebel success, but rather explained it away as 'ill fortune'. This was common for the British forces; they had difficulty admitting that the rebels were capable foes. The narrative went on to criticize the soldiers in the rear lorry, saying that if it had stopped immediately instead of continuing on into the ambush sight, they could have out-flanked the rebel positions. This, of course, does not take into consideration the flank guards placed by Moylan the day before, assuming that the British knew of their presence, which is unclear from their reports. They also noted that the rebels had an affinity for ambushes laid in bends in the road and cited the Ballyvourney Ambush as further evidence.[72]

The *Record of the Rebellion*, of about eighteen months later, generally took the same view as the early British reports; the narratives of the events were almost identical, but in its conclusion it admitted this was one of the 'worst reverses suffered by the army and, making all allowance for the elaborate and undoubtedly skilful preparations made by the rebels', that British forces walked right into it. The authors pointed out that the East Lancs must have let their guard down when they found the original ambush site vacated. Still, they decried the fact that if the armoured car had not been knocked out of action, the results probably would have been different. They fall short, however, in saying what the driver should have done instead;[73] it is hard to imagine that they would have wanted him to run over his brigade commander (who was also the regimental commander of the East Lancs). In this instance, it is difficult to see where the army could have done anything better given the situation, speed of travel and spacing of the vehicles, thus proving again the need for discipline in interval between the vehicles on the move. This ambush was successful despite the failure of the rebel IEDs and Moylan's hasty movement out of the prepared site. The reason for the second bomb failures was never explained, but the most likely cause was damage while being buried at the original site, retrieved there, carried by hand over land and re-emplaced.

Proper placement of the IEDs proved difficult for the inexperienced rebels; little information was available to them on how to conduct ambushes, let alone how to use explosives in conjunction with these attacks. The problem was not just the situating of the weapons themselves; it was also proper concealment, cover for the operator and means of detonation. Much of this depended on the weather. Since cold was a problem for

Figure 6.7 Seán Moylan's Report to Brigade OC

Clonbannin Attack

On receipt of your permission to cooperate with Kerry No. 2, the Brigade Q.M. and myself proceeded to Kerry on Wednesday, 2nd March. The intelligence reports there showed that on the 3rd of each month, two pay lorries of Auxiliaries came from Killarney to Rathmore. It was our intention to ambush these lorries three miles west of Rathmore, at Stagmount.

We selected our position, laid several mines on the road, got our men in position on the hills overlooking the road, got our sections to cover our flanks, and placed signallers.

We remained in position until 6 o'clock on Thursday evening without result, and therefore decided to hang on until Friday. In the evening, intelligence arrived from Killarney that General Strickland would probably travel from there towards Cork on Friday. This news strengthened our desire to remain on until Friday. Our men got into position on Friday morning, and remained there until 12 o'clock, when a scout arrived with the news that our positions and objectives were known to the enemy. After some discussions, we placed a section of riflemen and engineers in charge of the mines and made new dispositions, extending our flanks and forming our front into a narrow shape. By this means we hoped that in the event of an attempt to encircle us to fight an orderly retreat towards the mountains, and in case of a report that the enemy were notified of our positions being unfounded, our men would, on the explosion of the mines, be able to advance into their old positions and engage the enemy. There was, however, no result to our waiting on Friday, and as the fact of our party being in ambush was known to the whole countryside, owing to our being in position for two days in a thickly-populated district, we decided that our position could no longer be held with safety or hope of success.

After some consideration the B.Q.M. and myself came to the conclusion that we would move our men east, and take up a position between Rathmore and Banteer. Our forces now consisted of 30 men of the 4th and 6th Battalions, A.S.S.; 20 men of the 7th Battalion, A.S.S.; and 20 men from Kerry No. 2.

At 10.30 a.m. three Crossley lorries went west, and took no notice of our positions. At 2 o'clock a convoy consisting of three lorries, one touring car, and one armoured car came east. We attacked, but our mines failed to explode owing probably to the knocking about in the journey from Kerry. Our men opened fire on the leading lorry, and stopped it by killing the driver. This lorry contained Black and Tans. The second lorry pulled up, and the touring car and armoured car almost dashed into it. This can be explained only by the fact that the driver of the touring car was hit, and also the driver of the armoured car. The rear lorry came on until stopped by our rifle fire. There must have been a big roll of casualties in this car, as a very effective rifle fire was poured into it from north and west. After a two hours' fight, in which the enemy machine guns searched the whole countryside, and which finally developed into a series of skirmishes over a wide area we retreated in good order, after inflicting heavy casualties on the enemy and without suffering any on our side. I enclose a rough sketch of position (*vide* Map 2). The first and last lorries were about 700 yards apart. We could have done much better had we put the houses on the roadside in such a position that the enemy could not occupy them. Our signallers worked well, and the result impressed on me the necessity of paying particular attention to this department. We also need to train more section leaders. It is difficult to keep in touch with all sections during an extended fight. The leader of one section showed a regrettable lack of initiative. All the men fought well. The Brigade Q.M. proved himself to be an exceptionally fine leader. The result of this scrap has been to raise the moral [sic] of all the men. I am confident we would have made a big capture were it not for the armoured car, but better luck (Strickland) next time.

(*Signed*) Acting Vice-Commandant

most of the high explosives of the time, especially gelignite, one had to be careful with how long one left a mine in the ground. More than a few hours could mean the difference between success and failure under the coldest circumstances. Similarly, the mine had to be waterproof, or at least water resistant. Finally, the means of detonation determined where the mine could be placed and where the operator had to position himself. Electrically detonated mines were not a problem, as long as everything worked properly. Pressure detonation required little after the mine was buried, but flame ignition was problematic and there is little evidence that the IRA ever used this type for an ambush, if for no other reason than that it would have eliminated surprise. Of course, retrieving unexploded mines was even more problematic for the rebels then, as now, due to the somewhat haphazard construction of the bombs and their lack of experience. Still, they could hardly leave them in the ground since, being made of explosives sensitive to moisture and cold, they became even more unstable over time.

Rathcoole Ambush, 15 June 1921

While IEDs were of questionable reliability during the war and one must assume that prudent IRA leaders must always have been concerned about IED failures, there were few attacks where the road mines were crucial, rather than ancillary, to the attack itself. One of the more spectacular uses of mines by the IRA in an ambush occurred during an attack on a rationing party of L Company, ADRIC,[74] on Friday, 16 June 1921 near Rathcoole, Co. Cork, on the road from Millstreet to Banteer. It would appear that the ambush was, in fact, laid around the mines rather than their being mere additions to the attack. Furthermore, this shift in ambush doctrine was in response to the more numerous armoured vehicles in use by both police and military. Lastly, the local ADRIC were forced to use a limited number of routes due to IRA destruction of roads and bridges, thus funnelling the police into the ambush site.[75]

Under the command of Brigade Quartermaster Patrick O'Brien, approximately 130 rebels from elements of the IRA Cork No. 2 Brigade, including their flying column and men from five battalions, ambushed a group of twenty-five Auxiliary cadets who were transporting supplies for their company.[76]

Lynch explains that the Cork No. 2 Brigade leadership had made special efforts during the spring of 1921 to train their men in IED construction and use, bringing in an outside instructor for this purpose. They knew that the ADRIC had to travel on this road to obtain their supplies. The policemen used an armoured convoy several times a week for their supply missions. Lynch claimed that the Crossleys were armoured and had mounted machine guns, the other sources, including witnesses, make no mention of the armour or machine guns. It is difficult to know where the machine guns could have been mounted, but unmounted machine guns could easily be mistaken.[77]

O'Brien broke his group into eight sections and spread seven of them out along the woods on the southern side of the road, while he placed the eighth on the north side at the far western end of the ambush site. The rebels buried six five-to-seven-pound mines in the unpaved road, evenly spaced for about 150 yards; each mine had one section of Volunteer riflemen covering it.[78]

After letting the convoy come through the area several times (they made multiple trips that day), in the hope that the policemen would become lackadaisical, the Volunteers finally engaged the cadets around 1800 hours. The police came in four Crossley Tenders, maintained proper spacing – 300 yards apart – but had no flanking guards. When the convoy came into the ambush site, the rebels waited until the last lorry reached the easternmost mine and then detonated it. The Crossley was disabled, but not destroyed, according to Lynch, because the bomb-makers did not take into account 'the soft, boggy foundation of the road', which absorbed much of the blast. The rebels opened fire on this lorry almost immediately. The dazed cadets tried to dismount, but were unable to due to the withering fire from the Volunteers, even though their Hotchkiss gun jammed after the first burst. The second and third lorries stopped where they were when the first blast went off, but were in between mines and too far from them to be affected, so the nearest rebel sections opened fire on them too.[79]

The first Crossley was speeding west towards the last mine, as well as the eighth section, when it turned around to assist. The rebels held off attacking it until it stopped – on the next to last mine, the Volunteers detonated it. The blast lifted the vehicle up and to one side. Remarkably, the mostly uninjured policemen began to dismount, whereupon the rebels opened fire on them. Lynch said that the ADRIC cadets were able to get their machine gun into action and that this allowed them to hold off the rebels.[80]

At this point, as Abbott has pointed out, the two lorries in the middle were trapped. The men from the second and third lorries attempted to hold the rebels off the fourth; when a group of them rushed towards that lorry, the rebels supposedly set off one of the remaining mines. The Volunteers claimed this killed the ADRIC men as they went to the fourth lorry, but other accounts said the mine damaged the third vehicle. The rebels said that the engagement lasted about an hour and that when they realized the ADRIC machine guns were preventing them from inflicting further casualties, they decided to retire along their pre-planned lines of retreat. The army and police agreed that the IRA would have inflicted great casualties on the convoy, but that they retreated at the chance appearance overhead of an RAF aircraft.[81] Most republican accounts do not mention an aircraft, but this is difficult to account for since, as mentioned earlier, the IRA had disproportionate reactions whenever encountering aircraft in flight. This was due to airplanes' relative novelty at the time and the propaganda about their capabilities from the First World War and the inter-war inter-service rivalries. All aircraft in Ireland were unarmed, but the rebels did not know that, and so retreated quickly. If the machine guns had kept the rebels at bay, the British either did not know about it or discounted the effect.

Although the mines succeeded in halting the convoy, they did not kill large numbers of Auxiliaries probably due to the relative size of the mines; they did not completely destroy the vehicles. This was due to the rebels' still relative inexperience with bomb-making. The republican sources list twelve killed, but Abbott and the official history list two killed and four wounded. Since Abbott could name the two killed,

Figure 6.8 Rolls Royce Armoured Car

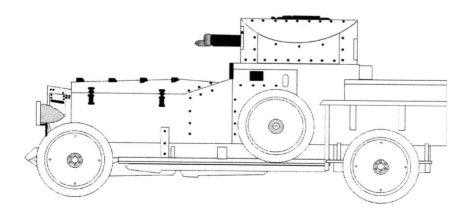

Cadets William A.H. Boyd and Frederick E. Shorter, Abbott's and the British are more likely to be the accurate versions.[82]

That the rebels had sufficient forethought to place the mines in a sequential manner so that they could detonate them individually at will, thus halting and attacking the convoy at certain locations and trapping the other vehicles, demonstrates an increasing sophistication with IRA ambush operations, and especially IED deployment. This placement, with appropriately sized bombs, could have destroyed the entire convoy without firing their small arms at all. Why they did not have more explosives available during this attack probably had more to do with supply, transport and skill than desire. As Lynch said in his write-up of the incident: 'The IRA leaders had brought all the experience at their disposal to bear on this operation'.[83] This appears to be an accurate statement; while not experts, the IRA were learning quickly.

Employment of IRA Improvised Explosive Devices
It would appear, then, that much of the IRA's success and failure in their use of explosives came down to two factors; construction and employment. As noted already, construction was problematic at best. There were two methods of employment for IRA IEDs in Ireland: by hand and by emplacement. For the former, these amounted to hand grenades. The records are unclear about which 'bombs' were factory-made grenades and which were improvised during an engagement. The IRA grenade factories produced products that were easily the equivalent of those manufactured by 'professionals' for the military. Those not manufactured in the factories, or stolen from the British forces, were usually truly improvised with flame ignition. Of course, this made them unstable and of varying power.

The emplaced devices were of three types: anti-personnel, anti-vehicle and breaching. There appear to be few incidences of anti-personnel mines in Ireland during this conflict, although they became all too common in the later 'Troubles' of the 1960s and to the end of the millennium. The incident that comes to mind first with regard to anti-personnel mines was one in which the Cork IRA attacked elements of the 2nd Bn, Hampshire Regiment on their way to a shooting range for marksmanship practice. Headed by members of their band, the rebels attacked the formation with a mine placed in a wall next to the road. As the formation reached the mine, the IRA detonated it and, according to press reports, threw grenades and fired into the column. Seven soldiers died and twenty-one were wounded; the rebels appear to have taken no casualties. Also killed was the driver and horse of the Rev. T. Roche, a Catholic priest on his way to celebrate Mass, who was hit in the foot by a stray bullet.[84] What

Figure 6.9 Excerpt from *Record of the Rebellion*

Hampshire Regiment Band Blown up by a Mine.

A carefully planned attack on the Hampshire Regiment was carried out on the 31st May at Youghal, where a mine in a wall was exploded as they were marching to the range. The full force of the explosion was felt by the band, who had seven killed and 21 wounded. The only sign of the attackers was two men, who were seen running away in the distance, and the wonderful account of the battle written up afterwards by the rebels merely goes to show that they themselves were really ashamed of the tactics which they had been compelled to resort to.

---

is not clear is whether this mine was significantly different in design from the road mines.

The breaching mines were primarily used against RIC barracks' walls during the numerous arms raids against them, the attempts to seize them or attempts to destroy them. These mines were much like the road mines in that they were of varying quality and they had a high failure rate as a result. As with all improvised explosives, the resulting weapon was only as good as its components, the assembler, the person who placed it and the person who fired it.

There were two main reasons for failures: mechanical failure, where the mine failed to detonate; and design failure, where the weapon went off, but was not powerful enough to breach the wall. The causes of mechanical failure occurred anywhere in the construction, assembly or employment phases. These issues of a failure to breach concerned the size of the weapon and the type of explosives. There were any number of reasons why the yield could be insufficient for the task, from strength of the explosives to the construction of the wall; not the least of these was the experience of the people involved.

Although they did not see widespread use for the rest of the war, mines remained an ever-constant threat. In Cork, the IRA converted used shell casings from British shore coastal artillery batteries into IEDs. This is quite reminiscent of the use of unexploded bombs by the Viet Cong and of 105mm howitzer rounds by the insurgents in Iraq as components and casings for IEDs in those conflicts. On Sunday, 10 April 1921, on the Youghal Road at Ballyedikin Cross, North Churchtown, republican sources claim that Volunteers, under Charlie Hurley, detonated a mine made from these shells, killing several soldiers. Likewise, they claimed a similar incident on Sunday, 3 July 1921 at Carrigshane Cross on the same road. After both incidents, rebels claimed there were violent reprisals by British forces.[85]

Mines against movement were not just against roads; there were several bombings of trains in transit in 1921, the worst of which occurred on 24 June when the IRA, using a mine, derailed the train carrying the squadron of the 10th Hussars on its return from Belfast for the state opening of the Northern Ireland Parliament. The resulting crash killed four Hussars and two railway employees, injured about twenty others, while almost eighty horses were killed or put down.[86]

The IRA tried this explosive derailment again in July on the Killaloe–Limerick railway line when, on the 8th, the Royal Welch Fusiliers discovered a mine set to open an ambush on the train. They did not know it was an ambush until such time as the rebels opened fire on the Fusiliers, who had by that time disarmed the bomb; one Fusilier was wounded.

The timing of this campaign using explosives came at the end of the Munition Strike in December 1920, which also was when the army received the last of its armoured vehicles. This, as with regular road mines and breaching charges, coincided with both O'Donovan's development of 'war flower' and the renewed, and increased, smuggling of explosives from the IRA Scottish Brigade, primarily in Glasgow, via the IRA Liverpool Battalion. These types of attacks were useful only for a limited time because these weapons were responses to the increased use of motor vehicles in general, as well as the increase in the number of armoured vehicles in convoys specifically.

As the British army learned to go 'cross-country' as part of their developing higher-level counterinsurgency doctrine in Ireland, the importance of mines lessened, although their use continued. This is not to say that the British halted convoy operations; they could not. The army's growing sophistication in counterinsurgency doctrine required them to use all modes of travel in support of their operations. This enabled them to advance on multiple axes of advance, as at Crossbarry or Kishkeam (see Chapter 8) in 1921.

NOTES

1. General Staff, Irish Command, *Record of the Rebellion*, vol. IV, p.209 (NA PRO WO 141/93).
2. The common modern military (both UK and US) term 'roadside' does not mean to imply that all of these devices were literally sitting by the side of the road, but that they were in, on, under or next to the road.
3. See War Diaries in general (NA PRO WO 35/90–3). It is important to note that these records are not exhaustive and also over-represent the Dublin District.
4. These latter were commercial devices using flint and steel sparks to ignite the fuses in a manner similar to a Zippo lighter.

5. Fitzgerald was mistreated in his captivity by Const. Edward Bolger; see Hart, *The IRA and its Enemies*), pp.70–1.
6. Deasy, *Towards Ireland Free*, p.155; Barry, *Guerilla Days*, p.28; C. Crowley, 'West Cork Column Taught the Essex a Lesson at Toureen', *Rebel Cork's Fighting Story* (1947), pp.102–3. No further mention of these men is made in the usual sources, so it appears that they survived the war.
7. Deasy, *Towards Ireland Free*, pp.155–6; Barry, *Guerilla Days*, pp.28–9; and Ryan, *Tom Barry*, pp.40–1.
8. Some sources note Dickinson as a captain or temporary captain.
9. General Staff, Irish Command, *Record of the Rebellion*, p.164 (NA PRO WO 141/93); Deasy, *Towards Ireland Free*, pp.155–6; Barry, *Guerilla Days*, pp.28–9; Ryan, *Tom Barry*, pp.40–1; and Crowley, 'West Cork Column', p.103.
10. General Staff, Irish Command, *Record of the Rebellion*, p.164 (NA PRO WO 141/93); Deasy, *Towards Ireland Free*, pp.155–6; Barry, *Guerilla Days*, pp.28–9; and Ryan, *Tom Barry*, pp.40–1.
11. General Staff, Irish Command, *Record of the Rebellion*, p.164 (NA PRO WO 141/93); Barry, *Guerilla Days*, p.30.
12. See 'Fifth Infantry Division Standing Orders for Armed Parties Moving by Lorry, and for Lorry Convoys', 20 June 1921.
13. Barry, *Guerilla Days*, p.75.
14. Crowley, 'West Cork Column', p.103.
15. Abbott, *Police Casualties*, p.164 and General Staff, Irish Command, *Record of the Rebellion*, p.211 (NA PRO WO 141/93). The official history records one death and twelve wounded, but Abbott has only eleven wounded.
16. See G. White and B. O'Shea, *The Burning of Cork* (2006).
17. R. Bennett, *The Black and Tans: The British Special Police in Ireland* (2002), pp.141–3.
18. Dublin District Memorandum No. S/124/G., 19 July 1920 (WO 35/90/1/35).
19. 'Report on the Situation in Ireland by the General Officer Commanding-in-Chief', 4 December 1920 (NA PRO CAB 27/108/310–11 SIC 61); see also 'Mechanical Transport, Armoured Cars and other forms of Protection for Troops in Ireland', 7 December 1920 (PRO WO 32/9541) 2; QMG to Secretary of State for War, 26 October 1920 (WO 32/9540); and T. Jones, *Whitehall Diary, Vol. III* (1971), 1 December 1920, p.43.
20. General Staff, Irish Command, *Record of the Rebellion*, Vol. IV, p.50 (NA PRO WO 141/93).
21. Ibid., p.236.
22. D. Begley, *The Road to Crossbarry* (1999), p.81.
23. Dublin Brigade Memorandum No. S/26/G. MT, 30 August 1920 (NA PRO WO 35/90).
24. Mark Sturgis to Assistant Treasury Secretary, 4 January 1921, Min. No. 20142/20; A.P. Waterfield to Under Secretary, Dublin Castle, 14 February 1921, Min. No. T.I.45/21 (NA PRO T 192/41); and 'Protection of Military Touring Cars', Dublin District Memorandum No. S/G.1.A., 3 February 1921 (WO 35/90, pp.1–2).
25. 'Protection of Military Touring Cars', Dublin District Memorandum No. S/G.1.A., 5 February 1921 (NA PRO WO 35/90).
26. Mark Sturgis to Assistant Treasury Secretary, 4 January 1921, Min. No. 20142/20; A.P. Waterfield to Under Secretary, Dublin Castle, 14 February 1921, Min. No. T.I.45/21 (NA PRO T 192/41) and L.H. Officer, *Five Ways to Compute the Relative Value of a UK Pound Amount, 1830–2006* (2008).
27. Statement of Cmdt L. Haugh, Collins Collection (MA A/0181, p.15).
28. One should keep in mind that most career army officers at the time regarded guerrilla warfare with contempt. The Second World War did much to change this view, but special operations forces did not really gain acceptance even in the U.S. military until well after the Vietnam Conflict (1961–75).
29. Railway Situation Reports (PRO CO 904/157). These ranged from May 1920 to July 1921 and covered only railways and bridges; they did not normally report on roads and road bridges.
30. RIC IG Report for King's County for May 1921 (PRO CO 904/115); K. Jeffery, *The British Army and the Crisis of Empire, 1918–22* (1984), pp.88–90; and Statement of Captain E. Gerrard (MA WS/348). For information on Royal Engineers in the war, see General Staff, Irish Command, *Record of the Rebellion*, Vol. IV, Appendix VII, p.226 (NA PRO WO 141/93).
31. See RIC IG Monthly Confidential Report for February 1921 for Co. Longford (NA PRO CO 904/114).
32. 'Mechanical Transport, Armoured Cars and other forms of Protection for Troops in Ireland', 7 December 1920 (NA PRO WO 32/9541); Dublin District Memorandum No. S/124/G., 19 July

1920 (WO 35/90/1/35); 'Operations Summary, Dec 1920' General Staff, Dublin District, 'O' Branch, (WO 35/90/1, p.7), 2 January 1921; Jeudwine, 'Report on the Situation in Ireland', 7 December 1920 (WO 32/9534); 'Operations Summary, Dec 1920' General Staff, Dublin District, 'O' Branch, 1 February 1921 (WO 35/90); General Staff, Irish Command, *Record of the Rebellion*, Vol. I, pp.32, 37 and Vol. IV, pp.69 and 236 (NA PRO WO 141/93).

33. The British feared the possibility of such weapons being used; see 'Protection of Transport', Dublin District to ADS&T, GHQ, Ireland, Memorandum No. S/847/G, 12 May 1921 (NA PRO WO 35/90/2).

34. See IRA Engineering Circulars No. 5 'Electrically Exploded Mines' and No. 7 'Protection of Mines from Damp', both dated April 1921; and Dublin District Weekly Intelligence Summary, No. 103, for week ending 27 February 1921 (NA PRO WO 35/90, p.6). Worse, frozen gelignite was unstable after thawing.

35. See for instance, Appendix A, 'Hostile Acts or Outrages', 5th Division War Diary for December 1920, 30 November 1920 (NA PRO WO 35/93A, p.1) and Appendix IX, '5th Divisional Intelligence Summary', Memorandum No. B.868/67.G., 18 December 1920 (WO 35/93A).

36. Statement of James L. O'Donovan (MA WS/1713); and C.D. Greaves, *Liam Mellows and the Irish Revolution* (1971), p.228.

37. Sometimes this is mistakenly rendered 'Wall Flower'. O'Donovan used the term 'War Flour' in his typed 13 December 1957 witness statement to the Irish Bureau of Military History.

38. Statement of James L. O'Donovan (MA WS/1713).

39. Kerry No. 2 to Collins, Collins Papers, (MA A/0507); Collins to O'Daly 21 December 1920, 17 February 1921, 4 March 1921 and O'Daly to Collins 11 January 1921, 17 January 1921 and 26 May 1921, Mulcahy Papers (UCD AD P7/A/3, P7/A/4, and P7/A/5) and Cardiff Papers (UCD AD P113/6–7). For more in-depth examination of IRA arms smuggling, see Kautt, 'Logistics and Counter-Insurgency', PhD thesis, University of Ulster at Jordanstown, 2005.

40. Mulcahy Papers (UCD AD P7/A/2 and P7/A/3).

41. Plunkett Statement (NLI MS 11981), pp.23–8; Statement of Joseph V. Lawless (MA WS/1043); and Director of Munitions to Minister of Defence, July 1921 (MA A/0606); Operation Summary for December 1920, General Staff, Dublin District, 'O' Branch, 2 January 1921 (NA PRO WO 35/190/1, p.4); Weekly Intelligence Summary, Dublin District, for week ending 13 December 1920, p.2 and for 20 December 1920, p.1 (WO 35/90).

42. *Dublin Brigade Review* (Dublin: Cahill, 1939), pp.40–1 and 'Sinn Fein and the Irish Volunteers', undated [probably 1920] (PRO WO 141/40).

43. Extract of Statement by Mr Michael Lynch, Superintendent of the Dublin Abattoir, 2 November 1935, Collins Papers, (MA A/0271/6); Statement of Daithi O'Brien, O'Malley Papers (UCD AD PR/6/40). The Volunteers at Rushbrooke Dockyard, Co. Cork had a similar operation established where they cast metal bomb cases in sand moulds in the yard. See Statement of Séamus Fitzgerald (MA WS/1737).

44. Kerry No.2 to Collins, undated, 1920, Collins Papers (MA A/0495/I).

45. Kerry No.2 to Collins, undated, 1920 and Mid-Tipperary Brigade to Collins, undated, May 1920, Collins Papers (MA A/0495/1 and A/0507/6) and Vise to Collins, 27 September 1919 (UCD P7/A/11).

46. See War Diaries, Irish Command, in general (NA PRO WO 35/90–3).

47. Bidwell and Graham, *Fire-Power*, p.125.

48. He also was unable to purchase mortar tubes or ammunition; see Collins to O'Daly, 21 December 1920 and 20 May 1921; O'Daly to Collins, 2 January 1921; Collins to Vise, 26 May 1920 and 9 April 1920; Mulcahy Papers (UCD AD P7/A/3, P7/A/5 and P7/A/11); Plunkett Statement (NLI MS 11981), pp.23–4; and Greaves, *Liam Mellows*, p.221.

49. RIC IG Report for February 1921 for Co. Longford (NA PRO CO 904/114) and General Staff, Irish Command, *Record of the Rebellion*, Vol. IV, p.50.

50. It is important to remember that the IRA did not want to escalate the conflict and so kept a steady and constant pressure on their true target, British governance.

51. Information drawn from RIC Inspector-General Monthly Confidential Report for January 1921 (NA PRO CO 904/114) and Abbott, *Police Casualties*, pp.179–91.

52. The IRA regularly raided post offices and postmen for money in the mail and for intelligence.

53. The Ulster Special Constabulary was formed to maintain greater security in the north in order to free army units to serve in the south. Since they were loyalists and unionists the 'Specials' were a problem and so did not free any army units. Their reputation was one of extreme anti-Catholic and anti-nationalist violence until they were disbanded in 1970.

54. RIC IG Report for Co. Longford for February 1921 (PRO CO 904/114); General Staff, Irish Command, *Record of the Rebellion*, Vol. IV, p.50 (NA PRO WO 141/93); and Abbott, *Police Casualties*, p.193.

55. RIC IG Report for Co. Longford for February 1921 (PRO CO 904/114); General Staff, Irish Command, *Record of the Rebellion*, Vol. IV, p.50 (NA PRO WO 141/93); and Abbott, *Police Casualties*, p.193.

56. RIC IG Report for Co. Longford for February 1921 and General Staff, Irish Command, *Record of the Rebellion*, Vol. IV, p.51 (NA PRO WO 141/93).

57. Department of State, 'Convention with Respect to the Laws and Customs of War on Land'; 29 July 1899, TIAS no. 8407, *United State Treaties and Other International Agreements*, vol. 1. 'Annex to the Convention: Regulation Respecting the Laws and Customs of War on Land and Department of State, Convention with Respect to the Laws and Customs of War on Land'; 18 October 1907, TIAS no. 8407, *United State Treaties and Other International Agreements*, vol. 1.

58. See Barry, *Guerilla Days*, p.122 and General Staff, Irish Command, *Record of the Rebellion*, Vol. III, '*Law*' (NA PRO WO 141/93).

59. RIC IG Report for Co. Longford for February 1921 and Abbott, *Police Casualties*, 194.

60. In addition to Houghton and Craven being killed-in-action, Cadets George Bush and Harold Clayton, DSM, died later of their wounds; see Appendix A.

61. General Staff, Irish Command, *Record of the Rebellion*, Vol. IV, p.51 (NA PRO WO 141/93).

62. See Abbott, *Police Casualties*, p.194, Mrs McGrath's letter sited on pp.181–2. Strangely, in his witness statement, Moylan mentioned that he was sentenced to fifteen years' imprisonment (*In His Own Words*, p.136).

63. The ADRIC was noted for carelessness with both alcohol and firearms; indeed they had the most accidental self-inflicted wounds of any organization on either side in the war. Leeson notes: 'Thirty-five police were accidentally or mistakenly shot and killed in the Irish War of Independence; five of these victims accidentally shot and killed themselves.' In the army, there were 159 accidental shootings in 1921: 95 were in Ireland (the highest); the second highest was Mesopotamia at 16. This was out of a total strength of 258,000 soldiers worldwide, with 58,000 in Ireland. The ADRIC never numbered more than 3,000. See D. Leeson, 'Death in the Afternoon: The Croke Park Massacre, 21 November 1920', *Canadian Journal of History* (April 2003), pp.43–68. Leeson also cites Abbott, *Police Casualties*, pp.315–20 and 'Precautions in the use of fire arms', RIC circular D.642/1921, 7 July 1921 (NA PRO HO 184/127) and RAMC Annual Medical Returns for 1921 (NA PRO WO 115/1–2).

64. RIC IG Reports for May and June 1921 for Co. Cork (PRO CO 904/115); and General Staff, Irish Command, *Record of the Rebellion*, Vol. IV, pp.194 and 50–1. The veracity of British reports of women participating in actual combat operations of is less than clear; for more on the desire of women in the republican movement to participate actively under arms, see Bennett, *Black and Tans*, p.208 and M. Ward, *Unmanageable Revolutionaries: Women and Irish Nationalism* (1995) generally and S. McCoole and M. Ward, *No Ordinary Women: Irish Female Activists in the Revolutionary Years, 1900–1923* (2003), p.82.

65. The Irish Command order of battle varied throughout, the major formations being the 5th and 6th Infantry Divisions and the Dublin District. The divisions had several brigades, some of which were almost independent at various periods. By 1921, the Galway Brigade's elements were reorganized under provisional infantry brigades and the Belfast Brigade became the 1st Infantry Division, while, late in 1921, the Dublin District gained a second brigade (provisional).

66. 'War Diary of General Staff, GHQ Ireland', p.1, 5 March 1921 (NA PRO WO 35/93A); *Record of the Rebellion*, Vol. IV, pp.179–82 (NA PRO WO 141/93); 'The IRA (from Captured Documents Only)', pp.33–5 (PRO WO 141/40); Moylan, *In his own words*, p.104; and Statement of Con Meaney (MA WSS/787), Statement of William Reardon (Billings) (WSS/1185), Statement of James (Jimmy) Hickey (WSS/1218), Statement of Humphrey O'Donoghue (WSS/1351), pp.40–1, Statement of Matthew (Matty) Kelleher (WSS/ 1319), p.46, Statement of Dan Coakley (WSS/1406), pp.51–2, and Statement of Matthew (Matty) Murphy (WSS/1375), p.57, in *The 'Boys' of the Millstreet Battalion Area: Some personal accounts of the War of Independence* (Cork: Aubane Historical Society, 2003), pp.18, 25 and 31.

67. Moylan, *In his own words*, p.104; Moylan, 'Clonbannin Attack' Report, nd, contained in *Record of the Rebellion*, Vol. IV., pp.181–2; and Lynch, 'First British General to take Civilian Hostages on his Lorries Killed in Action at Clonbanin', *Rebel Cork's Fighting Story*, pp.149–50.

68. Lynch, 'First British General', pp.152–3 and Moylan, *In his own words*, p.106.

69. General Staff, Irish Command, *Record of the Rebellion*, Vol. IV, pp.179–80 (NA PRO WO 141/93)

and Lynch, 'First British General', p.154. There were, in fact, no ADRIC in the convoy as claimed by Moylan.

70. 'The IRA (from Captured Documents Only)', p.33; Lynch, 'First British General', p.154; Moylan, *In his own words*, p.106; Statement of Con Meaney (MA WSS/787), p.18; Statement of William Reardon (Billings) (WSS/1185), p.25; Statement of James (Jimmy) Hickey (WSS/1218), p.32; Statement of Humphrey O'Donoghue (WSS/1351), pp.40–1; Matthew (Matty) Kelleher (WSS/ 1319), p.46; Statement of Dan Coakley (WSS/1406), pp.51–2; Statement of Matthew (Matty) Murphy (WSS/1375), p.57. Moylan incorrectly identified the Vickers as a Maxim; in his defence, the weapons were similar; Meaney correctly identified the gun in his statement.

71. General Staff, Irish Command, *Record of the Rebellion*, Vol. IV, pp.179–82 (NA PRO WO 141/93); 'The IRA (from Captured Documents Only)', pp.33–5; and Lynch, 'First British General', p.155.

72. 'The IRA (from Captured Documents Only)', pp.34–5 (NA PRO WO 141/40).

73. General Staff, Irish Command, *Record of the Rebellion*, Vol. IV, p.182 (NA PRO WO 141/93).

74. Abbott identified the ADRIC Company as C (pp.256–7, but the *Record of the Rebellion* lists it as L (p.203). These sources also differed on the date – the former used 16 June, while the latter used 15 June.

75. Lynch, 'Lorry-Borne Auxiliaries Hit Hard by North Cork Men at Rathcoole', *Rebel Cork's Fighting Story*, pp.172–5; Statement of Con Meaney (MA WSS/787), pp.1–20; Statement of William Reardon (Billings) (WSS/1185), p.25; Statement of James (Jimmy) Hickey (WSS/1218), p.32; Statement of Cornelius (Neily) Barrett (WSS/1405), p.36; Statement of Matthew (Matty) Kelleher (WSS/ 1319), p.46; Statement of Dan Coakley (WSS/1406), p.52; and Statement of Matthew (Matty) Murphy (WSS/1375), pp.58–9.

76. Lynch, 'Lorry-Borne Auxiliaries', pp.173–4. Abbott lists the battalions as: Charleville, Kanturk, Mallow, Millstreet and Newmarket, *Police Casualties*, p.256, while Meaney stated that his Millstreet Battalion used companies B through J in the attack and that ' 'B', 'C', 'D', 'G', 'H', 'I', and 'J' Companies supplied the 76 men for the barricades' (Statement of Con Meaney [MA WSS/787], p.20).

77. Lynch, 'Lorry-Borne Auxiliaries', p.173; Statement of Con Meaney (MA WSS/787), p.20; Statement of William Reardon (Billings) (WSS/1185), p.25; Statement of James (Jimmy) Hickey (WSS/1218), p.32; Statement of Cornelius (Neily) Barrett (WSS/1405), p.36; Statement of Matthew (Matty) Kelleher (WSS/ 1319), p.46; Statement of Dan Coakley (WSS/1406), p.52; and Statement of Matthew (Matty) Murphy (WSS/1375), pp.58–9.

78. Statement of Con Meaney (MA WSS/787), p.20; Statement of William Reardon (Billings) (WSS/1185), p.25; Statement of James (Jimmy) Hickey (WSS/1218), p.32; Statement of Cornelius (Neily) Barrett (WSS/1405), p.36; Statement of Matthew (Matty) Kelleher (WSS/ 1319), p.46; Statement of Dan Coakley (WSS/1406), p.52; and Statement of Matthew (Matty) Murphy (WSS/1375), pp.58–9; Lynch, 'Lorry-Borne Auxiliaries', pp.173–6; Abbott, *Police Casualties*, p.256; and General Staff, Irish Command, *Record of the Rebellion*, Vol. IV, p.203 (NA PRO WO 141/93).

79. Lynch, 'Lorry-Borne Auxiliaries', p.177; Abbott, *Police Casualties*, p.256; and General Staff, Irish Command, *Record of the Rebellion*, Vol. IV, p.203 (NA PRO WO 141/93).

80. Lynch, 'Lorry-Borne Auxiliaries', pp.176–7.

81. Ibid., p.177; Abbott, *Police Casualties*, p.256; and General Staff, Irish Command, *Record of the Rebellion*, Vol. IV, p.203 (NA PRO WO 141/93).

82. Lynch, 'Lorry-Borne Auxiliaries', p.177; Abbott, *Police Casualties*, pp.256–7 and General Staff, Irish Command, *Record of the Rebellion*, Vol. IV, p.203 (NA PRO WO 141/93); see also M.A. Hopkinson, *The Irish War of Independence* (2002), p.113; and '300 Sinn Féiners in Ambush', *New York Times*, 17 June 1921.

83. Lynch, 'Lorry-Borne Auxiliaries', p.176.

84. General Staff, Irish Command, *Record of the Rebellion*, Vol. IV., p.194 (NA PRO WO 141/93); and Hopkinson, *Irish War of Independence*, p.113. The use of bombs continued to the end of the war, a patrol of the Cameronian Highlanders tripped a mine at Midleton on 3 July 1921, with one man seriously wounded.

85. General Staff, HQ, Irish Command, War Diary, 3 July 1921 (PRO WO 35/93/p.1); Pádraig Ó Ciosáin, 'East Cork roads mined', *Rebel Cork's Fighting Story*, pp.195–6. See also 1st Cork Brigade Timeline (http://homepage.eircom.net/~corkcounty/Timeline/First%20Brigade.htm).

86. General Staff, Irish Command, *Record of the Rebellion*, Vol. I, pp.43 and 61 (NA PRO WO 141/93); General Staff, HQ, Irish Command, War Diary, 24 June 1921 (WO 35/93/p.4).

Seven

IRA Urban Operations

Up to this section, the focus has been on attacks in the countryside, but IRA ambush operations were not just rural affairs; they conducted frequent attacks in Dublin, Belfast, Cork and other major towns throughout the country. There are, however, few examples of *deliberate* and large-scale IRA ambushes within cities, as shall be seen, but Dublin, especially, provided some telling ones. That said, there were so many smaller attacks in Dublin that British troops pointedly referred to Aungier Street as the 'Dardanelles'.[1] These actions were remarkable for their rarity, but demonstrated the difficulties of conducting operations within city limits for both sides. That said, it should be mentioned that most IRA offensive operations within cities and towns were rarely anything that could be considered 'combat'; they consisted of intelligence and arms gathering, intimidation of civilians, transportation activities (especially once they had the information or munitions) and assassinations. It is important to understand, for instance, that of the police casualties that occurred in cities and large towns during the conflict – eighty-seven killed and twenty-seven wounded – thirty-nine (44.8 per cent) were killed and eight (29.6 per cent) wounded in random attacks or as what could be termed 'targets of opportunity'. Further, only the attack at Dillon's Cross (Saturday, 11 December 1920) and the fight at Parnell Bridge (Tuesday, 4 January 1921) – both in Cork City, with the former killing one and wounding nine and the latter killing two and wounding nine, along with five civilians also wounded – were anything approaching what could be called a real battle. Yet of those eighty-seven killed and twenty-seven wounded, twenty-three (26 per cent) were assassinated, while four survived attempts. The republican legend talks about large operations and their 'glorious' battles, but in the cities, fully one-fourth were single actions of chance or designed with multiple attackers striking a lone or small group target of three or fewer. Of those (twenty-three men) assassinated, eleven died and two were wounded under circumstances where they had no realistic chances of defending themselves;

essentially, they were executed. This was not 'war', but was the reality on the streets of the cities and towns of Ireland during this period.[2] It is also important to note that the author has deliberately left out any discussion of the propriety of these types of actions, as this is irrelevant and outside the scope of this study.

Offensive or violent IRA activities in cities and towns came in three basic forms: ambushes, assassinations and patrolling. Ambushes and deliberate assassinations[3] shared a common specificity; the former were rebels lying in wait for a known group, while the latter targeted a specific person. Both targeted or used known routes and also shared a generally known time frame, since they usually knew when they expected their target to be in a given area. Although assassinations of individuals were fairly common in cities, deliberate ambushes of groups in urban areas were rather rare. It was in the preparation for these attacks that the famed rebel intelligence system under Michael Collins demonstrated its exceptional capabilities, since rebels surveilled each target until they knew the routines. Without this information, rebel operations would have been significantly less effective.

Another, more common, IRA activity in cities, mostly Dublin, was 'patrolling', or an armed offensive movement by a large group, up to thirty or forty rebels, in accord with a defined area, usually a district or several city blocks, frequently within the assigned IRA battalion areas. In contrast to specified ambushes or assassinations, these patrols engaged unknown or unspecified military or police targets although they generally knew the patrol and other movement patterns of the enemy within their areas. They attacked targets of opportunity: individuals or small groups. It was in this category that most urban attacks by large groups of rebels fell, even when their tactics appeared to be similar to those of ambushes. Of course, it was also possible for these patrols to kill specific individuals whenever they encountered them. What differentiated these operations was not that they engaged and killed their enemies, but that they had no definite prearranged plans to kill specific individuals before setting out. Rather, they went out in the hope of simply 'engaging' the enemy. The major difference between a patrol ambush such as that on Great Brunswick Street (see below) and the deliberate killing of Assistant Commissioner William Redmond, DMP, in January 1920 (both in Dublin) was that the killers specifically targeted Redmond, whereas they did not know the two police victims, Cadet Beard or Constable O'Farrell, who died on Brunswick Street, nor did this matter. It is important to note that this type of operation was only possible in an urban environment, since such an action in rural areas could have been suicidal. In a city or town, the rebels, being local inhabitants, had the advantages of looking like everyone else in normal crowds and knowing the urban terrain itself. Rural operations needed to be mostly deliberate attacks, or at least 'more deliberate', due partly to the expansive rural areas. Rebel units in urban areas were usually weaker in number in proportion to the local population and also had to deal with the compact nature of the terrain. Further, the rebels deliberately used their civilian appearance for cover; looking like everyone else allowed them to approach with less risk to themselves. Knowing the terrain could mean the difference between life and death if things went wrong, a line of retreat was both necessary and available. At the same time, the urban environment also meant that they could not carry rifles because they had to look like everyone else, as well as move unhindered to their rallying points. Of course, this also limited their firepower and thus both their flexibility and capabilities.

Cities were dangerous places and there were sixty-eight separate attacks in urban environments that produced police[4] casualties between 1919 and 1922. The records for army attacks are primarily the war diaries of the Irish Command; these listed about 130 ambushes within Dublin.[5] Not surprisingly, Dublin was the centre of police assassinations (both RIC and DMP), having some 61 per cent of pre-planned IRA killings. This amount was probably higher, but it is difficult to determine directly. Further, it is important to note that the nine DMP men killed or wounded between 20 July 1919 and 20 April 1920 were almost exclusively the only deliberate urban police casualties for that nine-month period; the exception was Constable Joseph Murtagh, RIC, at Pope's Quay in Cork City on 19 March 1920.[6] The reason for Murtagh's death is unknown; he was killed on his way home from a funeral of another constable who was killed in action. This was probably simple opportunity. It is also interesting that 90 per cent of the total police casualties in the city of Dublin were among the unarmed DMP. The most likely reason for this was that these DMP casualties were primarily among their intelligence gathering G Division. Thus, they were a threat to the IRA, and while not directly violent, were no less 'military'.

While Dublin was the centre of police assassinations, in terms of violence against the police, Belfast was more dangerous than elsewhere, but violence against the police there was also more random (75 per cent) and this continued after the war.[7] Also of note was the sectarian nature of much of the violence in Belfast; most of the RIC rank and file in the north were Gaelic Catholics and so may have been part of the targeted social group.[8] While a policeman was more likely to be attacked in

Belfast, Dublin had more fatalities; 94 per cent of Dublin's police casualties died, but a still high 81 per cent of Belfast's casualties were killed outright. Most of the wounded policemen in Dublin later died of their wounds. Although the majority of the urban police casualties were attacked while they were in transit, only 15 per cent of these were in preplanned ambushes; 62 per cent were wounded. This suggests that the deliberately planned ambushes were deadlier than those of opportunity. Interestingly, three constables were killed by gunfire in Belfast while actually riding or sitting in Lancia Armoured Cars, where they, ironically, were sitting for safety. Assassinations aside, it was the relatively random IRA patrol actions that made the difference for most police urban casualties; they constituted 75 per cent of the total in the war.

Figure 7.1 Dublin, ca. 1920

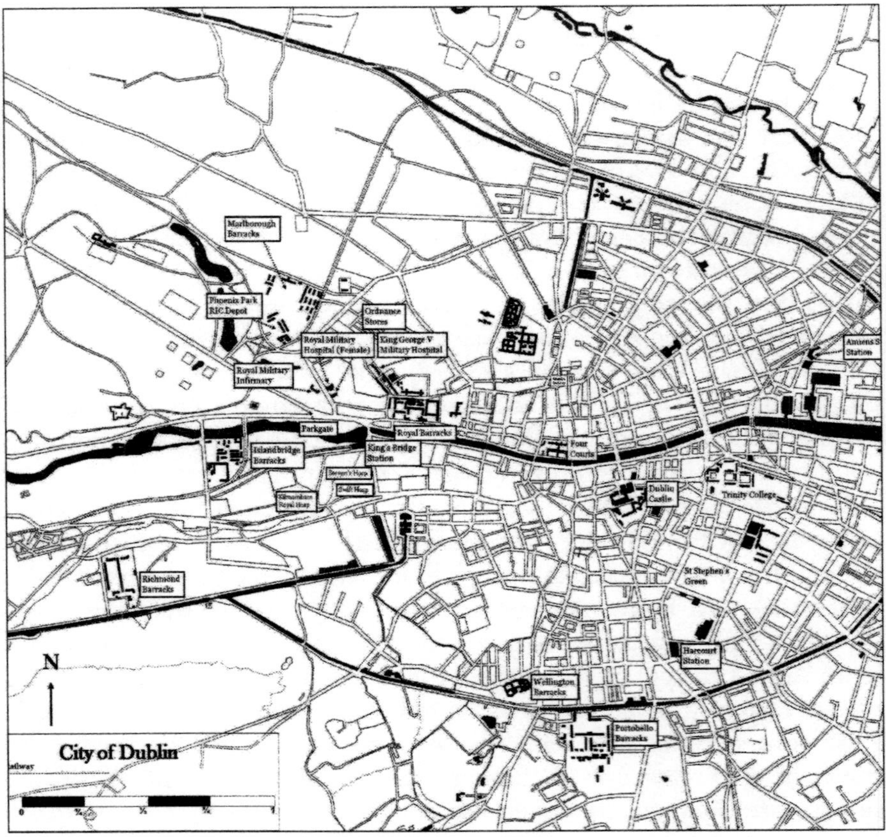

Another characteristic of IRA urban operations in general was the compression of both time and space. Where rural ambushes might have lasted for hours, or patrolling for days or weeks, in the cities this was simply not possible; they could last for no more than a couple of hours at the most. The availability of aid for police or military, along with the obvious closeness of the area, the compression of time and space, seem also to have increased the ferocity of these attacks. Another problem was that rebel attacks in cities were usually with handguns and bombs; the shooter or bomber could approach in a crowd and rejoin it after attacking, so the convoys were more vulnerable in crowds. Crowds in Dublin, even today, are difficult to avoid; literally anyone could have closed in with a pistol or bomb.[9] The IRA preferred pistols for their concealability in urban environments because at the time, the recently developed submachine guns such as the German Bergman MP-18 and the American Thompson 'Tommy gun' were very difficult to acquire, and so they saw only limited use in the war.[10] These weapons, especially handguns, necessarily closed the maximum range of the attacks. Thus, it would appear that the closer the proximity, the more intense or ferocious the fighting became.

Movement through the City of Dublin was dangerous for British forces; one of the earliest references to the concepts of modern force protection came from the Dublin District during the conflict. The Irish Command's Dublin District, recounting its wartime experiences in the official history, mentioned the movement of fourteen battalions through their brigade area of responsibility and that the 'protection of these [mostly combat] troops, devolved whilst in the district to the Dublin District Headquarters'. This small paragraph mentioned the means implemented in the city 'for the protection of these troops during their final move through it, now by march route' by sending out patrols, establishing guard posts and placing snipers on the line of march, measures similar to today. They claimed success, taking only two casualties during the movement of the battalion-sized units in a two-month period, although it is unclear how the two men were injured since there is no mention of enemy action and the Irish Command medical reports did not specify dates or locations.[11] This concept, that combat troops needed protection from enemy forces that they could not provide for themselves, or should not defend themselves due to a possible reduction in combat capability, was rather new. Another reason for not wanting combat troops to undertake their own defence is that they did not know or understand the local conditions and might have succumbed to overreaction or some other inappropriate response.

Probably the most obvious measure for British forces in the city was awareness that they were likely to be attacked. As late as October 1920, the Dublin District had to warn their troops that they were likely to experience 'resistance', be it random shooting or actual sniping.[12] This, specifically, was in regard to patrols and raids. In this case, the warning was not as obvious as such a warning would be to other formations of troops, because a patrol or actual raiding party carried more troops than, say, a supply convoy and was more likely to have an armoured vehicle with machine guns.

There was more to this warning in that, by issuing it, the army was acknowledging an increased threat from the IRA. They recognized that the rebels were not merely attacking less dangerous supply convoys, but that they were willing to engage offensive-capable groups. This also suggested that IRA arms were more ubiquitous than previously identified and that the rebels were more inclined to use them. This warning was, indeed, accurate; through the remaining nine months of the conflict, attacks on British forces within the City of Dublin (as well as the rural areas of the county) increased, in some cases to a daily occurrence.[13]

It is telling that five months earlier, in May 1920, Dublin District issued a list of twelve 'Bad Areas' in the city in terms of high levels of rebel activity or danger:

Inchicore District	Portobello Bridge & District
Fairview & District	Harrington St & District
North Wall & Amiens St District	Aungier St & District
Glasnevin District	Black Pits & District
All turnings off Upper Sackville St	Blessington St & District
Parnell St & Capel St & side turnings	North King St & District

Considering the scope and scale of this list, one wonders how much of the city was left to be considered 'good' or 'moderate'.[14]

The basic vulnerability for British forces came from the reality that they still had to move about in and around the city in order to function on a day-to-day basis. In October 1920 the army established requirements that each battalion have a platoon always on alert to perform escort duty within fifteen minutes' notice. The battalions would rotate through primary responsibility during the month and have two 'lorries and one Armoured Car' fuelled, armed and ready to move.[15] This, of course, meant that these three vehicles were unavailable for other duties, such as obtaining supplies, which, in turn, meant that the army in cities required more vehicles since protection/escort duty decreased the amount of space or total number of vehicles available for transporting supplies due to the necessity of protective forces.

At the same time, however, the British army also recognized that being attacked in such a manner provided an opportunity to engage the rebels. In the same memorandum that warned them of attack, the district also mentioned that troops should be trained to draw the rebels in or to fix their attacker by use of an armoured vehicle once the rebels engaged in force.[16] At the same time, there was no mention of attempting to cut off rebel lines of retreat; perhaps they did not recognise that the IRA was sophisticated enough to have pre-set lines of retreat.

Obviously, maintaining the standard 200 yards between vehicles and perhaps placing advance, flank and rear guards was not possible in the crowded streets of Dublin, but there were other measures they could take to make their convoys safer from rebel attack. First and foremost was using armoured vehicles. As with their rural operations, the armoured cars made mistakes less costly (or more 'recoverable') and gave the soldiers and policemen time to exit the vehicles to take action. Further, the firepower that an armoured car could bring to the fight made a difference, especially in the city where the security forces already outgunned the rebels due to the latter's reliance on handguns. Dual-mounted .303 (Vickers or Hotchkiss) machine guns added an element with which the IRA usually did not want to deal, because if the rebels did not take out the machine guns in the first attack, they would have had to retreat, likely without achieving their objective.[17] Still, opening fire in a crowded area with rifles, let alone machine guns, was never a preferred option for the military or police, especially since harming innocent bystanders could only help republican propaganda. Contrary to republican legend, the British forces rarely lost control or opened fire wantonly during actual operations. Such outbreaks usually occurred later.[18]

The vehicles could also be a hindrance in urban operations in that they did not permit proper pursuit, if permitted by the convoy's mission. If the rebels fired from cover, they also had an almost built-in line of retreat that permitted a man on foot to disappear quickly. There were (and are) many areas within urban districts in Ireland impassable to large motor vehicles. There was also the threat of people in the upper floors of buildings dropping bombs into the open backs of vehicles.[19] One need not be on top of a building or in an upper storey to lob a bomb into the back of an open lorry, and so the army covered most of their lorries with wire mesh, as mentioned earlier, against the threat.[20] So part of the answer lay in not allowing crowds to come close or approach the vehicles.[21] Of course, this was not a good solution, but it was better than nothing. Most of the army's Dublin Brigade orders were simple vigilance; there was little else

Figure 7.2 Standing Orders for the Crews of Armoured Cars

Standing Orders for the Crews of Armoured Cars.

24.ii.1921
In Action.
   S/83/G.

1. Casualties.

   All crews must understand the importance of not allowing a car to fall into the hands of the enemy. If all the crew become casualties they must contrive to put the car into such a position that it cannot be moved by the enemy before assistance arrives.
   It is preferable to destroy the car rather than to lose it.

2. Reliefs.

   During long operations the crew may relieve one another for meals, etc.
On Rolls Royce cars one man will always remain on the car.
On Peerless cars two men will always remain on the car.
The remaining men of the crew will remain in sight of and within easy distance of the car.

3. Precautions.

   Doors of cars will always be kept shut and the car closed down as for action. Cars will not remain stationary except when necessary.

4. Command.

   Drivers of cars will take orders only from the Officer in charge of the car or the Officer under whose orders he was placed before proceeding to the scene of operations.

5. Smoking. No smoking is allowed inside an armoured Car.

IN BARRACKS.

   Cars will be locked up before being left in Military or Police Barracks.

General Staff, Dublin District

they could do. In this sense, killing the right target was sufficient to the mission, but virtually any violent action by British forces, however justifiable, helped enemy propaganda. Killing an innocent person had two effects: turning that person's family against the government and providing more propaganda.

Coinciding with the British advantage of having plentiful reinforcements near to hand in Dublin, since army barracks and police stations ringed the city, was that communication within the city was easier than for the isolated detachments of police and military in the countryside or in small towns and villages. Many RIC barracks had telephones, but the IRA learned to cut the phone lines during their barracks attacks. This became so common that whenever the phones went dead in a police barracks, the constables braced for attack.

Interestingly, while both the British 5th and 6th Infantry Divisions discussed IRA operations extensively in their official histories of the war, the Dublin District (Dublin Brigade)[22] hardly discussed countermobility operations, except for some off-hand remarks about having problems and their dealing with them by simply issuing new instructions and standing orders (see Appendices). One issue in Dublin was that there were almost no large ambushes in the city, and so there is little upon which to draw, but examination of some of the few instances provides interesting conclusions.

One of the earlier ambush-type incidents targeting the British army in Dublin was an attack by the Dublin IRA Brigade on a rationing party of the 2nd Bn, The Duke of Wellington's Regiment on Tuesday, 20 September 1920. The group, consisting of one NCO and six enlisted,[23] was loading bread into their Ford van at Monk's Bakery on King Street when it was attacked by a group of rebels (see Figure 7.3). The Volunteers called on the soldiers to put their hands into the air and surrender, but when they did not do so instantly, the rebels opened fire at close range. The soldiers immediately returned fire. The engagement was over in a matter of seconds, with the rebels fleeing. Private Washington died on the spot, Ptes Whitehead and Humphries had mortal wounds, while Bandsmen Smith's and Noble's wounds were minor. Immediately after the shooting stopped, a civilian pointed to a young man under the van who was trying to clear his jammed pistol (a 9mm 'broom-handled' Mauser Parabellum automatic) and the soldiers took him prisoner.[24] He was Volunteer Kevin Barry (eighteen years old), a medical student at University College Dublin and a killer. Of the other IRA attackers, three were wounded, but escaped. Barry was tried by

Figure 7.3 King Street, Dublin

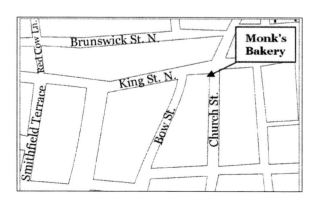

court-martial, convicted, sentenced to death in October and hanged on 1 November at Mountjoy prison amid a great public outcry. He became a 'poster-child' for the republican cause because of his youth, although the army was upset at this hypocrisy because some of the men he had helped to kill were as young as he was.[25] The British army seems to have learned little from this incident, although they appear to have improved their use of sentries.

Although contrary to the laws of war,[26] the British began carrying 'hostages' in their convoys in December 1920. They selected 'prominent' republicans and posted the names in the press prior to these trips in the hope that this would deter the rebels from attacking. The term 'hostage' is somewhat a misnomer in that they never intended to harm the person directly. Indeed, there is some evidence to suggest a more cordial relationship; the troops referred to them as 'mascots'. In one instance, a hostage wrote a humorous letter of complaint saying that riding everywhere was making him gain weight. While Macready noted that it offered 'some slight deterrent to outrages', there is little evidence that this deterred attacks.[27]

Drumcondra Road Ambush, 21 January 1921
One of the first pre-planned urban ambushes of 1921 took place on the morning of Thursday, 21 January, when eight men of the IRA Dublin Brigade 'active service unit' (ASU), commanded by its first lieutenant, Frank Flood, established an ambush site in north Dublin near the bridge over the Royal Canal, where Dorset Street Lower becomes the Drumcondra Road (see Figure 7.4). According to the IRA account, Flood and his men were going to attack a police vehicle that was expected to come through the area, but it arrived too early and sped through the position on to its destination in Collinstown to the north. Neither the police nor the IRA accounts explain how the car got through, for the rebels apparently attacked it, or at least fired on it, but, of course, the Volunteers were spotted.[28]

Flood, instead of retreating, moved his men some 600 yards north to the Drumcondra Bridge. This bridge, over the Tolka River, came near the intersection of Millmount Road (from the north-west), Millbourne Avenue (from north-north-west), Richmond Road (to the south-east) and Drumcondra Road (now the N1 motorway leading out of Dublin). At the intersection lay St Patrick's Primary School on the north-western corner and opposite that was the Drumcondra Petty Sessions Courthouse, which had an open field to the east.[29]

As one may well imagine, all of this rebel movement attracted attention, and so a 'traitor' gave the information to the ADRIC, who in turn sent out a large force (of unspecified size) from F and I Companies, ADRIC to attack the rebels. But the British did not reveal the sources of their information. The police plan was simple: approach from two directions at once and 'envelop' the ambush site. At around 0945 hours, as the Volunteers were still setting up, a police lorry carrying ADRIC from Gormanstown to the Phoenix Park RIC depot drove through the intersection heading south. These cadets met one of the ADRIC patrols about 100 yards away and gave warning as to the rebels' position. Two rebels fired on the car without orders, but it continued on its route and rendezvoused with one of the ADRIC columns heading north and warned them of the rebel presence.[30] At this point, the Volunteers should have retired, but Flood, inexplicably, chose to remain.

When the ADRIC column arrived on scene, the rebels opened fire from behind the walls surrounding the school as well as from the wall around the courthouse. The Auxiliaries returned fire, killing Volunteer Michael Magee and putting the rest to flight. It is unclear where the rebels from the school ran, but the rest went down Richmond Road and were swept up by the other ADRIC column as it arrived. Of the seven surviving rebels, five were captured and put on trial. The five, Thomas Bryan of 11 Henrietta Street, Patrick Doyle of 1 St Mary's Place, Flood (of 30 Summerhill Parade), Bernard Ryan of 200 Phibsboro Road, and Dermot O'Sullivan of 23 Glengarriff Parade, were found guilty of treason and sentenced to death.[31] A sixth man, Michael Magee of 20 Ostman Street, died of his wounds on 21 January shortly after his capture. On Monday, 14 March 1921, Bryan, Doyle, Flood and Ryan were hanged by a hangman brought in especially from England for the executions. Dermot O'Sullivan's death sentence was commuted to hard labour due to his youth (aged seventeen).[32]

From this attack, the British army reminded its men that many of the same security precautions in urban environments were the same as in rural ones. They stressed the importance of varying times and routes. They also said that 'Single vehicles containing a large number of men are particularly vulnerable, unless armoured, as only a portion of the weapons can be used effectively in defence and a concentrated target is afforded to the attackers.'[33] These precautions were the same as for movement in the countryside, but the British never seem to have been able to get their men to comply.

The British chalked up their success in this incident to timely, actionable intelligence, rapid but thorough planning, as well as its timely execution of the plan.[34] Further, their ability to manoeuvre tactically with

Figure 7.4 Drumcondra Road Ambush

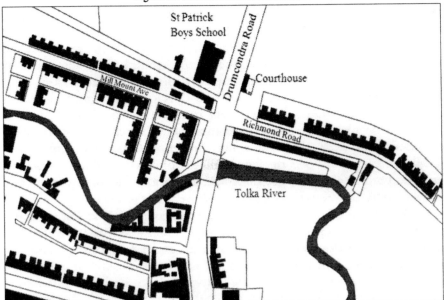

vehicles, especially in two different columns, made their success possible. The difficulty of manoeuvring with these separated columns without tactical radios or other communication should not be underestimated. Coordinating their movement was dependent on timing, planning and luck. Had the second column come up later, they might not have captured the rebels; had it come too early, they might have sprung the trap prematurely. While it is not appropriate to 'plan' for luck, what else could they have done, aside from establishing a firing line across Richmond Road, perpendicular to the river? Even this might not have been appropriate since it would have taken time to establish, and, if seen, might alert the rebels. If out of sight from the rebel positions, they might also have been too far off the rebel line of retreat. In the end, it appears that the old adage of luck favouring those who are well prepared was borne out.

Terenure Road Ambush, 29 January 1921

The first IRA patrol attack targeting the army in a city was in south-central Dublin. On Saturday, 29 January 1921, at 1900 hours, the ASU of the IRA 4th Battalion, Dublin Brigade readied for their patrol of the battalion area – about a two-mile square area adjacent to Portobello Barracks south of the Grand Canal in the Rathmines District of Dublin.

Figure 7.5 Dublin District Report on Drumcondra Ambush, 21 January 1921

S E C R E T.   S/G.1.A
                                                               23/1/21.

  Subject:- Special report on Ambush near DRUMCONDRA BRIDGE,
  21/1/21.

General Headquarters (G).   O.C. 'F' Coy. Aux. Div. R.I.C.
                    (I)   G.O.C.
Police Adviser.   'Q' Branch.
Inspector General R.I.C.   'A'
Chief Commr. D.M.P.   Raid Bureau
Hqrs. 24th (P) Inf. Bde.   A.P.M. (Room 22).
      25th (P) Inf. Bde.

At 1015.hrs. on the 21st inst., information was received at this Headquarters that an ambush was being set and patrolling columns of 'F' and 'I' Coys. Aux. Div. R.I.C. together with an Armoured Car were forthwith despatched to the scene. Just before their arrival a lorry of Aux. R.I.C. proceeding from GORMANSTOWN to The Depot, PHOENIX PARK was ambushed from behind a loopholed wall next to DRUMCONDRA Petty Sessions Court House. The occupants of this lorry warned the patrolling party of 'E' Coy. whom they met about 100yds. further down the road. These were fired upon by the Ambushers from the Allotment opposite ST. PATRICK'S School; fire was promptly returned, and one of the attackers fell, the others ran across the fields and five were captured by the 'I' Coy. patrol.

The five were all in possession of revolvers and bombs, all the revolvers being charged with dum-dum and split bullets. Two detonated bombs were found in the line of the wounded man's flight.

This man, who has since succumbed to his wounds, disclosed the fact that Capt. O'MALLEY, whose address has not been located, was in charge of the ambush and had handed over the hand grenades. (This is probably the Capt. O'MALLEY who was formerly Staff Captain of the now defunct Fingal Brigade I.R.A.).

The residences of the six captives were subsequently searched; nothing was found at any of them except at Frank FLOOD'S, 30 SUMMERHILL PARADE, where a revolver, sundry articles of equipment and garrotting cords were discovered.

Lr. Castle Yd.,   *D.C.W. Curtan, Lieut*
DUBLIN,   *for* Colonel Commandant
                                     Commanding Dublin Distr

They gathered at the battalion arms dump in Mount Argus near Harold's Cross Road and issued weapons and ammunition, at the same time giving out assignments. There were three IRA officers and twenty-six Volunteers. Three men were assigned to be unarmed bicycle scouts and they moved throughout the patrol area, generally moving south. Another pair was armed as hand-grenadiers, with only two grenades each (no specific type mentioned), and the rest of the force had various revolvers and automatic pistols. None were armed with rifles, sensible in the city, or with shotguns. All had between eight and twenty-five rounds per man. The six men armed with automatics had the greater amount of ammunition, presumably because they would fire and reload more quickly although they may simply have had more automatic rounds.[35]

The cycle scouts moved out at 1900 hours and the rest of the patrol followed at a quarter after. They established eight positions, six on the upper part of Terenure Road North, just south of where it becomes Harold's Cross at Brighton Square Road (see Figure 7.6). The seventh group took their position on Eaton Road to the west, about halfway between Terenure Park and Terenure Road North. Finally, the unidentified rebel OC placed himself at the southern end of the street where the three 'Terenure' streets – Road, East and North – all converge at 'Terenure Cross'.

Figure 7.6 Terenure Road Ambush

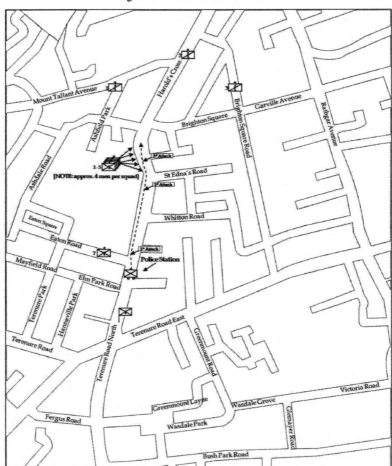

Around 2020 hours, one of the scouts reported to the IRA OC that an 'enemy' (2nd Bn Royal Berkshire Regiment)[36] lorry was parked on the east side of Terenure Road North at a police station opposite Elm Park Road. The OC took the scout's bicycle, going forward to see for himself, and found the lorry parked, with the engine off and no lookouts or sentries posted, in contravention of standing orders.

He said that the 'only point of attack appeared to be from corner where I left men at points 40 yards up road'[37] (marked as the seventh squad on Eaton Road). He and the ASU's second lieutenant discussed what to do, the latter feeling that the squad's position was too exposed and there were too few of them to make an effective attack. The OC was concerned that the lorry might go east on Whitton around to Rathgar Avenue and thereby avoid their other positions altogether.[38] As he started south again, apparently still not having decided, the lorry started up – the soldiers must have been inside the whole time since the canvas sides were rolled down – and started north up the street.

Decrying the slowness of half of the seventh squad, the OC said that the second lieutenant, with two grenades in hand, moved forward towards the lorry and tried to remove the arming pins from his grenades but could not. A second man, with a single grenade, armed and threw it, hitting the lorry, which appears to have stopped – the report does not say. At the same time, three of the rebels, with the lieutenant and his companion, opened fire on the lorry with their handguns. The unseen soldiers returned fire and the five men on Eaton Street, being significantly out-gunned, pulled back. Meanwhile, the remaining five men of the rebel squad had been too slow to act. The lorry started moving again (apparently not significantly damaged by the attack meant to force it to halt) and was attacked by two of the squads to the north with gunfire and the remaining grenade. When the soldiers again returned fire, the rest of the ASU retreated towards Crumlin Road to the north-west.

The IRA took no casualties, while the army stated that nine men (one officer and eight enlisted) were wounded in the attack. In his report, the ASU OC said two rebels 'opened ineffective fire at tops of houses while attack was on. Otherwise their conduct was reasonable.' He offered no explanation, but this may suggest that their behaviour might have been due to the stress of combat. He also mentioned that '3 men with automatics fired only 5 rounds. One man had a misfire at start, No. 2 a jam after 2 shots, No. 3 a jam after 3 shots – short parabellum, long parabellum Mauser, 30-bore pistol respectively.'[39] The Parabellum referred to is now the 9mm x 19mm NATO round. It would seem that there were problems with the operation of weapons with this round even in 1921;

of course, it is most likely that the IRA QMGs did not perform the maintenance that the weapons required. It is also significant that the rebels
using handguns during the attack did not have the sufficient firepower,
in terms of both calibre and volume of fire produced, to press their attack
in the face of British rifle fire. Pistols were the preferred weapon in
Dublin (and other large towns) due to their concealability, but also due
to their disposability – they were easier to throw away than rifles. With
the exception of close-quarters fighting and assassinations, however,
hand-gunners were at a distinct disadvantage against the .303 SMLE
Service Rifles. The most obvious counter for the intermediate distances
was the shotgun, but the IRA generally held the shotgun in contempt as
the weapon of 'mere' farmers. This attitude appears to have remained
throughout the war, despite logic, obvious effectiveness of the weapons
and combat experience.

Clearly, the Royal Berks were not obeying the standing orders, as
they did not deploy sentries while stopped, nor lookouts on board the
lorry. The *Record of the Rebellion* admitted this, stating that they 'were
caught with insufficient covering at the back'. Deploying the appropriate lookouts would certainly have decreased the response time from the
soldiers and may have prevented the grenade attack altogether or
stopped it by shooting the approaching grenadiers. Further, they did not
have the canvas sides in the rear of the lorry rolled up, also in contravention of standing orders, unless, perhaps, if they were transporting a 'high
value' prisoner, but they were not. Further, this attack demonstrated the
soundness of the standing orders and that, although they may have been
mere common sense, they were still useful.

Rebel operations in Dublin continued, and, to a careful observer,
demonstrated that the IRA were learning. For instance, at the Rathmines
Church (Dublin) ambush a week later on Saturday, 5 February 1921, the
British army learned the valuable lesson that the IRA Dublin Brigade
was sufficiently sophisticated in their operations to manoeuvre multiple
columns or patrols into any urban area to conduct coordinated attacks on
British forces. Further, they found that the IRA bicycle scouts were
highly effective, just as at the Terenure Road ambush earlier. In this
attack, as with Terenure, the rebels had trouble maintaining fire discipline. The IRA report on the incident, however, mentioned that the
returning fire from the soldiers was somewhat ineffective, coming in '2
or 3 intense bursts, seemed to be rather panicky and lacking deliberation,
and ceased almost suddenly on Company reaching cover on retreat'.
Strangely, despite the statements in the captured report, the British
army felt that 'The fire from the lorry appears to have been effective,

Figure 7.7 Patrol Report of 2nd Bn The Royal Berkshire Regiment, Terenure Street Ambush[40]

Report on Patrol of the 2nd Bn The Royal Berkshire Regt, Ambushed near Terenure Police Station on night of January 29/30, 1921

Orders were received on the 29th of January to raid CULLENSWOOD HOUSE at 1930 hours on that date and search for arms, seditious literature and wanted men.

Instructions to the effect that this house would have been raided by 'F' Coy of the Auxiliaries at 1330 hours were received at the same time, but that they would have searched for wanted men only. These instructions together with a notification that two lorries would report here at 1830 hours were contained in a written message from the Brigade Major, 25th (Prov) Infantry Brigade. No. of Message W.B.76/1 of 29.1.21.

One lorry only reported here at 1830. This vehicle was not 'protected' in any way, not having even a tarpaulin over the body.

Lieut. Newton with one Sergeant, one L/Cpl and eleven Privates exclusive of the driver left Barracks at about 1850 hours in this lorry. They called at Rathmines Police Station where they picked up a Constable. Thence they proceeded to CULLENWOOD HOUSE. On arrival they found that there was a party of Auxiliaries already there raiding the house, so Lieut. Newton went back with the lorry to Rathmines Police Station and left the Constable there.

From there they went to Terenure Police Station inside which Lieut. Newton spent about twenty five minutes.

On leaving Terenure Police Station, Lieut. Newton's intentions must have been to return to Barracks as he had no other raid to do before 2200 hours.

Both the lorry driver and the Sergeant are in agreement except in some details as to what followed.

It appears that just after the lorry had left Terenure Police Station (about 30) a bomb was thrown into the back of the lorry and fire was opened upon it from some ruins on the left of the road. This wounded eight out of the twelve men in the lorry. After the bomb burst the lorry went on and the firing ceased. After a short interval which appears to have been of only a few seconds duration, fire was opened again on the lorry from behind a wall on the left hand side of the road and Lieut. Newton was hit in the face by a revolver bullet and rendered unconscious. At the same time another bomb was thrown which the driver of the lorry said burst at Lieut. Newton's feet at the front of the lorry; but which probably did not fall into the lorry at all as neither the officer nor the driver was hit. The driver then put on all speed and drove to Portobello Hospital where the wounded were attended to before being sent to King George V's Military Hospital.

The only discrepancies between the report of the Sergeant and that of the Lorry driver are that:-

(i) The driver states that he stopped his car after hearing the first bomb burst. Whereas the Sergeant said that he stopped it after the second one.

(ii) The driver states that three bombs were thrown but the Sergeant only heard two.

(iii) The driver states that he thought the first bomb was a very loud backfire and that he stopped the car, jumped down, discovered it was a bomb and at once mounted again and started off.

Dublin.   NM McCormack Lieut. Colonel.
30.1.21   Commanding. 2nd Bn The Royal Berkshire Reg

inflicting 4 casualties and doubtlessly spoiling the aim of ambushers.'[41] This would seem incongruous, until one considers that the army took only one 'slight' casualty. At the same time, the army probably recognized that the fire ceasing when the rebels reached cover was a demonstration of good fire discipline.

Figure 7.8 Rathmines Ambush[42]

THE RATHMINES CHURCH AMBUSH, 5TH FEBRUARY, 1921.

A lorry containing troops was passing Rathmines Church when it was fired on. Fire was returned. The results as reported by the troops were: –
> 1 Officer slightly wounded.
> 2 civilians wounded and picked up.
> 2 revolvers and 2 bombs picked up.

The captured account is as follows: –

REPORT ON AMBUSH AT RATHMINES, 8.55 P.M., SATURDAY, 5TH FEBRUARY, 1921.

I append a rough sketch giving my positions from 7.30 p.m., Saturday, 5th instant, to 8.55 p.m., when Company came into action.

My patrol consisted of 22 officers, N.C.O.s and men. There were 4 bombers, 15 revolver men (9, .450; 4, .38; 2, .32), 2 cyclists and 1 first-aid man.

At 8.45 p.m. in consequence of information supplied by my cycle scout on right, I had placed my men. Sections 1 and 2 on right, and Sections 3 and 4 on left of gate in front of Rathmines Church. The bombers were placed, 2 in centre and 1 on each flank. The cover from view and fire was good, but in the only way of retreat the sections on right had to cover a space open to fire of about 7 or 8 yards.

One of my men on right, through excitement presumably, fired off 1 shot, obliging me to open attack with bomb on side of lorry instead of rear as I had intended. There were 3 explosions, 2 simultaneously, 1 separately. One bomb, so far as I have gathered up to the present, failed to explode. One bomb, at least, exploded inside lorry, and as to others there can be discovered no marks of bomb explosions either on street, or on wall opposite. The firing of Company was good, being marked by deliberation and regularity. The sections on the right retreated, according to instructions, first, their passage over open ground being covered very thoroughly by the fire of sections to be rather panicky and lacking deliberation, and ceased almost suddenly on Company reaching cover on retreat. All our men got away, one, subsequently, through a form of stupidity that none could foresee, being arrested hours later.

We had 4 casualties, all slight except one, an injury to foot.

We lost 1 revolver, which was dumped in a bad place by a man who was slightly wounded.

> CAPTAIN A. IV.
> H.Q., Dublin.

To A.G.

Herewith report of ambush at Rathmines from O.C., A. IV.

> ACT. BRIGADE ADJUTANT.

In this account it is interesting to note that the rebel patrols move about in certain areas, taking up different positions to attack Crown Forces according to information received from cycle scouts. The fire from the lorry appears to have been effective, inflicting 4 casualties and doubtlessly spoiling the aim of ambushers.

For the RIC, February 1921 started poorly; in the first three days, they sustained twenty-three casualties in seven separate attacks and all but three died. Centred primarily in the south, the regular RIC, the Black and Tans and ADRIC men died brutal deaths. The worst of these was at Dromkeen, Co. Limerick, where eleven men of a thirteen-man patrol were killed by the combined ASUs of the East and Mid-Limerick IRA Brigades on Wednesday, 3 February 1921.[43] It was unusual that ASUs combined instead of their columns. There is no mistaking that only two of these attacks were in urban environments (Const. Samuel Green in Balbriggan, Co. Dublin and Const. Patrick Mullany[44] on Trinity Street, Dublin, both on Tuesday, 2 February) and both of these were closer to being simple assassinations than any type of ambush. It is not that urban environments were safer – they were not – but the rebels were simply able to mass in rural areas in greater safety due to the dispersing effects of the terrain. It is also interesting that for the rest of that short month, three more RIC men (of the twenty-six further casualties of February) were killed in Dublin in an ambush at the corner of Parliament and Essex Streets in what appear to have been targets of opportunity.[45]

Figure 7.9 Amiens Street Station Ambush[46]

The Attempted Ambush near Amiens Street Station on 7th February, 1921.

This account is one of an ambush that did not succeed. An attempt was made to draw Crown Forces into an area strongly held by 165 rebels by the dispatch of a bogus telephone message. Information from police sources having reached Dublin Castle, however, to the effect that a train had been held up in Amiens Street Station, a police forces was dispatched at 22oo hours to the station and not to Seville Place, as desired by the rebels. This appears to have disconcerted their leaders, and the 'battalion' made off, having effected nothing.

The 'accompanying sketch' referred to by the rebel leader was unfortunately not captured, and a diagram has accordingly been attached.

The captured document state:—

Headquarters, 2nd Battalion.
12th February, 1921

To O.C., Dublin,
I am instructed by O.C. this Battalion to forward to you a *report on operations carried out by Battalion II on Great Northern Railway on 7th February*, 1921.

At 7.30 p.m. on Monday, 7th February, 1921, a telephone message was dispatched, per G.H.Q. Intelligence, to Dublin Castle, to the effect that there was "great activity around 100, Seville Place," and that apparently someone of importance was expected there, as a number of men was noticed going in. The sender also remarked that there was a means of escape at the rear of the house.

The reply from Dublin Castle stated that the message would receive immediate attention, and gave the sender to understand that "forces" would be promptly on the scene.

The object of the above message being sent was to endeavour to draw the enemy as near as possible to the Railway Bridge which crosses Seville Place.

The choice of number 100 was made for two reasons, viz.:—(*a.*) That as front and rear are immediately below the bridge, our forces could easily attack both in Seville Place and the end of Seville Lane (*see* accompanying sketch). (*b.*) Since these premises are owned by the St. Lawrence O'Toole's Club, they have been under constant observation by the enemy for some time, and so would be likely to receive attention on this account.

The preliminary arrangements were : At 7.35 p.m. 3 officers and 19 men from "C" Company entered the railway lines by the steps at end of Coburg Place (*see* map). Their task was to hold all cabins, offices, sheds and approaches, dismantle telephones and see that no persons communicated with outside.

The plan of operations was as follows: At 7.40 p.m. sharp 2 officers and 35 men from "B" Company entered the bridge by Coburg Place and took up their position facing Oriel Street and also the side wall opposite Coburg Place (*see* map). This force was to open fire on the enemy approaching from Oriel Street direction. At exactly the same time 3 officers and 38 men from "E" Company, 3 officers and 10 men from "D" Company and 1 officer and 7 men from the Cyclist Company all entered by the Guilford Place gate and took up positions in the following manner:—

Forty men armed with shot-guns and grenades commanded the bridge facing Portland Row (main point of attack). 10 men armed in the same manner manned the bridge at end of Seville Lane (rear of 100).

Three men held gate at Guildford Place. 2 men remained on guard at cabin at Newcomen Bridge.

Besides the above, a force of 3 officers and 40 men from "F" Company were placed in Portland Row (facing Seville Place), extending along North Strand Road out to Annesley Bridge. These men were armed with rifles, grenades, &c. This was planned with the object of attacking the retreating enemy and incidentally to cover the retreat of forces actually on the railway.

However, after a period of over half and hour's waiting, there appeared to be no sign of the enemy approaching the vicinity of our positions, with the exception of two armoured cars (fitted with searchlights), began to play on the railway line as if endeavouring to locate the position of our men. This was at 8.05 p.m., and at 8.15 p.m. it was deemed advisable to begin to retire.

"B" Company advanced in front as an advance guard. Next come "D," "E" and Cyclist Companies, and "C" Company came up in the rear to cover the retreat. The direction lay along the Great Southern and Western Railway. At West Road, "E" Company was directed by O.C. Battalion to dismiss and get safely off the line.

The remaining force pushed on, crossed the railway bridges at North Strand and Ballybough Roads, and alighted without mishap at St. James Avenue (Clonliffe Road). This was at 8.30 p.m., and the men were accordingly dismissed by O.C. Battalion.

Total number of officers engaged	..	..	16
Total number of men engaged	..	..	149

(These include "F" Company who commanded Portland Road, &c.)

Officers in charge of the various positions were as follows:—

1st and 2nd "E" Company, were in command of main point of attack (front of bridge).

O.C., "E" Company, was posted at rear of 100.

O.C., "B" Company, was in charge of position on bridge facing Oriel Street.

O.C., "F" Company, commanded forces in Portland Row, North Strand, &c.

O.C., "C" Company, was responsible for the cabins, approaches, &c.

O.C., Battalion, was in command of whole operations and remained with main body on bridge from where he directed operations.

NOTE.—All the forces engaged both on railway and on patrol carried small arms.

(Act) ADJUTANT
Battalion II.

Though of an indecisive action, the account is interesting in showing up the mentality of the I.R.A. Telephoning to the headquarters of their opponents was not outside their imagination. They were not afraid of assembling 165 men, armed with such visible weapons as shot-guns, in a busy part of the city. Their dispositions were carefully thought out. But, as always when they have been in position for any length of time, they soon became nervous of discovery and departed without firing a shot.

Great Brunswick Street Ambush, Dublin, 14 March 1921

March started little better than February for the RIC; they lost twelve men killed in action and seven more wounded[47] in eight separate attacks in the first half of that month. The last two of these died in Dublin during an IRA patrol attack on the evening of Monday, 14 March 1921, where a gunfight broke out in central Dublin on Great Brunswick Street around 2030 hours between about thirty-eight members of B Company, 3rd Battalion, IRA Dublin Brigade and some sixteen Auxiliary policemen and an unknown number of police of the DMP. The British claimed that the ADRIC had received intelligence about a meeting of over 100 high-ranking republicans at the St Andrew's Catholic Club at 144 Great Brunswick Street, with B Company providing security, and so attempted to raid the meeting to capture as many of the senior rebel leaders as they could. The IRA company commander, acting Capt. Peadar O'Mara, however, stated in his captured report that he and his men were simply conducting normal patrol operations within his company area when the Auxiliaries unexpectedly came in.[48] Whatever the reason, clearly the area was important since 'the Club', as it was known, sometimes served as an IRA headquarters during the war.[49]

The Volunteers split into four separate squads in the area around the Club around 1855 hours that evening. O'Mara said he and his detachment apparently inflicted no casualties when they attacked some members of the DMP shortly thereafter, but that one of his men was hit by hostile fire. It is unclear where this fire came from since the DMP was an unarmed police force.[50] There were no DMP members reported as casualties that night.

This attack succeeded in drawing British forces into the area, a goal stated in the captured IRA document,[51] when two Crossley Tenders and an armoured car (of unknown type, but with a mounted machine gun) arrived on the scene from Beggar's Bush Barracks (approximately three-quarters of a mile away to the south). The British army account implied that the arrival of the Auxiliaries[52] occurred at the beginning of the engagement, while the IRA clearly saw this as the final phase of their operations that night. In any event, the Auxie cadets dismounted and engaged on foot after five of their comrades were wounded in the opening volley of rebel fire. Although taking fire from four directions, the

ADRIC spread out, likely with supporting fire from the machine gun on the armoured car, and counterattacked the rebels.

The IRA account of inflicting heavy casualties is demonstrably incorrect; only five ADRIC were wounded, although two of them died later of their wounds – Cadet Bernard J.L. Beard, MC and T/Const. James J. O'Farrell[53] – there were no other British casualties in the engagement.[54] Interestingly, the RIC inspector-general's monthly confidential report for March does not report this incident, also singular considering a constable was killed; for that same month in Dublin, he reported the killing of a sergeant and head constable, the wounding of two more constables and the attempted murder of a district inspector, but nothing about this action on the 14th. Normally, the inspector-general did not report ADRIC actions, but O'Farrell was a real 'Black and Tan' driver, although the British army reports call him a cadet, so the neglect in not reporting his death is puzzling, unless he 'slipped' through because he was a temporary constable assigned as a driver with the ADRIC.

The IRA sustained four casualties that night – three killed, one wounded and two captured. The two captured Volunteers were Thomas Traynor and the wounded Jack Donnelly. Both were tried for murder and sentenced to death. The IRA in Co. Tipperary kidnapped RIC District Inspector Gilbert N. Potter[55] on 22 April 1921 and offered to exchange him for Traynor. The British refused and hanged Traynor on 26 April; Potter in turn was executed by the IRA on 27 April.[56] Donnelly, also sentenced to death, was spared the gallows by the Truce of July 1921. Why the British did not execute him along with Traynor is unclear, but his wounds may

Figure 7.10 Great Brunswick Street Ambush

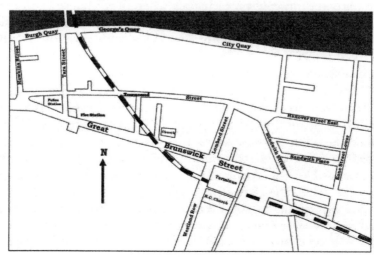

not have sufficiently healed to hang him (governments hesitate to execute wounded prisoners). He survived the war and ensuing Civil War, dying of old age in 1988.

Figure 7.11 IRA Report of the Great Brunswick Street Ambush

O.C.'s Report

On Monday, the 14th March, I paraded 'B' Company, Battalion 3, for patrol in Company area. The parade was divided in the following manner: First Lieutenant and his men for the south portion of the area; O.C., 'B' Company, for the north portion of the area. Instructions were issued to attack all enemy in the Company area, each patrol keeping in touch with Cyclists, and to scout the area with unarmed men. This was done at 6.55p.m. I proceeded *via* Gt Brunswick Street to Westland Row and got in touch with enemy who were operating in the easterly portion of the area. The enemy were searching people in the streets. I sighted a Staff car in the vicinity of the General Police Station and at once moved my patrol in that direction, *via* Tara Street, to Burgh Quay, meaning to encircle the enemy in Hawkins Street. I was too late for this car, and proceeded down Brunswick Street by the Police Station. Private ... [57] suggested presenting the D.M.P. with a grenade, which might bring the enemy into the area. This I thought was an admirable suggestion and we proceeded to arrange our method of doing same: 2 men of my patrol on the north side of Brunswick Street, 2 men on the south side to cover our retreat if we were fired on. Private ... then threw the grenade which struck the wall and rebounded on to the footpath before exploding. We then ran down Brunswick Street. Before the grenade exploded I looked back and saw Private ... lying on the street. The two men on the north side of the street proceeded to stop a cab which was going down Tara Street; the driver refused to stop. I rushed at the horse and stopped it. When we had stopped the cab I looked towards where Private ... was and saw that a tramcar had ridden down on him; he was under the fender as far as I could see. The Corporation ambulance came along and he was taken to Mercer's Hospital, where he is at present detained and his leg has been amputated. He was armed with a revolver (.45), which, I believe, has fallen into enemy hands. (This I am not satisfied is a fact.) After he was taken away I moved my patrol down Brunswick Street and got in touch with the squad under a Section Commander. I instructed the Section Commander to cover the Club (144, Brunswick Street) by placing his men at the north corner of Sandwith Street (both corners) and also Erne Street.

1st Lieutenant reported at the Club, and was ordered to send his patrol to the Club in two batches, sending them by south side of Sandwith Street and Erne Street. The first squad of the Lieutenant's patrol had come into the Club when there was an explosion and revolver firing in the street. Two Tenders of Black and Tans had opened fire on the Club and the patrols were engaging them from four points (the corner of Sandwith Street and Erne Street) and from the door of the Club. This was about 8.15p.m. when it was time to dismiss the patrols owing to 9 o'clock curfew.

I would like to bring to your attention the coolness of Privates ... who covered the retreat of the men from the Club, closing the hall door when the last man had retreated to the rear of the Club. The men scaled the walls at the rear of the Club, and got in touch with each flank fighting all the time. There were no casualties in the Club. In the scaling of the walls a handbag containing three revolvers and some ammunition was lost. This was found by the enemy when they searched the premises later in the night (about 11p.m.). Whilst this was taking place an armoured car and two more Tenders came on the job. These were responsible for the casualties to the I.R.A. which were Private ... wounded in the hip and Private ... (First Aid) was knocked out in Sandwith Street by a bullet wound in the back. Lieutenant ... had him taken to ... When the second party of Black and Tans arrived they then retreated as they went. It was in the retreat that we sustained the heaviest casualties losing Private ... as a prisoner in the hands of the enemy. (This I only learned on the 15th March) Also 3 other men, 1 wounded and 2 dead (This information I received from the driver of the Fire Brigade Ambulance who states that 2 men were taken up dead at the corner of Sandwith Street (north side), and from a conversation overheard in King George's Hospital. The names of the missing men are as follows: – ... These men have not reported or their whereabouts have not been discovered up to the time of dispatch. Being on the south side of Brunswick Street and in the fight and excitement I was not aware of any casualties until I checked the roll, which was done as soon as possible on the 15th March.) in the retreat up Sandwith Street. Privates … covered the men and prevented any closing in by the enemy; the fighting at this point was of a very hard nature and was carried on for a considerable time. Two grenades exploding in one of the Tenders caused it to stop, and this was one of the causes for the heavy casualties inflicted on the enemy. The men emptied their guns into them and only retreated when under machine-gun fire from the armoured car. They dispersed on the arrival of reinforcements of the enemy up side streets and lanes, and in two cases they got on the roofs and potted at the enemy if they tried to come too near. The B. and Ts. giving those a wide berth did not try to close in, thus enabling the men to move freely in their own neighbourhood and get safely away. I might report that Stephen Clarke, ex-soldier, 13, Queen's Square (killed), was under observation by Company Intelligence Officer for some time, as he was a tout for the enemy.

The two dead men and one wounded prisoner picked up at Sandwith Street were taken by the enemy to King George's Hospital, also all enemy wounded. The engagement ended about 10 o'clock. Estimated enemy casualties: – 7 killed and 8 wounded.

The following instructions were issued to patrol leaders: – All enemy to be engaged and if possible wiped out. In the event of a patrol coming in contact with the enemy, all patrols to concentrate on that sector of the area to begin the fight, as the men had not been in action before with one or two exceptions. Cyclists to be used as connecting links in order to keep in touch, unarmed men to be in advance of patrols as scouts. Patrols to move in files, 2 men on each side of the street and 5 paces between each file. First-Aid men to move at the rear of each patrol, 2 First-Aid men with each patrol. Bombers to keep on the outside of each file, each bomber to be with a gun-man. Unarmed men to fall back with First-Aid men, in the event of getting in touch with enemy.

Strength of the parties: – 1st Lieutenant and 16 men, this patrol to be divided into 2 parts.

O.C. and 20 men – this patrol was divided into 2 parties, 12 men under a Section Commander, and 7 men under O.C.

Total strength of party – 2 officers, 2 N.C.O.s and 34 men.

The British noted this incident as a good example of IRA urban operations. The open formation of the patrols and their movement/screening with bicyclists was common. Further, since the use of bicycles was so common, one could never know if a bicyclist was a scout or not. The British after-action report noted that in response to rebel attack, 'immediate and resolute [counter] attack is the policy the IRA like least'.[58] Another significant factor upon which the British did not touch was that the IRA used bombs and pistols only in this attack. This helps to explain the relatively low casualties among the British forces that day considering the sizeable forces involved. Yet the British army appears not to have noticed this factor, except to mention their advantage of concealability; the fact that the IRA were significantly outgunned on the streets of Dublin was an important point to the counterattack options, as well as effective engagement ranges.

Figure 7.12 Dorset Street Ambush Patrol Report[59]

At about 1905 hours on the 18th March, a lorry containing an escort was bombed going north from Upper Sackville Street. The escort opened fire. A second lorry, some hundred yards in the rear of the first, also opened fire on men seen to be engaged in the attack. The captured report states:—

PATROL REPORT.

Date..............................18.3.21
15 men.
Time.............................6.30—7.45 p.m.
   (Proposed.)
1st (Engra) 5.
Time.............................6.30—7.0 p.m.
(J.D.) Adjutant in charge.
   (Actual.)

Procedure.—Ambush party to be in vicinity of selected positions, majority on east side, and to take their places on sighting enemy ore receiving information of approach.

Scouts to watch approaches and report presence of enemy and their strength.

When engaging, Western Force to fire up street and Eastern Force down, so as not to endanger party operating opposite.

Disposal of men.—8 men with 45's and 5 bombs in lane above L.S.E. Garage. 7 men with 45's and 6 bombs in lane below opposite side. 8 unarmed scouts in positions shown in attached sketch.

Information re *enemy.*—Cycle scout in position south of Parnell Square reported approach of 2 military lorries at 6.57 p.m. Cycle scout at Berkley Road corner reported lorry draw up near by about 7.30 p.m. and remained a few minutes. Back of lorry opened and at least 2 motionless bodies lying at rear of car. A pool of blood formed during state of lorry.

Information re *our men.*—General behaviour good. Over anxious to engage and advancing too far from cover. Some men very excited after engagements.

Result.—At least two casualties inflicted.

Ammunition expended.—4 bombs, 14 rounds 45.

Casualties.—5 (3 men with superficial wounds, 2 more serious).

Remarks.—One bomb failed to explode. Excitement of men after engagement probably due to the fact that this was the first occasion on which the majority had been under fire.

(Sd.)   M.C., O.C.
                                                    11 a.m. 20th March, 1921.

Handed in as instructed.
Rough sketch of positions attached.

This report admits 5 casualties. There were no military hit. The value of parties travelling in two or more vehicles at a distance is shown here. Either the ambushers must, then, abstain from attacking all but the last vehicle or expose themselves to men in later vehicles. Convoys travelling slowly are less liable to attack than those travelling fast.

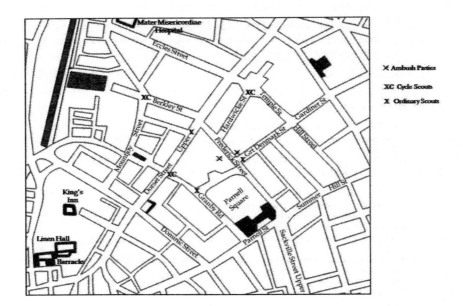

Figure 7.13 Dorset Street, Dublin

There was little that was spectacular about the IRA attack on Dorset Street four days after the Great Brunswick Street fight, but the excerpt above is a good example of IRA after-action reporting and also of how the British army dealt with the information they captured.

Military Abattoir Raid/Ambush, 14 May 1921

As mentioned above, the Irish Command's GHQ, transportation and barracks were all centred in the west of Dublin at Parkgate. Right next to the Phoenix Park RIC Barracks and Depot, and just behind the Military Hospital, Military Prison and Royal Barracks, was the Military Abattoir, which itself was just south of the Cattle Market on Aughrim Street. The abattoir supplied meat to the seven barracks, four military hospitals, several depots and other military facilities in Dublin. There is also evidence to suggest that they supplied meat to other military camps in Ireland as well.[60] Although this incident, from late in the war, does not quite meet the exact criteria of the classical ambushes in this volume, if one assumes that the victims must be in motion, it demonstrates the dangers posed by the IRA to British forces and also the effects of poor security practices.

On the evening of Friday, 13 May 1921, Lance Corporal J. Whetstone, 2nd Bn, East Essex Regiment, came down on the duty roster to be the NCO in charge of abattoir lorry delivery escort duty for the next day.

Whetstone was warned that same evening by his section sergeant, Sgt F. Walker, that he had heard rumours that the armoured car on abattoir escort duty would be attacked in the near future. Sgt Walker did not offer the source of his information, stating that it was 'private information', but added that he 'did not give any great weight to this warning ... as the information was vague' and that he had heard many rumours in the past.[61]

Early the following morning, around 0600 hours, L/Corp. Whetstone paraded his assigned crew, Privates Ruck and Harvey (RASC drivers) and Wheeler and Jordan (Hotchkiss machine-gunners), and checked to see that they had their side arms and other assigned equipment. Departing in Peerless armoured car No. 18, they escorted the meat delivery lorry to the abattoir and then to Broadstone Station on Harcourt Street before returning to the abattoir at 0730. They reloaded and then proceeded to the Esplanade Detail Issue Store at Royal Barracks by 0800 hours, made the delivery and breakfasted at the mess there.[62]

Figure 7.14 Dublin Brigade Instructions for Peerless Armoured Cars

Special Instructions for Peerless Armoured Cars.

1. The crew of a Peerless armoured car consists of one officer or N.C.O. (not below the rank of corporal) in charge, two gunners, one first driver, and one second driver.

2. No car will go out without its full crew.

3. The following ammunition will always be carried on the car: –

4 boxes of 24 belts of 50 rounds each	1,200 rounds.
1 box S.A.A. in bulk (sealed)	1,000 "
12 rounds per man .455	60 "
In bulk .455	40 "

4. Gunners will have their heads *only* through the opening in the turret, and will not expose more than their heads. One gun will point to the front and one gun to the rear.

5. The rear driver must always have his revolver drawn and near flap open sufficiently high to allow him to keep a look-out. All prisms must be kept clean.

6. Cars to be kept clean and sufficiently lubricated. Chains, springs and shackle pin greasers must always be well filled.

7. The lower part of the front driver's flap must always be up. The driver's side must be opened at an angle of 45 degrees.

8. Hotchkiss guns will always be loaded, locking handle at safety.

They returned to the abattoir, having picked up the delivery lorry at the Esplanade Issue Store, at 0930 and parked along the south-east side of the meat shed. Immediately before, the delivery lorry had passed through the main gate and backed up to the loading area. The turret machine gunners (Wheeler and Jordan) had to close the tops of their turrets as they entered the gate as it was too low to accommodate them. This severely limited their view; one of their main functions was to act as lookouts for the rest of the crew, since they were on top of the vehicles. The driver, Pte A Walker (615th M.T. Company, RASC), dismounted the vehicle and proceeded down the stairs to the below-ground kitchen for breakfast. When the attack began, he remained there because he was unarmed (in contravention of Dublin Brigade Standing Orders).[63]

Figure 7.15 Dublin Brigade Special Instructions for Rolls Royce Armoured Cars

Special Instructions for Rolls Royce Armoured Cars. [Dublin Brigade]

1. The crew of a Rolls Royce armoured car consists of one officer or N.C.O. (not below the rank of corporal) in charge, one first driver, and one gunner.

2. No car will go out without its full crew.

3. The following ammunition will always be carried on the car: –

Vickers Gun.		
3 boxes of 250 rounds	750 to 1,000 rounds.	
1 belt of 250 rounds on gun	250	"
Hotchkiss Gun.		
1 box of 6 belts of 50 rounds	300	"
Revolver.		
12 rounds per man in car	36	"
In box	64	"

4. Cars, whenever possible, will carry two spare wheels.

5. Tyres must be kept at a pressure of 95 lb. per square inch on the Shraeder gauge for rear wheels, and 85 lb. for front wheels, subject to tyre, weather, and road conditions.

6. Cars to be kept clean and sufficiently lubricated according to Rolls Royce handbook.

7. When on escort duty, cars must regulate their pace to suit themselves, and not use excessive speed in order to keep up with the vehicle being escorted; it must regulate its pace to that of the armoured car.

8. Under no circumstances will the speed of an armoured car exceed 20 miles an hour. Officer or N.C.O. i/c will be held responsible for any accident that may occur to, or be occasioned by, their cars while travelling at excessive speed unless they have a written order from a superior officer, who will forward a written report to the Company Commander immediately, giving details of the necessity of exceeding the speed limit.

9. Officers and N.C.O.s i/c cars must check the speed of cars and report non-compliance with orders at all times.

10. Drivers must, on return to the garage, examine their tyres for glass, nails, flints, etc., which may be embedded in the tread, and remove same.

11. If a tyre punctures, the gunner must remain inside the car ready for action.

12. Cars will be started once a week from inside with the hand-starter.

13. The Officer or N.C.O. in charge of car is responsible that no-one sits outside the car except those authorized to do so by Company Headquarters. Persons authorized must be properly dressed, and will be warned that they may not smoke or behave in a slovenly manner.

14. Armoured cars will always keep at least 50 yards distance from each other, or 10 yards behind vehicles that they are escorting.

15. Safeguarding of arms on Rolls Royce armoured cars: –
    (*i*) Revolvers will only be left on armoured cars by order of the Section Commander. Failing such order all revolvers will be handed back into the Section Store on completion of duty.
    (*ii*) When revolvers are on armoured cars, except when on duty, they will be invariably locked up on the chain issued for this purpose to each car. The officer or N.C.O. in charge of car is responsible that this is done on completion of duty, and that the key is in possession of first driver *or* that all revolvers are returned to store.
    (*iii*) In addition, when revolvers are left on armoured cars on the chain, the first driver will ensure that all doors are securely fastened and all port holes closed and pinned.

What the British soldiers did not know was that Michael Collins' infamous Squad was targeting them. The officer commanding the Squad, Paddy Daly, told the rebel special missions group to prepare to break rebel Séan MacEoin, commander at the Clonfin ambush in early February (see Chapter 6), out of Mountjoy Prison in Dublin. MacEoin was awaiting trial for murdering RIC District Inspector Thomas J. McGrath in January 1921. The Squad prepared to steal the armoured car and were deployed to the abattoir several times before getting the signal to proceed – a shade left up in a window in the superintendent's house. They saw the lorry arrive, which was then followed by the armoured car. They waited several minutes to allow the crew to get about its normal routine, and then entered the compound.[64]

As soon as the armoured car had stopped, Pte Jordan dismounted from his machine-gun turret, with Whetstone's permission, and went to the latrine. He saw a soldier in walking-out dress come out of the entrance to the kitchen stairs. He heard a shout of 'Hands up!' and then a shot; the soldier collapsed on to his back. Jordan ran back to the armoured car, mounted his turret, without giving the warning, and was bringing it into action when he heard the call, 'Hands up!' Whetstone had got out of the vehicle to speak to the meat lorry driver (Walker), but was held up by a rebel from the front. Whetstone claimed to have drawn his sidearm and was preparing to fire when another rebel 'jabbed a revolver into my ribs from behind'. This rebel took his weapon and held up the remaining group from every direction at once. When Jordan heard the call to surrender, he pulled his service revolver and fired one round at the raiders, one of whom returned fire with a pistol, hitting Jordan once in the left side of his chest. Jordan fell to the floor of the armoured car.[65]

The rebel who shot Jordan took the wounded man's pistol and two rebels took Jordan to the meat shed. Strangely, Jordan said that the man took his service revolver, unloaded it, pocketed the weapon and discarded the bullets. This was unusual since the IRA was always short of ammunition. Yet, when the army found the armoured car abandoned on the Malahide Road near Clontarf, Co. Dublin, the Hotchkiss guns were missing, along with some of the ammunition, but the rebels had left behind about 1,500 rounds of .303 rifle/machine-gun ammunition, the two spare barrels and four of their pistols (one with an expended round). The other armoured car driver, Pte Harvey, was able only to hide his sidearm in his overalls pocket before obeying Squad member Patrick McCrea's order to dismount the vehicle. McCrea told Pte Harvey that he should not worry, 'it's not you we want, it is your tin can'. The other soldiers were lined against the wall. Another rebel took Pte Ruck over to the armoured car and had him demonstrate its operation.[66] Ruck did not tell them that the armoured car was having fuelling problems and was running on emergency reserves. The rest of the rebels mounted the vehicle and drove out the front gate.[67] From there they drove to Mountjoy Prison where they tried, unsuccessfully, to get Séan MacEóin released to them by posing as British army officers.

The rationing party had violated many of the standing orders and procedures that morning, although it is questionable if they could have prevented the theft of the vehicle. Certainly, vigilance would have resulted in a gunfight, especially if the machine gunners had remained at their posts. Yet, they were supposed to be safe in 'friendly' territory; for it was only there that they let down their guard. Still, Whetstone reported in his statement that he violated several standing orders: allowing more than one man to leave the vehicle at a time; leaving the access door open when he dismounted (it was from this door that Jordan was shot; if it had been closed, he might have been able to bring the Hotchkiss gun into action);

and having both machine guns loaded, with one pointing forward and one rearward. Pte Ruck also had left the vehicle to check the oil, but had left his sidearm lying on the front seat. Ruck did not explain why he had it out of his holster. The court of inquiry felt that at least twenty rebels had to have been involved and that they simply walked into the compound from some low-lying fenced areas, whereas in truth, the operation was carried out by just the few men of the Squad. To be fair, the Squad comprised some of the most dangerous rebels in Ireland, having been specially chosen for their capabilities. Squad member Michael Kennedy was so cool that when the abattoir's office phone rang, he calmly answered it, took an order for the Curragh Military Camp and asked them 'to ring back in about twenty minutes and they would get all the meat they required. He then cut the telephone cord.'[68]

Furthermore, one must point out that by this period, and aside from the violations of security practice, the IRA had made the transportation situation so difficult that the military abattoir could only deliver its meat daily through military armoured convoy, including an armoured car with two machine-gun turrets. How serious had the situation become when meat could only be delivered by armoured vehicle? There were, indeed, several ambushes against rationing parties during the war. The threat was substantial.

The Peerless armoured car was found the same day by Lieut C.B. de la Mare, 5th AC Company, Tank Corps, at Donnycarney House on the Malahide Road around 1130 hours. The reason the rebels abandoned the vehicle was due to 'the failure of the petrol supply incident upon a defect in the auto-vac connection from the main supply tank and that the rebels concerned were compelled to abandon the car at the gates of ... owing to lack of petrol fuel'. What was rather remarkable was that they took the two Hotchkiss machine guns and the ammunition in the weapons, but left behind three pistols and more than 1,500 rounds of .303 Lee-Enfield ammunition in boxes.[69] Perhaps they did not notice it or were unable to carry it on foot when the vehicle broke down, but they did not even try to hide it elsewhere for later retrieval. This was one of the only cases where the IRA actually captured such additional supplies of ammunition from a military or police vehicle during the war, yet, on this occasion failed to exploit it.

The men of the IRA Dublin Brigade had one more surprise for the British forces – the Thompson submachine gun, the 'Tommy gun'. Developed by Col. John F. Thompson, of the U.S. Army Ordnance Corps, the Thompson was intended to break the deadlock on the Western Front. Firing a .45 ACP[70] cartridge, the Tommy gun was outstanding for urban combat. It made its combat debut on 16 June 1921 against the West Kents, who had just arrived in Ireland, in a train ambush.[71] The war ended before the Thompson could be used in greater numbers or have greater effect.

Rebel attacks in urban areas were sudden, but short. This was due to the terrain; in Dublin, the British had such vast and various forces spread throughout the city that help was always relatively close at hand. The rebels certainly knew this and acted accordingly, breaking contact quickly and/or refusing prolonged attacks. What is clear from IRA urban operations is that basic security and common sense was the best defence for the British. As noted already, most of the urban police casualties were killed or wounded singly, leading to the obvious conclusion that assassination was a solitary event for the victim. Movement in large, armed groups made a difference; armoured convoys faced a lower likelihood of attack than two men on foot. There were significant military requirements: lowering casualties while maintaining control. Controlling the city was difficult and the British did not learn how to do so, using both motor vehicle and foot patrols in tandem, until it was too late.

There were times, however, when sound policing or military doctrine required small groups to move through and operate in the urban areas. These were in danger, since assassination or attacks on small groups were such a real possibility in the cities. These threats could have been mitigated by training, equipment and weapons, and coordination. These men should have been well armed and prepared for any eventuality, giving them an extra edge to hold off a rebel attack until help could arrive. Greater coordination of British forces with each other would have allowed relief forces to be more readily available to move in quickly when needed. Although full answers to these issues were not always forthcoming, common-sense security and offensive spirit frequently made the dangers more manageable.

The IRA's urban attacks demonstrated that operations in cities, especially movement, were dangerous. The closed-in area, with high buildings and narrow, crowded streets, limited the available view of potential threats. Further, these also limited the earlier countermeasure of speed for safety, even for patrols supply convoys (which were frequent and at regular intervals). High buildings gave the rebels the advantage of the 'high ground', but also proved a liability if the ambushed group counterattacked and pursued – there was nowhere for the rebels to go if surrounded in a building.

Rebel patrols were good at exploiting British vulnerabilities, especially since they had ample time to observe and take notes on their targets. The idea of countersurveillance did not yet exist, although the rebels advocated basic security measures such as unpredictability in movements.[72] At the same time, British forces, especially the DMP and RIC, never seem to have understood that travelling alone and unarmed was lethal. Worse, even with the stunning increase in fatalities, many in both police forces *refused* to carry arms. When the police or military did not use common-sense security measures within cities, the seemingly omnipresent IRA were able to *exploit* their vulnerabilities. These were opportunities handed to the IRA that they might not otherwise have had.

Helping the IRA was the fact that the rebels did not have to control the ground, except for the duration of an attack. But then, what did 'controlling the ground' actually mean in an urban environment? Was it an issue of controlling the streets *and* the buildings, or just the former? The rebels only had to control their immediate area and then make good their escape, while letting the British simply react. The British forces, necessarily concerned with the legitimacy of their government, had a tougher job. They had to engage the enemy, and were eager to do so, but not harm the innocent. Further, the IRA was frequently unconcerned with collateral damage, since the liberals and the press blamed the government for any killings.

An obvious answer to these attacks was for British forces to move in large and well-armed groups. Rebels were less likely to attack the police or army when they were obviously ready for a fight. It is interesting, but not surprising, that the litany of IRA urban attacks rarely included a well-armed, eager British army or police unit being ambushed. When these attacks occurred, the IRA usually came out second best. A common-sense approach would have been to use both lookouts and scouts, even in the cities. The former could potentially prevent or stop an attack, while the latter provided not only reconnaissance, but added the unknown element to the rebels of a screening or even reserve force. These, of course, had to be adapted to urban terrain. The obvious problem was, could they function in an overcrowded street with limited sight or communications? In what sizes would they operate? If they were not large enough, the rebels might have simply targeted them rather than the main body. This would have been good, but only as long as the main body's mission supported this. At what size does the main body become overshadowed by the advance guard's size? That is a more difficult question, for which bicycles or motorcycles were perhaps a partial answer.

Something else that was part and parcel of being in a large, well-armed party was its inherent ability of counterattack. In all of the instances of urban attacks on groups, the rebels retreated quickly, but did so more quickly when the response was a fast and violent counterattack; indeed, as noted above, the rebels criticized weak responses from their enemies. One reason such counterattacks worked well in cities was the consistent weakness – being outgunned – of the IRA groups relative to their prey. Further, the IRA did not normally stand and fight for too long since the army and police were well positioned throughout the city. Thus, whenever the first shots or explosions rang out, reinforcements were on the way, and this increased their chances of being surrounded, which meant death or capture (which eventually might lead to death too).

The Dublin District instituted greater patrolling in response to the rebel urban threat. They divided the city by battalion, much as the IRA had done, and left it to each battalion commander to figure out how best to patrol his battalion area. In many cases, the answer was a vehicle patrol, but they also instituted foot patrols and used the ADRIC in plain clothes. In many respects, they adopted the methods of the IRA. There were incidents of the plain-clothed Auxiliaries coming into contact with other British forces and a number of 'friendly fire' incidents. The official history noted that the most effective patrols were on foot; this is hardly surprising, because one frequently finds that adopting the guerrilla method is often as disruptive to the enemy guerrillas as operations against them.[73] In the case of Dublin, the army found that increased patrolling affected the IRA's ability to establish ambushes because of the constant movement of vehicle-mounted and dismounted patrols throughout the city. Further, increasing the randomness of these patrols and conducting them in conjunction with observation posts on tall buildings tended to worsen the situation for the rebels.[74]

There were several other means available to the British forces to retard rebel movement within the urban environment; among these were patrolling, road blocks and checkpoints, and observation posts. While these were not specific countermeasures to just ambushes, they made all IRA operations more dangerous and more difficult for the rebels.

Road blocks and checkpoints searched people and vehicles according to the randomness of their movement through the picquetted area. They also enabled enforcement of the various motor permit orders throughout the conflict. Of course one could also track the movement of various vehicles in this manner.[75] These certainly made transportation of arms and documents more problematic for the rebels.

The Dublin District ordered that the picquets be comprised of not less than fifteen soldiers and one policeman, the latter being the one actually conducting the searches. The blocked area was to be in a defendable position in case of rebel attack. While the IRA rarely attacked these checkpoints, there were occasions where the troops had to open fire on rebels attempting to break through or escape.[76]

Observation posts were similar to piquets in that they could surveil a given area for long periods. Unlike piquets, however, observation posts had no real offensive capability; indeed, they had little defensive capacity. Their primary function was to provide early warning to defenders of the area under their purview.[77]

Another measure was increased searches and raids. British forces conducted these operations around the clock to ensure that the rebels received no respite. Although one may not consider the effects of darkness on military operations today due to the ready availability of low-light equipment such as night vision goggles, as recently as the 1970s, most armies had no such kit. In Ireland, the situation was no different; if British forces wanted to see at night, they had to bring sufficient equipment to do so. If they were conducting extensive raids or a 'cordon and search' at night, only searchlights were going to help.[78] The problem in 1920 was that they had no such searchlights.

In October 1920, the Dublin District identified this shortfall, most likely because they were conducting more urban operations. They initially tried to use the lights from Austin armoured cars,[79] and Lucas lamps inside the building. The memorandum directing this use also ordered the battalions to conduct practice training at night in barracks by platoons, in order not only to train the troops but to identify further requirements for kit.[80]

Since there were no light-producing units, the army experimented by mounting Aldis Lamps on vehicles. The Army Council baulked a little at first, hoping to use acetylene lamps instead of the Aldis, due in all likelihood to cost and availability, but the Irish Command pressed for the Aldis.[81]The War Office acquiesced. The British forces' countermeasures began to tell, but, as with much of this conflict, the political solution prevented validation of either side's claims to success.

NOTES

1. 'Dublin District Weekly Intelligence Summary', No. 63, for week ending 1 February 1921 (NA PRO WO 35/90, p.1).
2. See Abbott, *Police Casualties*, for information on each.
3. As opposed to targets of opportunity.
4. Either RIC or DMP, and, in one instance, a Special Harbour Constable in Belfast. There were actually sixty-nine shooting incidents, but one RIC constable was killed by the army by mistake on 6 November 1920 on Foyle Street in Londonderry; Abbott, *Police Casualties*, p.317.
5. See War Diaries in general (NA PRO WO 35/90–3). It is important to note that these records

are not exhaustive. These reports over-represent the Dublin District.

6. See Abbott, *Police Casualties*, pp.64–7.
7. Abbott took his study to the end of the Irish Civil War of 1922–3.
8. The most serious sectarian violence in the early twentieth century began in Belfast in 1912 as a result of the Orange and other Unionist groups targeting Catholics as a result of the home rule movement. There were also riots associated with the various large factories and shipyards; probably in order to force Catholics to leave Ulster. For more on the unrest in the north, see K. Jeffery and P. Hennessy, *States of Emergency: British Governments and Strikebreaking since 1919* (1983).
9. See, for example, HQ Dublin District Memorandum No. S/712/G, 1 April 1920 (NA PRO WO 35/90/1/17, pp.1–2) and 'Dublin District Weekly Intelligence Summary,' 1 February 1921 (WO 35/90, Copy No. 63, pp.1–2).
10. 'Dublin District Weekly Intelligence Summary', No. 63, for week ending 1 February 1921 (WO 35/90, pp.1–2). Submachine-guns were also wasteful in ammunition, which was consistently in low supply. There was an incident, late in the war, where New York police found and raided a shipment of 500 Thompson submachine-guns in a ship bound for Ireland in 1921. Submachine guns saw greater use during the Civil War of 1922–3. See J.B. Bell, 'The Thompson Submachine-Gun in Ireland, 1921', *Irish Sword*, no. 8 (Winter, 1967) pp.98–101; P. Jung, 'The Thompson submachine gun during and after the Anglo-Irish War: the new evidence,' *Irish Sword*, 21, 84 (Winter, 1998), pp.191–218; and P. Hart, *The IRA at War 1916–1923* (2004).
11. General Staff, Irish Command, *Record of the Rebellion in Ireland in 1920–21, and the Part Played by the Army in Dealing with It* (1922), vol. IV, p.251 (NA PRO WO 141/93); Dublin District Memorandum No. 3/386/1/G, 3 May 1920 (NA PRO WO 35/90/1/21); and Dublin District Weekly Intelligence Summary No. 119, Copy 83 for week ending 19 June 1921 (WO 35/91). See also Irish Command Annual Medical Returns for 1921 (WO 115/1).
12. Dublin District Memorandum No. S/G.1, 19 October 1920 (NA PRO WO 35/90/52, p.1).
13. See Dublin District War Diaries for October 1920 to July 1921 (NA PRO WO 35/90 to 35/93).
14. Attachment to Dublin District Memorandum, 'Bad Areas', No. S/813/1/G, 2 May 1920 (NA PRO WO 35/90/1/20).
15. Dublin District Memorandum No. S/G.1, 19 October 1920 (NA PRO WO 35/90/52, p.1).
16. Ibid.
17. See Appendices B through E for Dublin Brigade orders for armoured vehicles.
18. This does not deny that some British forces broke discipline and engaged in brutal reprisals, but these were *usually* after the events which provoked them rather than during regular operations. See, for instance, Dublin District Memorandum No. S/813/G, 15 August 1920.
19. Although this was not common, there were only three reported in the war diaries; one at Merrion Gates in February 1921, one at the intersection of Capel St. and Parnell St. in March 1921, and another on Camden St. also in March. See 'Operation Report', Dublin District Memorandum No. S/G.1.A, 13 February 1921, (NA PRO WO 35/90, p.2); 'Operation Report', Dublin District Memorandum No. S/G/1/A, 3 March 1921 (WO 35/90) and 'Weekly Intelligence Summary', No. 106, for week ending 20 March 1921 (WO 35/90, pp.7–8).
20. There were stories that the IRA overcame the wire mesh by attaching hooks to their bombs so they would entangle in the wires.
21. Operation Summary for December 1921, General Staff, Dublin District, 2 January 1921 (NA PRO WO 35/90/1, p.5.
22. The Dublin District, under the command of Brig.-Gen. Gerald F. Boyd, was variously part of the 5th Infantry Division with one brigade and independent during the war; by June 1921, the District's AOR increased to encompass several additional counties and so they received an additional brigade.
23. They were Sgt Archer Banks, Pvts Henry Washington, Matthew Whitehead, Thomas Humphries, Bandsmen William Smith and Frank Noble and an unnamed driver who was likely a member of the Royal Army Service Corps attached for transportation.
24. There has been the accusation that Barry was carrying 'flat-nosed' bullets in his Mauser, with the implication that they violated the Hague conventions. This depends on what one means, there is nothing illegal about flat, conoidal *fully-jacketed* (also called 'full metal jacket or FMJ) rounds because they do not cause any more horrific wounds than standard military 'ball' ammunition. 'Dum-dum' bullets, where the full metal jacket has been altered or removed to expose the lead core, or hollow-pointed bullets, where the metal jacket is cast to leave the tip exposed to cause expansion, are illegal in war. These were rare at the time; one must use a file

to remove the tip of the jacket. Flat-nosed FMJ ammunition, while uncommon at the time, would explain the multiple jams that Barry experienced, but were not illegal in war.

25. J. Ainsworth, 'Kevin Barry: The Incident at Monk's bakery and the Making of an Irish Republican Legend', *History*, 87, 287 (2002), pp.373–4; see also D. O'Donovan, *Kevin Barry and His Time* (1989).

26. See 'Laws and Customs of War on Land (Hague IV)', 18 October 1907.

27. 'War Diary of General Staff, GHQ Ireland', p.13, 19 December 1920 (NA PRO WO 35/93A); Sir N. Macready, *Annals of an Active Life*, Vol. II (1925), pp.503 and 525; and General Staff, Irish Command, *Record of the Rebellion*, Vol. I, p.30, Vol. II generally and Vol. IV, p.170 (WO 141/93).

28. 'War Diary of General Staff, GHQ Ireland', p.6, 21 January 1921 (NA PRO WO 35/93A); 'The IRA (from Captured Documents Only)', p.35 (PRO WO 141/40); *Record of the Rebellion*, Vol. I, p.39 (WO 141/93); and RIC IG Report for Dublin for January 1921 (CO 904/114).

29. 'Operation Report' Dublin District Memorandum No. S/G.1.A., 23 January 1921 (NA PRO WO 35/90).

30. 'The IRA (from Captured Documents Only)', p.35 (NA PRO WO 141/40); General Staff, Irish Command, *Record of the Rebellion*, Vol. I, p.39 (PRO WO 141/93); RIC IG Report for Dublin for January 1921 (CO 904/114) and 'Operation Report' Dublin District Memorandum No. S/G.1.A., 23 January 1921 (WO 35/90).

31. 'War Diary of General Staff, GHQ Ireland', p.6, 21 January 1921 (NA PRO WO 35/93A); 'Operation Report', Dublin District Memorandum No. S/G.1.A., 22 January 1921 and 'Operation Report' Dublin District Memorandum No. S/G.1.A., 23 January 1921 (WO 35/90).

32. The executions brought large protests and the Very Reverend Archbishop of Dublin, Joseph Walsh, argued that it was unjustified since no police were killed in the ambush. This was unusual since most of the hierarchy of the Catholic Church had condemned the conflict. The success in the commutation of O'Sullivan's sentence may have been a result of the backlash from Kevin Barry's execution the previous autumn.

33. 'The IRA (from Captured Documents Only)', p.36 (PRO WO 141/40).

34. Ibid., p.35; General Staff, Irish Command, *Record of the Rebellion*, Vol. I, p.39 (NA PRO WO 141/93); and RIC IG Report for Dublin for January 1921 (CO 904/114).

35. 'Patrol Report', OC, Company G, 4th Battalion, IRA Dublin Brigade, 'The IRA (from Captured Documents Only)', pp.35–6 (PRO WO 141/40).

36. See General Staff, Irish Command, *Record of the Rebellion*, Vol. IV, p.245 (NA PRO WO 141/93).

37. 'Patrol Report', OC, Company G, 4th Battalion, IRA Dublin Brigade, 'The IRA (from Captured Documents Only)', pp.35–6 (PRO WO 141/40).

38. He did not explain if this was just a fear in general or that this might be the normal route to take due to the traffic conditions of the day.

39. 'Patrol Report', OC, Company G, 4th Battalion, IRA Dublin Brigade, 'The IRA (from Captured Documents Only)', pp.35–6 (NA PRO WO 141/40). See also *Record of the Rebellion*, Vol. I, p.39 (WO 141/93).

40. 'Report on Patrol of the 2nd Bn. The Royal Berkshire Regt, Ambushed near Terenure Police Station on night of January 29/30, 1921', 31 January 1921, Memorandum No. S/G88/A (NA PRO WO 35/90). The Dublin District report went on to state that Lieut. Newton's 'wounds are described to-day as severe, but not dangerous'; Patrol of the 2nd Bn. The Royal Berkshire Regt, Ambushed near Terenure Police Station on night of January 29/30, 1921', 31 January 1921, Memorandum No. S/G1A (WO 35/90).

41. 'Report on Ambush at Rathmines', IRA HQ, Dublin, nd, from 'The IRA (from Captured Documents Only)', pp.36–7 (NA PRO WO 141/40).

42. 'The IRA (from Captured Documents Only)', pp.36–7 (NA PRO WO 141/40).

43. RIC IG Report for Co. Limerick for February 1921 (NA PRO CO 904/114); Abbott, *Police Casualties*, pp.194–6; and General Staff, Irish Command, *Record of the Rebellion*, Vol. IV, p.174 (WO 141/93).

44. Const. Samuel Green, (#75477), b. Middlesex, England, 26 December 1898, d. Balbriggan, Co. Dublin, 3 February 1921 (he was mortally wounded on the 2nd and died on the 3rd) and Const. Patrick Mullany (#65685), b. Co. Cavan. 31 October 1886, d. Trinity St., Dublin, 2 February 1921. J. Herlihy, *The Royal Irish Constabulary: A Complete Alphabetical List* (1999), pp.183 and 209 and Abbott, *Police Casualties*, p.192.

45. These three men, Constables Martin Greer, Daniel Hoey and Edward McDonagh, were couriers *en route*.

46. 'The IRA (from Captured Documents Only)', pp.37–8 (NA PRO WO 141/40).

47. These wounded were not named in any of the available sources.
48. 'The IRA (from Captured Documents Only)', pp.38–9 (NA PRO WO 141/40).
49. P. Quin, 'Battle of Brunswick Street', in J. White, ed., *Dublin's Fighting Story 1913–21, (1947)*p.159. If the British were correct about this supposed meeting, one must give B Company more credit as the British stated that they captured none of the meeting's participants due to the resistance of the IRA men in the street. In that, they would seem to have accomplished this mission.
50. The injured IRA man was severely wounded or injured (it was unclear) in the leg, which was later amputated at Mercer Hospital. 'Operation Report', Dublin District Memo No. S/G1A, 15 March 1921 (NA PRO WO 35/90); 'Dublin District Weekly Intelligence Summary', No. 106 for Week Ending 20 March 1921 (WO 35/90, pp.5–6); 'Dublin District Weekly Intelligence Summary', No. 60 for Week Ending 3 April 1921 (WO 35/90, p.1); 'War Diary of General Staff, GHQ Ireland', p.1, 14 March 1921 (WO 35/93A); 'The IRA (from Captured Documents Only)', pp.38–9 (WO 141/40).
51. It is difficult to accept the British claim of a meeting if the IRA report was correct, since deliberately drawing in British forces would obviously endanger the meeting.
52. Called 'Black and Tans' in the IRA report, it was not uncommon for the people to refer to the Auxiliaries as 'Black and Tans' although that term technically applied only to those non-Irishmen serving with the regular RIC.
53. See Appendix A, Police Casualties.
54. 'Fortunes of War', *An t–Óglác*, III, 2 (1 April 1921), p.149; Abbott, *Police Casualties*, p.208 and Herlihy, *Royal Irish Constabulary*, pp.15 and 371.
55. See Appendix A, Police Casualties.
56. 'Execution at Mountjoy Prison', DMP Memo No. 8766.S, 25 April 1921 (NA PRO WO 35/90). Traynor's last words were reported as being: 'Fight on not for vengeance but for Freedom. I hope that some young man who has not yet realized his duty to his Country will fill my place.' *An t–Óglác*, III, 7 (6 May 1921).
57. The IRA did not normally use proper names in their reports to safeguard the identities of their members. The British, when transcribing IRA reports, frequently left out the names of the IRA men.
58. 'The IRA (from Captured Documents Only)', p.39 (NA PRO WO 141/40).
59. General Staff, Irish Command, *Record of the Rebellion*, Vol. IV, p.40 (NA PRO WO 141/93).
60. Statement of Joseph Byrne (MA WS/461); Statement of Seán Fitzpatrick (MA WS/1259); 'Gormanstown Camp Meat Contract', 31 May 1923, Dáil Éireann Debates, Vol. 3. See also Dáil Éireann Debates, Vol. 8, 27 June 1924; Vol. 13, 16 December 1925; and Vol. 124, 8 March 1951; and Dublin District Weekly Intelligence Summary, No. 114, Copy No. 60, for week ending 15 May 1921 and Appendix E, p.3 of same summary (NA PRO WO 35/90/2).
61. Statement of Sgt F Walker and Statement of L/Corp J. Whetstone (NA PRO WO35/56B, pp.5–6).
62. Statement of Statement of L/Corp J. Whetstone (NA PRO WO35/56B, p.6).
63. Court of Inquiry Summary and Statement of L/Corp J. Whetstone (NA PRO WO35/56B, pp.4–6). The *An t–Óglác*, account did not mention the full circumstances of the action, III, 10 (27 May 1921).
64. Statement of Joseph Byrne (MA WS/461).
65. Statement of Pte F Jordan (NA PRO WO35/56B, p.6).
66. The British later captured a Patrick Reynolds whom they believed was the driver of the armoured car; see 'Operation Report', Dublin District Memorandum No. S/G1A, 19 May 1921 and of 22 May 1921 (NA PRO WO 35/90/2).
67. Dublin District Weekly Intelligence Summary, No. 114, Copy No. 60, for week ending 15 May 1921 (NA PRO WO 35/90/2); Court of Inquiry Summary, Statement of Pte S. Ruck, Statement of Pte Harvey and Statement of Lt C.B. de la Mare (WO35/56B, p.4–9) and Statement of Joseph Byrne (MA WS/461).
68. Statement of Joseph Byrne (MA WS/461).
69. 'Testimony of Lt. C.B. de la Mare, 5th Armoured Car Company, Tank Corps, to the Court of Inquiry', 19 May 1921 (NA PRO WO 35/56B). The lieutenant also stated that damages to the vehicle were £299.11.4. Although the IRA were quite experienced at arson, they were unable to get the vehicle to catch fire. This would suggest that the rebels were rushed, but the means attempted took too long to set up to support that conclusion.
70. Automatic Colt Pistol.

71. Hart, *The IRA and its Enemies*, pp.178–93; Bell, 'The Thompson Submachine Gun in Ireland, 1921', *Irish Sword*, no. 8 (Winter, 1967) pp.98–101; P. Jung, 'The Thompson submachine gun during and after the Anglo-Irish War: the new evidence,' *Irish Sword*, 21, 84 (Winter 1998), pp.191–218; and P. Ó Snodaigh, 'The Thompson submachine gun: a few footnotes', *Irish Sword*, 22, 89 (2001), p.348. The problem with the Thompson was that, with a cyclic rate of fire of around 600 rounds per minute, the weapon was hard to control and used too much ammunition, which was always in short supply.

72. 'Notes of General Officer Commanding's Conference Held at Dublin District Headquarters', 27 March 1920 (NA PRO WO 35/90/1/2, pp.1–2).

73. General Staff, Irish Command, *Record of the Rebellion in Ireland*, Vol. IV, p.250 (NA PRO WO 141/93).

74. Appendix B, Dublin District Weekly Intelligence Summary, No. 114, Copy No. 60, for week ending 15 May 1921 (NA PRO WO 35/90/2); Dublin District Weekly Intelligence Summary, No. 118, Copy, No. 83, for week ending 12 June 1921 (WO 35/91); and Dublin District Memorandum No. S/712/G/1, 17 May 1920 (WO 35/90/23, p.3).

75. 'Permits', Dublin District Memorandum No. S/26/GMT, 22 November 1920 (NA PRO WO 35/90/1/57).

76. 'Dublin District Instruction for Picqueting Roads', Dublin District Memorandum No. S/871/G.B, 24 June 1920. (NA PRO WO 35/90/1/29, pp.1–2); and Operation Report, Dublin District Memorandum No. S/G/1/A., 3 March 1921 (WO 35/90).

77. Dublin District Memorandum No. S/712/G/1, 17 May 1920 (NA PRO WO 35/90/1/23, p.2).

78. Dublin District Weekly Intelligence Summary, No. 103, for week ending 27 February 1921 (NA PRO WO 35/90, p.7; and Operation Report, Dublin District Memorandum No. S/G/1A, 24 March 1921 (WO 35/90, p.1).

79. One assumes they meant to use the headlights, but there is no indication in the records as to why just the Austin and not other motor vehicles.

80. Dublin District Memorandum No. S/G1, 19 October 1920 (NA PRO WO 35/90/1/52, p.1).

81. The Aldis signal lamp was the signal light the navy used for signalling between vessels at sea; it produced a bright light that could be seen in daytime. *An t–Óglác*, III, 17 (16 July 1921); 'War Diary of General Staff, GHQ Ireland', p.3, 10 January 1921, and p.5, 18 January 1921 (NA PRO WO 35/93A).

Eight

Conclusion: British Tactics, Techniques and Procedures

The only plans to end the conflict on the British side were either maintaining the status quo, which was failing, or full-scale war. Macready, the GOCinC, Ireland, forwarded a plan to the British Cabinet in 1921, the foundations of which had been laid by police and military officers as early as late 1919, to attack the rebels without cease, to hound them to submission by capturing or killing the rank and file and their leaders. Macready wanted to sweep from one end of the country to the other with infantry on foot and in vehicles; horse-mounted cavalry; armed[1] RAF aircraft acting as scouts and as a screening force; with the various police organizations conducting raids; bringing in shallow-draft boats for riverine patrols (also having begun in 1921 under army direction) and the Royal Navy blockading the entire island. Finally, they would have sufficient support forces from the Royal Engineers and logistics support from the Royal Army Service Corps.[2]

This was a bold plan, but would it have worked? Macready did not get all the additional infantry battalions he wanted. But he already had the RAF support and would likely have received enhanced engineer capabilities in addition to an extra cavalry brigade. It was not that the Cabinet did not want to give Macready all the forces he needed – they pulled infantry battalions from as far away as Egypt in preparation – they simply did not have enough men to meet their global commitments. Yet while this plan would likely have succeeded in purely operational terms, there is little to suggest that it would have led to long-term peace since it did not deal with the underlying problems in Ireland that continue, in various forms, to the present. It is hard to accept that this plan would have done anything more than prolong the conflict for another generation – or longer.

While this is not meant to be a work on counterinsurgency theory, it is important to note that the doctrine itself would have worked. The army tested its tactics in the relatively quiet county of Sligo in March 1921 and again later in Co. Wexford in April, as well as others. But before Macready could marshal sufficient forces, the IRA started a new offensive unexpectedly – they stood down their largest brigades in the south in order to reorganize them into divisions in May 1921. At the end of that month, the new divisions were ready and launched an offensive. The rebel offensive of late May and June was by no means devastating, but it made some important political gains. At the same time, British troop strength peaked at over 53,000 in July 1921. Macready hoped to begin his sweeps in mid-to-late summer, but then the Cabinet suddenly agreed to a ceasefire, formally signing a truce, effective on 11 July 1921. Five months later, after a shaky peace and tense negotiations, the Anglo-Irish Treaty of December 1921 formally ended the war.

At this point it is appropriate to ask what the British learned from this traumatic experience. There seem to be essentially two schools of thought here; some say that, judging by their actions in the inter-war years on the North-west Frontier, the Mandates, especially Mesopotamia (Iraq) and Palestine, the British learned little. This view seems a bit harsh, but the other side could assert that Churchill, for instance, was impressed by the IRA and that he used them as an example for the founding in 1940 of the British organization that assisted the resistance movements in the Second World War, the Special Operations Executive (SOE).[3] Indeed, one of the founders and leading lights of the SOE, Maj.-Gen. Sir Colin McVean Gubbins, served in Ireland during the war and supplied the artillery Collins used on the Four Courts in 1922. As tantalizing as this is, there has yet to be any significant evidence to support this assertion. Both schools would probably agree that the British lost much of any specialized knowledge they had gained of combating countermobility operations in counterinsurgencies by the end of the Second World War. But while the issue of what they actually learned and used later is enticing, is not the question relating to what they could have learned from Ireland more important?

The generalized counterinsurgent lessons one might draw from the British experience in Ireland from 1919 to 1921 are many: the importance of unity of command was always at the top of the list for the British leadership almost in the same breath as having clear, measurable objectives established by the civil government. It is important to realize just how difficult the situation was; the British army in 1920 was no scalpel, yet this blunt instrument's leadership was expected to develop an answer to a *political* problem, and then expected to implement it. A more modern way to put this is that they wanted a clearly defined exit strategy. How were they supposed to measure success? How were they supposed to know when they were finished? The republican legends of the 'Tans' being driven out are demonstrably false; the British fighting forces were perfectly ready and, in many respects, willing to continue the war, and fully expected to do so after the hiatus of the truce (as did the IRA themselves). Although the government largely capitulated in the sense of conducting formal negotiations with those with whom they vowed never to do so, British forces seemed to have learned to fight in this environment. They later called for the implementation of total martial law and insisted on the necessity of large numbers to provide a high ratio (1:40) of soldiers to population (roughly 4 million total) of well-trained, highly disciplined, flexible troops. They expected timely, accurate and, to use the modern term, 'actionable' intelligence; the establishment of safe areas for troops and loyalists, and control of information, all topped the list. They wanted to know what to do and to have a clearly defined enemy; what they got in the early, and perhaps most critical, years of the war was much different. Still, through trial and error, they learned. But there were other, more immediate and proactive measures to take which relate more directly to this study.

There are many examples of post-operational reports, or after-action reports (AARs) following incidents during the war from both sides, and it is clear that the AAR 'process' was a critical factor on both sides. The IRA passed what they learned primarily through their general orders (policy), engineering circulars, their *Engineering Handbook*[4] and, most importantly, their bi-weekly (later, weekly) journal, *An t-Óglác*, (tactical and operational information and practices). The British forces, primarily the army, passed information through standing orders (policy), weekly intelligence summaries, conferences,[5] their publication 'The Irish Republican Army (From Captured Documents Only)' of June 1921, and late in the war, the first counterinsurgency school of the twentieth century. Dissemination of information remained a problem within the army and was even worse within the police forces. For the latter, this was somewhat resolved with the appointment of Brig.-Gen. Sir Ormonde de l'Epée Winter as chief of

Figure 8.1 Map of Sandford Road Ambush

police intelligence in August 1920. He created 'Raids Bureaus' to central-
ize analysis and exploitation of captured rebel documents.
Unfortunately for the British, 'O', as he was called, did not have sufficient time to implement his changes fully.[6]

Figure 8.2 IRA Patrol Report of Sandford Road Ambush

	PATROL REPORT
8:50 P.M. 19-4-'21	7 men 'E.' Coy. III 1st Lieut. M
PROCEDURE	The Patrol was instructed to attack any enemy lorry, foot-patrol or convoy they met in the Company area. The attack was to be opened by bombs, if possible and sustained by revolver fire.
DISPOSAL OF MEN	The patrol was stationed on both sides of Sanford Road, Ranelagh: three men including O.C. patrol armed with bombs on one side of the road and four men armed with revolvers on opposite side in pairs.
INFORMATION ABOUT ENEMY	The enemy was in convoy; six [Crossley] Tenders and one Ford car. The latter appeared first travelling from city in direction of Dundrum. The attack was opened on the Ford and the following Tender. One bomb fell right behind the first Tender injuring three of its occupants and damaging the car. Upon the attack being opened, the remaining Tenders halted and the occupants started to search the xxx wood. Another Auxiliary R.I.C. man was wounded in Hollybank Avenue, when following one of the [IRA] patrol.
INFORMATION ABOUT OWN	The patrol retreated through the houses on the road; one man carrying a .45[5] Webley was held up and searched by an MENAuxiliary who was so excited that he failed to discover the weapon and let the man go.
AMMUNITION EXPENDED	Two bombs – 19 rounds .45[5] revolver amm.[unition].
CASUALTIES Our men had none.	There were 4 known enemy casualties.
REMARKS	The patrol fought a splendid action.
(By hand)	Signed – O/C E. Coy Time 7.0 p.m. 20-6-'21

The British army knew that the IRA used an after-action reporting system to examine and improve their attacks; not only had they captured the reports, rebel doctrine and TTPs had developed and improved

accordingly.[7] Thus, the IRA's IED use, for instance, became deadlier and the army specifically warned, after the Millstreet Road ambush in Bantir, Co. Cork on 16 June 1921, that the IRA 'are becoming effective [with their IEDs] and [the IEDs] can be fired with fair accuracy and precision from a concealed [electric] battery placed at a considerable distance'. They continued, saying that the rebels 'are likely ... to hold considerable frontage and to distribute their mines along some distance of road'.[8] In response, the British divisional headquarters issued instructions, reports and standing orders dealing with security and protection. They based these on experience gained through their own after-action review process. Yet, due to a lack of centralized effort at the General Staff level of the Irish Command, this information remained mostly localized within the divisions until the publication of 'The Irish Republican Army (From Captured Documents Only)' by the Irish Command in June 1921. This was the first attempt by the Irish Command to produce a work that applied over all of Ireland, not as a regulatory document but rather as a means to inform the planning and execution of operations in Ireland. Issued with another study, called simply 'Sinn Fein', 'The Irish Republican Army (From Captured Documents Only)' permitted British soldiers a view into rebel operations not normally available to them. Yet, with this went a larger conceptual problem for the British leaders; they needed to admit that the IRA was capable of succeeding. Although the Irish Command did not collate the techniques and procedures into the publication until late in the war, the information comprising that publication existed in various fora as early as the summer of 1920. Further, the divisional and RIC concepts mirrored each other, although it is unclear if this was by accident or design. It is certainly true that there was no compendium manual about the IRA's doctrine and tactics until that of June 1921.

Through trial and error, the British discovered that patrolling and escorting, cordon and search, and using checkpoints were effective means of dealing with many types of rebel activity, including ambushes. Of these, however, the rebels feared the patrols and escorts because they were highly mobile. Checkpoints at random locations also caused anxiety, but it appears that the rebels were usually able to avoid cordons. These latter operations were primarily good for capturing war materiel.[9]

One of the first details to come from the British post-incident report process was the importance of preparation and planning; half-measures or haphazard preparation were lethal. One had to know the route and its terrain completely, all of its choke points, blind spots, and the locations of other dangerous areas. In early summer 1920 the army began to stress the need to vary convoy and patrol routes. This, combined with varying departure times, would lessen the likelihood of pre-planned ambushes making contact. Unfortunately for the British forces, in some areas with fewer roads, especially in the countryside, there were frequently fewer routes available to a given locale. The IRA exploited these problems or, indeed, created them, with their systematic trenching of roads throughout Ireland. Yet, Tom Barry later expressed surprise that the Auxiliaries in the Kilmichael ambush (28 November 1920) used such a well-known and travelled route. The truth was that the British leadership was incapable of enforcing these ideas among their military and RIC officer corps. Although the road network in Ireland was poor, there were usually other routes available, even if they were longer or more difficult. So by the spring of 1921, when the rebels had largely succeeded in blocking many of the roads through more or less permanent obstructions and thus reducing the availability of multiple routes, the army got around this lethargy by instructing the troops to patrol the route with large offensively capable groups incessantly at different times, day and night. This, of course, prevented the IRA knowing if an advancing convoy was filled with supplies or armed troops. Further, the constant, but irregular, patrolling kept the rebels from surreptitiously establishing their ambush sites, which, by 1921, were usually well prepared and frequently used IEDs, but necessarily required them to be present. The problem was that if one travelled or patrolled a route frequently, one displayed its criticality to the IRA.[10]

Another preparatory factor was training for drivers, mechanics and regular soldiers. As mentioned in earlier chapters, driving was still a rare skill and the army had an eight-week course to train drivers, but unlike today, the trainees usually had no previous driving experience, leaving them only basically qualified. In 1921, leaving routine accidents aside, when the skill of the driver may have meant the difference between life and death, an eight-week driving course was inadequate. In the case of men with no previous driving experience, the opportunities for gaining such experience under safe conditions were rare. This shortfall was deadly in a campaign where mobility was important.

Figure 8.3 IRA Incendiary Device

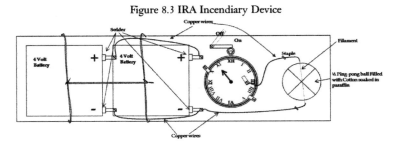

The complexity of motor vehicles today is rapidly making 'tinkering' impossible; but the engines in 1920 were as complex for the average contemporary soldier as modern, computer-controlled engines are now. This was due primarily to a general lack of mechanical experience among the populace. This placed all but the simplest repairs out of reach of the untrained. Worse still, with the internal petrol-powered engine literally only a couple of decades old (not to mention poor-quality parts and bad roads), reliability was a factor and breakdowns were frequent. Much could and did go wrong with these machines, aside from rebel action.[11]

One could deal with most emergencies with well-trained, disciplined troops; unfortunately for the British, the army was not always producing these. One could instil discipline and handle training issues at the unit level, but this took time and experienced NCOs, neither of which were available. Yet, even the best troops can become ineffective if they do not know the mission and contingency plans. Briefing one's soldiers in detail before an operation is standard practice today, but the British army has not had a reputation for explaining itself, especially to other ranks in the 1920s, when class distinctions between officers and enlisted were greater than today. On the one hand, they frequently did not see any reason to explain the operations to the other ranks, while on the other, they might have felt that the private soldier was not intelligent enough to understand potentially complex operations. Therefore, the standing orders gave explicit instructions that the commander would ensure that *every* soldier was briefed and knew the mission, his position and role in it, and what to do if the group came under attack. What was radical about these instructions was that there was an internal, unstated realization that in many instances, the soldiers might have had to take the initiative and act without orders. These decrees tried to ensure that the private soldier understood his mission in order to provide him with the knowledge to inform those actions. He was also to impress upon them the necessity for alertness, obedience and calmness. While not quite the recent phenomenon of the so-called 'strategic corporal', these soldiers were certainly his ancestor.[12] Finally, the commander had to ensure that the other officers and NCOs also knew their functions and responsibilities.

After-action reports and standing orders also led to the introduction of 'lorry drill', or actually practising physically what to do when attacked, and derivations based on different eventualities.[13] Again, a dry run before starting may seem obvious today, but this type of conflict was almost entirely new to the men fighting it and they had little pre-existing doctrine or training with which to work. Since the majority of the experienced troops came from the trenches of the First World War, this went mostly against their existing training and experience. Lorry drill was practice for getting into a position to defend and, perhaps, to counterattack (if the mission allowed). It was to take place *before* starting the mission, or shortly thereafter while still in friendly territory. The orders stressed the need to do this before *every* mission to prevent complacency.

There were other preparations to make. After the mission brief, and normally before the lorry drill, the commander personally inspected *each* man in the convoy (including other ranks, NCOs and officers) and vehicle in the group. Every soldier had to carry his normal combat kit: .303 SMLE Mark III service rifle, bayonet (unfixed), steel helmet and Mills bombs (fragmentation grenades). Each man had his magazine fully charged (ten rounds) and extra clips.[14] The magazine was loaded, but no round chambered. All pistols, normally .455 Webley Army Service Revolvers, were to be fully loaded, while automatic pistols were to have a loaded magazine, but no round chambered; all firearms were also to be set on 'safe'.

Going on a patrol or taking a convoy into rebel-infested areas with rifles and pistols without rounds chambered may seem somewhat over-cautious, but one must remember that these men were technically serving at 'home', and therefore not legally at 'war'. British law did not protect soldiers who were called out to deal with civil disturbances; nor did Common Law recognize states of rebellion. So when the troops were sent out to 'aid civil power', they had no real legal protection: they could be charged with a civil crime if they fired on a rioter or rebel, *even when obeying a lawful military order to do so*. The soldier was caught in a nightmarish position. If he fired, he could be charged with murder; if he did not obey a lawful order, it was still a 'lawful' order and he could be court-martialled. Normally, parliament prevented this problem by passing an act of indemnity, which decreed soldiers not to be liable under civil law, but this was done individually for each 'disturbance'. Parliament did not, however, pass an act of indemnity for the Irish conflict until after the war in 1922, so the soldiers fighting there were subject to *local* criminal prosecution and there were instances of killings by soldiers being ruled 'murder' by republican-influenced coroners' juries.[15] As a result, commanders, who felt they would be held responsible for any mishaps, took precautions against accidental discharges to try to prevent innocents being hurt or killed, of which there were still surprisingly many.

Each vehicle, depending on make and type, was to carry specific equipment, which the convoy commander also had to inspect before each mission. This included: a shovel (or two if only one vehicle was going out); a steel cable 'for towing purposes or dragging away road obstructions'; 'hand-ax' [sic]; crosscut saw; a crowbar; wire cutters and twelve field dressings. In addition, they carried two (or four for just one vehicle) eight by four-foot metal pieces of expandable bridging, which the IRA promptly learned to defeat by extending the length of their trenches.[16] They also carried extra gas, oil, water, spare parts and lights for each vehicle, while the lead vehicle carried two charges (with caps and detonators) of the high-explosive ammonite for clearing obstacles. Certain vehicles also carried several thousand additional rounds of .303 Lee-Enfield ammunition for the rifles and machine guns. Finally, the commander was required to carry a map and a copy of the standing orders. If anything was missing, the commander could proceed on his own authority, but was to report the deficiencies to his headquarters, giving the name of the driver and vehicle number. The vehicles usually belonged to the RASC, and so were the responsibility of a separate organization, which also performed all the required maintenance and other upkeep. With all the equipment they had to carry, one wonders how much room was left for troops and supplies.[17]

The minimum number of men permitted in an escort was five enlisted men and one NCO, 'except in case of a single Ford van sent out on urgent tactical duty (no other means of conveyance being available) ... five other ranks may be sent exclusive of the driver'.[18] Sending out small groups was less preferable as the war progressed, so these numbers were merely the minima and troops preferred to go out in force. The larger the force, the less likely they were to be attacked. Of course, the drivers probably also wanted to go out in force for the same reason and also because losing one's vehicle to the enemy was a court-martial offence.

The convoy, where sufficient vehicles existed, was to have an advance guard, main body and rear guard. If the advance guard was a lorry, it was to have at least one NCO, five enlisted men, a driver and carry the obstacle-breaching equipment mentioned above. In addition to the advance guard, if there were motorcycles available, they would send forward a vanguard to scout ahead. If there was an additional motorcycle available, he was to maintain communication with the other parts of the convoy, radios in vehicles were not available due to size and weight, and so there were none in the vehicles in Ireland. These measures reduced the likelihood of being surprised while increasing the odds of defeating an attack by providing a force capable of counterattack. The important, but frustrating, point was that the forces screening the convoy's movement were to counterattack, but any pursuit phase could follow only as far as the mission permitted; supply convoys could only go so far, while offensive patrols permitted a greater pursuit. Offensive patrols were less valuable targets than supply convoys for the continually supply-starved rebels.

Travelling not less than 300 yards behind the advance guard came the main body. If this had more than one vehicle, the convoy commander had to be in the lead vehicle and the interval between them was to be at least 20 yards. Following the main body by no less than 200 yards was the rear guard. Importantly, they were to be as strong as the advance guard. If there were more men than could be placed in the advance guard, the balance was to be divided between the rear guard and main bodies.[19] These forces, depending on the size of the guard force, could also be capable of the types of pursuit mentioned above. The rear guard also helped the commander maintain the formation, integrity of the column and interval. Part of the problem was communication between vehicles, especially on the narrow and winding roads of Ireland (usually with high hedges on either side); hence the need for motorcyclists.

The distances between the sections of the convoy not only prevented it appearing as a mass target, but also kept it from entering the ambush site all at once. If the convoy was long, the lead vehicles should have been clear of the site, and therefore out of range, as the last of the vehicles entered it. This created a tactical problem for the attackers, because one would normally want the entire convoy covered and inside the ambush site so that all parts of it would come under fire at once, to prevent anyone from escaping. Of course, if they were all in the ambush site, any counterattack was less effective since the counterattackers, too, were already under fire. Further, any counterattack from outside the ambush site was potentially more dangerous since the rebels would likely not have been able to find an ambush site which afforded good position to attack from and to defend, while offering a poor position for the victims' counterattack from inside the site and from without. These variables were almost impossible to achieve.

By lengthening the convoy, the army would force the rebels to cover more frontage and thus have to spread themselves out to cover it. This necessarily reduced the numbers of available gunmen in the increased number of attacking rebel sections. Tackling such targets necessarily required more men and, at the same time, increased the likelihood of detection by British forces; hence, the size increases in Tom Barry's 3rd West Cork Brigade flying column.

There were also supposed to be flank guards, but the instructions, beyond determining the use of bicycles if motorcycles were not available, did not explain how these men were to keep up with the convoy – a flaw in their doctrine. At Crossbarry, Lieutenant Tower used men on foot, but this was hardly practical over long distances or when speed was important. Even Tower appears to have become impatient with his slow progress that morning. Their mission was to check all walls and hedges on both sides of the road and any civilians they met along the route, as well as 'enfilading the enemy' or 'outflanking the enemy' in case of attack.[20] The instructions seemed to assume that these guards' mere presence would do more than their numbers would achieve in a normal fight. Judging by the incidents where similar methods were employed during the war, this view was likely accurate against regular IRA Volunteers, but against the flying columns was frequently a different proposition altogether. Yet their employment, not possessing sufficient transport, bicycles, motorcycles, possibly horses, was a hole in the normally detailed instructions and demonstrates the limited depth and breadth of the doctrine. It was one thing to call for a given solution, but if the supply of transport did not support it, then the doctrine was not useful. They eventually worked out that they needed flank guards, but did not necessarily know how to get the job done. Part of this was the general deficiency in motorcycles (for longer-range operations), which only exacerbated the weaknesses of armoured vehicles. One does not normally consider that armoured vehicles had drawbacks, but in addition to the limitations in size (both length and girth) and weight, they were slower, had greater turn radii, limited sight range, increased petrol expenditure and longer stopping distances. Only motorcycle-mounted flank guards (or supposedly bicycle-mounted with a sufficiently slow convoy) could make up for this deficiency at the time. But, clearly, the use of proper formations and maintenance of communications was still critical.

Each vehicle was to be under the command of an NCO and each section of the convoy was also supposed to have a commander. If there was only one NCO on a lorry, he was *never* to ride beside the driver, but always in the rear. This prevented the loss of the only leader on the vehicle being killed in an opening attack, since those in the driving compartment were the most vulnerable due to the compacted space and limited ability to move. The cab was also the most obvious area to attack to stop the vehicle. The commander was also responsible for the lookouts on the lorry, especially those in the rear, presumably because that was his most likely location too. Those not specifically assigned duties in the convoy were to keep their weapons handy, but stay out of the way.

There were four lookouts on each vehicle (unless there were more than ten men, in which case they added another one to either side). In the driving compartment next to the driver an officer or NCO sat acting as the front lookout (unless they were the only officer/NCO present). There were two side lookouts and one rear, at the tailgate. Each of these men was to have his rifle ready for 'immediate action' – round chambered with the safety on, muzzle outward or up. The tarp sides in the rear were always to be rolled up, but they also placed wire mesh around and on top (if there was no tarp) to prevent grenades or bombs being thrown in. Presumably, they felt the grenade threat was greater than the loss of mobility or escape in the rear, for with the wire mesh one could not jump over the side. The orders also directed that the tailgate be down or removed on the lorries, with no reason given, but likely for ease, speed and safety of dismounting for immediate action under fire.

The commanders were supposed to ensure that the lookouts were relieved frequently; the convoy had to stop every hour for ten minutes in the 5th Division orders, while the Dublin District stated that they should stop for 'meals and purposes of nature' as needed.[21] This difference was likely due to the shorter distances and narrower lanes travelled within the Dublin District Area. Since communications were difficult, the front and rear lookouts relayed hand signals and reported breaks in the formation of the convoy. Finally, one lookout was detailed to fire off the distress signal indicating an enemy attack, usually with a flare or sound rocket.

Since the state of tactical communications was so primitive at this time, the convoys carried several carrier pigeons with which they could send messages in case of attack. Commanders recognized that they might not have time to write a message before releasing the birds, so in July 1921 they decided to treat 'the arrival at a loft of a pigeon carrying no message ... as an S.O.S. signal'.[22] Of course, they also used sound rockets and flares for signals, as mentioned above, depending on the location of the convoy. If they were far from friendly support, rockets and flares did little good.

To maintain the integrity of the convoy's formation and safety of civilians, speed was limited to twelve miles per hour in the countryside and eight in towns. This was actually a departure from the earlier (1919–20) policy of moving at faster speeds to thwart the rebel ability to stop vehicles with gunfire. This means worked until the IRA learned to trench roads, but there were several instances of innocent bystanders and pedestrians being run down inside the narrow streets in towns and cities. The orders also stated that the slowest vehicles should be placed near the head of the column and that the 'speed of the convoy will be that of the *slowest* [emphasis original] vehicle', obviously to maintain the integrity of the column's formation.[23] The lead vehicles were also to slow down when rounding corners, since this was one of the more likely spots for rebel obstructions.[24]

Lookouts were told to be suspicious of supposedly harmless-looking parties of civilians on the roadside, since everyone was potentially dangerous. They were to stop and search them. Security and safety demanded they do this but 'stress was laid upon the necessity for exhibiting the greatest care and consideration for law-abiding people, women and children'. They preferred to let the police search, and since they frequently worked together, this was possible, but when this was not possible, only an officer was supposed to conduct the search. Further, the military was not permitted to arrest women, whom only female police searchers (specially hired) were permitted to search.[25] Obviously, the IRA exploited these limitations, primarily to transport documents and munitions. From Kilmichael, British forces learned constant vigilance: 'From the accounts of this operation the necessity for an advance guard to any force on the roads is shown to be imperative. Furthermore, it shows troops must be on their guard against being led into traps by persons with plausible stories, even in British uniforms.'[26] Since rebels could be tried and executed for capital crimes if caught, changing uniforms and other perfidy were certainly acceptable to them, as at the abattoir/Mountjoy jail raid and as *alleged* at Kilmichael.[27]

Even surrounded by a potentially hostile population, the army's most common transport problem was mechanical breakdown, either accidental or contrived by the IRA. After coming to a halt, the convoy commander was to post a guard of a least six soldiers. They would defend the vehicle against any attack, a common problem even when the breakdown really was accidental, and prevent civilians from approaching it. The standing orders specifically mentioned that the guard should be established in the best defensive position covering the vehicle. At odds was the fact that civilians used the road too and so, if they had to approach, the orders were to search them and permit them to proceed singly. This was likely the reason for using so many soldiers, having enough men to defend the site and to search the passers-by at the same time.

In the event of a breakdown, the commander was to send out an unarmed soldier to the nearest 'friendly' area. He was to be unarmed because it was less likely that the IRA would harm him. Were he armed, they would probably use force against him to get his arms and ammunition. Yet, considering the 'disappearances' and developments during the war, one should question the propriety of deliberately sending a solitary soldier into or through potentially enemy territory, especially if he was also to be unarmed.

Figure 8.4 British Commentary on Mourne Abbey Ambush, 15 February 1921[28]

THE MOURNE ABBEY AMBUSH, 15TH FEBRUARY, 1921.

On 15th February, 1921, a successful operation was carried out by parties of troops against rebels located in ambush. But for the delayed arrival of one of these parties a big capture of rebels must inevitably have followed. Numerous reports having been received to the effect that an ambush was being prepared in the vicinity of Mourne Abbey, a combined military and police operation was organized. A party of R.I.C. and of the East Lancashire Regiment were ordered to move out in lorries to the vicinity of Ballinvuskig, and at 1000 hours to move in small parties across country towards Jordan's Bridge. At the same time parties of the same regiment from Buttevant were to move across country from the direction of Pendy's Cross Roads.

It so happened that a patrol of 27 men of the Manchester Regiment were also operating at this time along the Cork–Mallow road, and at about 1100 hours reached Jordan's Bridge. Here they noticed carts drawn across the road. Their cars stopped and the men advanced, extended on either side of the road. Several armed civilians were then seen running both east and southwest. They were fired on. Those that went east were intercepted by the parties from Mallow, and all killed or captured. The majority went southwest and escaped owing to the fact that the troops advancing from Pendy's Cross Roads had not had time to close.

Some 53 rebels appear to have been engaged according to their account. The map mentioned in this account was not captured. A plan has accordingly been prepared and attached.

The casualties admitted by the rebel leader were four killed and five prisoners. The latter were subsequently tried by Court-Martial and sentenced to death or penal servitude. Numerous others were seen to be hit and were carried off by their companions.

The Crown casualties were nil.

Four shot-guns were captured.

The captured account of this action is given below in full: –

Figure 8.5 Rebel Report on Mourne Abbey Ambush, 15 February 1921

MOURNE ABBEY ROUND-UP

Headquarters, No. 2 Brigade,
4th March, 1921.

To C.S.

1. I attach copy of report from Mallow Battalion on above; also map showing position.

2. In all we had four A.S.U. that day in four different positions watching for Enemy Generals and their Staffs, and Divisional Commissioners, as there was a Conference of same being held in Cork. We also had men on trains.

3. We have it from a reliable source that the Officer in charge of enemy at Pendy's Cross took his men towards Creamery instead of to A and B. A Court-Martial was held over this. Owing to this mistake the A.S.S. got away without a scratch.

4. Credit is due to O.C., A.S.S., as he did not withdraw until all shot-gun men had left, and also for keeping his section intact and retreating in good order.

5. ... is the young lady mentioned; one of her brothers was killed, and one wounded and is a prisoner.

6. It was bad that that Volunteer from Mallow was so slovenly and was held up by the patrol before reaching O.C. It still may have been better, as enemy must have been more or less in position. Scouting must be done in future in a wider area.

7. *Casualties.* –

(*a*.) In action –

Patrick Dorgan	..	..	Killed.
Patrick Flynn		..	Murdered.
Michael Looney	..	..	Died of wounds.
Thos. Mulcahy	..	..	Wounded and prisoner.
Cornelius Mulcahy	..	..	Prisoner

Patrick Ronan	..	..	Prisoner.

(*b*.) Not in action –

Edmond Creedon	..	..	Murdered.
Michael Creedon	..	..	Wounded and prisoner.
Bart. Riordan	..	..	Prisoner.
*Daniel Jones	..	..	Prisoner. Not I.V.
*David Hassett	..	..	Prisoner. Not IV.

Flynn was murdered by H.C. McGill, Tralee. Thos. Mulcahy, though wounded and his hands up had his finger blown off by an Officer when he would not give the names of his Officers. Edward Creedon was murdered by Serjt. Burke, R.I.C., Mallow.

8. As yet I have not held an enquiry into the whole affair, but will do so as soon as possible. In the meantime we hope to track down the informer.

9. Enemy machine guns failed to work at Monee and Greenhill side.

COMMANDANT.

* These men were not tried.

REPORT ON A.S.U. ACTIVITY, 2ND BATTALION, FOR 15TH FEBRUARY, 1921.

Headquarters,

Cork No. 2 Brigade.

3rd February, 1921.

To O.C., Cork No. 2 Brigade.

1. On the morning of 15th February, at 7 a.m. (before daybreak), on order received from Battalion Commandant, 13 men of the A.S.S. with 40 men from "A" and "G" Companies went into position on the Cork road on the boundary line of "A" and "G" Companies' area, at a point known as the rock between Abbey Stores and Mourne Abbey Station.

2. *Position of Men.* – 13 men of A.S.S. took up a position overlooking the road at a range of 80 yards at the right hand side of the road leading to Cork. On the opposite side of the road 6 shot-gun men held a position at 15 to 20 yards from the road.

3. At the Abbey Stores, a distance of about 300 yards from the riflemen and about 200 yards from the shot-gun men on the rock, 5 shot-gun men held a position inside the ditch overlooking the road at the left hand side. At that point a barricade had been arranged consisting of two carts to be run across the roads to intercept motor traffic only.

4. A cycle scout was posted on the road on the Cork side of the Abbey Stores and two men were posted at Mourne Abbey where there is a cross roads. Two armed men were posted at Burnfort Railway Bridge. Two signallers were on the Castle, a distance of about 400 yards from the riflemen on the Mallow side. These men had a view of the main road leading to Mallow for about two miles.

One man was watching a Protestant's house at this place. Two armed men were posted in position at the cross roads over Mourne Abbey Creamery, leading to Dromore and Dromohane. Two armed men were in position at Sheehand's Public-house at Athnaleenta, commanding a cross roads.

Four shot-gun men held a position on a quarry on the Athnaleenta Road overlooking Jordan's Bridge on the main Cork Road. Two men (one armed) were guarding Corry's house, which is about 200 yards from the position held by the riflemen. This man was held up early in the morning as the sections were taking up their positions and ordered home.

There was also a signaller with the riflemen. A man was placed on Jordan's Bridge and two men on the Athnaleenta Road.

5. The duties of the different men in position. – The riflemen were under orders to watch a Convoy conveying Staff Officers of the enemy forces to Cork. If the officers were in a private touring car with the Convoy we were to concentrate all our fire on the touring car. The shot-gun men were under the same orders. (Men on rock opposite riflemen).

6. If the enemy travelled in a private car without a Convoy the barricade was to be run out from the Abbey Stores at a given signal, and the shot-gun men in this position were to hold up the occupants of the car, and if possible to take them alive. All private motor cars were to be held up at this point.

7. The two men at Mourne Abbey Post Office were to allow nobody to pass in the direction of Mallow.

8. The men on Burnfort Bridge were under the same orders.

9. The cycle scout was to patrol the Cork Road, of which he had a good view, and give word if any motor traffic was approaching.

10. There was one man on Jordan's Bridge to direct pedestrians or traffic that was not allowed to pass a point on the Athnaleenta Road, where they were to be held prisoners by three armed men.

11. The four men on the quarry were under orders to fire on any of the enemy forces who attempted to cross Jordan's Bridge in the direction of Athnaleenta from which point the riflemen could be surrounded.

12. Two men were guarding Corry's house with order to allow nobody to leave the house.

13. Two men at Sheehan's Public-house were under orders to allow no traffic or pedestrians to enter Mallow from this side.

14. The man on the Castle was to signal to the man with the section when any lorries were approaching from Mallow.

15. A man was guarding a house here to allow nobody to leave.

16. The two men at the cross roads leading to Dromohane and Dromore were to hold up all traffic entering Mallow from this point.

17. About 10.20 a.m. a merchant's motor lorry coming from Cork was held up at the barricade by the shot-gun men and taken up the Athnaleenta Road. The barricade was then withdrawn.

18. About 11 o'clock the men on the Castle signalled the approach of a private motor car from the direction of Mallow. The barricade was again run out, but the car stopped at Mourne Abbey Public-house where it remained for some time. This was a local car.

19. Immediately after this car stopped the approach of a military lorry from Mallow was signalled. At this time the barricade had not been withdrawn, as we were awaiting the approach of the private car.

20. The man on the Castle then signalled that the lorry had also stopped at Mourne Abbey. Just as the signal was received shots rang out from the direction of Jordan's Bridge and the Abbey Stores. We then retired to take up a position on the Athnaleenta Road. We has proceeded about one field when rifle fire was opened on us from the direction of the Abbey Stores and Corry's Yard, as at this time the enemy were in Corry's Yard.

21. We kept on until we were within two fields of the Monaparson Road, when machine-gun fire was opened on us. We wheeled to the right in the direction of the Castle. Having heard no more about the lorry that came on to Mourne Abbey, we decided trying to cross the Castle Road before firing, as, in our opinion, if we fired where we were we could easily be surrounded, as we were in between four roads, viz., Athnaleenta Road on our left, Monaparson Road in front of us, Castle Road on our right, and the main road to Cork on our rear. If we were cornered on the Castle Road we would have fought our way across and made for Clashmorgan Glen, as it was our only chance of escaping.

22. As we were proceeding towards the Castle Road continual fire was directed on our left from the machine gun and rifles, but, as we saw our way open to escape, we decided on keeping on and retreated in the direction of "H" Company area.

23. Before we left our positions overlooking the main road all the men on the left side of the road had retreated from their positions.

24. About 10 o'clock a volunteer from "B" Company came to Mourne Abbey with the information that six lorries had left Mallow about 9 o'clock and proceeded in the direction of Cork, three going the old Cork Road and three going the new Cork Road. They had proceeded about a mile from the town when they returned.

25. From this information a young lady from Mourne Abbey district proceeding from Mallow to business was held up by the men at this point (Mourne Abbey cross roads), but she being friendly towards the Republic was allowed to proceed the old road to Mallow.

This young lady met the three lorries coming the old Cork Road, and they afterwards passed her before she reached Mallow on their return journey. She, being suspicious that the lorries must have found out that something was about to happen, sent this Volunteer to Mourne Abbey with an account of the military activity; but he did not get to us soon enough, as he was held up by our patrols and delayed. It was when the firing began that he reached us and gave this information later on as we were resting.

26. When we reached "H" Company area we rested for a short time. While we were here six lorries came from the direction of Mallow, and we again had to retire and kept on until we reached "D" Company area.

27. Owing to the illness of the A.S.S. Adjt., this report was written by the Batt. Adjt., who is with the A.S.S.

(Sd.) BATT. ADJT.,
Cork No. 2 Brigade.

In this action the elaborate arrangements made by the rebels are interesting. Though in numbers not greatly inferior to the crown forces engaged, they put up no fight. They were disposed so as to pour a murderous fire into an unsuspecting convoy, not to fight an operation. As has been shown on many other occasions, the IRA will never stand to fight a party of crown forces advancing in extended order.

If the vehicle could not be repaired on the spot or towed at the time, the convoy commander was to transfer as much of its cargo as possible to other vehicles and to use his best judgement as to whether to leave a guard behind or not. This depended on the threat he perceived in addition to available manpower and mission requirements. In any event, the driver was to remain with the vehicle. One would assume he, too, would be unarmed for the same reasons as the messenger from above. It made little sense, however, to leave the driver behind, as, even if armed, there was little he could do against multiple attackers; in such an instance, they would lose a valuable trained man and the vehicle. While one might get used vehicles, trained drivers, as has been demonstrated, were in short supply. This simply made no practical sense.

The standing orders actually said little about obstacles or obstructions, giving only a list of their types and saying that the convoy commander should be ready to deal with them. The list consisted of:

(*a*) Trees felled across the road

(*b*) Stone walls (loose or cemented) across the road

(*c*) Trenches (covered with camouflaged material or left open)

(*d*) Barbed-wire entanglements

(*e*) Damaged, or destroyed, bridges, or culverts.[29]

This was uncharacteristically vague when considering the level of detail of the rest of the order. They had, apparently, been given separate instructions for clearing some of these. One would assume that precautions such as those for breakdowns were to be used. Despite the scant attention paid to them in the orders, coming upon obstructions had to be stressful for the men of the convoy, given that obstacles were frequently used to begin an ambush.

There were differing options when dealing with ambushes that depended on several factors, such as mission, cargo, number of troops, types of vehicles, terrain, and so on. The responses generally divide into the two vehicle categories: unarmoured and armoured. The early lessons, as noted above, were fairly simple – speed and not stopping. Both the army and the IRA found that on an unobstructed road, speed saved passengers' lives. This frustrated the rebels until they recalled a lesson from their earlier campaign against RIC barracks. These attacks brought with them a need to delay or halt relief forces with the natural counter to speed, trenches (especially when camouflaged). Once the IRA learned to obstruct roads effectively, they increased the frequency of their ambushes, which were also more effective. In one case, the chief of intelligence for the police, Brig.-Gen. Winter, jumped his 'large American car' over a trench at a potential ambush site but split his head open on landing, as there were no seatbelts; still, he escaped what would have been a major coup for the rebels.[30] Most military vehicles in Ireland could not jump the obstacles, so the British forces needed other means to get through or across them.

The increase in rebel attacks on motor vehicles led to the other two early TTPs that the British developed: no turns and not stopping. The latter meant not assisting damaged vehicles (and potentially abandoning comrades). This was highly controversial, as one can well imagine; no one liked leaving 'friendlies' behind, but sometimes the mission might have been too important to stop, as was the case at Toureen/Ballinhassig in October 1920, although the records available do not indicate if this was ever done again. Not turning around came about due to the fact that, in several instances, drivers attempted to turn around to lend assistance, but only succeeded in getting stuck or blocking a line of retreat. This was likely due to the drivers' inexperience, since backing up would have achieved their goals, but by blocking the route, they took away the commanders' flexibility and so they had to stay and fight. The other probable issue, perhaps in addition, was the size and weight of the vehicle on a narrow inadequate road.

By late 1920 the emergency procedures had advanced to take armoured vehicles into consideration and how best to employ their offensive and defensive capabilities. This was really no different if it was an armoured vehicle or an armoured car with turret-mounted machine guns, the latter being more offensively capable. Further, there appear to be no regulations about where the armoured vehicles were supposed to be in the convoy. The procedures they established worked well and should not be unfamiliar today. These men were aware whether their convoys' mission permitted counterattack. If it did, when attacked, assuming the vehicles were forced to stop, the lookouts immediately (and without orders) opened fire in the belief that a good volume of fire would 'disconcert the enemy'. While they did this, the other troops were to dismount and immediately counterattack, again without awaiting orders; or as the standing orders put it, 'go for the enemy'.[31] Permitting enlisted men to act independently was rare for the time, but they believed not waiting was key, for, 'as has been shown on many other occasions, the IRA will never stand to fight a party of Crown Forces advancing in extended order'.[32] Once their cover allowed the other troops to dismount the vehicle, the lookouts either joined the counterattack or provided security. Obviously, an armoured lorry provided greater protection, but the armour plate was only a preventive measure and had limited endurance. Its main function was to keep the troops alive through the first volley of fire from the rebels, or to provide some protection against the IEDs (a job for which it was less suited). One-inch armour could stop a .303 rifle round, but not indefinitely. The soldiers in the front and rear of the column had special orders; they were to attempt to turn the rebels' flanks, which were their most vulnerable part. The IRA was not always very proficient at protecting its flanks or placing security during their operations. Much of this was due to poor (in most cases, no) training, but also to low numbers and insufficient arms. Meanwhile, depending on the terrain and location, the drivers were supposed to attack too, 'so as to support the [counter]attack and inflict the heaviest casualties on the enemy'.[33] In the case of turret-mounted machine guns on the armoured cars, the gunners were to remain with the vehicle to provide supporting fire. Unmounted machine guns were used in the squad-level actions as appropriate to infantry tactics.

Although unstated, one has the impression that after counterattacking, pursuit was highly encouraged. The army also noted that the IRA could bring together considerable numbers of armed men, but that the longer these men were marshalled, or, in the case of a flying column, remained in one area, 'they soon became nervous of discovery and [frequently] departed without firing a shot'.[34] To the British, and they appeared to be correct, aggressive counterattack was the key; for this, another example proves useful.

Tourmakeady Ambush, 3 May 1921

As demonstrated earlier, just because instructions on convoy procedures are issued does not mean the troops will obey them, but the incident in Tourmakeady demonstrates what obedience to sound doctrine could accomplish. Late in the war, Tuesday, 3 May 1921, the IRA ambushed a police supply convoy in the southern environs of Co. Mayo on the shores of Lough Mask. The choice of location, the little village of Tourmakeady, was good; the only approach from the north-west had an almost ninety-degree turn in the road, which, of course, required vehicles to slow down. However, as well as its being a good tactical site, the village may have been chosen because it was mostly owned by Protestants and the military and police convoys rarely expected trouble there.[35] So the rebels decided to ambush the supply convoy coming from the RIC district headquarters in Ballinrobe to the RIC station at Derrypark (see Figure 8.6). It is unclear how the rebels acquired their information or by what means they received it, although they claimed intelligence came from an IRA informant.[36]

Tom Maguire, commandant of the IRA South Mayo Brigade, took his flying column and combined it with some local Volunteers, bringing the ambush force to about sixty men. Dividing his force into three sections, Maguire placed the first under his adjutant,[37] Michael O'Brien, at the Fair Green at the north-west end of the village. He placed the second under Patrick May on the west side of the road just opposite the gate to the vacant Drimbawn House on the south end. Maguire led the third in the centre of the village as a command post and reserve. The rebels originally expected three vehicles in the convoy, but received word that it had only two (not ideal by British standards, but acceptable according to the standing orders).[38]

Displaying their usual operational security, the rebels rounded up the villagers, about a dozen people (this was only possible because the village was so small), and held them in the home of known local loyalist Thomas Robinson. They kept the postmaster, William Billington, at the post office to answer any phone calls.[39] Strangely, the rebels did not block any of the roads. Normally, they would have trenched the south section of the road; that is the only place where such an obstacle made sense, since it left only an entrance via the bridge at the northern end of the village while preventing escape via that route. If nothing else, they should have blocked the main road from the south to prevent reinforcements from Derrypark, about seven miles distant, thus providing more security to their exposed rear. They also normally would have dug a trench, thus securing the rear. Likewise, had the rebel force been large enough, they could have left a detachment to hold that road against any relief force. They had the doctrine, labour and time, but did not take advantage of this opportunity. Famed rebel leader Ernie O'Malley claimed that Maguire thought the policemen would surrender quickly, but this is unconvincing because this late in the war, as events actually proved later that day, there was little reason for the constables to surrender. Further, the RIC knew that they could send out a distress signal and the twelve policemen at Derrypark would respond. Maguire, an experienced commander, knew this and must have expected reinforcements or a relief force.[40] Considering the events of that day, Maguire's lack of preparation bordered on reckless negligence, unless he decided not to force the issue if the convoy was larger than the two lorries and single car he expected.[41]

For their part, the police at the Ballinrobe RIC district headquarters actually were not intending to send a supply convoy to Derrypark that day, but since their vehicles would be out when the supply convoy came due, Sgt Henry Gouldon suggested sending the convoy early. Head Constable Martin Frawley agreed, but switched with Gouldon on the duty roster, taking command of the convoy himself.[42]

Table 8.1 RIC Supply Convoy to Derrypark, Co. Mayo, 3 May 1921

Ford Touring Car		
Sgt John Regan	Vehicle Commander	b. Co. Roscommon, 1874 – KIA
Const. Christopher O'Regan	Driver	b. Co. Clare, 22.xii.1894 – KIA
T/Const. Herbert Oakes	Passenger	b. London, 25.iv.1897 – KIA
Const. Patrick Flynn	Passenger	b. Unknown – WIA
Crossley lorry		
Head Const. Martin Frawley	Vehicle & Convoy Commander	b. 1890 – d. 1922
Const. Bruce	Driver	
Const. William Power	(Passenger, driving compartment -centre)	b. Co. Waterford, 1882 – KIA
Const. John Morrow	(Passenger, driving compartment -left)	WIA
Const. 'Ted' Donaghue	(Passenger, rear)	
T/Const. Wright	(Passenger, rear)	
T/Const. John Coughlan	(Passenger, rear)	
Const. Slevin	(Passenger, rear)	
Const. Cruise	(Passenger, rear)	

The police moved off at noon and, in accordance with standing orders, the Ford touring car was 300 yards in the lead. They demonstrated sound doctrinal precaution when they reached the bridge; the three passengers dismounted the car and crossed the bridge on foot. Interestingly, Maguire expected the Ford car to lead, which demonstrated he had a detailed knowledge of British convoy standing orders and doctrine.[43] They remounted when they reached the other side and, as they drove through the village, the first two rebel sections remained under cover. As the Ford reached May's third section, a single rebel with a shotgun stepped into the road from the Ford's right and fired one round into the driving compartment, killing Const. O'Regan, the driver. This was perfectly natural as driving in Ireland is on the left, so O'Regan was on the right side of the vehicle. The car swerved to the left and crashed into a gate pillar of Drimbawn House. The impact ejected the survivors. May's men opened fire and cut down the three men. T/Const. Oakes lay dead and both Sgt Regan and Const. Flynn were badly wounded and laying on opposite sides of the vehicle. Flynn stated that he heard a rebel walk up to Regan, say something and then fire point-blank with a shotgun into Regan's stomach, killing him. Flynn survived by pretending to be dead.[44]

When May's group fired on the Ford, the lorry to the rear, having already crossed the bridge without dismounting since the Ford had found no problems, tried to stop, but one IRA rifleman fired and hit Const. Power, killing him. Power was sitting in the centre of the cab and slumped over to the right on to the driver, Const. Bruce. A second round hit Const. Morrow, sitting on the left side, in the arm (later amputated). Bruce brought the lorry to a halt and the men poured out, collected their casualties and took shelter in a building (identified as a hotel, but this is not definite). From there, they immediately returned fire with rifles and rifle grenades. Meanwhile, Maguire sent half of his section to help May, while he took the rest to aid O'Brien.[45]

The police from the lorry were in a strong position that they could hold. Further, the rebels were in a poor tactical situation because prior to the attack they had only six rifles and had gained only four more from the Ford, and thus were ill-equipped for a siege. Since Maguire failed to block the road south to Derrypark, they did not know if help was coming or not. So as the policemen held their position, the rebels lost heart, or made a sound tactical decision, and withdrew to the north of the village into the mountains along their pre-planned line of retreat.[46]

The British official history claimed that the IRA forced postmaster Billington to send a telegram to the army at Ballinrobe giving news of the attack. With the rebels in retreat, it is unlikely that they sent the message.

It is more likely that Head Const. Frawley did this. In response to anonymous news, the RIC at Ballinrobe sent about a dozen men in four commandeered cars, while sending word to the local army garrison, the 2nd Bn. Borderers. Lieutenant Geoffrey Ibberson, acting O/C of C Company, 2nd Borderers, set out with a group of sixteen men and two officers in several Crossleys. Sending a Lt. Smith with eight men to approach from the south, Ibberson took the rest to Tourmakeady directly. After arriving, he sent a message to other army forces in Castlebar and Capt. A. V. H. Wood led another force of men in four lorries to the scene.[47] These three columns moved on the rebels from three directions (north, south and east) in the hope of enveloping the rebels. Capturing a rebel flying column would have been a coup for any battalion.[48]

The force was unable to envelop the rebels, although Lieutenant Geoffrey Ibberson, leading the army column on the far right wing (east), made contact with the Volunteers. It was Ibberson who shot both Maguire and O'Brien, killing the latter.[49] The former was evacuated to the nearby Goat Hotel at the northern end of Lough Mask. This running fight ended when the West Mayo flying column, under Michael Kilroy, arrived to fight a rear-guard action to cover the South Mayo column's retreat.[50] It is unclear how Kilroy found out about this ongoing fight. It was also unusual that the columns were in such close proximity, but his intervention clearly saved them.

In the end, the British lost four policemen killed-in-action and one army officer and two RIC wounded; the rebels lost three men killed-in-action, one wounded and two captured. The police and army claimed the Volunteers threw their weapons away as they ran, indicating they were not retreating in good order, but the rebels denied this. The army strenuously denied the IRA's claim of inflicting heavier losses on them.[51]

This ambush was important, despite the failures by the rebels to follow their sophisticated ambush doctrine. They inflicted heavy losses on the lead vehicle – 100 per cent casualties – because Head Const. Frawley neglected to send out flank guards, probably due to the belief that the village was 'safe' (or perhaps Sgt Regan disobeyed Frawley's orders). Yet at the same time, this attack demonstrated the reliability of the developing British counterambush doctrine in that the police in the lead car paid dearly for their complacency, thus their disobedience demonstrated the soundness of the standing orders. Would the situation have unfolded differently if the Ford car had deployed the passengers as advance or flank guards? It is difficult to see how they could have failed to discover the first section under O'Brien, which then would have negated the trap of Maguire's command post/reserve and May's southern section. In such an event, the constable discovering O'Brien's position would have been in immediate danger, but he also would have given the others time to respond and they, in turn, would have been able to support him. Three men with rifles against twenty rebels, who were variously armed, was a fairer fight than what they got, especially when one considers Const. O'Regan and the Ford. O'Regan might have been able to use the car as an offensive or defensive weapon. In addition, considering the rebels knew that at least one more vehicle was coming up with more men, they would likely have retreated, especially since they knew this to be a supply convoy and thus pursuit was not part of its remit. More importantly, this demonstrates the delicate balance between the numbers of men one could carry versus how many more were needed for proper defensive movement – capacity of the vehicles and men available were the two primary factors.

When the second vehicle, the lorry, was hard-hit by the opening of the attack on it, the policemen's obedience to their doctrine there saved them. By keeping his wits, Head Const. Frawley, subsequently decorated (although later killed in action in 1922), was able to get his men to dismount, take their wounded, and move into a defensible position, all while under fire, with few orders and without further casualties. One

Figure 8.6 Map of Tourmakeady Ambush, 3 May 1921

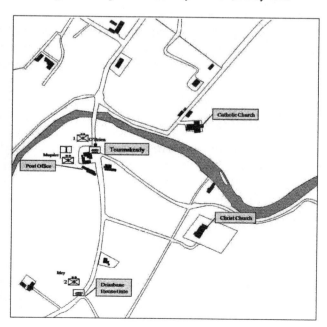

must point out that the police were in a supply convoy incapable of prolonged counterattack. Further, their doctrine was defensive (the only real departure from the army doctrine), and thus, instead of immediately counterattacking, they took up defensive positions. It is likely that the army doctrine of counterattack without regrouping in a defensible position would not have worked in this circumstance. In such a situation, the prudent course of action might very well have been to take the defence, regroup and then counterattack.

Regardless of the issues surrounding the RIC counterattack/defence of their position and the army's pursuit, the important point is that there was a successful defence and a later pursuit. Had the second group under Frawley not been prepared, or had Frawley been in the lead vehicle, they likely would have taken greater casualties and there would have been no pursuit. British doctrine, when followed, worked. In this case, it saved lives.[52]

The attack at Tourmakeady was proof that the British could develop useful doctrine against the IRA, but they also passed their information in ways other than the standing orders, which helped in the process of developing new doctrine at the same time.

There were other means for the British to fight back; the first of these was training. Officers and NCOs studied many of these types of lessons at the 5th Infantry Division's Guerrilla Warfare Course at the Curragh Military Camp in Co. Kildare. After October 1920, at the height of the British counteroffensive and when many of the IRA ambushes became more successful, Maj.-Gen. Jeudwine, GOC, 5th Infantry Division, decided his officers and senior NCOs needed training to deal with guerrilla warfare. So the seasoned British officers and NCOs created a three-day course. The programme was so successful it became mandatory for all officers entering the 5th Infantry Division, and many officers and NCOs of the 6th Infantry Division, the Dublin Brigade, as well as the police, also attended.[53]

The training, the first of its kind, taught the soldiers how the IRA operated and then taught effective counters to them based on experience. It stressed mobility, flexibility and operational security. Most of what has already been covered in this book was contained in their curriculum, so there is no need to reiterate that here. Finally, the school stressed that taking the offensive was key to victory.

Another offensive countermeasure the British tried was with their so-called 'Q Lorries', which were based on the warships disguised as merchant vessels during the First World War.[54] When rebels were at their greatest levels of attack against broken-down vehicles, the army decided to develop a heavily armed lorry as a decoy. The decoy, the Q lorry, was surreptitiously filled with armed troops and would appear to break down on a road to draw in the rebels. On 4 September 1920, one such vehicle 'broke down' near the Ballyvourney area of Co. Cork. 'The rebels soon collected and commenced firing. Two rebels were killed and three others were wounded.' After another such operation in Co. Limerick, 'the rebels soon became wary, and broken-down lorries were given a very wide berth. It was not unusual to see the rebels leave the road and run across country when they saw one.'[55] Strangely, republican sources do not mention these decoys. If nothing else, this was an effective psychological tool against the IRA.

The British army in Ireland were not operating in a military conceptual vacuum, so their desire to restore manoeuvre to the battlefield was well grounded in the operational concepts being debated at the time. The issues came about in response to the experience of the static, stagnant defensive combat in the First World War. This is not to suggest that the Western Front was always defensive, but while most officers seemed to remain members of the 'cult of the offensive', their views on its implementation necessarily matured. As a result of these experiences, the officer corps understood that the restoration of tactical and operational manoeuvre in war was critical.

The British eventually learned that motor vehicles generally, and armoured vehicles specifically, were not *the* answer to their troubles, but were part of a larger response. These vehicles provided only one element; without the others, especially doctrine explaining how to use vehicles in actual operations, they were almost useless. These issues were just as problematic in counterinsurgent operations in Ireland and affected both the offensive and defensive aspects of their campaigns.

In the case of the former, armoured vehicles helped to protect the forces in transit to their embarkation points, although most of the troops rode in unarmoured vehicles. Merely having an armoured car with two dual-mounted machine guns in the convoy increased the available firepower, thus further safeguarding the convoy. Yet these vehicles, by themselves, were an insufficient answer to the mobility problem since, due to their noise and large size, they deprived the British of arguably one of the most important factors in counterinsurgent operations: surprise. Since they could be seen and heard at great distances, especially at night, motor vehicles, including armoured vehicles, were not usually effective offensive weapons. By the time an armoured vehicle arrived on the scene, the rebels would have flown. So the doctrine of actually using an armoured car in an offensive mode, driving forward against the rebels, under fire, was impractical. For if the rebels stood their ground against such an assault, a prudent commander would have known that the rebels would be expecting to knock out the vehicle in some manner – explosives (primarily mines), a tank trap, or dropping a bridge – and thus, any decision to move forward under such a threat would certainly be imprudent, if not downright reckless.

The offensive doctrine developed into one of using motor transport to cover distances quickly, then dismounting and closing in on foot, which, although running the risk of getting lost in the dark, usually maintained the element of surprise. A variation of this included using bicycles to cover most of the remaining distances, as already covered.

The use of armoured vehicles in the latter of the two aspects of British counterinsurgent operations in Ireland, defensive operations, was more straightforward and similar to their use in the offence. British forces needed supplies and transport, which the Royal Army Service Corps provided. This needed to function in a secure manner, and since it was not an offensive operation, surprise was not an issue for the troops involved. The vehicles, then, were more useful from beginning to the end of the missions. And, as mentioned previously, the armoured vehicle in a supply convoy provided greater protection as well as some ability to counterattack or increase the volume of defensive fire available, in the event of an ambush.

The Kishkeam Raid, 14–16 May 1921

A final operation, this time British, serves as a good example of how the crown forces learned from their enemy. Although the British experienced setbacks during and after the Kishkeam operation of May 1921, the official history of the conflict used it as an example of a good operation and to illustrate that, while parts of the operation did not go as planned, continuing with the commander's intent for the operation led to success. The 6th Infantry Division decided to conduct a raid deep into a rebel 'stronghold', whose objective was to capture Seán Moylan, then newly appointed commander of the IRA Cork No. 2 Brigade and on-scene commander at the Clonbannin ambush in March of that year.[56]

In the second week of May 1921, the 1st Bn Gloucestershire Regiment at Kanturk, Co. Cork, part of the 6th Infantry Division's Kerry Brigade, received intelligence (citing 'various sources') that Moylan was staying in the Kishkeam area of Co. Cork, about a mile from Knockavoreen, where he had been spotted by a source. They decided to mount an operation to try to capture him.[57]

The army realized in early 1921 that bicycles were frequently better than horses or motor vehicles due to their flexibility. They had some problem with this, however, as bicycling was not common in Britain and so their men did not always have the skill, which took time to develop. By the end of the spring, they began using bicycle-mounted forces more frequently. The importance here was not that motor vehicles were too noisy to maintain surprise or that bicycles gave mobility, but that stealth, combined with mobility and speed, was a winning combination then as it is today. The IRA took notice of this as well.[58]

So, knowing that their motor vehicles and bicycles frequently gave away their movements when they were trying to maintain surprise, the Glosters decided to send a foot-bound force in early and then close in with a bicycle-mounted force after the first was in position. Starting off from Kanturk at 2330 hours on Saturday, 14 May, the five officers,[59] fifty-eight men and four RIC marched off, but made only five miles through the countryside in seven hours due to the difficult terrain (which they had not expected). They remained under cover about three-quarters of a mile from the town of Boherbee during the daylight hours of Sunday, the 15th. A local farmer stumbled on their position that afternoon, but did not give away their presence. A British cyclist patrol reconnoitred the area around 1700 hours on Sunday and captured two rebels – Maurice Clancy and Patrick Cronin. The overland force continued its march under cover of darkness that evening and arrived in the Kishkeam area around 2345 hours. The rebels had seen their approach and set off audio alarms, but the night was so dark that the British force's actual where-abouts, as well as its objective, remained unknown to the rebels.[60]

At 0230 hours on 16 May the cyclist force, consisting of two officers and sixty men, set out. They too were hampered by the terrain and poorly maintained roads and did not arrive in the Kishkeam area until 0430 hours. Meanwhile, the dismounted force took up their positions and started establishing a cordon to surround the rebels and ensure that none escaped. Dividing into four groups, they placed one officer and six soldiers approx-imately every 400 yards in the cordon. Before this first group could finish, the rebel alarms sounded anew while the fourth group, two officers and eighteen men, were moving north up a low road towards a farm, when at 0440 hours they were fired on by approximately three men. They returned fire and the rebels moved off. There were no casualties on either side. As they continued on, a man appeared in the road moving towards them at 0450 hours. They called on him to halt and he raised his hands, but then bolted. They fired, but did not hit him.[61]

The cyclists arrived at 0445 hours; their advance slowed when the shooting started, and both forces began the round up. How they made contact safely with each other in the darkness was not discussed.

Figure 8.7 Kishkeam Operation, 14–16 May 1921

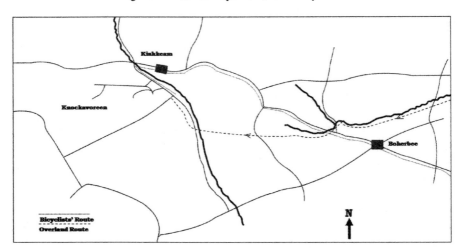

Capturing dozens of weapons and a stockpile of equipment and ammunition, the soldiers also arrested a dozen men, including Séan Moylan, who was the solitary man they fired on earlier. At 0900 hours, the Glosters began the march back to their barracks, sending out the cyclists and flank, advance and rear guards – perfect according to standing orders and doctrine. There were no British casualties that night, while the IRA lost twelve men, including one of their best brigade commanders.[62]

This operation was well executed, but the Glosters made some mistakes; the official history mentioned that this operation demonstrated that reconnoitring was absolutely critical and that maps were insufficient when trying to identify and choose concealment. They also mentioned that one must allow for difficult terrain and that foot-bound forces must travel lightly. Timing was critical, but while the cordon could be established in the dark, the advance should only begin during daylight – obviously, this is less important today with modern technology. Finally, the difficult route taken by the marching column confused the enemy, even when the alarms sounded. The British army suggested that this was key to a successful operation. This area remained disputed for the rest of the war. Most importantly here, the British obeyed their doctrine and carried out a successful, albeit difficult, raid deep in rebel territory.

The purpose of this work has not been to give a definitive list of 'lessons' for use today, but rather to provide an example of the development of successful doctrine of countering operations against manoeuvre. Clearly, the British army learned from their foes, but never seem to have had the opportunity to demonstrate this fully. As mentioned above, the war ended abruptly, but not due to military failure on their side; indeed, this outcome led to feelings of being betrayed by their government.

What is also clear is that these lessons would have assisted greatly in the British military counterinsurgent campaigns between the world wars. Why these TTPs did not make it out to the other commands in the British army was likely due to the parochial nature of the inter-war British army. Although beyond the scope of this study, it is also probable that many of the other commands (Mesopotamia, Khartoum, the North-west Frontier and Palestine) developed their own TTPs for dealing with their peculiar threats and needs.[63] Cross-pollination, by bringing together representatives from each of their theatres of operation, would have created a tremendously useful manual, but how does one achieve this in an army at war dispersed around the world? One could point out that this is what counterinsurgents need today, and that the internet makes this possible. While there are some official agencies to help in this, soldiers tend to use what works rather than just the 'official' means; these agencies should remain in a supporting function rather than taking the lead. Soldiers in the field are the ones who really develop and modify doctrine and TTPs; they should be at the forefront of disseminating their lessons too. One problem in Ireland was that many of the important studies put together by the army were limited in their distribution and so could not have greater effect.

Something British commanders never seemed to learn was that their own sense of superiority, which oozed thickly from their reports – both police and military – kept them from seeing that their enemy was good at his job. This was part of a general condescending view of the Irish by the British soldiers at the time, and also of guerrilla warfare by regular troops in general. By not seeing their enemies as skilled, ingenious, dedicated and willing to sacrifice, the British leadership blinded themselves to many possibilities.

Finally, something that training and procedures could not overcome was that no matter how 'ready' the troops were, or how well led, casualties were inevitable. The 'perfect' operation was not necessarily the one with the fewest friendly casualties. This does not mean that one would not try to prevent friendly loss of life. It is incumbent upon the leadership, both military and civilian, to ensure that sacrifices are only made when absolutely necessary and that they are not made in vain. At the unit level, one will do everything possible to prevent loss, but there must be a realization that one will ultimately fail in this attempt while achieving the objective against a determined foe. Well-armed convoys, those ready for a fight and capable of inflicting significant damage on the enemy, were not 'safe' from ambush, but rather were safer.

A Final Ambush – Béal na mBláth, 22 August 1922

In many respects the last important ambush by the IRA occurred in Cork in August 1922 during the Irish Civil War, where the IRA fought its former comrades who had accepted the Anglo-Irish Treaty, ending the War of Independence. In this infamous ambush, the former leader of the IRA, General Michael Collins, commander of the new Irish Free State National Army, was killed. His death allowed Irish politics and society to develop in a manner different from what they would have and permitted Éamon de Valera, the man many blamed for Collins' death, to retain the honour of being the rebel with the highest standing to survive these wars. This, in turn, gave de Valera a political advantage for the rest of his life.

What is interesting about this ambush is not that it was well planned, as it was; or that it occurred in Collins' home county, which it did; or that Collins was well known personally to the men who killed him; that it was done with weapons that he had smuggled into the country; or that his killers actually held him in high regard.[64] No, what is interesting is another irony: Collins, the agent and catalyst of so much violence and pain during these wars, was an inexperienced guerrilla. He was adept at moving about Dublin unarmed and in plain sight without getting caught, but there is little evidence that he, personally, killed anyone after 1916. He certainly ordered many deaths, but had no personal experience in killing during the War of Independence. This also meant that a mastermind of some of the most violent elements of the conflict had no first-hand experience in ambushes until the last day of his life.

Collins spent the war directing, smuggling, stealing, and so on. He read about and corresponded on most of the ambushes in the war, as indeed he had read about most actions and operations, but he had no actual experience with ambushes. It is to the IRA rebels – who had fought the British by attacking their manoeuvre, who were now fighting the fledgling Irish Free State and its National Army and who had spent from 1919 to 1921 (and later) ambushing – that the credit must go for teaching the first commander of the National Army a final lesson in ambushes.

NOTES

1. Up to 1921, RAF aircraft in Ireland were unarmed for political reasons.
2. 'Proceedings from a Conference of Ministers', 8 June 1921 (NA PRO WO 32/9522); Wilson to

Arnold Robertson, 30 March 1921,*The Military Correspondence of Field Marshal Sir Henry Wilson*, ed. K. Jeffery (1985), p.250; General Staff, Irish Command, *Record of the Rebellion in Ireland in 1920–21, and the Part Played by the Army in Dealing with It* (1922), vol. I, p.43 (WO 141/93); M.L.R. Smith, *Fighting for Ireland: The Military Strategy of the Irish Republican Movement* (1995), p.39; and K. Jeffery, 'Colonial Warfare 1900–39', in *Warfare in the Twentieth Century* (1988), p.34.

3. See, for instance, D. Stafford, *Churchill and Secret Service* (1997) and M.R.D. Foot, 'The I.R.A. and the Origins of the SOE', *War and Society: Historical essays in honour and memory of J.R. Western 1928–1971* (1973).

4. IRA Engineering Staff. *Engineering Handbook* (Dublin, 1920).

5. See, for instance, 'Notes of General Officer Commanding's Conference Held at Dublin District Headquarters', 3 June 1920 (NA PRO WO 35/90/1/5, p.2) for an examination of the IRA's operational thinking.

6. For more on Winter's efforts, see Sir O. Winter, *Winter's Tale: An Autobiography* (1955). For Winter's evaluation of the intelligence situation and the Irish Command's attempt to blame him, see 'A Report on the Intelligence Branch of the Chief of Police, Dublin Castle from May 1920–July 1921', in P. Hart (ed.), *British Intelligence in Ireland, 1920–21: The Final Reports* (2002). Historian Peter Hart accepts the Irish Command's version that Winter was more of a problem than a solution. While not the topic of this work, the current author rejects this view since Winter's policies and organizational changes were sound from a modern intelligence points of view.

7. 'Notes of General Officer Commanding's Conference Held at Dublin District Headquarters', 3 June 1920 (NA PRO WO 35/90/1/5, p.2) and IRA Operations Memorandum No. 1, 'Enemy Transport', 1921. There were more formal after-action reviews, some reproduced here. These were for the IRA leadership. Another means to report was through various periodicals, especially *An t–Óglác*. This served to get information out of the Volunteer rank-and-file; these reports were generally action-oriented, giving advice rather than merely reporting, as with the more formal reports.

8. Addendum 1 to 'The Irish Republican Army' Chapter 5: 'Operations', of June 1921, pp.1–2.

9. 'Operation Report', Dublin District Memorandum No. S/G/1/A, 3 March 1921 and of 27 June 1921 (NA PRO WO 35/90) and War Diary of the 36th Bde, RFA, 15 June 1921 (WO 35/93A).

10. See, for instance, 'Weekly Intelligence Summary', Dublin District, for week ending 20 December 1920 (NA PRO WO 35/90, p.2).

11. This analysis derives mostly from 'Standing Orders for Armed Parties Moving By Lorry, and for Lorry Convoys', 5th Infantry Division, 20 June 1921; 'Standing Orders for Armed Parties Moving by Lorry, and for Lorry Convoys', Dublin District, undated; 'Battalion Standing Orders for Armoured Cars in Ireland', Dublin District, undated; 'Special Instructions for Peerless Armoured Cars', Dublin District, undated; and 'Special Instructions for Rolls Royce Armoured Cars', Dublin District, undated.

12. The 'strategic corporal' is the idea that the actions of a single soldier can have a strategic impact in modern war due to the omnipresence of the news media.

13. The rebels too saw value in this practice and so, after examining a captured copy of the British order, directed that ambush units should practise 'anti-lorry drill' in preparation for the ambush. See *An t-Óglác* III, 3 (8 April 1921), p.145.

14. The .303 SMLE had a detachable magazine, but the normal means of loading was to recharge the magazine *in situ* with 'stripper clips' (a strip of metal with the rounds clipped to it, which then sits in a housing over the magazine well and allows the rounds to be pushed down into the well in one motion). For this reason, soldiers did not normally carry additional magazines.

15. Sir S. Hare, 'Martial Law from the Soldier's Point of View', *Army Quarterly*, vol. VII (October 1923 and January 1924), p.297; C. Townshend, *Britain's Civil Wars: Counterinsurgency in the Twentieth Century* (1986), pp.19–24. See also 'Court of Inquiry in Lieu of Inquest', 5 May 1921 (PRO WO 35/149A); Macready to Secretary of State, 1 September 1920 (PRO WO 32/9537); and T. Jones, *Whitehall Diary. Vol. III*, 31 May 1920, p.18.

16. *An t-Óglác*, III, 14 (24 June 1921). The additional shovel in a single vehicle was to ensure there were at least two available, likewise the additional bridging equipment was so that at least two sets were available.

17. See 'Standing Orders for Armed Parties Moving By Lorry, and for Lorry Convoys', 5th Infantry Division, 20 June 1921.

18. Ibid.

19. Ibid.

20. Ibid; 'Notes of General Officer Commanding's Conference Held at Dublin District Headquarters', 3 June 1920 (NA PRO WO 35/90/1/5, p.3); 'Summary of a Conference Held at Dublin District Headquarters', 3 May 1920 (WO 35/90/1/3, pp.3–4); and 'Weekly Intelligence Summary', Dublin District, for week ending 20 December 1920 (WO 35/90, p.1). See also 'The Irish Republican Army (From Captured Documents Only)', p.186.
21. 'Dublin District Standing Orders for Armed Parties Moving by Lorry, and for Lorry Convoys', undated.
22. General Staff, Irish Command, *Record of the Rebellion*, Vol. IV, p.42 (WO 141/93).
23. 'Standing Orders for Armed Parties Moving By Lorry, and for Lorry Convoys', 5th Infantry Division, 20 June 1921.
24. See IRA Engineering Circulars No. 1, 'Road Obstructions', July 1921 and No. 12, 'Warning re Road Trenches – Bridge Demolitions', May 1921.
25. General Staff, Irish Command, *Record of the Rebellion*, Vol. IV, p.6.
26. 'The Irish Republican Army (From Captured Documents Only)', p.27.
27. From mid-1920 onwards, the mere possession of arms or munitions was a capital offence throughout the southernmost counties. Further, while the British army decried the fact that the IRA did not follow the laws of war, since the wearing of the IRA (Irish Volunteers') uniform was a capital offence, as was the possession of arms, there was little incentive for the IRA to bother abiding by the laws of war since, in effect, they received no quarter from the British.
28. These reports come from 'The IRA (From Captured Documents Only)', pp.29–31.
29. 'Standing Orders for Armed Parties Moving By Lorry, and for Lorry Convoys', 5th Infantry Division, 20 June 1921.
30. Winter, *Winter's Tale*, p.311
31. 'Standing Orders for Armed Parties Moving By Lorry, and for Lorry Convoys', 5th Infantry Division, 20 June 1921.
32. 'The Irish Republican Army (From Captured Documents Only)', p.31 – speaking of the so-called 'Mourne Abbey Ambush', 15 February 1921.
33. 'Standing Orders for Armed Parties Moving By Lorry, and for Lorry Convoys', 5th Infantry Division, 20 June 1921.
34. 'The Irish Republican Army (From Captured Documents Only)', p.191
35. Statement of J.H. Gouldon (MA WS/1340). Of course it would have been difficult for the police to retaliate against the loyalists living there.
36. D. Buckley, *The Battle of Tourmakeady, Fact or Fiction: A Study of the IRA Ambush and Its Aftermath* (2008), pp. 35–8.
37. Deputy commander.
38. Statement of J.H. Gouldon (MA WS/1340); E. O'Malley, *Raids and Rallies* (1982), p.118; R. Abbott, *Police Casualties in Ireland, 1919–1922* (2000), pp. 228–9.
39. At the time, the Post Office controlled both the telegraph and the telephone services throughout the UK.
40. Statement of J.H. Gouldon (MA WS/1340); O'Malley, *Raids and Rallies*, p.121. Buckley's excellent examination questions where the civilians were held.
41. An t-Óglác, 19 August 1921 (in Buckley, *The Battle of Tourmakeady*) pp. 107–10.
42. Statement of J.H. Gouldon (MA WS/1340).
43. Buckley, *The Battle of Tourmakeady*, p.43.
44. This must have required great resilience as Flynn was not only badly wounded, but the rebels collected the weapons and equipment from the constables as well as rifling their pockets. Maguire claimed the RIC men fought back. Statement of J.H. Gouldon (MA WS/1340); O'Malley, *Raids and Rallies*, p.118; Abbott, *Police Casualties*, pp 228–9.
45. Statement of J.H. Gouldon (MA WS/1340); O'Malley, *Raids and Rallies*, pp.120–1; Abbott, *Police Casualties*, p.229.
46. Statement of J.H. Gouldon (MA WS/1340), O'Malley, *Raids and Rallies*, pp.120–1; Abbott, *Police Casualties*, pp.229 and *An t-Óglác*, III, 12 (10 June 1921) p. 2 (19 August 1921).
47. Buckley, *The Battle of Tourmakeady*, pp. 71–2. Wood's force was of unknown size. Buckley said that it could carry up to 100 men if the lorries were fully loaded, but this could be true only if they were 3-ton lorries. If they were Crossleys, the force could only be about half that size.
48. General Staff, Irish Command, *Record of the Rebellion*, Vol. IV, p.53 (NA PRO WO 141/93). O'Malley agreed that the police sent the message; see O'Malley, *Raids and Rallies*, p.121.
49. Republicans claim Ibberson shot O'Brien while the latter was rendering first aid to Maguire, something he vehemently denied.

50. Statement of Maj. Geoffrey Ibberson (MA WS/1307); Statement of J.H. Gouldon (MA WS/1340), O'Malley, *Raids and Rallies*, pp.120–1; Abbott, *Police Casualties*, pp.229; and *An t–Óglác*, III, 12 (10 June 1921).
51. General Staff, Irish Command, *Record of the Rebellion*, Vol. IV, p.179; and *An t–Óglác*, III, 12 (10 June 1921).
52. The IRA rightly claimed a strategic success too since the ambush led to the withdrawal of British forces from Cuilmore, Kinnury and Derrypark; see P. O'Farrell, *Who's Who in the Irish War of Independence and Civil War, 1916–1923* (1997), p.67.
53. General Staff, Irish Command, *Record of the Rebellion*, Vol. IV, p.68 (NA PRO WO 141/93); see also Appendix F, 'Notes on Guerrilla Warfare in Ireland'.
54. These were ships that acted as unarmed merchant vessels to lure German submarines. Once within range, the armed ships attacked the submarines. For more see D. Lake, *Smoke and Mirrors: Q-Ships Against the U-Boats in the First World War* (Stroud: Sutton, 2007).
55. General Staff, Irish Command, *Record of the Rebellion*, Vol. I, p.61 and Vol. IV, p.159 (NA PRO WO 141/93); and N. Browne, *The Story of the 7th* (2007), pp.36–7. Browne stated that the British killed only one rebel and that the other man killed was an innocent civilian.
56. S. Moylan, *Seán Moylan In His Own Words* (2003), p.130–1.
57. General Staff, Irish Command, *Record of the Rebellion*, Vol. IV, p.191 (NA PRO WO 141/93).
58. Of course, the IRA felt that they had created this problem for the British ('From Lorry to Bicycle', *An t–Óglác*, III, 5 (22 April 1921).
59. Second Lieut. T.N. Grazebrook (battalion intelligence officer); Capt. Manley A. James, VC, DSO, MC, MBE; Lieut. G.W.V. Ladds; Lieut. Armine Morris; Lieut. Bertram Temple, MC; and CSM W. Reece. See Ladds, *Kishkeam*, 'Ireland, 15th May 1921', *Back Badge* (December, 1957)
60. General Staff, Irish Command, *Record of the Rebellion*, Vol. IV, p.192 (NA PRO WO 141/93).
61. Ibid., pp.192–3. It appears that the IRA expected this operation and the tactics used. Writing to Collins, Florence O'Donoghue said that the British came in as expected and that most of the important IRA men escaped before the cordon was in place, but that 'one of our best men [Moylan] in this area.' was captured. It turns out that Moylan deliberately exposed himself so that his officers could escape. See J. Borgonovo (ed.), *Florence and Josephine O'Donoghue's War of Independence* (Dublin: Irish Academic Press, 2006), pp.160 and 187 n.24; F. O'Donoghue, *No Other Law: The Story of Liam Lynch and the Irish Republican Army, 1916–1923* (1986), p.169; and Moylan, *In His Own Words*, p.131.
62. General Staff, Irish Command, *Record of the Rebellion*, Vol. IV, p.194 (NA PRO WO 141/93).
63. There was some transfer of knowledge from the Black and Tans and Auxiliaries to the Palestine police since many of them joined that force, while the last inspector-general of the RIC (Sir H.H. Tudor) became the chief of the Palestine police.
64. IRA prisoners and Free State guards in the Dublin prisons spontaneously knelt and prayed a rosary when Collins' death was announced; see A. Dolan, *Commemorating the Irish Civil War: History and Memory, 1923–2000* (2003).

Appendix A
Police Casualties

The following lists the names and details of the members of the British forces casualties named in this work and is not exhaustive.

Name	Service Number	Rank	Organization	Birth	Death or Incident	Incident	Remarks
Barnes, William	72849	Cadet	N°. 2 Sect, C Coy ADRIC		28.xi.1920	Kilmichael	KIA
Bayley, Cecil J.	72843	Cadet	N°. 2 Sect, C Coy ADRIC		28.xi.1920	Kilmichael	KIA
Baynham, Hubert L.	69949	DI	RIC	8.xii.1892	12.iii.1921	Callan, Co. Kilkenny	WIA
Beard, Bernard J.L. (Late B. Gen)	73551	Cadet	ADRIC			Great Brunswick St, Dublin	KIA
Beasant, James R.	74691	Constable	RIC		4.iii.1921	Cashel, Co. Tipperary	Deliberately Killed
Bradshaw, Leonard	72847	Cadet	N°. 2 Sect, C Coy ADRIC		28.xi.1920	Kilmichael	KIA
Bush, George	79943	Cadet	M Coy ADRIC			Clonfin	KIA
Cane, Arthur William	72068	T/Const RIC	F Coy ADRIC		25.ii.1921	Ballyvourney	KIA
Clayton, Harold	80248	Cadet	M Coy ADRIC			Clonfin	KIA
Cooper, Walter H.	74169	Constable	RIC		13.iii.1921	Victoria Square, Belfast, died of wounds at Royal Victoria Hospital	KIA
Crake, Col. Francis W.	72473	DI	N°. 2 Sect, C Coy ADRIC		28.xi.1920	Kilmichael	KIA
Craven, Lieut.-Cdr. Francis W.	80043	DI	M Coy ADRIC		2.ii.1921	Clonfin	KIA
Crooks, Robert	73850	Constable	RIC		11.iii.1921	Victoria Square, Belfast	KIA
Cumming, H.R.	Army	Col.	East Lancs		5.iii.1921	Clonbannin	KIA
Duddy, Joseph	75988	Constable	RIC		3.iii.1921	Cartacrooks, Co. Waterford	KIA
Falkiner, Walter	79207	Cadet	H Coy, ADRIC		12.iii.1921	Turbid Railway Station, Co. Kerry	KIA
Forde, Frederick H.	83047	T/Const RIC	N°. 2 Sect, C Coy ADRIC		28.xi.1920	Kilmichael	WIA
Gleave, James C.	72825	Cadet	N°. 2 Sect, C Coy ADRIC		28.xi.1920	Kilmichael	KIA
Graham, Philip N.	72813	Cadet	N°. 2 Sect, C Coy ADRIC		28.xi.1920	Kilmichael	KIA
Green, Samuel	75477	Constable		26.xii.1898 Middlesex	3.ii.1921	WIA Balbriggan, Co. Dublin, 2 Feb, died of wounds at Steeven's Hosp, Dublin	KIA
Greer, Martin J.	67768	Constable	RIC		23.ii.1921	Parliament & Essex Sts, Dublin	KIA
Guthrie, Cecil J.	72863	Cadet	N°. 2 Sect, C Coy ADRIC		28.xi.1920	Kilmichael	KIA
Hoey, Daniel	66287	T/Const	RIC	3.iii.1888	23.ii.1921	Parliament & Essex Sts, Dublin	KIA
Houghton, John A.	80249	Cadet	M Coy ADRIC			Clonfin	KIA
Hugh-Jones, Stanley	72307	Cadet	N°. 2 Sect, C Coy ADRIC		28.xi.1920	Kilmichael	KIA
Hugo, Frederick	79333	Cadet	N°. 2 Sect, C Coy ADRIC		28.xi.1920	Kilmichael	KIA
Humphries, Thomas	Army	Private	2d Dk/Wellingtn		20.ix.1920	King St, Dublin	KIA

Name	Service Number	Rank	Organization	Birth	Death or Incident	Incident	Remarks
Jones, Albert G.	72818	Cadet	N°. 2 Sect, C Coy ADRIC		28.xi.1920	Kilmichael	KIA
Jordan, F	3903947	Private	1st SWBs		14.v.1921	Aughrim St, Dublin	WIA
Lucas, Ernest W.H.	72845	Cadet	N°. 2 Sect, C Coy ADRIC		28.xi.1920	Kilmichael	KIA
Maguire, James	54713	Sgt	RIC		6.iii.1921	Kilmallock, Co. Limerick	KIA
McDonagh, Edward	69370	Constable	RIC		24.ii.1921	Parliament & Essex Sts, Dublin, died of wounds 23 Feb.	KIA
McGrath, Thomas J.	65788	DI	RIC	30.viii.1890 Rathkeale, Co. Limerick	7.i.1921	Ballinalee, Co. Longford	KIA
McIntosh, John	76247	Constable	RIC		11.iii.1921	Victoria Square, Belfast	KIA
Mullany, Patrick	65685	Constable	RIC	31.x.1886 Co. Cavan	2.ii.1921	Trinity St, Dublin	KIA
Murtagh, Joseph	57783	Constable	RIC		19.iii.1921	Cork City	Deliberately Killed
Noble, Frank	Army	Bandsman	2d Dk/Wellingtn		20.ix.1920	King St, Dublin	WIA
O'Farrell, James J.	75984	T/Const	ADRIC			Great Brunswick St, Dublin	KIA
Pallester, William	79151	Cadet	N°. 2 Sect, C Coy ADRIC		28.xi.1920	Kilmichael	KIA
Pearson, Horace	71615	Cadet	N°. 2 Sect, C Coy ADRIC		28.xi.1920	Kilmichael	KIA
Poole, Arthur F	73356	Cadet	N°. 2 Sect, C Coy ADRIC		28.xi.1920	Kilmichael	KIA
Potter, Gilbert N.	59414	DI	RIC	10.vii.1878 Dromahair Co Leitrim	22.iv.1921	Kidnapped at Clogheen, Co. Tipperary (executed by IRA)	KIA
Redmond, William C.F.	NA	Asst Com	DMP	1874	21.i.1920	Dublin	KIA
Riley, Ernest J.	79407	Constable	RIC		12.iii.1921	Callan, Co. Kilkenny	KIA
Saggers		Private	RASC		14.v.1921	Aughrim St, Dublin	KIA
Seafield-Grant Maj. James	79885	Insp.	F Coy ADRIC		25.ii.1921	Ballyvourney	KIA
Smith, William	Army	Bandsman	2d Dk/Wellingtn		20.ix.1920	King St, Dublin	WIA
Soady, Clevel L.	79905	Cadet	F Coy ADRIC		25.ii.1921	Ballyvourney	KIA
Somers, Nicholas	71336	Constable	RIC		8.iii.1921	Shronebaha, Co. Cork	KIA
Taylor, Frank	72824	Cadet	N°. 2 Sect, C Coy ADRIC		28.xi.1920	Kilmichael	KIA
Wainwright, Christopher	72850	Cadet	N°. 2 Sect, C Coy ADRIC		28.xi.1920	Kilmichael	KIA
Washington, Henry	Army	Private	2d Dk/Wellingtn		20.ix.1920	King St, Dublin	KIA
Webster, Benjamin D.	79332	Cadet	N°. 2 Sect, C Coy ADRIC		28.xi.1920	Kilmichael	KIA
Whitehead, Matthew	Army	Private	2d Dk/Wellingtn		20.ix.1920	King St, Dublin	KIA

Appendix B
Notes on Guerrilla Warfare in Ireland[1]

The following notes and instructions are the result of practical experience in the field and of tactical exercises carried out at guerrilla warfare classes at the Curragh.

Orders
1. All Officers and N.C.O.s require practice in giving orders before carrying out an operation. No party will leave barracks without having received orders as to what they are going to do and how they are to act in the event of being ambushed and, if possible, having practised it.

Lorry drivers will invariably be present when orders are being issued to troops, as the decision as to where the lorry should be halted in order to allow the troops to descend and go into action depends on their grasp of the situation and nerve.

Orders for raids on houses and areas will be illustrated by plans on a black board, or sketch, to all taking part in the operation.

However urgent the call may be for troops to move, it will be found that the time expended in the issue of short and concise orders before moving is not time wasted.

Secrecy
2. The leakage of information in Ireland is very great, and it may be generally accepted that no inhabitant or civilian employee is really to be trusted.

The orders for an operation will be issued to the troops taking part in it, immediately before they start out, so as to obviate any chances of conversation with outsiders and consequent leakage.

The importance of blocking telephone and telegraphic communications temporarily is obvious.

Rebel Tactics
3. The tactics employed by the rebels are those of ambush. These

ambushes are dependent on secrecy, which is easily obtainable owing to the fact that they are dressed as civilians and move amongst a population of sympathizers similarly attired. These ambushes are dependent for their success on surprise and fire effect at close range, and do not aim at further offensive action; the rebels having small stomach for fighting at close quarters or suffering heavy casualties.

Individuals cutting peat in the bog may not be as harmless as they appear to be.

Our Tactics

4. However small the party engaged in an operation, the idea of at once taking active offensive will be in the mind of all ranks. With this end before him every Commander will always have a striking force available, however small.

Whether moving on foot, on bicycles, or in lorries, every force will have an advance guard and a main body, and if possible, a rear guard.

Foot and bicycle patrols will never be of less strength than 10 other ranks.

Lorry patrols will always consist of at least two motor vehicles.

Reconnaissance

5. Much practice is required by Officers and N.C.O.s in the making of reconnaissances of buildings, especially for operations at night. The report will include a plan of the house and outbuildings showing entrances, windows, etc., and the best ways of approach. These reports, if not required for immediate action, will be filed under the suspects' names in the black list and utilized for raids at a later date, thus obviating the necessity of making a further reconnaissance and increasing the chances of effecting a surprise.

Bicycle Patrols

6. Bicycle patrols have been found most useful – especially where quietness is required, as for instance in making raids at night, or in places where the approach of a patrol is given away by the noise made by motor vehicles. In order to be successful the following points require attention:

(a) Bicycles must be kept in good condition and must be carefully inspected before starting out, to ensure that they are in thorough order throughout, and that pumps and mending kits are available;

(b) Cyclist patrols will not allow civilian bicycles or motor cycles to pass them on the road for fear of information being given of the approach of the patrol;

(c)   Rebels cycle scouts at road junctions must not be allowed to get away.

7. Lorries are particularly easy to ambush and the greatest vigilance is required.

Lorries should be so disposed in depth that it becomes difficult for the ambushers, without employing a large force, to ambush the whole column. The principles of protection are the same with a column of lorries as with any other column of troops, i.e., an advance guard, main body and rear guard should be formed if possible.

There are officers who consider that the order giving 300 yards *minimum* distance between leading and following lorries cannot be applied in practice on dusty or winding roads or where there is danger of following lorries down the wrong road. If the leading lorry has to change its road, or arrives at a tricky turning it will be halted and a man sent back to direct the following lorries as to what road is to be followed. Drivers and N.C.O.s directing lorries must have maps with them with the route they are taking marked on it. If care is taken there should be little chance of going wrong. Mistakes which occur are usually due to the man with the map not looking ahead and noting tricky places, and to vehicles being driven too fast, thus missing turnings.

(a)   Lorries should be carefully inspected before starting to ensure that they are in decent running order and are supplied with spare petrol, water and oil, and that headlights are working and tools for clearing obstructions are carried.

(b)   The success of lorry raids is dependent on speed rather than secrecy. Consequently, the 15-cwt. lorry, owing to its greater speed, is better suited to this type of work than 3-ton lorries.

(c)   Both 15-cwt. lorries and 3-ton lorries should have seating accommodation for the men, so that they face outwards and are ready to fire.

(d)   The Commander of a lorry party will travel in the body of the lorry with his men and not on the driver's seat. If he is in front, owing to the intervening partition, he is unable to issue orders to his men.

(e)   The Commander should never be in the *leading* lorry, but with his main body.

(f) Communication by signal must be maintained between lorries on the move. For this purpose Verey lights or signal grenades will be employed. They and the means of firing them must be ready to hand for *immediate* use. One signal should be utilized to show that a lorry is attacked and another to show that a halt is needed owing to breakdown or other cause. Whenever the attack signal is seen, the occupants of other lorries should dismount and take the offen sive against the ambushers. Whenever the halt signal is seen, or a halt ordered, lorries will halt and not close up. Side look-outs will picquet the column outside the hedges and off the road.

Dress

8. All patrols and escorts will be as lightly equipped as possible. Activity and agility are what are required. Spare ammunition and rations will be carried in lorries in bulk and not on the men.

Armoured Lorries

9. The main object of the armour is to ensure the safety of the men from the first concentrated outburst of fire. Armoured lorries, if not blocked by an obstacle, should push on through an ambush to a point at which the party can dismount to take the offensive without being under close fire. The lorries may then be used offensively against the ambushers as the Commander may decide.

Care must be observed in ascertaining whether the armour on lorries is bullet proof or only proof against long range pistol fire and slug. Both these types are in use and the subsequent action of the armoured lorry after the party having dismounted will depend on which type of armour the lorry has.

Armoured Cars

10. As soon as any portion of a column with which an armoured car is moving is attacked, the armoured car will move on the ambushers and pin them to their position by fire, while the rest of the party dismounts and attacks the ambushers in flank and rear under cover of this fire.

Searches

11. Whenever possible, searches are carried out by the police accompanying military parties. But cases are not infrequent where soldiers have to carry out the search themselves owing to no police being available. The following are some of the places in which documents, arms and ammunition have been found concealed:

(i) *Pedestrians*.

(*a*) Man wearing a hat – underneath the hat; (*b*) under the had riband; (*c*) hollow heels and soles of boots; (*d*) dispatches rolled in cigarettes; (*e*) in collars; (*f*) hollow walking sticks; (*g*) in socks; (*h*) sewn into garments; (*i*) parcels.

(ii) *Vehicles*.

Motor lorries, motor cycles and cycles –

(*a*) Under bonnet; (*b*) behind cushions; (*c*) in lockers under seats; (*d*) tool boxes; (*e*) folds in hood; (*f*) petrol tins, tyres, pumps, etc.; (*g*) petrol tanks; (*h*) saddle pillar, pedals, handle bar, handle grips; (*i*) special mud guards and mud flaps; (*j*) harness, whip cups, lamps; (*k*) removable spokes.

(iii) *Various*.

(*a*) Removable horn on a cow; (*b*) in animals' ears; (*c*) in mangolds, turnips, etc.

(iv) *Houses*.

(*a*) In flues, cooking pots, up chimneys; (*b*) under table cloths; (*c*) on the under side of table tops; (*d*) under seats of earth closets; (*e*) in ornamental vases and clocks; (*f*) rolled up blinds; (*g*) under coal, wood, turf, etc.; (*h*) pushed out through skylights.

Whenever a house has been searched a receipt should be obtained from the inhabitant to the effect that no damage has been done and nothing taken away with the exception of the arms or documents seized.

General

12. Offensive action should always be taken against the flanks and rear of ambushers. It must be remembered that the rebels are not highly disciplined troops and that a threat to their line of retreat usually makes them bolt. This tendency must always be borne in mind when efforts are made to round them up. The rebels use a considerable amount of cunning both in their raids and ambushes and have a well-organized system of intelligence which works easily owing to the fact that the population are sympathetic. Raids, patrols and escorts by troops in order to be successful must employ every ruse and camouflage that can be thought of, such as starting in the wrong direction and using a detour to reach the objective – sending out men hidden in a lorry to be dropped and hidden in the country while the lorry returns apparently full to where it came from – sending out bicycles hidden in a lorry and dropping a bicycle party for the purpose of carrying out the raid.

It may also be useful for a party to march by night across country, bog or mountain and lie up by day.

In short the one essential condition for success in raids, searches and drives is *surprise* and every ruse by which surprise can be obtained should be studied and practised. Without the element of surprise the most perfectly organized operation will be ineffective.

Appendix C

GENERAL HEADQUARTERS, DUBLIN, DEPARTMENT OF
ENGINEERING, 6th January, 1921.
Circular No. ½ 4½

ROAD OBSTRUCTION

In general there are two methods of obstructing a highway; by placing an obstacle or making it impassable by excavating or demolition. Both the methods to be effective must be carried out in a large scale. In other cases it may be possible to block a road to wide vehicles while allowing the passing of narrower.

Obstacles placed on a roadway may be anything from a light barricade of hurdles, brushwood or carts to masonry backed with earth. Masonry walls at frequent intervals make a good obstruction, while small vehicles may be allowed to pass by placing one wall across the road, leaving a small gap on the extreme left. The next wall a short distance behind the first will leave a small gap on the extreme right. Such pairs of walls should be at frequent intervals.

This idea may be carried out with lighter walls or with other variations.

The subject of variation is to remove just enough of the surface to make it impassable for vehicles above a certain size to pass or to block the road to all wheeled traffic.

Considering first a scheme for complete obstruction, alternate squares, triangular or irregular patches or strips of the road surface are removed. These are explained in the attached sketch. Figures 1 to 4 show examples of complete blockage. The shaded portions are cut out of the surface. No. 1 is probably the best as it is the hardest to fill in. In all work of this kind no excavation material should be left about and the walls of the excavation should be as nearly vertical as possible.

Figure 5 shows a good example for a partial stoppage. Figure 6 is a modification.

In choosing a position to block a road, a narrow main road without alternative routes is desirable. Other points to look for are roads bounded by strong hedges or strongly built masonry walls or a road which is a cutting or embankment, the former being the better of the two. The possibility of bringing a vehicle into the fields on either side of the road and so around the obstacles should not be overlooked. To meet this, such a position as is shown in Figure 7 would be advisable. This shows ditches with hedges or other such obstacles at right angles to the road, & position should also be chosen if possible where suitable material for filling up the excavation is difficult to obtain.

Figure 8 shows another method. This is a cross section. The dotted line showing the original surface of the road, the portion shown shaded is excavated, leaving a new roadway below the original level and narrower so that wide lorries etc, cannot pass.

DIRECTOR OF ENGINEERING

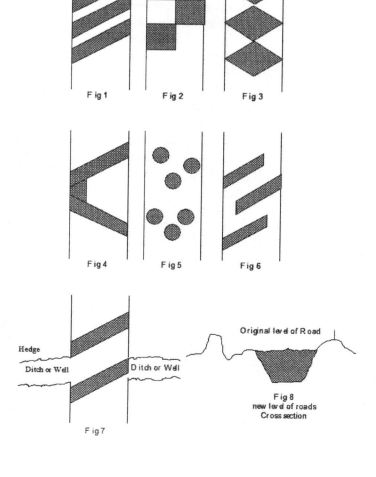

Fig 1   Fig 2   Fig 3

Fig 4   Fig 5   Fig 6

Original level of Road

Hedge

Ditch or Well   Ditch or Well

Fig 8
new level of roads
Cross section

Fig 7

Appendix D

AMBUSH OF MOTOR BOAT PATROL, 17 OCTOBER 1920

(*b*) *Ambush of a Motor Boat on the River Shannon near Athlone on 17th October*, 1920: A party of officers and men under Major C. F. Adams, Brigade Major 13th Infantry Brigade, went by motor boat from Athlone to search certain islands in Lough Ree for arms. On the return journey, when the boat was in the river close to the latter's debouchment from the lough, fire was opened on it by a party of rebels concealed on the banks. The account of this operation is given in full in Appendix XIII, and is of interest because it led to an application being made to General Headquarters for the provision of armed naval launches for use on the Shannon, Loughs Ree and Berg, and on Lough Corrib in Co. Galway.

The correspondence which went backwards and forwards between General Headquarters, the War Office, the Admiralty and the Naval Commander-in-Chief, Queenstown, eventually filled a large file; several reconnaissances were made of the Grand Canal, the Shannon and other Loughs by naval and military officers; Lough Corrib was pronounced impracticable for naval launches owing to out-jutting rocks and sudden storms; and the results, by 11 July 1921, were that two naval harbour launches, destined with their crews for Athlone, were in the estuary of the Shannon below Limerick ready to take advantage of a rise in the river and a renewed outbreak of 'activities' to reach their final destination. The history of these launches will be referred to again in Chapter V; but the islands of Lough Ree have remained unsearched by troops to this day.

AMBUSH OF MOTOR BOAT PATROL NEAR LOUGH REE, 17TH OCTOBER, 1920

Headquarters,
5th Division

1. I now forward fuller details of the attack on a motor boat patrol on Lough Ree on Sunday, 17 October 1920, and strongly recommend the names of the following officers and non-commissioned officer for recognition under GHQ letter No 2/24746/MS, dated 18 September 1920: Lieut. H. Cannon, Royal Army Service Corps (MT), Capt. C.L.D. Tully, 13th Infantry Brigade Intelligence Officer, Lce.-Corporal H.R. Cantrill, 1st Bn. The Leicestershire Regiment (attd. Armoured Cars).

2. It was very largely due to the personal courage, coolness, and initiative of the above named that the party was able to reach safety.

Major Adams and Lieut. Hodson were hit almost by the first volley, Major Adams receiving a severe wound in the shoulder, which was very nearly fatal, and Lieut. Hodson being disabled in one hand and wounded by splinters in the face. Both did all they could to help, and Lieut. Hodson, in spite of his wounds, was able to give much assistance, but the command practically fell on Captain Tully and Lieut. Cannon, whose behaviour throughout was admirable.

3. Certain leading townspeople are anxious that I should receive a deputation, but so far I have declined. There is a good deal of nervous tension in the town and its neighbourhood, which may be to advantage.

I propose to see them if they still desire on Saturday.

4. I have reason to think more serious attacks may be made. It is not yet clear whether the attempt to throw a bomb into the RIC barracks at Athlone, on the evening before, and an attempt to get into the Workhouse by night, which was stopped by the sentries' fire, were directly connected with the motor boat affair, but it is quite probable that the plans for a serious effort, which had been intended, were altered during the morning, when the motor boat was seized and seen to be patrolling the river.

(*Signed*) T.S. Lambert, *Brigadier-General*
Commanding 13th Infantry Brigade

Athlone,
20 *October* 1920

NARRATIVE

1. On 17 October 1920, about 7.30 a.m., a party consisting of Major C.F. Adams, Brigade Major; Captain C.L.D. Tully, Intelligence Officer; Lieut. Hodson, 1st Leicestershire Regiment; Lieut. Cannon, RASC (MT), with six NCOs and men, Royal Dragoons, and six NCOs and men 1st Leicestershire Regt. (attached Armoured Cars), with two Hotchkiss guns, left Athlone Barracks with orders to requisition two motor launches and search three islands, Inchturk, Inchbofin, and Inchmore, in Lough Ree (and others if desirable), in search of arms believed to be concealed there. The officers were in plain clothes, the men in uniform.

2. I considered it desirable that not less than two boats should be used, as the lough is not easy to navigate owing to hidden rocks and the strong stream.

3. It was found, however, that only one boat, that belonging to a Mr. Coen, was fit to go, the engines, or parts, having been dismantled from the others examined. It took some time to get Mr. Coen's boat ready, as the engine would not at first start. A large dinghy was also seized, and it was decided to proceed in Mr. Coen's motor boat, with the rowing boat towed behind.

4. The search on the islands was unsuccessful. They were fairly large and the inhabitants are known to be bad, but any arms or literature had been well hidden.

5. No previous idea of the intention to seize the motor boats or search the islands on Sunday could have leaked out, as it was known only to myself and a few officers, but there was plenty of time during the morning for the rebels to make their plans, though I think it probable that they had, in any case, arranged to assemble near Athlone for a bad purpose that day. Most of the roads were picqueted by their parties.

6. The motor boat returned from the lough to the river about 4 p.m., and had passed the beacon and was just opposite the Athlone Yacht Club Hut when the firing started. Just previously, Major Adams had seen two men of the Royal Dragoons on the right bank hidden in the reeds making facial signs to him, but he did not realize their intention. These two men had seen the Sinn Fein party and suspected it, but were hidden in the reeds and dared not disclose themselves. They afterwards saw some of them go away in boats. Major Adams also saw a man on a hillock (evidently a sentry) run to give notice.

7. At the first volley a bullet struck Major Adams in the left shoulder, inflicting a severe wound and practically incapacitating him. He fell across the engine control and was afterwards put into the cabin. The bullet was a large one, possibly from a Snider, and made a large hole.

8. About the same moment, Lieut. Hodson was wounded in the hand by a bullet, and in the face by a splinter. Major Adams' servant was struck in the wrist and another man was also hit. Several had narrow escapes, one man falling overboard as a shot hit the taffrail just beneath him. He scrambled back.

9. The chain of the steering wheel was cut, and the wires of the magneto wrenched off, and the petrol supply put out of action. The boat therefore stopped.

10. The firing came from a ridge and wall close to the Yacht Club Hut, and probably also from the bushes and perhaps the reeds nearer. The two soldiers of the Royals above referred to afterwards saw a boat come up from here. The distance from the wall to the boat was 150 to 200 yards. Most of the enemy were well hidden.

11. Captain Tully at once told Lieut. Cannon to do all he could to get the boat moving again, and brought the two Hotchkiss guns and all available rifles into action. He himself scrambled along the boat to superintend the firing and behaved with the utmost gallantry, himself using a rifle. He was wounded in the face by a splinter.

12. Lieut. Hodson, though wounded and bleeding freely, gave him much assistance, using his revolver and helping others with his one available hand. He showed much gallantry. Lance-Corporal Cantrill also gave much help and kept his head well. Other NCOs and men also did much excellent work.

13. Lieut. Cannon first carried Major Adams into the cabin and quickly mended the magneto wires, but then found there was no petrol supply. The engine had two pairs of cylinders, with separate carburettors. Fortunately, he had previously noticed an auxiliary petrol tank and had it filled when starting. Finding the engine would not work he put this into action and started the engine again. He then found the steering control was completely cut and out of action. By lying along the stern he therefore controlled the rudder by hand all the way. All this was done under heavy fire and necessitated constant movement. All ranks speak in the highest terms of his absolute self control, quickness, and the manner in which he got the boat going again and steered it. But for him matters might have been very serious.

14. When the two Hotchkiss guns opened up the enemy's fire became more erratic, but for fear of exhausting ammunition too early it had to be carefully controlled. Altogether 229 rounds were fired from rifles and guns. The boat was hit many times and an electric light bulb in the cabin exploded like a bomb.

15. Later news points to over 150 enemy being present. They came mostly from the Ballymahon side and from Coosan. An officer driving back from Longford met a full carload and a number of others on cars and bicycles were seen going away. The affair is thought to have been organized from IRA Brigade Headquarters, the Tang, Drumraney, and Coosan Companies being used.

16. The country was searched carefully afterwards and four arrests made, but no definite proof of their being concerned was found, though they had suspicious documents, etc. Two of these have been since released. Many of those in the attack were wearing khaki, and khaki clothing was found in one of the houses.

17. A rough barn, known as the Sinn Fein Club, at Coosan, was burnt down later, but it is not known by whom, as no troops were in the vicinity for some time.

18. There are report that eight of the enemy were wounded, three of them seriously, but they have not yet been traced.

> *(Signed)* T.S. Lambert, *Brigadier-General*,
> Commanding 13th Infantry Brigade

Athlone,
20 *October* 1920

Secret (3932/44.G.)
GHQ
Forwarded

I concur thoroughly with Brig. General Lambert's recommendations.

I have to-day seen Major Adams in hospital, and he warmly endorses the commendation of Lieut. Cannon's conduct.

Major Adams cleared up one or two points which the attached report leaves doubtful. For instance, he states:

(*a*) that the two men of the Royals who attempted to give him warning by making faces were being covered by the rebels, who warned them that they would be shot if they gave any signal;

(*b*) that there was no lack of ammunition, as might be inferred from para. 14 of the narrative;

(*c*) that the boat was hit about 40 times.

Recommendations are being forwarded under a separate letter on AF W.3121.

> (*Signed*) H.S. JEUDWINE, *Major General*,
>   Commanding 5th Division

22 *October* 1920

NOTE

1. Appendix XXVI, *Record of the Rebellion*, Vol. IV, pp. 129–31.

Bibliography

PUBLISHED SOURCES

Abbott, R. *Police Casualties in Ireland, 1919–1922* (Cork: Mercier Press, 2000)

Akenson, D.H. and Fallen, J.F. 'The Irish Civil War and the Drafting of the Free State Constitution,' *Éire-Ireland: A Journal of Irish Studies*, 5, 2 (Earrach/Spring 1970), pp.42–93

An t-Óglác: The Official Organ of the Irish Volunteers, 1918–1921

Augusteijn, J. *From Public Defiance to Guerrilla Warfare: The Experience of Ordinary Volunteers in the Irish War of Independence, 1916–1921* (Portland, OR: Irish Academic Press, 1998)

Augusteijn, J. (ed.), *The Irish Revolution, 1913–1923* (Basingstoke: Palgrave, 2002)

Augusteijn, J. Review of Hopkinson, M. *War of Independence*, in *American Historical Review*, 108, 4 (October 2003), pp.1218–19

Ball, S. (ed.), *A Policeman's Ireland: Recollections of Samuel Waters, RIC* (Cork: Cork University Press, 1999)

Banerjee, N. and Hart, A. 'Soldiers Saw Refusing Order as their Last Stand', *New York Times*, 18 October 2004, p.1

Barry, T. *Guerilla Days in Ireland: A Personal Account of the Anglo-Irish War* (Boulder, CO: Roberts Reinhart, 1995)

Beadon, Col. R.H. *The Royal Army Service Corps: A History of Transport and Supply in the British Army* (Cambridge: Cambridge University Press, 1931)

Begley, D. *The Road to Crossbarry: The Decisive Battle of the War of Independence* (Bandon: Deso Publications, 1999)

Bell, J.B. 'The Thompson Submachine Gun in Ireland, 1921', *Irish Sword*, no. 8 (Winter 1967), pp.98–101

Bell, J.B. *The Secret Army: The IRA, 1916–1979*, 4th edition (Cambridge, MA: MIT Press, 1983)

Bennett, R. *The Black and Tans: The British Special Police in Ireland* (New York: MetroBooks, 2002 [first published 1959])

Bidwell, S. and Graham, D., *Fire-Power: British Army Weapons and Theories of War, 1904–1945* (London: Allen & Unwin, 1982)

Borgonoro, J. *Spies, Informers and the 'Anti-Sinn Féin Society'* (Dublin: Irish Academic Press, 2008)

Bowden, T. *The Breakdown of Public Security: The Case of Ireland, 1916–1921, and Palestine, 1936–1939* (London: Sage, 1977)

Boyce, D.G. *Englishmen and Irish Troubles: British Public Opinion and the Making of Irish Policy, 1918–1922* (Cambridge, MA: MIT Press, 1972)

Boyle, J. 'Irish Labour and the Rising', *Éire-Ireland: A Journal of Irish Studies*, II, 3 (Autumn 1967), pp.122–31

The 'Boys' of the Millstreet Battalion Area: Some Personal Accounts of the War of Independence (Cork: Aubane Historical Society, 2003)

Bracevich, A.J. 'Rewriting the Last War: What New Pentagon Papers Reveal', *National Review*, 5 June 2000

Breen, D. *My Fight For Irish Freedom* (New York: Anvil, 1964)

Brewer, J.D. *The Royal Irish Constabulary: An Oral History* (Belfast: Institute of Irish Studies, QUB, 1990)

Brinton, C. *The Anatomy of Revolution* (London: Vintage, 1965)

Brown, I.M. *British Logistics on the Western Front, 1914–1919* (Westport, CT: Praeger, 1998)

Browne, C. *The Story of the 7th: A Concise History of the 7th Battalion, Cork No.1 Brigade, Irish Republican Army from 1915 to 1921* (Ballydehob, Co. Cork: Schull Books, 2007)

Buckley, D., *The Battle of Tourmakeady, Fact or Fiction: A Study of the IRA Ambush and Its Aftermath* (Dublin: Nonsuch, 2008)

Carey, T. and de Búrca, M. 'Bloody Sunday 1920: New Evidence', *History Ireland*, 11, 2 (Summer 2003)

Carroll, F.M. 'All Standards of Human Conduct: The American Commission on Conditions in Ireland, 1920–1921', *Éire-Ireland: A Journal of Irish Studies* (Winter 1981), pp.59–74

Carroll, F.M. *Money for Ireland: Finance, Diplomacy, Politics, and the First Dáil Éireann Loans, 1919–1936* (Westport, CT: Praeger , 2002)

Caulfield, M. *The Easter Rebellion* (New York: Holt, Rinehart & Winston, 1963)

Clarke, Lieutenant F.A.S., DSO, 'Some Further Problems of Mechanical Transport', *Army Quarterly*, vol. VI (April & July 1923), pp.377–85

Clarke, Lieutenant F.A.S., DSO, 'Memoirs of a Professional Soldier', unpublished manuscript, 1968 (Liddell Hart Centre for Military Archives, Clarke Papers) [Brigadier Frederick Arthur Stanley Clarke, DSO]

Clausewitz, C.M. von *On War*, edited and translated by Michael Howard and Peter Paret (Princeton, NJ: Princeton University Press, 1984)

CIA World Factbook

Collins, P. *British Motorcycles Since 1900* (Shepperton, Surrey: Ian Allen Publishing, 1996)

Connolly, S.J. *The Oxford Companion to Irish History* (Oxford: Oxford University Press, 1999)

Coogan, T.P. and Morrison, G. *The Irish Civil War* (New York: Seven Dials Press, 2001)

Cronin et al., 'Activities of Ballingeary IRA 1920–21', *Ballingeary History Society Journal* (1998)

Crozier, Brig.-Gen. F.P., CB, CMG, DSO, *Impressions and Recollections* (London: T. Werner Laurie, 1930)

Curran, J.M. 'Ireland since 1916', *Éire-Ireland: A Journal of Irish Studies*, I, 3 (Autumn 1966), pp.14–28

Dáil Éireann Debates: vol. 8, 27.6.1924; vol. 13, 16.12.1925; vol. 124, 8.3.1951

Dangerfield, G. *The Damnable Question: A Study in Anglo-Irish Relations* (Boston: Little, Brown, 1976)

Davies, N. *White Eagle, Red Star: The Polish–Soviet War, 1919–1920 and 'The Miracle on the Vistula'* (New York: St Martin's Press, 1972)

De Vere White, T. *Ireland* (New York: Walker, 1968)

De Watteville, Lieut.-Col. H. 'The Employment of Troops Under the Emergency Regulations', *Army Quarterly*, vol. XII (April & July 1926)

Deasy, L. 'The Beara Peninsula Campaign', *Éire-Ireland: A Journal of Irish Studies*, I, 3 (Autumn 1966), pp.63–78

Deasy, L. 'The Schull Peninsula in the War of Independence', *Éire-Ireland: A Journal of Irish Studies*, I, 2 (Summer 1966)

Deasy, L. *Towards Ireland Free: The West Cork Brigade* (Cork: Royal Carbery Press, 1992)

'Declaration on the Use of Bullets Which Expand or Flatten Easily in the Human Body', 29.vii.1899, Declaration of St Petersburg of 29.xi.1868

De Jomini, Baron A. *The Art of War*, translated by Capt. G.H. Mendell and Lieut. W.P. Graighill (Westport, CT: Greenwood Press,1862)

Dening, Major B.C., MC, RE, 'Modern Problems of Guerilla [sic] Warfare', *Army Quarterly* (January 1927), pp.347–54

Department of Defense Dictionary of Military and Associated Terms, 9 May 2005

Dolan, A. *Commemorating the Irish Civil War: History and Memory, 1923–2000* (Cambridge: Cambridge University Press, 2003)

Dublin Brigade Review (Dublin: Cahill, 1939)

Duff, D.V. *Sword for Hire: The Saga of a Modern Free-Companion* (London: John Murray, 1937)

Dwyer, T.R. *Michael Collins: 'The Man Who Won the War'* (Cork: Mercier Press, 1990)

Dwyer, T.R. *Tans, Terror and Troubles: Kerry's Real Fighting Story, 1913–23* (Cork: Mercier Press, 2001)

Echevarria, A.J. II, 'The Trouble with History', *Parameters* (Summer 2005)

Edwards, O.D. & Pyle, F. (eds), *1916: The Easter Rising* (London: Macibbon & Kee, 1968)

Fitzpatrick, D. 'Strikes in Ireland, 1914–21', *Saothar*, vol. 6 (1980)

Fitzpatrick, D. *Politics and Irish Life, 1913–1921* (Dublin: Gill & Macmillan, 1977)

Fitzpatrick, D. *The Two Irelands 1912–1939* (New York: Oxford University Press, 1998)

Flanagan, P. *Transport in Ireland, 1900–1910* (Dublin: Transport Research Associates, 1969)

Foot, M.R.D. 'The IRA and the Origins of the SOE', *War and Society: Historical Essays in Honour and Memory of J.R. Western 1928–1971* (New York: Harper & Row, 1973)

Fortescue, J.W. *The Royal Army Service Corps: A History of Transport and Supply in the British Army*, Vol. I (Cambridge: Cambridge University Press, 1930)

Foster, R.F. *Modern Ireland: 1600–1972* (London: Penguin, 1988)

Foy, M.T. *Michael Collins's Intelligence War: The Struggle Between the British and the IRA, 1919–1921* (Charleston, SC, 2006)

Gallagher, F. *The Anglo-Irish Treaty* (London: Hutchinson, 1965)

Garven, T. *Nationalist Revolutions in Ireland, 1858–1928* (Oxford: Clarendon Press, 1987)

General Staff, Irish Command, 'The Irish Republican Army (From Captured Documents Only)', (Dublin, June 1921)

General Staff, Irish Command, *Record of the Rebellion in Ireland in 1920–21, and the Part Played by the Army in Dealing with It*, vol. I, *Operations* (London: War Office, 1922) (PRO WO 141/93)

General Staff, Irish Command, *Record of the Rebellion in Ireland in 1920–21, and the Part Played by the Army in Dealing with It*, vol. II, *Intelligence* (London: War Office, 1922) (PRO WO 141/93)

General Staff, Irish Command, *Record of the Rebellion in Ireland in 1920–21, and the Part Played by the Army in Dealing with it*, vol. III, *Law* (London: War Office, 1922) (PRO WO 141/93)

General Staff, Irish Command, *Record of the Rebellion in Ireland in 1920–21, and the Part Played by the Army in Dealing with it*, vol. IV, Part I – 5th Division, Part II – 6th Division, Part III – Dublin District (London: War Office, 1922) (PRO WO 141/93)

Giap, General V.N. *People's War, People's Army* (Hanoi: Foreign Languages Publishing House, 1961)

Graham, D. 'The British Expeditionary Force in 1914 and the Machine Gun', *Military Affairs*, 46, 4 (1982), pp.190–3

Greaves, C.D. *Liam Mellows and the Irish Revolution* (London: Lawrence & Wishart, 1971)

Gregory, A. 'The Boys of Kilmichael', *Journal of Contemporary History*, 34, 3 (July 1999)

Her Majesty's Stationery Office (HMSO), *Statistics of the Military Effort of the British Empire During the Great War, 1914–1920* (first published by HMSO 1922, reprinted 1999 by Naval And Military Press)

Her Majesty's Stationery Office, *The Irish Uprising: 1914–21* (HMSO, 2000)

Hachey, T.E. 'The Irish Question: The British Foreign Office and the American Political Convention of 1920', *Éire-Ireland: A Journal of Irish Studies*, III, 3 (Autumn 1968), pp.92–106

Hague IV, 'Laws and Customs of War on Land', 18.x.1907

Hare, Maj.-Gen. Sir S., KCMG, CB, 'Martial Law from the Soldier's Point of View', *Army Quarterly*, vol. VII (October 1923 and January 1924)

Hart, P. (ed.) *British Intelligence in Ireland, 1920–21: The Final Reports* (Cork: Mercier Press, 2002)

Hart, P. 'The Geography of Revolution in Ireland, 1917–1923', *Past & Present*, no.155 (May 1997), pp.142–73

Hart, P. *The IRA at War 1916–1923* (Oxford: Oxford University Press, 2004)

Hart, P. *The IRA and its Enemies: Violence and Community in Cork, 1916–1923* (Oxford: Oxford University Press, 1998)

Harvey, A.D. 'Who Were the Auxiliaries?' *Historical Journal*, 35, 3 (1992), pp.665–9

Hayes, K. *A History of the Royal Air Force and United States Naval Air Service in Ireland 1913–1923* (Dublin: Irish Air Letter, 1988)

Herlihy, J. *The Royal Irish Constabulary: A Complete Alphabetical List of Officers and Men* (Dublin: Four Courts Press, 1999)

Herlihy, J. *The Dublin Metropolitan Police: A Short History and Genealogical Guide* (Dublin: Four Courts Press, 2001)

Herlihy, J. *The Royal Irish Constabulary: A Short History and Genealogical Guide* (Dublin: Four Courts Press, 1997)

Hood, F. *The Military Impact of Counter-Mobility* (Salisbury: Defence Science and Technology Laboratory, 2002)

Hopkinson, M.A. *The Irish War of Independence* (Ithaca, NY: McGill-Queen's Press, 2002)

Hoppen, K.T. *Ireland since 1800: Conflict and Nationalism* (London: Longman, 1989)

House, J.M. *Toward Combined Arms Warfare: A Survey of 20th-Century Tactics, Doctrine, and Organization*, Research Survey No. 2 (Fort Leavenworth, KS: Combat Studies Institute, 1984)

House, J. M. *Combined Arms Warfare in the Twentieth Century* (Lawrence, KS: University Press of Kansas, 2001)

Huber, T. *Compound Warfare: That Fatal Knot* (Fort Leavenworth, KS: US Army Command and General Staff College Press, 2002)

Irish Free State, *Status and Constitution: Document Submitted to the Fourth Assembly of the League of Nations*, Geneva, 1923

Jeffery, K. 'British Military Intelligence following World War I', in K.G. Robertson (ed.), *British and American Approaches to Intelligence* (London: Macmillan Press, 1987), pp.55–84

Jeffery, K. *The British Army and the Crisis of Empire, 1918–22* (Manchester: Manchester University Press, 1984)

Jeffery, K. 'Colonial Warfare 1900–39', in *Warfare in the Twentieth Century* (London: Unwin Hyman, 1988), pp.24–50

Jeffery, K. 'Ireland and War in the 20th Century', Parnell Lecture, delivered at Magdalene College, Cambridge, 10 November 2003

Jeffery, K. (ed.), *The Military Correspondence of Field Marshal Sir Henry Wilson* (London: Army Records Society, 1985)

Jeffery, K. and Hennessy, P. *States of Emergency: British Governments and Strikebreaking since 1919* (Boston: Routledge & Kegan Paul, 1983)

Jones, T. *Whitehall Diary, Vol. III, Ireland, 1918–1925*, edited by Keith Middlemas (Oxford: Oxford University Press, 1971)

Jung, P. 'The Thompson Submachine Gun during and after the Anglo-Irish War: The New Evidence,' *Irish Sword*, 21, 84 (Winter 1998), pp.191–218

Kautt, W. *The Anglo-Irish War, 1916–1921: A People's War* (Westport, CT: Praeger, 1999)

Keegan, J. *Face of Battle* (London: Penguin, 1976)

Keegan, M. (ed.), *Rebel Cork's Fighting Story, from 1916 to the Truce with Britain* (Tralee: The Kerryman, 1947)

Kerry's Fighting Story, 1916–21: Told by the Men Who Made It (no bibliographic information given)

Knox, M. and Murray, W. *The Dynamics of Military Revolution, 1300–2050* (New York: Picador, 2001)

Leeson, D. 'Death in the Afternoon: The Croke Park Massacre, 21 November 1920', *Canadian Journal of History* (April 2003), pp.43–68

Leeson, D. 'The "Scum of London's Underworld"? British Recruits for the Royal Irish Constabulary, 1920–21', *Contemporary British History*, 17, 1 (Spring, 2003)

Lowe, Brt. Maj. T.A. 'Some Reflections of a Junior Commander upon the Campaign in Ireland', *Army Quarterly*, 5 (Oct. 1922–Jan. 1933)

MacCarthy, P. 'RAF and Ireland, 1920–22', *Irish Sword*, 17, 68 (1989)

Macready, General the Rt. Hon. Sir N., Bt., GCMG, KCB, *Annals of an Active Life, Vol. II* (London: Hutchison & Co., 1925)

Maher, J. *Harry Boland* (Boulder, CO: Irish American Book Company, 1999)

Mao Tse-tung, *On Guerrilla Warfare*, translated by Brigadier General Samuel B. Griffith, USMC (Ret.) (Westport, CT: Praeger, 1961)

Mao Tse-tung, *Selected Works, Vol. IV, 1941–1945* (New York: International Publishers, 1956)

McBride, L.W. *The Greening of Dublin Castle: The Transformation of Bureaucratic and Judicial Personnel in Ireland, 1892–1922* (Washington, DC: Catholic University of America Press, 1991)

McCarthy, Colonel J.M. (ed.), *Limerick's Fighting Story: From 1916 to the Truce with Britain* (London: Anvil Books, nd)

McConville, S. *Irish Political Prisoners, 1848–1922: Theatres of War* (London: Routledge, 2003)

McCoole, S. and Ward, M. *No Ordinary Women: Irish Female Activists in the Revolutionary Years, 1900–1923* (Madison, WI: University of Wisconsin Press, 2003)

McInnes, C. and Sheffield, G.D. *Warfare in the Twentieth Century: Theory and Practice* (London: Unwin Hyman, 1988)

Meehan, N. 'After the War of Independence: Some Further Questions about West Cork, April 27–29 1922', *Irish Political Review*, 23, 3 (2008)

Mitchell, A. and Ó Snodaigh, P. (eds), *Irish Political Documents, 1916–1949* (Dublin: Irish Academic Press, 1985)

Mockaitis, T.R. 'The Origins of British Counter-Insurgency', *Small Wars and Insurgencies*, 1, 3 (December 1990)

Mockaitis, T.R. *British Counterinsurgency, 1919–60* (London: Macmillan, 1990)

Moylan, S. *Seán Moylan in His Own Words: His Memoir of the Irish War of Independence*, 3rd edn (Cork: Aubane Historical Society, 2003)

Murray, W, and Millett, A. R. *Military Innovation in the Interwar Period* (Cambridge: Cambridge University Press, 1996)

Newman, P. *Companion to Irish History: From the Submission of Tyrone to Partition, 1603–1921* (New York: Facts on File, 1991)

O'Callaghan, S. *Execution* (London: Muller, 1974)

O'Connor, E. *A Labour History of Ireland, 1824–1960* (Dublin: Gill & Macmillan, 1992)

O'Connor, the Rt. Hon. Sir J. *History of Ireland, 1794–1924, Vol. I* (London: Edward Arnold, 1971)

O'Connor, R, McMahon, T. and Plunkett, J. (eds), *Engineering Handbook* (IRA, Dublin, 1921) (O'Malley Papers – AD UCD P17a/154)

O'Connor, U. *Michael Collins and the Troubles: The Struggle for Irish Freedom, 1912–1922* (New York: W.W. Norton & Co., 1996 [first published 1975])

O'Donoghue, F. *No Other Law: The Story of Liam Lynch and the Irish Republican Army, 1916–1923* (Dublin: Irish Press, 1954)

O'Donovan, D. *Kevin Barry and His Time* (Dublin: Glendale Press, 1989)

O'Farrell, P. *Who's Who in the Irish War of Independence and Civil War, 1916–1923* (Dublin: Lilliput Press, 1997)

O'Farrell, P. *Ireland's English Question: Anglo-Irish Relations, 1534–1970* (New York: Schocken Books, 1971)

Officer, L.H. *Five Ways to Compute the Relative Value of a UK Pound Amount, 1830–2006* (Measuring Worth, 2008)

O'Halpin, E. 'British Intelligence in Ireland', in C. Andrew and D. Dilks (eds), *The Missing Dimension: Governments and Intelligence Communities in the Twentieth Century* (Urbana: University of Illinois Press, 1984), pp.55–77

O'Halpin, E. *The Decline of the Union: British Government in Ireland, 1892–1920* (Syracuse, NY: Syracuse University Press, 1987)

O'Mahoney, S. *Frongoch: University of Revolution* (Killiney: FDR Teoranta, 1987)

O'Malley, E. *Raids and Rallies* (Dublin: Anvil Books, 1982)

O'Riordan, M. 'Forget Not the Boys of Kilmichael!', *Ballingeary Historical Society Journal* (2005)

O'Snodaigh, P. 'The Thompson Submachine Gun: A Few Notes', *Irish Sword*, 22, 89 (2001), p.348

Paret, P. (ed.), *Makers of Modern Strategy: From Machiavelli to the Nuclear Age* (Princeton, NJ: Princeton University Press, 1986)

Reynolds, D.J. *Inland Transport in Ireland: A Factual Survey*, Economic Research Institute, Dublin, Paper No. 10, November 1962

Ryan, M. 'Tom Barry and the Kilmichael Ambush', *History Ireland*, 13, 5 (September/October 2005)

Ryan, M. *Tom Barry: IRA Freedom Fighter* (Cork: Mercier Press, 2005)

Selth, A. 'Ireland and Insurgency: The Lessons of History', *Small Wars and Insurgencies*, 2, 2 (August 1991), pp.299–322

Sheehan, W. *British Voices: From the War of Independence, 1918–1921* (Cork: Collins Press, 2006)

Smith, M.L.R. *Fighting for Ireland: The Military Strategy of the Irish Republican Movement* (New York: Routledge, 1995)

Stafford, D. *Churchill and Secret Service* (New York: Overlook Press, 1997)

Stephens, J. *The Insurrection in Dublin* (New York: Macmillan, 1916)

Stewart, A.T.Q. *The Ulster Crisis: Resistance to Home Rule, 1912–14* (London: Faber & Faber, 1967)

Swindlehurst, J.E. *The Maintenance of Roads in Urban Districts* (London: William Clownes & Sons, 1894)

Taber, R. 'The Offensive and the Problem of Innovation in British Military Thought, 1870–1915', *Journal of Contemporary History*, 13, 3 (1978), pp.531–53

Tery, S. 'Raids and Reprisals: Ireland: Eye-Witness (1923)', translated by Marilyn Gaddis Rose, *Éire-Ireland: A Journal of Irish Studies* (Summer 1985), pp.32–9

The Northern & Western Motorway: Its Aims and Objects (London: Northern & Western Motorway, 1923)

Townshend, C. *Britain's Civil Wars: Counterinsurgency in the Twentieth Century* (London: Faber & Faber, 1986)

Townshend, C. *The British Campaign in Ireland, 1919–1921: The Development of Political and Military Policies* (Oxford: Oxford University Press, 1975)

Townshend, C. *Political Violence: Government and Resistance Since 1848* (Oxford: Clarendon Press, 1983)

U.S. Army, Field Manual (3-24: *Counterinsurgency Operations* (Washington, DC: Headquarters, Department of the Army, 1 December 2006)

U.S. Army, Field Manual, *Countermobility* (Washington DC: Headquarters, Department of the Army, 1 October 2004)

Vickery, Lieut.-Col. C.E., CMG, DSO, RFA, 'Small Wars', *Army Quarterly*, 6 (April and July 1923), pp.307–17

Ward, M. *Unmanageable Revolutionaries: Women and Irish Nationalism* (London: Pluto Press, 1995)

War Office, *Manual of Military Law* (London: Harrison & Sons, 1914)

White, G. and O'Shea, B. *The Burning of Cork* (Cork: Mercier Press, 2006)

White, J. (ed.), *Dublin's Fighting Story, 1913–21: Told by the Men Who Made It* (Tralee: The Kerryman, nd)

Wimberley, Capt. and Brevet-Maj. D. 'Military Prize Essay', *Army Quarterly*, 26 (April and July 1933)

Winslow, B. *Sylvia Pankhurst: Sexual Politics and Political Activism* (London: UCL Press, 1996)

Winter, Sir O. 'A Report on the Intelligence Branch of the Chief of Police, Dublin Castle from May 1920–July 1921', in P. Hart (ed.), *British Intelligence in Ireland, 1920–21: The Final Reports* (Cork: Cork University Press, 2002)

Winter, Sir O. *Winter's Tale: An Autobiography* (London: Richards Press, 1955)

Wyatt, H. *Motor Transport in War* (London: Hodder & Stoughton, 1914)

ELECTRONIC SOURCES

Ainsworth, J. 'Kevin Barry: The Incident at Monk's bakery and the Making of an Irish Republican Legend', http://www.eprints.qut.edu.an/247/1/Ainsworth_Kevin.PDF

Beresford Ellis, P. 'The Mental Toll of Revolution', *Irish Democrat* (23 January 2004)

Cronin, J.P. and Cronin, J.D. 'Activities of Ballingeary IRA 1920–1921', *Ballingeary Cumann Staire/History Society Journal* (1998), pp. 53–4 http://homepage.eircom.net/%7esosul/page51.html

Crossley Motors Ltd (http://www.crossley-motors.org.uk/history/WW1.html)

Fox, S. 'Chronology of Irish History 1919–1923', http://www.dcu.ie/~foxs/irhist/index.htm

Gaughan, J.A. 'Listowel Police Mutiny', 1974, Garda Síochána Historical Society website: http://www.esatclear.ie/~garda/listowel.html

Hart, P. '"Operations Abroad": The IRA in Britain, 1919–23', *English Historical Review*, vol. 115, no. 460 (February, 2000)

Marrinan, R. 'The War of Independence in West Clare', Clare County Library, nd, http://www.clarelibrary.ie/eolas/coclare/history/west_clare_woi/west_clare_woi.htm

Royal Dublin Fusiliers Association, 'Ireland and the War: Women and IVA', http://www.greatwar.ie/ire-war-down/4femdw.rtf

Royal Navy History website, http://www.royal-navy.mod.uk

Sagall, Sabby, 'Solidarity Forever', *Socialist Review* (September 2002), http://www.socialistreview.org.uk

UNPUBLISHED MATERIAL

Costello, F.J. 'The Anglo-Irish War, 1919–1921: A Reappraisal', PhD thesis, Boston College, 1992

Doyle, E.J. 'The Employment of Terror in the Forgotten Insurgency: Ireland 1919–1922', MS thesis, Defense Intelligence College, 1969

Fierro, M.R. 'British Counterinsurgency Operations in Ireland 1916–1921: A Case Study', MA thesis, US Naval War College, 1997

Kautt, W. 'Logistics and Counter Insurgency: Procurement, Supply and

Communications in the Irish War of Independence, 1919–1921', PhD thesis, University of Ulster at Jordanstown, 2005

Kostal, D. 'British Intelligence in Ireland 1919–1921: Integration of Law Enforcement and Military Intelligence to Support Force Protection', MS thesis, US Joint Military Intelligence College, 2004

Leonard, P.B. 'The Necessity for De-Anglicising the Irish Nation: Boycotting and the Irish War of Independence', PhD thesis, University of Melbourne, 2000

Leeson, D. 'Imperial Stormtroopers: British Paramilitaries in the Irish War of Independence, 1920–1921', PhD thesis, McMaster University, 2003

ARCHIVES

Republic of Ireland
Archives Department, University College Dublin

IRA 2nd Southern Division Papers
Mulcahy Papers
O'Malley Papers

Cork Archives Institute, Cork City

Liam de Róiste Diaries
Séamus Fitzgerald Papers
Siobhán Lankford Papers

Military Archives, Cathal Brugha Barracks, Dublin

Bureau of Military History Chronology
Bureau of Military History Witness Statements
Maurice Aherne Statement
Gilbert Barrington Statement
Alice Barry Statement
Piaras Beaslaí Statement
Flor Begley Statement
Patrick Berry Statement
Joseph Booker Statement
F.S. Bourke Statement
Eugene Bratton Statement
Daniel Breen Statement
Timothy Brennan Statement

Éamon Bulfin Statement
Bernard C. Byrne Statement
James Byrne Statement
Joseph Byrne Statement
Tom Byrne Statement
Vincent Byrne Statement
Josephine Clarke Statement
Michael Cordial Statement
Edmund Crowe Statement
Patrick Crowe Statement
Tadhg Crowe Statement
Seán Culhane Statement
James Cullen Statement
Michael Cummins Statement
James W. Cunningham Statement
M.J. Curran Statement
Charles Dalton Statement
Patrick G. Daly, MD Statement
Una Daly Statement
Frank Davis Statement
Liam Deasy Statement
John J. Dolan Statement
Éamon Dore Statement
James Doyle Statement
John J. Doyle Statement
George C. Duggan Statement
Thomas Duggan Statement
Hugh Early Statement
Vincent Cornelius Ellis Statement
Dr James J. Enright Statement
Patrick Egan Statement
Michael J. Feely Statement
Patrick Fehilly Statement
Jack Fitzgerald Statement
Séamus Fitzgerald Statement
Michael Fitzpatrick Statement
Patrick Fitzpatrick Statement
Seán Fitzpatrick Statement
James P. Flood Statement

Michael Fogarty Statement
Peter Folan Statement
E. Gerrard Statement
Oliver St John Gogarty Statement
J.R.W. Gouldan Statement
D. Hales Statement
Dan Holland Statement
Geoffrey Ibberson Statement
Joe Lawless Statement
Michael Leahy Statement
Joseph Leonard Statement
Diarmuid Lynch Statement
Mrs Maisie McCarthy Statement
Patrick McCrea Statement
Patrick Meehan Statement
Patrick Mills Statement
Fintan Murphy Statement
Jeremiah Murphy Statement
Séamus Murray Statement
William Myles Statement
Seán Nunan Statement
Liam O'Brien Statement
Diathi O'Donohue Statement
Paddy O'Donohue Statement
James O'Donovan Statement
Patrick O'Dwyer Statement
Fergus O'Kelly Statement
William T. O'Keefe Statement
Mortimer O'Leary Statement
John O'Mahoney Statement
Edward O'Neill Statement
Stephen J. O'Reilly Statement
Patrick Ormond Statement
Seán O'Shea Statement
D. O'Sullivan Statement
Ms Mary O'Sullivan Statement
Patrick O'Sullivan Statement
Tadhg O'Sullivan Statement
John Plunkett Statement
Catherine Quinlon Statement
Bernard Reilly Statement

George Henry Roberts Statement
Joseph Rosney Statement
Michael F. Ryan Statement
Séamus Robinson Statement
Declan Slattery Statement
James Slattery Statement
Michael Staines Statement
Patrick Whelan Statement
Alfred White Statement
Mrs A.K. Wordsworth Statement

Bureau of Military History Contemporary Documents

Fintan Murphy Collection
George Gavan Duffy Collection
James Collins, TD Collection
Jeremiah Mee Collection
Leon Ó Broin Collection
Leopold H. Kerney Collection
Lt.-Col. John MacCarthy Collection
Michael Conway Collection
Monsignor J. Curran Collection
Mrs Aileen McNulty Collection
Mrs Erskine Childers Collection
Mrs Seán Collins Collection
Ms Dorothy McCardle Collection
Oscar Traynor Collection
Patrick Keegan Collection
Peter Paul Galligan Collection
Robert C. Barton Collection
Tadhg Kennedy Collection
Thomas J. Maldan Collection
Thomas Malone Collection
Thomas McInerney Collection

Collins Papers
Florence O'Donoghue Papers
National Archives of Ireland, Dublin

City of Dublin Tinsmiths and Sheet Metal Workers Society

Diaries of George G.H. Heenan
Irish Railways
Letter from Board of Public Works
Office of Public Works Papers
Rail Clearing House
Sinn Féin Files
Tyrone County Surveyor's Office

National Library of Ireland, Dublin

Robert Barton Papers
Dáil Éireann Papers
Dublin Brigade Papers
Gavan Duffy Papers
Frank Gallagher Papers
IRA Papers
Thomas Johnson Papers
Diarmuid Lynch Papers
Diary of Lord French
Joseph Magarrity Papers
Dr Patrick McCartan Papers
Minutes of the Irish Transport and General Workers' Union
Monteagle Papers
Colonel Maurice Moore Papers
Art Ó Briain Papers
William O'Brien Papers
Thomas O'Donnell Papers
Michael O'Dwyer Papers
Count Plunkett Papers
Southern Division Papers

United Kingdom
Imperial War Museum, London

Field Marshal Sir Henry Wilson Papers
General Sir Hugh Jeudwine Papers
General Sir Peter Strickland Papers

Liddell Hart Centre for Military Archives, King's College, London

Papers of Brigadier Frederick Arthur Stanley Clarke, DSO

Papers of Lieutenant Colonel Evelyn Lindsay-Young
Papers of Major General Charles Howard Foulkes

Public Records Office, Kew, Surrey

Admiralty Papers
Air Ministry Papers
Colonial Office Papers, Dublin Castle Records
Home Office Papers
Labour Ministry Papers
Metropolitan Police Papers
Ministry of Munitions of War Papers
Railway Company Papers
Railways Staff Conference Papers
Records of the Boards of Customs, Excise, and Customs and Excise
Records of the Cabinet Office
Records of the Special Operations Executive
Sturgis Diaries
Transportation Ministry Papers
Treasury Board Papers
Treasury Solicitor and HM Procurator General's Department Papers
War Office Papers
Board of Trade Marine Department Papers

The Tank Museum, Bovington

RH.87 RTC 5ACC: 8008 – '5th Armoured Car Company Historical
    Record 1920–33'

Index